NOTES OF A HANGING JUDGE

NOTES OF A HANGING JUDGE

Essays and Reviews, 1979-1989

STANLEY CROUCH

OXFORD UNIVERSITY PRESS
New York   Oxford

Oxford University Press

Oxford New York Toronto
Delhi Bombay Calcutta Madras Karachi
Petaling Jaya Singapore Hong Kong Tokyo
Nairobi Dar es Salaam Cape Town
Melbourne Auckland

and associated companies in
Berlin Ibadan

First published in 1990 by Oxford University Press, Inc.,
200 Madison Avenue, New York, New York 10016

First issued as an Oxford University Press paperback, 1991

Oxford is a registered trademark of Oxford University Press

Library of Congress Cataloging-in-Publication Data
Crouch, Stanley.
Notes of a hanging judge: essays and reviews, 1979-1989 / Stanley Crouch.
p.   cm.
ISBN 0-19-505591-8
1. United States—Race relations.   2. Afro-Americans—Civil rights.
3. Africa—Description and travel—1977-   4. Italy—
Description and travel—1975-   5. Crouch, Stanley—Journeys.
I. Title.
E185.615.C76   1989   305.8'96073—dc20   89-16138   CIP
ISBN 0-19-506998-6 (pbk.)

10 9 8 7 6 5 4 3 2
Printed in the United States of America

First of all and above all, to my mother Emma Bea Crouch, who introduced me to reading and has long supported my struggle with diction and word order, the essences of writing. To Bert Meyers in memoriam, a fine poet and a learned man of humor, earthiness, and honor. And, finally, to Rudy Langlais, who from the position of senior editor sent me south in 1979 and opened the way for me to write on the range of subjects that I did at *The Village Voice*.

CONTENTS

INTRODUCTION

BLUES TO YOU

These essays, reviews, and columns are largely concerned with the struggles and fascinations surrounding racism, sexism, and sexual orientation. The period given the most attention was kicked off by the Civil Rights Movement, which was as important to the direction and the evolving nature of this society as the fall of colonialism was to sovereign representation in the United Nations. The Civil Rights Movement was quite influential in raising the issues and setting the tone for much of the redefinition that has taken place in America over the last thirty years or so, redefinition that the country has been moving toward in one way or another from the moment explorers or chattels or immigrants began arriving on this continent. These changes of perspective touch me as a writer because I am primarily interested in those affirmations of human value that have brought about reconsiderations of history, the arts, and heavy-handed, demeaning, or soppy media images.

This rush of new definitions, of revisions, of repudiated stereotypes is part of what has led me to think of our century as The Age of Redefinition. We have either inherited or participated in, observed or been stupefied by, the monumental shifts of meaning engendered by work in the worlds of scientific research, technology, warfare, and social movements. Our international inheritance is one of inspiration, threat, and disappointment. We know an unprecedented number of things about our brains and our bodies, about the natural world of this hurtling sphere, and about the electromagnetic universe in which the small issues of time, flesh, and blood that constitute our lives mean absolutely nothing. Aerodynamics and environmental pollution cause us to now think differently about air, clouds, and space. The world wars gave us a fresh and shocking understanding of the relationship of barbarism to technology. The rise and decay of Marxism's promise resulted in sobering perceptions of slavery, bureaucracy, totalitarianism, and propaganda. And where Mao Tse-tung often described the West as a paper tiger, Third World revolution itself became a paper angel before the eyes of those who expected the fall of colonialism to make way for the emergence of societies driven by the innate good of the masses, societies that would show the Euro-American capitalist democracies how little they understood of the human soul. The cynicism that overwhelmed those who expected more than what they at first refused to believe says perhaps more about their naïveté than it does about the inevitable brutishness of human behavior.

Yet because of the new definitions born of science, blood, and argument, significant aspects of policy and perspective have been so altered that fewer the world over are limited by stereotypes. Even so, there is much unfinished business, especially in American affairs and in the way those affairs affect our vision of the Third World. Much has taken place that must be looked at closely, for we all still bear the burdens of recent history. My intention in this collection is to examine some of those burdens and some of the successes, which means that a writer of my interests must also look at the relationship between the uncertainty so central to democratic freedom and its influence on developments in the arts and politics. In surveying aspects of the era engendered by the Civil Rights Movement, a number of pieces discuss how much was improvised, how much was invented, and how shamelessly thorough assessment was avoided in the face of ill-conceived or irresponsible policies, actions, and philosophies.

Many of my evaluations are stern. In the years since 1979, when the first of these pieces was written, I have become something of a hanging judge, much like Henry Morgan, who sent many of his former pirate buddies to the gallows, certain that they deserved what they got. Experience has made me equally confident in my vision of how a noble movement went loco. Having been born in 1945, I consider myself part of an undeclared lost generation that ran into the xenophobic darkness, retreating from the complex vision of universal humanism that underlay the Civil Rights Movement. It was surely a flight that called for embracing black power, black nationalism, black studies, the racist rants that were known as "revolutionary black art," and a comical but tragic version of leadership that recently reiterated itself in the outlandish antics of the advisers in the Tawana Brawley case, all of whom were quick to call any Afro-American critical of their charges and tactics some sort of a traitor to the collective skin tone.

As I look back on it all now, I would say that I found myself moving from philosophical and active involvement with the Civil Rights Movement into the ethnic nationalism that began to take hold in my hometown of Los Angeles after the Watts Riot of 1965. It was then that I began earnestly reading the works of the Negritude writers, of African novelists and playwrights, of Franz Fanon, of LeRoi Jones, of the various Third World revolutionaries, and started publishing essays, poems, and reviews in *The Journal of Black Poetry, Liberator,* and *Black World.* But the work that this movement produced more often than not wasn't worth reading, much less reviewing or celebrating. I soon began to fall out with the movement and was often accused of having been too influenced by European or "Western standards," code for being a traitor to the revolution.

I was indeed a traitor to that movement and have since become even more hostile to its ideas, which helped send not only black America but this nation itself into an intellectual tailspin on the subjects of race, of culture, of heritage. Where there was not outright foolishness, there was a mongering of the maudlin and a base opportunism. Those qualities tainted a good deal of the writing that came out of that period and supported more than a few of the conceptions that many are only now coming to recognize as the self-destructive double standards they always were. What I frankly consider cowardice or intellectual dishonesty among Afro-American intellectuals and commentators allowed for the sustained power of more than a few silly ideas. Those men and women were more interested in getting along than stirring up discussion or debate, pretending that their lack of nerve was actually a feeling that the dirty drawers of the Negro community should never be held up for white people to look at. If not that, they might explain their concerns in empathetically careerist terms: since it was so hard for a man or woman of color to make it out here in America, they didn't want to give public criticisms that could impinge upon an individual's chance at economic success.

I accept none of this and believe that the issues surrounding Afro-American life are so crucial to any comprehensive understanding of this country and the directions of its policies that Negro intellectuals need to be as honest as possible. It is not, after all, as though no one else can see what is going on. In New York, where the black media hid under the bed as the fraud at the center of the Brawley case became clearer and clearer, it was obvious that few black writers or commentators in Manhattan were courageous enough to say what most close observers more than sensed. This is quite dangerous. It means that Afro-American leadership is embarrassed: after all these years of asserting that whites should vocally separate themselves from the racists, demagogues, and hysterics in their midst, few black people in positions of responsibility are willing to do what they demand of others. (Affirmative action, anyone?) It also erodes whatever confidence those most serious among us might have in the sustained moral significance of Negroes as symbolic or literal instigators of democratic responsibility.

If anything, when this book is not a celebration of those who found their way through the briar patches, sand dunes, and bogs of American challenges, it is a series of attacks on clichés, sentimentality, and the demagoguery that endangers the excluded as much as it does any other group. These essays, reviews, and columns look at the achievements of the Civil Rights Movement, at the forces that destroyed the thrust and substance of that epic point in American political history, at figures of enormous import such as Atlanta's Maynard Jackson, at the development of a pernicious crime culture in America's black communities, at some literary figures, a few books, a handful of plays, even a festival of racist cartoons. With the exception of the first piece, which was done for *The New Republic* but published there in a much shorter version, and "Aunt Medea," which also appeared there, all the essays of the collection were written during my stay at *The Village Voice*, where my position as a staff writer gave me great freedom, allowed me the benefits of Robert Christgau's superbly instructive editing, and made it impossible for me not to come face to face with the feminist and homosexual liberation movements.

It was at *The Voice* that my conception of the strengths and weaknesses of contemporary social movements expanded. I saw the connections between the motion of Afro-American politics and the rhetoric and actions of feminist and homosexual participants in two superficially removed orders of dissent. Much of what I read and heard from the paper's feminist ideologues and champions of homosexual liberation was quite familiar, reminiscent of what had been said when the Civil Rights Movement decayed into the mirror-licking of ethnic nationalism and condescending self-regard. The tragedy was that such politics failed to address the fact that the sort of communicative power Martin Luther King possessed resulted not only from his charismatic gifts but, and even more important, from his discovery of the intersection of mutual identification that allows those outside a minority or special interest group to fight for its principles. At *The Voice*, there was a great deal of self-righteous and separatist talk of the sort I had heard as the black nationalists and armed black revolutionaries took center stage in the second half of the sixties. One could hear things such as Andrew Kopkind's observation, "Straight men are out. The new alliance is between women and gay men." The wrongs of the world were the fault of heterosexual men whose dictates led to the restrictions at the centers of world religions, the family unit, the double standards of the workplace, and the educational system. Gaggles of Marxist chestnuts were re-roasted, and the homosexuals then advocated promiscuity and refused to be critical of the public sexual encounters that made parks off-limits to heterosexuals and children in places like San Francisco, where anything could go on at any time.

However silly most of those ideas were, there is no way I could dismiss the experiences I had at that remarkably uneven and frequently adolescent paper, for there were sometimes real thinkers there, and what they were examining in their writing and conversation helped me see the virtues of the movements they championed and better understand the role that democracy always finds indicated by the cards history deals into its hand. It is undeniable how important the feminist challenge was to this country, and the impact it has had is profound. Though one can sympathize with the problems of lesbians so battered to despair by social prejudice that they advocate separatist ideas as nutty as those of the Nation of Islam, it should be pretty obvious now that the farthest out of them were the Black Panthers and Weather Underground of feminism, pushing the more rational feminists, heterosexual or lesbian, to ludicrous positions of antagonism. And however much remains to be done, women have changed their images and their positions in the world so thoroughly that the redefinitions they have brought to our time are some of the most remarkable in human history.

It is obvious at this point that the progress of ethnic minorities and women has been enormous, but AIDs and the attendant taint of plague slowed the movement of homosexual liberation. AIDS has also changed the "lifestyle" of homosexuals. Living in Manhattan's Greenwich Village is now a very different experience than it was during the height of homosexual promiscuity, when one could see many strange phenomena taking place in the streets after dark or inside one's vestibule. Like the armed black cadres of the late sixties who threatened and taunted the nation with what now seems suicidal intensity, the cruising frenzy of homosexual life is over for the same reason: death. What the homosexual community has in common with the black saber rattlers is also a parallel indignation at the lack of identification with its plight on the part of a society it sneered at and baited. Though black revolutionaries stated their intention of overthrowing the government of the United States "by any means necessary," they never failed to leap beneath the covers of the Constitution when local police and government agents took them seriously and moved to wipe out the self-declared threat. The middle-class morality dismissed by the kinds of homosexuals Lionel Mitchell attacks in this collection's "Gay Pride, Gay Prejudice" is the very same morality now appealed to as more and more homosexuals pay the brutal costs that errant promiscuity levied on Mitchell himself. As Robert Christgau once said in an argument with a homosexual radical who thought all taboos against rampant promiscuity were only repressive vestiges of Judaeo-Christian morality, "No, absolutely not. Heterosexuals learned a long time ago—against their will, by the way—that if you go to bed with any and everybody you meet, you'll get sick."

As the plague set in and the doomed wore the emblems of purple welts, what had often seemed an essentially frivolous world took on a spiritual majesty that many besides myself probably thought beyond it. Where the homosexuals who dominated the radical assaults on sexual convention seemed advocates of a largely superficial and trend-oriented grasp of life, those men grew up as all human beings do when the terrors at the center of existence demand more of them than has been asked before. They embraced the dying and supplied them with extended families willing to clean their homes, take care of their correspondence, do their shopping, supply them with visits as regular as their health allowed, read to them, bring them flowers and recordings, and provide the human feeling that ennobles when morale is, finally, pointless. Once again, redefinition reared itself and revealed another depth of character that gave the troops at battle with man's fate fresh, unflinching reinforcements.

So my ambition here is to bring much of what George Steiner calls "the pressure of life" into pieces that take on the subjects of redefinition, sure that the Afro-American experience provides the appropriately corkscrewing path through the spiritual and intellectual thickets of our time, exposing us all to ourselves as often through art as politics. Central to what I bring to these discussions is an attempt at a morality large enough and stern enough to include the human qualities of good and evil that transcend all simple-minded categories. For that reason, the book opens with a long essay about Jesse Jackson's presidential campaign of 1988: the breadth of his political vision and the strengths and weaknesses of his character provide a perfect overture to the recurring themes of this book. After the Jackson piece, the collection moves backward to 1979, when I went to Mississippi for the fifteenth anniversary meeting of many who had participated in the Student Non-Violent Coordinating Committee's brave summer of voter registration in 1964. What I was thinking then is developed through a number of pieces, while one, "Aunt Jemima Don't Like Uncle Ben," is an early draft both technically and intellectually for what later becomes "Aunt Medea." Throughout, the reader will witness my working things out and my deepening confidence in the imperatives of the American social contract.

A great help in the changes I made when I began rejecting the strictures of black nationalism was the work and friendship of Albert Murray, who is not only my mentor but one of the most original thinkers and writers in America. My late friend Larry Neal, who was himself breaking away from the limitations of black nationalism when he died in 1981, introduced me to Albert Murray about 1970. In the process of reading Murray's books and putting his ideas together with those of Ralph Ellison, I was inspired to follow my own instincts about the most serious directions in Afro-American intellectual life, art, and politics. Those instincts are perhaps best expressed in a short address I wrote for a memorial service held for Larry Neal in Harlem.

I usually have no more interest in memorial celebrations than I have in funerals, since both bring out the hysterical nature of sentimentality, allow some to invent relationships and concerns they never had, and others to breathe more easily if an honest person will no longer be able to bear witness to their own lies. But Larry Neal was important, and his death is a tragedy because he was the only honest man I knew who was in New York during the upsurge of demagogues and the would-be-militant social clubs, replete with exotic costume ball regalia and name changes, that formed much of black nationalism. His passing was an occasion for deep sorrow because we will probably never know what really happened in terms of the dynamics, the deals, the confusion, the misue of mass naïveté, and the intellectual barbarism that passed for new perceptions. Such, unfortunately, is the nature of contemporary Negro American circumstances, for real examination has taken a backseat to the placation of the ignorant and those lacking enough courage to state the hard facts.

That Larry Neal was working on a criticism of that period was very important and we must hope that he finished enough to allow us to get a grip on the decisions and actions of a time that is constantly being rewritten by those who have fallen in love with yet another set of definitions and are trying to feed us the insect larvae that would replace our brain cells with the maggots of simplistic politics and postures. If there is any job before us, and Larry Neal was quite aware of this, it is to decide whether we shall go to the gym and train for the professional championships, or sloppily train, never move toward a professional contest but will demand prize monies and trophies on the basis of sentimental manipulation. The tradition from which we come is a grand one, and a bloody one, and one filled with struggle, inspiration, and disappointment. Yet if there is one person who is serious enough to try to be the very best he or she can be within the cold and lonely quarters of the chosen craft, addressing the desire Larry Neal had for troops who would not deal themselves out of games for which they helped design the cards, we may not come any closer to heaven, but we will be one man or one woman further from the hell of self-imposed exclusion. Thank you.

NOTES OF A HANGING JUDGE

1

READY ON MY MIND: THE CONTEXT
AND IMPLICATIONS OF JESSE JACKSON

I. THE RIDDLE

Such welcome and unwelcome things at once
'Tis hard to reconcile
Macbeth

Jesse Jackson's public image and his role in the course of contemporary affairs are perhaps more complex than those of anyone else in recent memory. In a number of ways by now quite obvious, he is very much like the magnetic rogues and hustler-heroes of films like *All Through the Night,* where Humphrey Bogart and a gathering of soft-shelled gangsters find themselves in the middle of a Nazi espionage plot but end up as patriots defending America against external demons who would destroy its ideals. Given all the accusations made about Jackson, mixed with his handsomeness, his wit, his seductive·arrogance, and his ability to lift the hearts of his listeners, the radiant reverend stands before us all as a man besmirched by his own conduct, his ambition, his willingness to make pretzels of the truth, but also as a figure who symbolizes American potential in his better moments and who has more populist appeal than anyone since the Kennedys and King.

Jackson can already do things no one before him could, and he has brought to the forefront of the discussion of American problems an agenda as influential on American politics as Louis Armstrong's innovations were on American music. (As Joe Klein observed in *New York* magazine before the 1988 New York primary, "both Gore and Dukakis have appropriated vast swatches of the Jackson canon and are beginning to sound like Jesse Lite.") Jackson has defined the issues to a large degree but he has also ventured into areas of criticism only he could get away with, unabashedly calling problems of individual conduct that bedevil the Afro-American community and the quality of urban life by extension. No white politician could presently challenge Negroes to get off dope, to raise the babies they make, to stop being lackadaisical in public school, and to work their ways out of problems rather than merely whine as they sullenly accept their conditions. Any white politician so bold would be shouted down as a racist, or as one given to dangerous generalizations. If not, said politician would be told that he or she didn't understand the dictates of the culture of Afro-Americans, which are so, so different from those of the majority. Because Jackson will have none of that, and because he has a reputation as an activist who has taken the field against sheeted or business-suited grand dragons, he cannot be dismissed when he says, "The rising use of drugs and babies making babies and violence is cutting away our opportunity." And since there is an unmentioned agenda in his presentation—the repudiation of black nationalism in its most racist and separatist extremes—Jackson has more than meager appeal to a good number of whites, whether or not they would like to see him hold high elected office.

By challenging Negro Americans to do and be better, and by making possible an atmosphere of multiracial coalition unrivaled since the most inspiring moments of the Civil Rights Movement, Jackson has changed the positions of his listeners from often disgruntled spectators to potential participants. He has provided in his rhetoric of inspiration what Georges Gusderf said of myth, "a spontaneous mode of being in the world . . . a way of grasping things, beings and oneself, a set of conduct and attitudes, an insertion of man into reality." Jackson calls this *common ground,* and the power of his conception is not only undeniable but fundamental to the American future. Its deepest human importance is always overlooked, however. When he says in one way or another what he did at the 1984 Democratic Convention, that "we experienced pain but progress," or "our heads are perhaps bloodied but not bowed," his vision carries with it a component of tragedy and, as such, is far less utopian than those who listen with the simplest ears ever hear. For any American politician to raise the issue of inevitable suffering as part of the engagement necessary to bring about a higher quality of life is exceptionally bold in peacetime. Yet it is the kind of boldness that commentators have consistently ignored when analyzing Jesse Jackson.

But for all the light that the radiant reverend offers at this time in our history, there is an undeniable element of darkness, ice-cold questions about his character and his methods, proof that he is a breathing idol who has, if not clay feet, a good amount of thick mud on his shoes. Let us now see if we can perceive him more clearly through the gauze of his glamour, the immeasurable gallons of newspaper ink, the sting of the flash bulbs, the glare of the television lights.

II. THE SOUND

It takes pleasure in changing its linguistic masks
as often as its hero changes his God-masks—the last
of which looks remarkably American. For it is the
mask of an American Hermes, a brilliant messenger
of shrewdness . . .

> Thomas Mann, foreword to
> *Joseph and His Brothers*

Jesse Jackson is a remarkable orator whose success has come from speaking to the disaffiliated and reiterating the myth that fuels all conceptions of heroes. Whether he is a hero or not, Jackson has the *sound* of a hero; he fills the air with a timbre that makes flame audible. Somewhere down inside that timbre is the sting of reluctant weeping, but the decibels of desire in that sound ring from a frequency that gives public voice to all those bored, enraged, and disillusioned by the alienation of racial paranoia, of gender and sexual persuasion, of collective greed, and the paralyzing cynicism that has formed so many pustules within the national sensibility. When Jackson says, "My constituency is the desperate, the damned, the disinherited, the disrespected, and the despised," he achieves a majesty of reference and a suggestion of intent, drawing upon the accumulated association of oral mood that calls back to King, but even further, even deeper in our history than most of us truly realize. What we hear are the weights and textures of the charismatic style that came of African and European fusings of rhythm and spiritual dignity. The result was the molten nobility of Negro religious emotion, which is the legacy of feeling from which Jackson pulls his power. That legacy speaks to all Americans; it is the spiritual tuning fork that has always brought the orchestra of domestic morality up to pitch, the tone that summons and guides the quality of the national epic.

That sound is epic because we know from which gore-smeared and sticky portal the Afro-American emerges, know of the slave trade's black gold and of the structured hysteria that was segregation, of the castration and lynching festivals held by the Ku Klux Klan, and of the well-documented and protean forms of injustice as well as the imposed modes of subservient conduct. We know that the Negro comes from a place in the American continent where the earth is, as Faulkner wrote in *Absalom, Absalom!*, "a soil manured with black blood from two hundred years of oppression and exploitation until it sprang with an incredible paradox of peaceful greenery and crimson flowers and sugar cane sapling . . . valuable pound for pound almost with silver ore, as if nature held a balance and kept a book and offered a recompense for the torn limbs and outraged hearts even if man did not."

It is that recompense, that balance, that ledger upon which the spiritual history of this country is written, added up and analyzed act by act, that speaks to us through the voice of the Negro. Said voice is the vernacular sound of majestic human engagement, whether personal or social, political or spiritual. And contrary to what many commentators seem to believe, it most definitely affects the sensibility of white Americans, having long resonated from one passageway of consciousness and psychology to another. That very sound has been close to the soul of the country at least since the Second Awakening, when whites marveled at the way Negroes would continue singing on into the night after the revivals and when everyone else had gone to bed. It was heard on the plantations and as far removed from them as whaling boats, was loved even in the crude mutilations that made minstrelsy the first enormously popular entertainment phenomenon in this nation, and still beguiles in the subsequent derivations that piled up fortunes for men as distant in style and demeanor as Al Jolson and Bruce Springsteen. It rose up in the work of the Fisk Jubilee singers, the music of ragtime, the invention of blues and the evolution of divas such as Bessie Smith, reappeared transmogrified in the rattling power of Marian Anderson and was given perhaps its most humbling nobility in the tragic depth and heroic optimism of Mahalia Jackson, while it was most secularly imposing in Louis Armstrong and Billie Holiday.

The overriding significance of that voice is lodged in a single fact, no matter its infinite variations: it has provided us with the most sterling sense of tragedy and has long proven that human beings need not be reduced to lower forms of animal life by great suffering. So what is most important in the Negro story is not the loss of life to murder, to mistreatment, to madness, but the sense of heroic optimism mentioned earlier. That optimism is what has ennobled the Negro American at his or her best, because it is the source of the willingness to take the field, to do battle, to struggle up from the sink holes of self-pity that exist just beneath the cynicism so many would encourage in Negroes and in all Americans, assuring them all that there is no hope within "the system," that "they" will never allow fairness to rise like steam through the grating of the society.

Optimism is the fulcrum with which Jackson moves those within his world. At its finest, Jackson's rhetoric is a repudiation of the shallowness that has come to exemplify so much Negro public statement. It has particular pungence at a time when sham glamour moves in line with the degradation of rap music and the demonic vulgarity of musicians like Prince, whose tunes are the squeaks of ungreased souls, are what William Carlos Williams called "the shriek of starvation." Jackson means something beyond materialism to so many who listen to his vision, however much that vision focuses on the economic problems that bedevil our society. It is therefore odd that any politician would assert a spiritual undertone that does not pander to the provincialism of those so overwhelmed by the modern age that almost any call for the reassertion of traditional values carries with it the prudish and sanctimonious bent which leads us away from the pluralism America must constantly struggle toward if it is to realize the vision of democracy set forth by our country's finest thinkers. Jackson intends to connect himself to those thinkers when he says, "The white, the Hispanic, the black, the Arab, the Jew, the woman, the Native American, the small farmer, the business person, the environmentalist, the peace activist, the young, the old, the lesbian, the gay, the disabled, make up the American quilt."

III. IN THE CENTER OF THE EPIC

Materially, psychologically, and culturally, part of the nation's heritage is Negro American, and whatever it becomes will be shaped in part by the Negro's presence.

Ralph Ellison, *Going to the Territory*

If in my high moments, I have done some good, offered some service, shed some light, healed some wounds, rekindled some hope, or stirred someone from apathy or indifference, or any way along the way helped somebody, then this campaign has not been in vain.

Jesse Jackson, Democratic Convention
Atlantic City, 1984

Those who found it odd that Jesse Jackson would take seriously the idea of running for President since he was an Afro-American, and who thought his Rainbow Coalition a pot-boiled oddity, showed their inadequate knowledge of American history. As a symbol at least, Jackson represents the deep relationship of Afro-Americans to the actions and ideas that have expanded our sense of democracy. There is no area of political, economic, or personal concern that is not traversed by the Negro over the entire length of the national epic. As slaves, Afro-Americans were obviously related in fundamental ways to the problems of exploited labor and even sexual harassment on the job; as those denied the vote, equal treatment under the law, and freedom of choice, they illuminated the contradictions of social policy engendered by discrimination. Therefore, the March on Washington stretched its historical hand back to the coalitions of abolitionists and fighters for women's rights, to the labor movement, and to those who had long argued against double standards, from John Quincy Adams's defense of the Africans who took over the slave ship *Amistad* to those who demanded women's suffrage and, finally, to the lawyers under the leadership of Thurgood Marshall who shaped arguments so convincing the Supreme Court decided to break with its leopard past and knock down the tenets of segregation. On the steps of the Lincoln Memorial Monument in the capital were gathered representatives of many who had previously been done wrong and many who were presently suffering. They formed a rainbow coalition that was soon lost in an electrical storm of xenophobia.

Jackson's repudiation of that xenophobia is central to his impact on his supporters, regardless of race, because it is probable that, after economic stability, the greatest single desire in this country is for a reduction in paranoia. Jackson's Rainbow Coalition also repudiates the reverse of the fall of populism's first thrust. Though many are reluctant to tell it as it was, what should seem rather clear at this point is how black nationalism sold out the populist dream of the Civil Rights Movement as surely as Georgia's Tom Watson sold out the original movement and became "one of the outstanding exploiters of endemic Negrophobia," as C. Vann Woodward describes him in *The Strange Career of Jim Crow*. Fomenting separatist hysteria and charging headlong into exotica, black nationalists splintered the movement and set the tone for what became a fragmented social agenda, suggesting that just as Afro-Americans have set high standards at their best, they also have the ability to fill the air with wrongheadedness. It is not at all farfetched to question whether or not the strained self-celebration of black nationalism helped trigger the so-called "me generation" which turned away from the challenges implicit in the country's vision of democracy. The obnoxious antipathy toward whites screwed up the country's clarity of dialogue, which was predicted when white workers were expelled from the Student Non-Violent Coordinating Committee and black power began to emerge. One social movement after another became a separate cell, though the model was clearly that of the Afro-American firebrands.

Jackson obliquely refers to this fragmentation when he says, "We are bringing the family back together. What we have is reunion. We forgive each other, redeem each other, regroup, and move on." In order to move on, Jackson seeks expansion of allies, even bringing into his camp movements that emerged in the wake of the battle for Negro civil rights, but that have historical forebears, literally or implicitly. So when Jackson sides with the women's movement and takes the position that homosexuals should receive equal treatment under the law and spouse equivalent benefits, he is actually reorchestrating the theme that was played almost one hundred and twenty-five years ago when Susan B. Anthony said at the Equal Rights Convention of December 6, 1866, "That the ballot, alike to the woman and the negro, means bread, education, intelligence, self-protection, self-reliance, and self-respect; to the daughter it means industrial freedom and diversified employment; to the wife, the control of her own person, property and earnings; to the mother equal right to her children; to all its means social equality, colleges and professions, open profitable business, skilled labor and intellectual development."

Jackson's reorchestration, his ambition to bring back together all of the forces that stood in agreement on that summer Washington day in 1963, is what underlies his homilies such as "Red, yellow, brown, black, and white, we're all precious in God's sight," which he tends now to chant with multi-racial groups of children, moving beyond the "I am somebody" wing of "black is beautiful" to a statement on the basic value of human beings in the grand vision of the society. In that direction, he attacks what he calls "escapism, militarism, and yuppieism," with sneering rejections of what used to be termed "looking out for number one."

The moral torpor that comes of greed, which is essentially narcissistic, is one of Jackson's favorite targets, from the ruthless corporate mogul to the Negro dope dealer, one willing to destroy the environment for profit, the other an agent in the granulation of community order, safety, and pride. The spiritual bile Jackson identifies has neither race nor class and its victims are the very rainbow of Americans he proposes should move in tandem to "make America better." This is the most remarkable aspect of Jackson's social thought when taken whole. His conception of so-called "economic violence" is balanced by his sense of the violence done to urban life by those whom he does not let off the hook because they can plead poverty. Everyone not deaf, dumb, and blind or brain-damaged is responsible to and for the society.

That is where Jackson is freshest and strongest: he demands the best of even those who live in the worst conditions. He challenges black people to engage their fates, "Don't cry your way out, sweat your way out, *work* your way out . . . We must revive our expectations of decency, honor, and dignity . . . I was born in the slum but in no way did I therefore earn the right to do less than my best . . . The first step in changing our condition is to change our mind . . . By your mind, you are transformed. Nothing is more powerful in the world than a made up mind." Jackson returns responsibility to the poor and the discriminated against and gives them a sense of mission and a vision of their own roles in their lives. That is so different from the buck-passing that has dominated too much political talk by black leaders, but it is also different from the usual tone of presidential candidates. What every presidential candidate since John Kennedy has said is that if you vote for him and he takes office, you can lie down and go to sleep: he'll handle everything. As Jackson said to his audience in Hempstead, Long Island, during the New York primary, the President could not stop the consumption of drugs, irresponsible sexual behavior, or poor performance in school. He could not legislate against laziness or a lack of commitment to one's community. Only through taking command of their own lives could the people lessen the power those problems had over them.

IV. IN THE WHITE GIANT'S EYE

Traveling with Jackson's campaign through Wisconsin, Arizona, Indiana, New York, one could easily see how poor the perception of the press is and how little reporters understand about this country. Their assumptions about white racism were publicly perforated through the privacy of the voting booths, especially those of Wisconsin, where Jackson took almost a quarter of the white electorate. Reporters obviously knew less about white people than they presumed. The popularity of everyone from Bill Cosby to Michael Jackson and Michael Jordan went right by them. The shock experienced at Jackson's popularity proved they had missed the fact that America has elected a good number of black mayors over the last two decades and that, as Pennsylvania Congressman Bill Gray has pointed out, "Half the black members of Congress represent mostly non-black constituents." When Jackson brought Lt. Goodman back from Syria and the airman traveled in motorcades with his white wife, there were no protests against their marriage. K. C. Jones taking over as head coach of the Boston Celtics didn't inspire the outrage many might have expected. Even the fact that Oprah Winfrey is front runner in the talk show race and that whites have become accustomed to seeing Negro men and women as co-anchors on news programs across the nation didn't alert the press to significant changes in the racial sensibility of the country.

Jackson symbolizes the democratic ideal of comfortable multi-racial assemblies. His speeches and the atmosphere he creates make racism unwelcome and relieves those whites who might have felt left out or alienated from politics involving black people. That is where Jackson's family theme is so effective because, for whites, it speaks to their desire to believe in the goodwill of Afro-Americans. Leaving a Jackson rally on Long Island, a white guy said to the woman he was with, "It feels good to go to an event that's not all white." In other words: It felt good to feel like an American. It is probable that reporters know few white people who are the friends of Negroes, or who socialize with them, or who take inspiration from their examples. One must assume that they know only white people like themselves—wrong-way cultural Corrigans.

Seeing Jackson get an enthusiastic response from students at the University of Wisconsin at Milwaukee took one back to the rallies of the sixties, but out in Janesville, where mostly white rural people gathered in a huge barn that had been used for hoedowns and jamborees and had waited four hours for him, the response the reverend got was startling even to this writer. They held up their children to see, teenaged blonde girls giggled and discussed his good looks, skeptics were drawn in, and by the conclusion of the address, they were chanting, "Win, Jesse, win! Win, Jesse, win!" But perhaps the most stunning example of how things turn around in this country was observed in Kenosha, Wisconsin, at a United Auto Workers rally for Jackson. A middle-aged white woman on a metal crutch, her hair in Shirley Temple curls, wore a hooded white sweatshirt which had the slogan across the front in red, green, and black letters, "Black to the Future."

In the bars and on the planes and buses, it was evident that the effect Jackson had on people touched many of the reporters who were guarding themselves against sentimentality. Even the Secret Service men told me one night in Milwaukee that they had never seen anybody who could heat up rallies like Jackson, not Nixon, not Ford, not Carter, not Reagan. But there is a reason why reporters must struggle to maintain emotional connection to what is happening in front of them: the candidates give essentially the same speeches over and over. And even though Jackson is Captain Charisma, the standardization and the sameness of delivery could spur the mind to float up out of the theater or out of the hall and into something very far removed from the words and the inflections one soon knew by heart.

Under the influence of a few drinks, however, many of the reporters implied they were actually rooting for Jackson secretly, so secretly that it might make their prose about him deadly. One of the reasons was that Jackson could deliver the same speech with the same authority over and over, sometimes snatching the spirit and making it come so alive that it seemed he was actually hearing it at that moment. Or he could improvise himself into a rhythm that would soften even the professionally hard-boiled. The other candidates didn't do that, which made the job a hard piece of work. "Al Gore," said one cameraman, "gave the speech so much the same way every time that we could get our job done very fast, film some reaction shots, and turn off the camera. We had it down in a matter of days. George Bush? Dukakis? Oh, my God. Whatever else is going on with the reverend, he never lets you doze off because he just *might* be spontaneous. You got to watch him. He's even that way with the people. The Secret Service has to be ready for him to almost dive into crowds. When he gets that look in his eyes, he's going for the hand-shaking almost as fast as the idea comes to him. The reverend is good with the press and with the people because he's been courting celebrity for a long time. He's got it down."

V. IN THE PRESENCE OF MINE ENEMIES

Courting celebrity is much like the ritual dance of kissing the cobra's head—it doubtless takes nerve and skill, but no matter how much finesse one brings to the undulating rhythms of that calculated smooch, the danger of snakebite is ever-present. Jackson was often nipped once he got to New York, but the idea that he was being treated differently from other candidates because of his color deserves ice-cold scrutiny, especially since those charges were made by Ronald Reagan and Edward Koch. In the March/April issue of *Extra!*, a leftist publication that is "The Newsletter of FAIR (Fairness & Accuracy In Reporting)," there was such an interesting comparison of the media's memory when it came to the President and when Jackson was the subject. The difference is so startling that the article "Jackson's 'Free Ride'" deserves lengthy examination:

> Nearly every significant piece on Jesse Jackson has contained the word "anti-Semitism" ("Jackson's perceived anti-Semitism," *Newsweek*, 12–14–87: "The taint of anti-Semitism," *ABC World News*,

2–15–88). His 1984 "Hymietown" remark and his past relationship with Louis Farrakhan are always cited. Most accounts go on to link these with Jackson's support of a two-state solution to the Israeli/Palestinian crisis—neglecting to point out that such a solution is endorsed by many prominent American and Israeli Jews. In a story typical of the genre appearing almost monthly in 1987—and daily in the weeks leading up to the New York primary—the *New York Times* (6–13–87) dredged up all the old news with the headline, "Three Years Later, Jackson Is Haunted by Anti-Semitism of Farrakhan; Despite Meetings with Jewish Leaders, Suspicions Persist." The story quoted two establishment Jewish leaders. Jewish supporters of Jackson were, as usual, ignored.

By contrast, one is hard-pressed to find a profile of Reagan in the mainstream media which contains the word "racism." The issue didn't haunt candidate Reagan in article after article. Yet Reagan had consistently opposed civil rights laws in the 1960s, as well as open housing in California. When blacks sought to move into whites-only neighborhoods, then-Governor Reagan told realtors that the blacks had "staged attempts to rent homes," but their real intent was "only to cause trouble." When Martin Luther King was assassinated, Reagan blamed the murder partly on King's civil disobedience: "This great tragedy began when we began compromising with law and order and people started choosing which laws they'd break." When poor blacks assembled in Oakland to receive free bags of groceries paid as ransom in the 1974 kidnapping of heiress Patty Hearst, Reagan quipped that he hoped for "an outbreak of botulism" among the food recipients.

Such comments were not made a campaign issue by the media. Nor has Reagan's association with racists burdened his political career. Former Reagan cabinet member Terrel Bell said that racist slurs (such as "Martin Lucifer Coon") were frequently uttered by White House staffers. After a racial remark led to the resignation of Interior Secretary James Watt (the White House expressed regrets over the departure), Reagan wasn't hounded by the media to denounce Watt for the next four years, as Jackson had been asked to denounce Farrakhan. The media never made a campaign issue of Reagan's 1982 letter praising Roger Pearson, a publisher of racist, anti-Semitic literature (*Village Voice*, 5–7–85). Nor has much been said about the 1980 endorsement of Reagan by the Knights of the KKK, who gloated that the Republican platform "reads as if it were written by a Klansman."

Blacks fear racism in high places as much as Jews fear anti-Semitism. Yet black concerns rarely get the same media attention. Reagan's presidential campaigns were not subjected to repeated articles bearing headlines such as "Four Years Later, Reagan Still Haunted by Perceived Racism; Despite Meetings with Black Leaders, Suspicions Persist."

Journalists like to pretend they are merely observers, not participants, even when their decision to focus on one campaign issue prior to the New York primary—"Jackson and the Jews"—undoubtedly influenced the course of events. Thus *NBC Nightly News* correspondent Bob Kur (4–11–88) could deadpan about "that lingering image" of Jackson embracing Yassir Arafat. Images have a way of lingering when TV producers decide to show them every day, as happened with the Jackson footage. If shown daily, the image of George Bush in Manila toasting Ferdinand Marcos as a committed democrat would also linger.

There are similar memory lapses on the part of media when it comes to Edward Koch, who once went on record saying that he felt most black people were anti-Semitic, but is not constantly reminded of it; who once donned an Afro wig for a party with the press and sang, "Ain't Nobody's Business What I Do," but is not constantly reminded of it; who said long before there was any evidence of Bernhard Goetz's character (e.g. "We need to get all the niggers off Fourteenth Street") that the subway shoot-ist should be acquitted, but is not constantly reminded of it; and so on. But the tone of Koch's attacks on Jackson was so venomous that Albert Gore, the country boy who came to the big city well turned and left in a barrel, had to distance himself from the man who endorsed him, that columnist after columnist opened up on the Mayor, as did the many Jews who suffered from the image of all Jackson opponents being hysterical. Felix Rohatyn, for instance, was angered by Koch's saying that all Jews and other supporters of Israel would be crazy to vote for Jackson. Rohatyn said that he had a number of disagreements with Jackson, but one did not choose a President on the basis of a single issue. He also made it clear that he resented Koch giving the impression that he was the voice of the Jew-ish community, adding that as a man who had escaped the Nazis with false papers, he wasn't in need of instruction about anti-Semitism.

Across the media, Jackson was criticized for visiting and praising Cas-tro, for ignoring human rights violations if they took place in leftist coun-tries, and for not having sufficient experience to govern a nation. *The City Sun,* a black weekly published in Brooklyn, declined to endorse the rev-erend because it claimed that he hadn't taken a strong enough stand on racial problems. That dubious trinity of rabble rousers, Al Sharpton, Al-ton Maddox, and C. Vernon Mason, continued to pretend that they rep-resented responsible black leadership and held a press conference that gave the impression, at least in the *Daily News* summary, that they had drafted the *City Sun's* Jackson editorial.

The most damning look at Jackson came a week before the election as a segment of the *MacNeil/Lehrer Newshour. If I mythologize myself I might become a hero,* appeared to be Jackson's philosophy. The candidate has recast a number of events in his life for the purposes of attention and is, according to Tyrone Brooks, who managed Jackson's Georgia campaign in 1984, out there for other than political reasons: "I think Jesse is run-ning to satisfy his ego." Jackson was not, as the segment proved, as poor as he claims—"Three room house, bathroom in the back, slop jar by the bed, wallpaper for windbreaker, not decoration"—but was, in fact, mid-dle-class. The young Jackson was always sharp and his home had an abundance of food. Though Jackson recently went to Selma, Alabama, to recount the terror of the famous march, no one who was there recalls seeing him, and his tall figure isn't in the footage. Since he is remembered for always standing close to King whenever there were cameras near, Jackson's claim to participation is at least dubious. The bullying of white businesses, the administrative disorder of PUSH and EXCEL, the attempt to silence the black press through demands of allegiance, and the willingness to overstate were also presented. Hosea Williams adamantly sneers at Jackson's tale of cradling the head of the dying King, saying that the reverend wasn't even there. Most disturbing was the rageful parading of a bloody shirt, first before reporters in Memphis, then into the chambers of the Chicago City Council. If the blood on the shirt *was* King's, then Jackson, as Gail Sheehy pointed out in *Vanity Fair*, committed a self-aggrandizing act of bibical intensity.

Though he gave rousing speeches and sustained his themes of common ground and bringing the family together, sometimes getting way up into a rhetoric of individual antiphony and refrains that was astonishingly lyrical, giving his ideas and the images of those in social trouble a tragic onomatopoeia, Jackson didn't handle his demons well. He neither confronted issues in the heroic way his rhetoric suggested he would, nor did he provide at least one large gesture that might have been extraordinarily risky but also might have shown that he was more interested in truly bringing the family together than seeming to avoid facing the cobra's head. As it happened, he took the nips in his buttocks, winning New York City but losing the state and the primary. Jackson's failure to meet with local Jewish leaders in Manhattan made him appear spooked or a man listening to bad advice. Instead of doing it himself, the reverend relied on his troops: the Jewish wing of the Rainbow Coalition took action. Labor leader Barry Feinstein attacked Koch for trying to make other Jews accept his definition of an anti-Semite. Members of Jewish Americans for Jackson took on the Arafat issue, saying that Jackson's trip to talk with Arafat came at Sadat's request and was for the purpose of getting the PLO leader to renounce terrorism, recognize Israel's sovereignty, and bring about negotiation.

Those were good moves but they lacked the dramatic power Jackson needed, a power that might not have won him the bulk of the Jewish vote but would have shown his determination to represent all the people. Though Jackson is far from a cowardly man, he didn't really address his own skills at meeting the protean challenges set before the democratic leader, he who must somehow be himself and some piece of everybody else in order to even get close to the throttle of actual power. Had Jackson gone to synagogue, put on a yarmulke, and prayed, he might have angered some of his followers who resentfully assumed that "the Jews want to string him up and make him kosher," but he would have put another mask over the many a democratic candidate must almost always wear, one under another, ever in place, ever ready to dominate when necessary.

A ten-gallon hat in Texas, a hard hat with construction workers, a sombrero in California, a yarmulke in New York.

Jackson just couldn't get it right, and made a series of mistakes. He allowed Spike Lee to direct a political commercial in which the reverend looked and moved like a cast member from *Dawn of the Dead*. The reverend was dispirited and stiff, possessing none of the fire that had so hopped up his audiences. It looked so dull and amateurish that it couldn't have done him any good. In the wake of the *MacNeil/Lehrer* segment on his leopard past, Jackson wasn't able to handle the questions it raised very well. On *The Phil Donahue Show*, he held questions about the bloody shirt at bay until the time ran out, giving the impression he had no appropriate answer, which he probably did not. Jackson's decision not to join the Manhattan parade celebrating Israel's fortieth anniversary might have come at the behest of the Secret Service, but it still didn't look good. Ironically, Koch called Jackson arrogant and insensitive as well as afraid of the heat. The second charge was not wild on the Mayor's part: Koch has never avoided speaking in hostile situations where he is sometimes drowned out by the shouts, boos, and hisses of those black people who see him as racism incarnate. A few days before the voting began, Jackson took an about-face on the question of negotiating and said he would not speak to the PLO, which gave the impression that he was running scared.

VI. THE FALLEN

Unlike all other forms of lutte or combat the conditions are that the winner shall take nothing;
neither his ease, nor his pleasure, nor any notions of glory; nor, if he win far enough, shall there be any reward within himself.

       Ernest Hemingway, *Winner Take Nothing*

The night Dukakis won the state of New York and Jackson took Manhattan, there was much gloom and anger in the ballroom of the Sheraton Hotel, a crowd of people who were prepared to be lifted into a livid state. But that was not what happened. Labor leader Stanley Hill, who had co-chaired Jackson's New York campaign, said that there had never been in his career of over thirty years a coalition of the sort he had seen gather around the reverend, and that none of it would have happened if it hadn't been for Jesse Jackson. When the reverend came to the microphone he commended Dukakis for running a campaign that was clean and above the fray of hysteria. He then said that a President must make America better, not bitter. "What must a President do? He must make history, not hysteria. We won Delaware tonight; we won Vermont tonight. We cannot become cynical, we have come too far. We can't be pessimistic, we have come too far. From Rosa Parks in Montgomery, Alabama to this ballroom, we have come a long ways. We must keep hope alive. We have come a long ways. We know this road. We will keep going. We must keep hope alive." And as he went on, the mood changed until the anger in the air had been ameliorated.

I realized then that Jackson was often at his best when he had been defeated and fought off any temptation to set a tone of hostility or rageful self-pity. The loss in Wisconsin, for instance, dropped a somber shroud over the reverend and his people. Brooding in defeat, he stood on the plane, blue shirt in tune with his mood, a sadness lying far from dormant in his gaze: it was the look of a fighter who had been not pulverized but outpointed, whose attunement to the sound of the crowd near his corner had been deceptive. But at the next stop, he did as was his habit, stood mulling near his seat, waited for the reporters to step from the plane, put on his jacket, and came down onto the runway with Secret Service guards fore and aft. At the podium, Jackson said that there had been no actual defeat because the right agenda was rising into plain sight, and the appropriate moral tone was emerging. It was the kind of speech not expected from a politician, and perhaps it wasn't a politician's speech. It was the talk of a poet, a mightily complex man who was continuing to prove that in a democracy you never know who the messenger will be or where the messenger will come from.

VII. ME AND THE DEVIL BLUES

Me and the Devil was walking side by side.
                              Robert Johnson

By the end of the New York primary, this writer concluded that Jesse Jackson would have a very difficult time if he ever intended to get to the White House, not because of race, not because of money, not even because of gaffes here and there. It seems that the ghost of King and the stain of his blood would haunt and damn Jackson whenever he attempted the long march to the Oval Office; they would rise up on the King holiday six months into the campaign, bloody shirt noosing itself around his chances of becoming President. It appeared that the radiant reverend would be forever doomed by his willingness to mythologize his life, his desire to immediately become the drum major for justice that King had called himself. It was one of those winching tragic ironies, that the holiday Jackson had fought so hard for, literally and symbolically, should come to thwart him. His 1984 campaign, as an example, inspired so much black registration in South Carolina that Strom Thurmond, Mr. Segregation himself, broke ranks with his ace-boon-coon buddy Jesse Helms over ratifying a day of national celebration that would always bring up something the Jackson of 1988—or '92 or '96 or 2000—would most surely like to put behind him.

So when we consider the space between what Jesse Jackson seems to be and what he is saying, we are again eyeball to eyeball with the tragic dimensions of the man and of our history itself. Though he has mythologized himself, has exaggerated his poverty and made his early life seem something far different from what it was, though he has neither seen, nor heard, nor spoken evil of those in business association with him, though he appears to still be struggling with an inclination to grandstanding and a stubborn refusal to publicly admit to some of his own whoppers, the reverend is still someone the nation must use in a large way or lose an extraordinary opportunity. As John A. Kouwenhoven observes under the section title, "America Is Process," in *The Beer Can by the Highway*, "Our history is the process of motion . . . up and down the social ladder—a long, complex, and sometimes terrifyingly rapid sequence of consecutive change. And it is this sequence, and the attitudes and habits and forms which it has bred, to which the term 'American' really refers." Jackson is in process and, like Lyndon Johnson the ex-segregationist, Hugo Black the ex-Klansman, and a bevy of others whom we must see as men who walked side by side with the Devil at times and left him later, should not be counted out nor forced to remain in the lesser ditches of his spirit if he has chosen to step out. If white men can grow, so can black men. If flawed men can do great things, we must not assume that those flawed men cannot be Negroes or men from any group usually outside the stations of official power. If we do, which may be the case with Jackson's purported anti-Semitism, as but one example, we deny ourselves the truth of human change in a society ever in process.

In Jackson's specific case we have a man who can speak across so many gaps of communication, who can give so many a sense of the nobility and the necessity of expelling the demons from themselves and from their communities, who can sometimes reach levels of such lyricism that the body politic itself seems some sort of poem still being born in heroic proportions. If this man cannot be used in some way by this country, through fusing his colossal ambition to the appropriate tasks, then there is a problem of political immaturity within us much greater than any we have faced thus far. For if it is all looked at in a military fashion, and if we truly examine the characters of many great Americans who have preceded Jackson, we find few—if any—who fit the unstained definitions the most naïve among us would demand of their leaders. Slaveholders or drunks, adulterers or racists, con men or manic-depressives, many of them—Washington, Jefferson, Grant, Roosevelt, Lincoln, Johnson, and Sherman, for instance—achieved things much greater in impact, more ennobling in vision, and of far more import than the detailing of their difficulties with themselves or with the values of exemplary human sensibility and conduct would tell us about the relationship of private inclinations to the democratic process.

Perhaps this is the best way to look at the potential of Jesse Jackson—as a man whose obvious power should not be left outside the centers of policy nor reduced to mere deal-making in which his weapon is the threat of taking the marbles of black votes out of the game. Jackson is, essentially, a scrapper, and he has committed acts of courage during this campaign that are not rivaled by any of the other candidates. When he spoke to over five thousand black churchgoers in Milwaukee's Mecca Auditorium, the reverend challenged his audience by going on at length about his participation in the Gay Rights March. Jackson knew well, as could anyone watching, that most of them did not want to hear that. When he talked of embracing homosexuals who were dying and who weren't addressed in person by *one* elected official, the feeling of recoil was in the air. It is not right, he said, it is not right. America can be better than that. We can be better. Since that audience was his the moment it walked in the door, Jackson didn't need to say what he did. It was an act of true courage and an example of a man who is determined to push his constituency beyond provincialism, to create that common ground any democratic leader must seek. A man like this must be used for large tasks. He could be the one who mediates the necessary alliances between Afro-American communities and the local police; the one who leads the war against drugs through the people themselves; the one who might so change the climate in lower-income neighborhoods that law and order becomes not only a passionate desire but an inspiration to active engagement; the one who could instigate and mediate reform in the public schools, raising them to the position they should have in a democratic society. Jesse Jackson should function as an empowered activist and nothing less.

Postscript in Blue:

The ways of Jesse Jackson are not to be understood simply, nor even optimistically. His performance during Chicago's mayoral race in the spring of 1989 was more than disappointing. After eight years of running on a multiracial platform, adamantly taking the position that an Afro-American could definitely represent more than racial interests, he yielded to the politics of skin tone and reduced his Rainbow Coalition, as one Chicago journalist wrote, "to one color." "In Chicago, it's black and white," says a campaign worker for Tim Evans, the black Democrat who ran as an independent when Eugene Sawyer lost out to Rich Daly for front position on the Democratic ticket. "Jackson backed Sawyer at first, but when it came down to going with Daly just because he was a Democrat, Jackson had to come behind Evans or he couldn't have run PUSH here in Chicago. He would have had to get out of town. If he stayed, he couldn't have been a black leader here anymore. That would have been over." When Jackson attacked his former campaign manager, Ron Brown, now chairman of the Democratic Party, for coming to Chicago in support of Daly, he went against the very idea that Brown should have gotten the job because he could address the complexities—and the disappointments— of political leadership beyond the province of race. Had Brown sub-

*mitted, as had Jackson, he would have given aid and comfort to any
eager to dismiss him as a serious, professional politician. At this point, it
seems that Jackson has great problems going beyond the position of a
great symbol and achieving the often painful identity of a truly great man.*

2

CIVIL RIGHTS BLUES
November 19, 1979

When I told people I was going to Jackson, Mississippi, some winced, others looked startled, some wished me good luck. They probably had never
thought it possible that Mississippi, which may still have the cumulative
record for lynchings, could advance to the point that a black person's life
would be in no more danger there than in Los Angeles, Boston, or Philadelphia, maybe in far less danger. But the extreme social chaos symbolized by the Ku Klux Klan heroes of D. W. Griffith is not easily forgotten.

Of course, Mississippi is the home of Theodore Bilbo, the patron saint
of modern racism and once governor of Mississippi, whose Depression-
era radio broadcasts made him our own loquacious and garbled Goeb-
bels. It is also the home of the late Fannie Lou Hamer, called by a veteran of the Student Non-Violent Coordinating Committee "the spiritual
leader of the Civil Rights Movement." Ironically, each died from cancer
and belied the stereotype of the southern gentleman on the one hand and
the dizzy black mammy on the other. But irony is basic to the matter of
Mississippi, and its symbols are everywhere especially in the land and the
pace. There is the exceptional landscape, a tropical human tempo one
associates with hospitality—an invitation through an easy and graceful mel-
lowness when not the sluggish coagulation of ignorance and fear. Mississippi, once called "the middle of the iceberg." I found myself contemplating how much it might have changed and what the conference on the
15th anniversary of the Freedom Summer of 1964—being held in Jackson—
would be like.

I knew there would be things I would encounter that would be hard to
communicate to New Yorkers, residents of America's sneer capital. What
they would think of is nostalgia, somehow forgetting—or never knowing—
that Mississippi is not New York State, and that Jackson is not Woodstock.
Historically, it means something of much greater dimension.

Behind the check-in counter at the Holiday Inn near Jackson State were two young men, one black and slender, the other white and stocky. More acquainted with the work and somehow still fresh with dawn at least three hours away, the young black guy got my reservation together and took me to my room. I asked him if there had been big changes in Jackson and in Mississippi. "A lot but not enough. Still, some of them oldtime crackers want to call you a nigger and get away with it. I don't let 'em forget I'm a man. I'm 21 years old, I was in the army four years. I worked my way up to sergeant and handled nearly 40 men, black and white. I don't take no shit. If they want to get physical, fine. I'm ready to die. I have to be just because I was in a position in the service where any day my life might be on the line to protect this country. If I was ready to die for a country and I'm not ready to die for myself, which is me *and* you *and* everybody else that look like us, shit, what the fuck I'm living for in the first damn place? And on top of that, I talk to any pretty girl I like."

I told him that I wanted to get something to eat and we took a quick drive in the inn's van through the poor black community near the colleges. He pointed to one corner that held a rundown pool hall and said, "So many muthafuckas used to get killed on this corner they shoulda painted it with ox-blood shoe polish to keep the corner from gettin' stained." At an all-night deli where the sandwiches are frozen, I got some Heineken and he told me he had never seen that kind of beer before. "That's some more I don't know. They didn't give me a good education here in Jackson, but I know how to work hard. I don't read too tough but I'm going to. I don't know much math and science but I'm going to. In four years, or however long it takes, Mississippi gonna have it an *educated* muthafucka on its hands!" he laughed. "They know what they doin'," he said, turning sober, "when they don't educate us. They wasn't crazy about keepin' people out of school for nothin.'"

As he said that, I looked at a dark and extremely muscular black guy of about 20 years and 200 pounds, standing in front of the deli in a sleeveless silk T-shirt, jeans, and tennis shoes, the elasticized plastic beret covering the pink pin curlers of his permanent, a comment on his desire for street-life dandyhood. Something futile and regular was going on in Jackson that was common to certain kinds of young people grappling for their glamour with clay-footed kitsch. I realized that there would be in this city a complexity shaped by the nationally familiar and the regionally particular. Jackson would have its urban sicknesses and its Southern glories, its Southern demons and its urban virtues; it would all be the result of information, myth, and the resultant deception of the simplified, the glib. The chains and wings of modern life rattled and flapped in Jackson as in every place where mass media orchestrated the broader meanings of the dreams that used to roll up from the pages of the Sears Roebuck catalogues, both Christmas master and classy outhouse toilet paper. I was prepared to be inspired, challenged, touched, and disgusted. It was the whirlpool of American identity and politics. I was to be repeatedly shown that we know far less about ourselves than we tend to think. Too, that the disillusionment and ruthless climbing which dismisses motion for serious change with cynical symbols, like new Moonie-admirer Eldridge Cleaver, are, at best, naïve when not self-serving.

The conference began the next day at Tougaloo College. Both Tougaloo and Millsaps were hosts and sponsors, each campus holding panels on alternate days. Most of Tougaloo's major panels were held in the campus chapel, a clean, sturdy, and old building that reflected the country quality of the campus, where even some Ph.D.s live in brick bungalow one-story apartments.

Millsaps is a more modern campus and the fact that it is primarily a white college helps it raise funds. Its major panels were held in both an auditorium and the recital hall of a large, recently built academic complex. Robert McElvaine, a white history teacher from New Jersey, conceived the conference after reading a book about the nonviolent movement. He organized a planning committee made up of many black and white people from or near Jackson and received funding from six foundations and WBLT, the local television station and the only one in America whose general manager is black. I suspect that even though many veterans of the movement were involved in the planning, the unhappiness shown by certain of the ex-troops was the reaction to a white man organizing a conference to discuss a moment of history where strategy and ideas came primarily from black men and women. One panelist had even defined it to his colleagues and students as "a Caucasian conference that doesn't have much to do with us." Some blamed McElvaine for not getting out sufficient information on Tougaloo's campus, thus accounting for the small attendance until the night black power was discussed. But the young crowd that turned out to hear the black power panel may have said as much about the regular lectures of Stokely Carmichael at Tougaloo as it did about disinterest or lack of information. However, students on the Tougaloo campus knew surprisingly little about the conference.

One student said to me, "I hear Dick Gregory is going to speak today. He's not? I might not come then. All I want to hear is something relevant. If it's not relevant I don't got time for it. But, tell me this—where y'all partying tonight? I can get to that. A party. But some stuff way back in the past, in the '60s, that ain't gonna help me get my degree and get out here and fight with these whiteys for a decent job."

Two students came up to us with the greeting, "Hello, Africans."

"Light as you are," I said to one, "you might be part Indian."

"But the Indians ain't gonna claim me!"

"Will the Africans?"

"Of course."

"Which ones?"

"Africa is one continent. It has to be united like Vietnam. *One* African people. Just like this is the red man's land; Africa is the black man's land. And we *will* be united. Eventually for armed struggle."

"That might sound good to you in the South," I said, "but in the North black people neither have guns nor are good shots. Speaking of Vietnam, what do you think about the squabbles between Vietnam, Cambodia and China?"

"That's Asian business. Asian business."

I realized somebody was still using black students' heads as fish bowls in which they dropped penny slogans. I could tell by the intensity of those young men that they represented the cannon fodder fringe and had they been unfortunate enough to have been the same age 10 years earlier, they might have been eulogized as they lay in black leather jackets covered with the tin mail of politician buttons. "The best humanity has to offer."

Ringing the colleges and the long debates and discussions that took place publicly and privately was a black community that seemed ambivalent about it all. In the streets and on the corners many I talked to felt betrayed, saying that having the right to sit down and eat some place didn't matter if you couldn't afford the food. The bloody shirt was waved at the middle class for gobbling up everything and moving away, basking in newly minted liberties while in Jackson one could still find shotgun houses, spavined dogs, functional illiterates, and filthy children. Many thought that an abundance of elected officials had sold out to white control and were but puppets of regimes that ignored the problems of lower-income communities, occasionally throwing up traffic lights and painting crosswalks. It appeared that every achievement of the nonviolent movement, from integrating public facilities to getting the vote and gaining the election of black candidates, was but an overture to the battle with poverty.

Still, there were many extraordinary people soberly examining the brilliant strategies of the nonviolent movement and how the movement was broken down: by internal disagreements, murder, abdications, discouragement, and tactical and philosophical blunders that descended to rabble-rousing. Whether contemplating other political and economic systems or working for economic leverage in this one, believing in multiracial alliances or distrustful of them, standing at the sidelines and advocating a return to Africa, or heatedly arguing over the tactics for change right here, they agreed on the necessity of organization and praised the movement for that. They uniformly saw their job as preparatory to action, if not improving action that was already taking place. This gave a freshness to the atmosphere and countered the pompously disillusioned and narcissistic constipation of much contemporary political discussion. Where many of the shills of Northern radical movements seem almost always to be seeking some form of therapy, if not the romance of anarchy, the people in Jackson, most of them Southerners, expressed an experienced seriousness that defined the talk. Even the talk that was totally ass backwards.

The question of white involvement stirred hot arguments that began on the first evening's panel. There emerged a recurrent feeling that white people were going to overstate their importance to the movement and rewrite history. Taking the stage, SNCC veteran Willie Peacock said, "We had a movement, a grass-roots based movement, and there were those of us who thought that when someone who looked like the oppressor told a black person to vote and that black person tried to register, it was only a continuation of the slave mentality. But if they responded like that to a black person, an advance had been made." Charles Sherrod, another black SNCC worker, pointed out that whites had been brought in because they would get the movement the attention it needed, that white people being beaten in the streets was a tactical move to get America's attention, and that those who volunteered knew why they were there. Beyond all skills they may have had, the whites brought television cameras and newspaper coverage.

Certain facts were clear, Mississippi was and is one of the poorest states in America. Since the end of Reconstruction it was totally controlled by white racists until local residents and students formed and worked with organizations, some of which, like the local NAACP under Medgar Evers, were more militant than their national leadership. The 1954 *Brown v. Board of Education* Supreme Court school desegregation decision and Rosa Parks refusing to give up her bus seat to a white man in Montgomery, Alabama, kicked off what became a movement that spread to Mississippi and culminated in the historic work of registering voters, the creation of the Mississippi Freedom Democratic Party, which tried to unseat the all-white delegation at the 1964 National Convention in Atlantic City, and the unprecedented indictments, through the brilliance of the movement lawyers, of Sheriff Lawrence Rainey and his cohorts, all of whom were eventually tried for the murders of movement workers James Chaney, Andrew Goodman, and Michael Schwerner.

Goodman and Schwerner symbolized the tactical decision to enlist white students that made the big difference and got the project workers the attention that had eluded them when all the workers registering voters in Mississippi were black. As Leslie McLemore, ex-movement worker and present chairman of the political science department at Jackson State, pointed out, the movement was run primarily by Northern students, because they were sophisticated and brought with their courage a larger vision of social possibility. It was the decision of Bob Moses that brought them there.

Arriving in the South in 1961, Bob Moses, through brilliance, courage, and discipline, rose to the top of SNCC. What made him so important, however, was his commitment to developing local leadership. Movement workers looked for leaders among the most influential community people, often the ones to whom others went to for advice. From those ranks came Fannie Lou Hamer, who was to become a candidate and prime mover in the Mississippi Freedom Democratic Party and serve as another of the strong female figures who were central to the success of the thrust.

Moses and Hamer were mentioned more than anybody else during the entire conference, he in the context of strategy and tactics, she in that of spontaneous poet and spiritual leader. Both were beaten and had attempts made on their lives. Moses eventually abdicated, some say, because he blamed himself for the deaths of Chaney, Goodman, and Schwerner. Joyce Ladner, a professor of sociology at Hunter College, said that had Moses not left SNCC for Africa, the entire history of the movement and the manner in which black power came into existence might have been very different. "Bob knew better, just like a lot of us did, than to run around talking about picking up guns and all that foolishness. We had their guns locked to their legs. They couldn't use them. But when all that stuff started with Stokely Carmichael and Rap Brown, the police and the FBI and the CIA were thrown right into the briar patch. They could do what they wanted all along. Kill us off. And they did."

Moses arrived in the South like a man destined to realize the mythic resonances of his name. He had been a comfortable math teacher, an intellectual with a great appreciation for philosophy and French literature, and a man for whom the future would probably never have included terrible beatings, assassination attempts, the laborious task of muting the fear of Southern black people, and the acceptance of tragedy that would come with direct action, all for $20 a week—if he had not gone south.

Much of his gift was his ability to communicate complex ideas to illiterate people and blunt, even poetic, insights about dignity and courage to Northern people. Fund-raising with him in California in 1964, I found that his technique was to transcend the blasé by asking a question no one would ask or by showing that charisma had to do with the ability to make people believe in themselves. Once, I recall, rather than give a speech, Moses said to an audience, "I'm not going to speak about what I'm thinking because that might not be what you want to hear. So, I'm going to ask for questions from the floor because we might find out that many people want to know the same things and the things they might want to know might be the things we all need to know."

The many stories about Bob Moses always reveal a man of courage and discipline. Moses would walk into the most dangerous of towns, calmly stride up to a door, and begin talking about registering to vote. He would be arrested and beaten, then released. He would wash up, check his teeth, his glasses, change clothes, and go back out to register people to vote. Whatever his complaints might be, he would keep them to himself, ever ready to change the subject from his misfortunes to something beautiful and poetic some delta man or woman had said, or a passage in some book he had found exciting. But it was quite obvious to Moses that, in a volunteer army where the ultimate sacrifice could be death, recruitment could best be done by example. Building an organization from the ground up, finding and grooming local leaders at every opportunity, was the only way a movement of that sort could ever actually be successful, for it would create a structure that could survive the murders of charismatic figures. But the movement had much more to survive than murder.

Allard Lowenstein, a New York lawyer with powerful political connections called in by Moses to help with the various legal problems that the confrontations presented, came to symbolize the kind of white control and arrogance about which many are still bitter. When Lowenstein rose to address the conference, a heavy-set white woman turned to a black man and whispered, "Why is *he* speaking? All he knows about the movement is that he tried to destroy it!"

Lowenstein began talking and before he could get far into his version of the movement, he made the mistake of saying, "The white people who came to Mississippi found a courage, a dignity, and a nobility in the black people that they didn't find in the white people." He then went on to mention the fact that whites had found new identities and new role models. Michael Thelwell, a Jamaican who came to America in 1959 and soon found himself in the movement, leaped up and said, "Al Lowenstein, I'm not going to let you change the movement's meaning! The movement came out of the culture, the needs, and the struggle of black people. It wasn't a 'touch me, feel me,' encounter group, or sensitivity session!" Thelwell also expressed a certain suspicion of Lowenstein's connections. I later found out many suspected Lowenstein of being some kind of informant for the government.

The hostility toward Lowenstein seemed to some white students present as no more than a form of anti-Semitic or anti-white feeling, probably because no questions of substance were asked him. There is a transcript of a meeting, however, contained in ex-SNCC tactician James Forman's book, *The Making of Black Revolutionaries,* in which it becomes clear that Lowenstein was moving for an influential role in the movement and was demanding that those white Northerners who footed the bills should be involved in policy, tactics, and strategy. Field workers, especially blacks, were angered by that attitude because it gave the impression that someone in the white North who had no knowledge of Mississippi might be able to sway the movement simply because he got some people out of jail. It is acceptance of money from the North which some workers think was the biggest mistake. "If we hadn't taken any of their money, we could have flooded the jails until they *had* to let us go or risk the overcrowding and crippling of their penal system."

The questions that arose about white participation during the early panels and during Lowenstein's speech exposed the roots of black power and the reason for the eventual splintering of the movement. Some blacks went so far as to say whites were totally irrelevant, describing them as "window dressing on the movement," while others often addressed the assembled as though there were no whites in the audience, usually speaking with extraordinary condescension. A few panelists seemed intent on denying the significance of white participation in black liberation movements throughout American history—as field workers, financial backers, lawyers, or as sometimes too-arrogant or paternalistic Pygmalions ever ready to mold ideas and set policy. It seems to me, however, that, whether anyone likes it or not, white people can point to a tradition of positive involvement in black history. It is undeniable that the major thinkers and strategists for the Civil Rights Movement were black and that the whites, as auxiliary as they were, were frequently brilliant and courageous. It seems a silly argument by those who deride the white workers from the North to think their presence in any way diminishes the heroism of the local Mississippians or the black students who initially came to work with them.

Disillusionment seems to have preceded the expulsion of whites from SNCC, a disillusionment connected as much to government resistance as it was to resentment of white patrons. In a startling paper, John Salter, who worked with Medgar Evers, accused the Kennedys of never supporting the drive for school desegregation, better jobs, and voter registration, unless there was the threat of public embarrassment or violence. He also claimed that the NAACP tried to thwart the Jackson movement in 1963 at the urging of its financial backers and the government. Add to that the fact that, as reported in *Southern Exposure,* an excellent magazine about the South, by October 1964 fifteen people had been murdered, four had been wounded, 37 churches had been bombed or burned, and there had been over 1000 arrests. The mood of discouragement deepened.

Bitterness began to erode alliances. Some began to resent whites coming to the movement because they would draw unnecessary racist attention. Most of all, however, the rise of black nationalism, the ideas of Elijah Muhammad and pre-Mecca Malcolm X, rife with science fiction, heckling of nonviolence, and xenophobia, increasingly influenced more people. The literate, sophisticated, and aggressive whites, who showed through their skills the extent of black oppression, eventually were the targets of resentment, especially white women, for they got most of the romantic attention of black men. Cynthia Washington, a SNCC veteran, wrote in *Southern Exposure,* "I remember discussions with various women about our treatment as one of the boys and its impact on us as women. We did the same work as men—organizing around voter registration and community issues in rural areas—usually *with* men. But when we finally got back to some town where we could relax and go out, the men went out with other women. Our skills and abilities were recognized and respected, but that seemed to place us in some category other than female. Some years later, I was told by a male SNCC worker that some of the project women had made him feel superfluous. I wish he had told me that at the time because the differences in the way women were treated certainly did add to tension between black and white women."

Finally, the whites were asked to leave SNCC and work in the white community, a directive that was not taken very well by the whites. Many of those workers were Jewish and had much greater difficulty identifying with poor whites than poor blacks, particularly since poor whites were quite often anti-Semitic and given to violence. This was the beginning of the end, not only for SNCC, but for most reasonable politics in the radical community.

It is ironic that those who became either black nationalists or thugs shaped into transparent Marxists and who accused the nonviolent leadership of hopeless fantasizing were the more conventional thinkers. Black nationalists seemed to get their manner from films showing off the decadent pageantry of popular potboilers set in Rome or Pompeii, depicting bush despots surrounded by the humble and the gruff, the servants and the palace guard. Nationalists loved drums and dancing, and martial arts displays, all of which revealed their being caught in the party scenes of the celluloid fantasies they claimed to abhor. The swagger and style of black revolutionaries was set and shaped by Westerns in which the gallant man is not the preacher ready to turn the other cheek, but the guy who grabs the villain's arm and knocks him down. Hollywood has long told us that nonviolence is good in idea but not in function. But that is what made the Southern movement so revolutionary: It was a set of variations on epic themes of the labor movement and Gandhi with the inflections and syncopations of black Bible belt oratory.

Black power and honky-baiting made the mass movement of black people that had been so responsible for change and had brought so many innovations seem futile. In fact, one could say that the most absurd aspects of black power led to the worst of black studies courses. Where black studies sometimes did enrich academic offering and open up fresh areas of study, calling into question conventional assumptions, at its worst the ideas of Elijah Muhammad were taught as genetic history. People were sometimes paid as much as $2000 to appear on campuses and call for the slaughter of whites, or Jew bait. Those rants in an academic context and the cheering of naïve black students may have more to do with the fights of Jewish organizations against affirmative action than has ever been discussed.

Maybe worst of all, the black power movement alienated the older black community. Consequently, unlike the Southern movement, black power was not connected to the people in any real way and did not make for the broadest of alliances. It was one of the greatest tragedies of African-American history.

By the end of conference, it was evident that there are black people who fear no alliances that make political and tactical sense, and that the face of future politics will demand more active participation than merely getting up one day to register and voting another. Absentee records will have to be studied as will voting records, and people will have to keep their feet in the asses of those whom they elect rather than roll over, go to sleep, and expect them to resist the pressure of corruption and intimidation. Julian Bond gave an excellent speech in which he called for more black registration, more marshaling of candidates and elected officials, which was echoed by Mayor Charles Evers, who said: "I blame white people for a lot of things, but I don't blame them because black folks won't get up in the morning to register and vote." And Leslie McLemore, during the last panel, added, "In 1979, we are on the verge of the election of the largest number of black officials since Reconstruction."

Still, traveling around the poorer sections of Jackson with John Reeves, PR director for the *Jackson Advocate* and a promoter of jazz concerts, it was easy to observe that the people of Jackson are far from satisfied and suffer from a lack of information about what they can do to change their fates. It can't be argued that massive changes have taken place in the South or that all of the objectives of the Civil Rights Movement helped to clarify the imposing gnarl of problems when racism becomes, as it is in the North, subtle and white sheets are worn only inside skulls or behind closed doors.

As I rode with Reeves to see the battlefield of Vicksburg, where Ulysses S. Grant had invented modern warfare, it came over the radio that, in Greensboro, North Carolina, where the sit-in movement had begun just 19 years ago, four people had been killed in a demonstration against the Ku Klux Klan. Given the violence in Boston, the regularity with which young black men are shot by white police officers; the killing of Eula Love, a black woman, by Los Angeles police; the terrain that must still be negotiated is obvious. When the time comes, those many who survived the movement in Mississippi with minds and spirits intact will know in most cases just what to do.

Of course, those kinds of events give fuel to the convention of dismissing the achievements of the Civil Rights Movement. But it seems to me the cynicism is misplaced and what is actually being criticized is the mediocrity of the thought, decisions, and action of a large number of black people who were able to take advantage of the monumental changes. Hustlers and frauds who are no more than xeroxed versions of the worst aspects of American careerism seem to dominate the picture. The upshot of it all is that Mississippi may have taught us that real change only comes about when the people themselves, in conjunction with the best minds from within and outside the community, *participate* in the realization of their ideals. When they do not, as when the movement was taken over by black power, effective strategy may be replaced with empty shouting or empty posturing of the sort that allows America the opportunity to avoid both identification with black people and the job of bettering this nation.

3

AUNT JEMIMA
DON'T LIKE UNCLE BEN
April 16, 1979

It was recently noted in the *New York Times* that the images of blacks one gets from television are consistently simplistic. Black women, like Louise Jefferson, are sentimental or obnoxious tubs of flesh, while black men, such as George Jefferson, are sentimental or childish or obnoxious buffoons, and both types of depictions cut through all class lines, proving their universality in the colored communities. Indications of the epic complexity of the black experience were realized in some episodes of *Roots: The Next Generations,* especially those concerning railroad workers, college students, and soldiers. But those were obviously exceptions.

Of late, the muddled ideas concerning black Americans that are gaining the most popularity are those focused for controversy and profit on male-female intimacy. One with an addiction to theories of conspiracy would probably say that some kind of backlash is in the offing. Although I don't believe that a conspiracy replete with smoke-filled rooms exists, neither do I believe that the august offices of book publishers, film, television, and theatre producers, or supposedly radical periodicals sit beyond racial trends in some objective space in the American sky. There is a backlash taking place in this country. Those whites within the media who felt betrayed or affronted by the anti-white, anti-Semitic and violent tendencies of black nationalism during the '60s are promoting a gaggle of black female writers who pay lip service to the women's movement while supplying us with new stereotypes of black men and women. The celebrations of the militant mediocrity and self-pity of Ntozake Shange and the horror stories of Gayle Jones, in which maddened black women bite off the penises of their black brutalizers, are part of that backlash, although I doubt either of them is aware of it. Michele Wallace's *Black Macho and the Myth of the Superwoman* is the latest in this series.

An excerpt from the book was published last year (1978) in *Ms.* magazine, which touted *Black Macho* on its cover as a work that would "define the '80s." Figuring that something superficial was in the works, I ignored it. But then curiosity about how the colored quarters of America were being weighed and measured led me to read it. I wasn't outraged or surprised, but I found the material a collection of un-realized ideas and victim-oriented sorrows connected to Wallace's fears of thwarted ambition. It sturck me as curious, however, that *Ms.*, a magazine given over almost entirely to the problems of middle-class white women, would go so far out on the limb in predicting the book's importance. Actually, I shouldn't have been surprised, because Albert Murray had pointed out in the social classic, *The Omni-Americans*, that ". . . Americans, including most social scientists, don't mind one bit what unfounded conclusions you draw about U.S. Negroes, or how flimsy and questionable your statistics, or how wild your conjectures, so long as they reflect degradation." This allows for the glibness, apparently informed stereotypes, and the condescension that typify most racial discussion. There was a period during the '60s when whites "accepted" the idea that they knew little or nothing about the African-American experience, yet they published books and produced films by blacks that, as more than a few critics pointed out, would have been considered racist and would have been shouted down had they been written by whites. The focus then was supposedly on the victimized black man. That was before the emergence of the women's movement. Now, the focus is on black women—if those women maintain ideas about being brutalized by black men.

I am sure that is the case, for no book titled, for example, *American Jewish Macho Identification with Israel and the Myth of the Yenta* would be so quickly accepted by *Ms.*, since everyone knows that things for non-black people are more complicated than that. And certainly no white woman only 27 years old who had written a book only 177 pages long would be held up as an expert not only on her generation but on her sex and the history of her people since 1619. But the assumption has always been that things are much simpler in the black community. Or some people would like them to be. Pimps, woman-beaters, dope fiends and dealers, ludicrous and pretentious buffoons and sentimental mamas dominating the images of black people seem to be the intellectual mint juleps that cool out summers on the culture plantations.

The ease with which such new stereotypes are accepted by both conservatives and liberals indicates their usefulness to both camps: they allow for the continued rationalization of the terrible conditions under which far too many black people now live and symbolize the resentment many whites feel toward what black advances have taken place over the last 25 years, beginning with the monumental Supreme Court desegregation decision of 1954.

Blacks have penetrated far into America since then, visibly at least, and have changed some relationships. It has been said of late that the ratings of television basketball have fallen off because there are "too many black players," and that the rise of interest in tennis, hockey, and gymnastics, has to do with the fact that these sports are still dominated by white men and women. Obviously, Caucasian America is not yet comfortable with heroic images of black people, which means that African-Americans haven't achieved the level of *universal* human symbols, where great accomplishment inspires national pride across the board rather than fear, envy, and enmity. It is also true that this is not the relaxed and affluent America of the last decade. Ex-radicals of all hues and hippies to boot are in the tight job market. There is an undeclared war between feminists and blacks for government funding of such things as small businesses. Black men are also under fire for having conducted real or imagined exploitative affairs with so many well-intentioned middle-class black and white women. And, perhaps most of all, they have proven as corrupt as anyone else in certain situations (e.g., Charles Diggs) and didn't save America as some loudly proclaimed they would, thudding their wet, clay feet on the clean ballroom floor, dancing the dance of the black paper tigers.

Observing how Michele Wallace was received at a book party and reading at Books and Co. on the Upper East Side led me to further conclusions about what is taking place. From the elegant, witty, and trivial manner with which Wallace answered questions and made small talk it was clear that she was a veteran of integrated cocktail parties and that she understood the artful balance of militance and laughing gas. It was also quite clear that she understood the dynamics of Lillian Hellman's comment in *Pentimento,* which Wallace used in her book to make too glib a point about hostility between white women and black women. Hellman's statement concerned following the orders of her black maid: "All my life, beginning at birth, I have taken orders from black women, wanting them and resenting them, being superstitious the few times I disobeyed." That is: She knows white women miss their mammies just as much as white men do and they are now kicking Uncle Ben out the front door of hip-shot ideas and letting Aunt Jemima in through the back—to the fanfare of publishing parties, readings, and *Ms.* magazine celebrity. If, however, Wallace is not aware that the attention given her and her book has little to do with literary merit, then she is in danger of falling for the ego-inflating game of letting whites tell her that she, like the Shadow, knows what evil lurks in the hearts of 25 million people. An intellectual conjure woman.

The terms "wonderful" and "marvelous" came up often at Books and Co. Every white I asked said things that had never been said before. One woman told me, "Those things about Norman Mailer romanticizing the primitive violence of black men and his ideas being picked up by Eldridge Cleaver and LeRoi Jones. Lillian Hellman and her maid. Those kinds of things are important." They all said the book was very touching and moving. Yet, when asked how they were able to evaluate its validity since they were neither black women nor black men and weren't privy to the inner workings of the organizations during the '60s that Wallace criticizes, they said things like "If one can read a book and that book is well-written, then one will learn. Besides, sexism is the oldest of national and international problems." While the whites were telling me this, the blacks there, most of whom hadn't read the book, were busy passing around a calendar of corny and pornographic cartoons of black men and women, which I found ironically hilarious. In the old days, I would have been slightly embarrassed. I guess I don't feel as responsible for every black person as I used to.

It struck me not too long after this party that many white women who are now in the feminist movement were politically or romantically involved with black men during the last decade. If they felt exploited—as many men and women were—and know they cannot express their bitterness because they'll be called racists, they probably cheer somewhere within the secret chambers of themselves when black men are held up to castigation, whether by an Ntozake Shange, a Gayle Jones, or a Michele Wallace.

If they felt guilty, they can know Wallace felt guilty, too. ("As I've said middle-class black children of my generation were plagued by a gnawing guilt. We were certain that there were other, poorer blacks who were taking our punishment in our stead. That was in part what made us rather uncomfortable about the attention that was given to the civil rights movement, it made us all the more conscious of that guilt.") If they had ideas about "noble savages," so did Wallace. ("In our simple-mindedness we had completely fallen for the popular definition of ghetto life: it was erotic, wild, free, intense, and liberating in its poverty and in the violence of its extremes. We did not go to the street to contribute; we came to pay penance and to extract, finally, a definition of ourselves—not unlike whites, even whites of Mailer's ilk.")

One of Wallace's conclusions is a perfect rationale for a white woman disenchanted by the black movement who had decided to go back to the middle class: "I got out when I realized there was nothing beautiful or worth saving about living in the ghetto, that its violence was not an indication of its liberation, but rather of the restrictions that pervaded all areas except the purely physical . . . the really entrenched ghetto dweller is one who is brutalized, so brutalized, in fact, that his every action, thought, word, emanates from a sense of his own affliction, from the consciousness of having been deeply and irreparably wounded . . . Surrounded by such human wreckage, one fears each day that the unbearable will occur, that finally one will be anesthetized, become a vegetable unable to recognize one's own pain." Are those monstrous blacks or are those some monstrous blacks?

It is also a recasting of favorite snobbish ideas about emergent black Americans. Since middle-class life almost totally symbolizes for white feminists the reduction of themselves to little more than extensions of household utensils (one white woman once told me she fantasized herself as a talking vacuum cleaner), it is easy to see why they so readily accept Wallace's simplistic attacks on the black middle class. I, for one, refuse to accept that when black Americans move beyond poverty they lose themselves in some way or become "less black." This is especially true when one realizes that many of the people who personify the idiomatic authenticity of the black community in thought, word, action, or style are not lower-class any longer, but upper-class—Muhammad Ali, James Brown, Marvin Gaye, Richard Pryor, Julius Erving, George Clinton, Chaka Khan, Millie Jackson, and so on.

Is it possible that what Wallace is saying forms part of a rejection of the idea that lower-class black people have any virtues at all? Isn't it a much better argument for building walls around black communities than involving city, state, and federal funds and expertise to bring about change? And if, as Shaw once said, hatred is the coward's revenge for ever having been intimidated, perhaps the condescension that Wallace now levels at both the black middle and lower classes is a repudiation of ever having been impressed.

I am always struck by the complexity involved in discovering the difference between the public and private person. Before an interview with Wallace last month, at her Village apartment, I expected, after being announced by the doorman, to find her ensconced in a pretentiously over-decorated apartment. I was wrong. It was spartan and contained a small but good collection of records and a library that bespoke a person with a literary education (Melville, Proust, Joyce). She was excited about being interviewed on television the next day in Philadelphia with Teddy Pendergrass. She settled down quickly and proved to be far more intelligent and articulate than her book had led me to expect. I'm sure the next book will be much stronger.

"My mother was always politically active and the kind of woman who, if she was involved in something, my sister and I were right there," she said. "Anti-war demonstrations, picketing museums (she was an artist who taught in the public schools), going to rallies. So I became aware at a very early age that things weren't what they were supposed to be. I tried to join SNCC in 1968 when I was 16 because I had fallen in love with Stokely Carmichael; he was a sex symbol to me.

"In the whole movement there was this mating game going on, but a strange one. I was meeting all these guys who were coming on to me with this heavy rap about black women being too domineering, matriarchal—a whole put-down. It was very intimidating because these guys were dating this 16-year-old—me—and they were implicitly making it clear that if I didn't toe the line, they were two minutes off getting a white woman."

With great wit, Wallace went on to describe the illusions many black men have about their sexual prowess. I told her that would make a perfect subject for a best-seller, especially since the success of *Rocky* and *For Colored Girls* showed there is a huge market for any material that seems to paint uppity black males as arrogant opportunists.

"But a better subject would be black women and white men." She laughed. "They would really love that. But you know the whole racial question as it enters feminism is very interesting. You see, I don't think there is much hope for black and white woman getting together right now because they don't like each other. A lot of black women don't know that a lot of white feminists envy and resent what they think has always been their independence. They also think we can dance better than they do, are sexier than they are, stronger, and much closer to liberation. They also think we look better. But, interestingly, black women think white women look better than them. Why do you think so many black women are going back to straightening their hair? They want to look like white women again. But at the same time, they often see white women as female counterparts of sissies—weak, neurotic, ineffectual, naïve, and incompetent. Yet one of the most ineffectual people in the world is the middle-class black woman in the business world. After all that loud superwoman talk, you should see those crocodile tears they shed when those white men snap at them. They fall apart. I find most of them fake and disgusting."

"Do you think your book could be used as part of a backlash against black men?"

"It could be. I know if whites like it, it has very little to do with anything that will do black people any good. White America wants to adopt everything about you that is effective so they can get rid of you. That's why they always try to pretend that some white woman or some white man who is imitating a black person is better than the original or at least as good. And, as for me, it's always about one play when there should be 1000 plays, one book when there should be 1000 books, one article when there should be many magazines. In fact, the way white people like it is that no black person should stay out there longer than three to five years. And if you do, they'll either change you, make what you did or said obsolete, or get rid of you. Look at the scene, you'll see what I mean."

THE ELECTRONIC GUARDIAN ANGEL
September 17, 1979

Just as Adolph Saxe opened a mighty door for African-American genius—quite unwittingly—through the invention of the saxophone, Jim Corbett did the same by mating boxing to dance. It was many years later when we would see in boxing what we now see in basketball—a dance beat and a rush of tempos in which the plasticity and rhythmic counterpoint define power by mobile grace. And just as the Continental Congress updated the monied European lords who bulldozed the Magna Carta through, Muhammad Ali, like the very finest black athletes, updates Africa, for his influence brings an audacity whose convention is unconvention.

Ali lives in a more complex world, one that allows his every move to become an international influence, joke, or magnet of dismay and disgust. Like all people living in the modern world, he knows of universes his ancestors could never have imagined. Not being a literate man, much of his information comes from hearsay, experience, and the media. The Greatest has obviously listened to the brilliant, the half-baked, the banal, and the ludicrous. That his ancestry is a gaggle of under-the-table miscegenation is not only the story of the South but of America and the Western world, since progress seems to come, finally, from ongoing mixtures of cultures and information.

Even in official retirement, celebrated last week in Los Angeles, Muhammad Ali is still as big as a mythic or religious force, ancient *and* modern. For instance, in the religion of particular Africans there exists the Orisha, the homemade god who is given celestial powers by the will and ritual of the people. The god is usually a community hero who has passed on and is given accoutrements necessary to create miracles for humanity. Ali is an Orisha now. He achieved the status of electronic guardian angel through the mass media and the attention so many people gave that communications complex when he entered it.

It is a dubious honor and a very costly one, for this is the century in which media figures of great achievement have become the last-ditch honor guard of our dreams and values, formal religion having been battered by Freud, technology, and ongoing social cruelties. So when a man has been promoted to the status of a god because he seems to do everything in his profession perfectly, an error or loss seems to resonate so that it jellies to national nausea, or, if the person is a perfect demon, to national glee. Throughout his boxing career, Ali has done both, and his presence, rife with improvised epic turnabouts, moved from the buffoonish to the breathtaking, like Louis Armstrong or Charlie Chaplin.

One could say that Muhammad Ali comes close to jazz and his art says some things about innovation in particularly American terms. Particularly American because many of the boldest shapers of this century have been Americans and have often had in common an arrogant and playful sense of the level to which they could carry a form, whether in science, society, or art. Performing sports are arts of the moment. Like the jazzman, the training of the great athlete has prepared him to manhandle the moment, to throw a saddle on the tornado and, like Pecos Bill, *break it!*

Breaker, trick rider, picador, and the heavyweight ring's fastest jockey, Ali has made ring time canter and canter, bow, leap over giant bushes, and move so much in his own terms that time became mutual with his grace. Truly the Professor of Boxing, he elasticized his profession, made daring and cunning and mystery part of the craft. Did we ever wonder as much during anybody else's fights what the champ was thinking? After the epic Foreman fight, we never knew whether or not he was hurt, or, if he was, how badly. So many of his fights were splendid and special physical projects, works of art created with punishing gestures.

He adds up at the end to an absolute hero—one who showed courage, wit, and brilliance as a young man, who was visited by disruption and tragedy, living out a third of a decade with one foot in oblivion, who came back, rallied, was humiliated, humbled, and rose to even greater stature. He gave us some of the greatest sports victories of the epoch— Zaire, the last Frazier fight, the taking of the crown for the third time. Some losses missed the book as well. I think he lost to Jimmy Young, whose sticking his head out of the ropes was a variation on the rope-a-dope. Maybe he did lose to Norton at Yankee Stadium, which proves the adage that one has to *kick the champ's ass* to win. And who can deny Leon Spinks his shower of glory? He did that.

Only Joe Frazier, however, can be discussed as a boxer near Ali's greatness, Ajax bringing up Achilles's rear. In Manila, they gave us *the* heavyweight fight. Never before had two men been better matched—the power, the stamina, the quirkiness of style, the legendary punches—each man's craft defined the other's limitations. They fought with a pace and a fury that awed. Men that size had never boxed with that kind of force for that long. It reminded me of those impossible movie fights in which every round is jammed with connecting jabs, hooks, and uppercuts. Fourteen rounds. Frazier's eyes were closed and he couldn't come out for the last round; Ali collapsed from exhaustion. John Wayne and Randolph Scott's mythic tangle in *The Spoilers* was blown away.

I became a Frazier fan that night, just as many did in the Apollo, the only place in Manhattan to see a closed-circuit Ali fight. Of course, Ali was still our man. Not only an innovative boxer, he was a Prometheus of speech, flipping the barbershop, pool hall, and locker room combination of braggadocio and the barbed skin-testing of the dozens into the athletic world in ways no one ever had before. Ali was the black schoolboy with plenty of eloquent sass for the stuffy white teacher, and when he broke their rules and replaced them with his own—not out of ignorance, but out of *knowledge*, he became the runaway slave whose very flight redefined speed and evasion. He introduced to boxing the concept of total war, where sportsmanship consisted *only* of never breaking rules like literally hitting below the belt—everything else was up for grabs, from the opponent's looks to his roles in movies ("We don't need no x-rated champion," he shouted of Ken Norton after *Mandingo*.)

But then Ali may have been telling us in another way that boxing is a cruel sport, if only because one wins by bashing and loses by being the more bashed, that it is a sport, like all those contact sports which pay big money, in which one risks becoming a cripple, imbecile, or corpse. And because the stakes are so high, we are attracted to it, for when human activity can symbolize that unstoppable force beautifully passing through an immovable object, the vision of the world is bettered, and our understanding of human will walks steadier ground.

5

CLICHÉS OF DEGRADATION
October 29, 1979

African-American attitudes toward homosexuality are very complex, and not solely because the joint role of stud and sexual butler has been imposed on black men and even voluntarily adopted in order to cuckold white males or use in lieu of significant social influence. Homosexuality has not meant just surrendering to a stereotypically threatening identity; it is mired in the smut and terror of the sexual Uncle Tom because the very act itself has so often taken place under circumstances absolutely connected to colonialism and other situations where *force* determines consent. In the historical backwaters of the Islamic sweep, the cultivation of gay, palpitating hearts in young African boys by colonialists who couldn't get away with it in Europe, the rapes and desperation connected to the least lit corridors of domestic slavery, or the constantly looming threat of erotic assault in American penal institutions—homosexuality is a form of identity so interwoven with exploitation and oppression that very few black Americans would connect it with liberation, regardless of the eloquence of its champions.

Consequently, gay black men are in a very strange position. Did they move aside false and conventional sexual natures—overthrowing the structures under which they were reared and taught—or are they simply perverse, even masochistic? Perversity and masochism are basic to the question because so much black thinking on the matter is shaped, again, by the threat of rape, which is so pervasive in penal institutions, and the debasing sexual slavery that often follows. (These attitudes have been reinforced by cases in which the sphincter muscles of certain men have collapsed and they were required to wear plastic underwear to avoid public embarrassment. However, writer Lionel Hampton Mitchell tells me that surgical updates have resolved that problem. One imagines that, like birth control, another blow has been struck against historical sexual terror.) Given the glib ideas about black self-hatred, connections to humiliation and submission in homosexual romances, particularly interracial ones, are obvious.

So when a black writer like James Baldwin steps into the noonday sun with a book about a black homosexual, he opens up not cans of worms but vats of super-charged eels. *Just Above My Head*, his newest novel, brooks even greater controversy because it talks about the homosexuality that sometimes takes place behind the wondrous robes and songs of the black church, where the secret and sometimes not so secret celebrations of Sodom bob and weave between the observances of the most holy who, to take off on Baldwin, might be closest to the most lost.

But Baldwin, though no longer projecting his preoccupations into the mouths, minds, and passions of white homosexuals, as he did in *Giovanni's Room* and *Another Country*, is confronted with a problem over which he does not gain literary dominion—the fact that, thus far, no black writer has been able to address or depict the experience of homosexuality, male or female, without recourse to making it seem some sort of religious order. Baldwin fails, as have LeRoi Jones, Aisha Rachman, and Ntozake Shange, by trying to prop up that form of sexuality with contrived ideas about greater tenderness and passion, all of which leads to some nearly elitist spirituality, suggesting that sex with no possibility of procreation is somehow more exalted than that which begets.

Still, homosexuality could provide for fresh material: It could, for example, reveal that more than a small percentage of pimps are woman-hating gays. It could make for a great novel about a notoriously gay and very great black boxer of the relatively recent past. It could show how one's specific sexual choices in that area can influence one's career for the better as easily as for the worse (this is what Duke Ellington meant by the faggot mafia, which is, apparently, as racist as its namesake, however). And so on.

But to do anything at all, the gay writer, black or white, has to fight off the same thing a major artist using rhythm and blues has to fight off— a strong predisposition for the maudlin. This has been the curse of the Irish, Jewish, black, and Hispanic-American writer since word one about the pertinent group, for massive doses of kitsch seem endemic to each heritage, from without and within, and as often improvised by the victims as imposed by the oppressors.

It is Baldwin's sentimental and poorly argued attempt to present homosexuality as some form of superior erotic enlightenment that continually slackens the power of *Just Above My Head*. The sentimentality results from a tendency to overstatement, pretension, and pomposity, as well as the creation of situations and responses the sole function of which is to prove the degradation of black people at the behest of racism and sexual convention. The degradation is wrought with existential clichés to demonstrate that suffering and alienation form the high road to awareness, and that he or she who is most painfully alienated is somehow most human and, as Robert Bone once angrily pointed out, stands as guiding priest or priestess at the intersections of human ambivalence. (One sometimes feels that Baldwin keeps reading *The Fall* over and over.)

Baldwin loves the black church for the depth of its music and its great feeling of collective exaltation, but hates it for its provincialism; he seeks in his writing to combine the language of the Bible and of his church people with that of Henry James and the hip argots of the streets and jazz. The results are frequently ineffectual especially when the characters are made to vent long monologues about love and danger, nakedness and loneliness, outrage and self-pity—the subjects Baldwin belabors most. Then his lecture voice takes over and everybody sounds about the same.

Yet there are many instances when the literary power that informed those fine and virtuosic essays in *Notes of a Native Son* comes through, and we are made ruefully aware of the struggle this writer is waging with his attempts to define his own life choices in a grand and heroic light. Writing of Joel, who incestuously rapes his daughter after his wife dies (the fashionable post-Bigger neo-brute is burned again in literary effigy), Baldwin's language moves from the Bible to the blues with actual eloquence: "Joel was still the zoot-suited stud of studs, fatigue beginning, perhaps, to undermine the jawline, an embittered bewilderment coming and going in his eyes, but the suit was navy blue, and so was the knitted tie; the shirt was white, the cufflinks gleamed like gold." But this same writer can also observe: "Love is a two-way street." You see the problem.

The 600-page novel moves across three decades, from the late '40s to the late '70s. It is narrated by Hall Montana, whose brother, Arthur, is a homosexual gospel singer who has died of a heart attack in a London bar at the opening of the work. As in *Moby-Dick*, or many films of 30 years ago, the narrator often moves beyond what he would actually know, providing both scenes and interior monologues that transform him into an omniscient story-teller.

Hall is much of the novel's problem. He is given to insubstantial observations about racial history, an ongoing series of sermons and homilies about the terrors and responsibilities of love, an irritating bitchiness, and claims of moral superiority to white people more often stated in a self-congratulatory fashion than proved. Then his sugary-salty Sunday school compassion takes on the tone of a professional mourner trying to be hip. Too, he is a very unconvincing heterosexual (with a few homosexual romances in the service): His descriptions of experiences with women are clay-pigeon fantasies glazed with effusive adjectives. The narrative can be effective, however, when Baldwin backs off from creating intensity by merely piling up words, and depicts situations he knows or imagines with clean authority.

The story is primarily about two families and a few careers. The families are those of Hall and Julia, the main female character, who is first introduced to the reader as a child preacher. Hall managed his brother's career for about 15 years, until Arthur's death, and has grown up with him in an uninhibited but religious family supported by their father, Paul, who plays piano in a local bar and grooms the gospel quartet in which Arthur first proves talent. Florence, the mother, is rendered well, though she sometimes takes on stilted Earth Mother qualities seemingly panhandled from Faulkner and Hattie McDaniels.

Julia is raped by her father, Joel, at around the age 13. Her arrogance and self-righteousness as a child preacher is partially responsible for her mother's death from unexplained complications brought on by a miscarriage. Rather than calling a doctor, Julia recommends a laying on of hands. Joel does not resist her because she is the family's main bread-winner—making him an interesting variation on the kept man. His anger at being dictated to erupts with his assault on Julia following his wife's death. Thereafter, Julia ceases preaching, becomes the sexual slave of her father, and a prostitute, later getting involved with Hall, going to Africa after a successful stint at modeling, and returning to New York with a long monologue about identity.

Arthur, however, is the central character of the novel, and most of what happens (through flashbacks) pivots around him. Arthur's life is supposed to be tragic, as are the lives of his peers, the other members of the gospel quartet, all of whom discover the soap opera beauties of homosexual love as teenagers. Each of them, in typical Baldwinesque fashion, is destroyed by racism or some other fatal blow to the spirit—a betrayal. Crunch, Arthur's first lover, returns from Korea, cannot face his sexual identity, and goes mad. Red returns from Korea and becomes a junkie. Peanut, a Civil Rights worker, is murdered in the South. Arthur himself becomes involved in the Civil Rights Movement, falls in love with Julia's younger gay brother, Jimmy, and eventually loses his grip on himself when he feels condescended to and despised for his sexual decisions.

Although Arthur is basically a very strong character, Hall and the others so swoon and moan over his difficulties that the reader is given little chance to feel anything at all. When this is not the problem, Arthur's language, filtered through Hall, so often changes at the demands of the writer that he sometimes seems no more than a literary dummy, ever ready to mouth speeches about dread and romantic terror. Yet, again, there are moments when the purple shrouds are removed, and some of Arthur's adult life carries authenticity. Arthur's brief romance with a Frenchman also seems authentic—though it, too, occasionally succumbs to sentimentality, and there is a fraudulent conversation in which Arthur lectures his lover on the horrors of being black in Western civilization.

Elsewhere in *Just Above My Head* are some of the finest scenes in recent American literature, some so precise and easefully evocative that one hopes Baldwin finds a strong and sympathetic editor next time out. Baldwin communicates superb insights about the buying of Christmas presents for loved ones and near-strangers, then artfully undercuts both the affection and the ambivalence with a finely orchestrated confrontation between Hall and a white worker in an expensive clothing store. Their animosity and suspicion are as charged as the best of Pinter or Thelonious Monk.

Another fine scene reveals Hall's and Arthur's mutual love as they kid and tease each other for hogging the bathroom and about the hopelessness of looking any better. Baldwin's depiction of a gospel competition among many gathered churches is exquisite. There are passages set in the South during the most dangerous days of the Movement that vividly express the tension, sense of community, and bravery of the people fighting for their rights. (But then the sermonettes intrude again, as when Baldwin pretends that every black man who goes south relives the horrors of some runaway slave ancestor with bloodhounds on his trail. How many of us are descendants of *actual* runaways?) Baldwin expands the territory of the black novel as he details the ambivalence of black people faced with the privileged dungeon of Madison Avenue success, and realistically— though too briefly—portrays black poverty-program opportunists. The irony, however, is that those are the people who benefit most from the kind of guilt Baldwin so continuously tries to impose on his white readers.

I think the guilt is all a waste of time, for guilt is not what black people need to inspire in white people, if, in fact, black people need to inspire anything at all in white people. What is needed is a breaking away by writers, readers, and various speakers for the black cause from simplistic, pot-boiled ideas, from the howling propaganda that is the Madison Avenue version of politics and social comment. This and opportunism are what locked too much black politics of the last decade into a treadmill of incoherence, and turned many into shills for a dispirited thrust bereft of its best minds by assassination and taken over by men and women dazed by French romance, whether that of Fanon or Rousseau or Genet.

No, I do not believe that as many black people are destroyed by poverty and racism alone as are destroyed—disabled—by educations that produce intellectual invalids unaware of the intricacy of their social context and of the many forms of actual change that can only be brought about through great study, dedicated action, and diligence. Nor do I believe that the world of a Nicky Barnes or a Richard Pryor is more real or significant than that of an Adam Powell, a Romare Bearden, a Max Roach, or a Donald McHenry. That kind of thinking can lead to an irresponsible snobbery wherein one could believe that black people, women, or homosexuals will, by some grace of special suffering, burst through the paper and metal chains that repress them and change our country for the better. Oh, it *will* be changed, and probably for the better—but not because the condition of the outsider guarantees enlightment. No condition guarantees that, which is something James Baldwin knows quite well. That he will ever successfully tell us this again, as he did so wonderfully in *Go Tell It on the Mountain,* is something we should hope for. Between a third and a half of *Just Above My Head* proves it is still possible.

CHITLINS AT THE WALDORF:
THE WORK OF ALBERT MURRAY
March 3, 1980

Far too many contemporary black writers produce work as though their function is to provide both blacks and whites with pots to pity in or gutters to guilty in, but Albert Murray is a man intent on providing his readership with the rich mulatto textures of American culture. His work is that of a writer who knows that to be all-American is to be Indian, African, European, and Asian, if only through cuisine. In fact, an American at his or her best can feel the cowboy (who is white, black, and Mexican), the Negro, the Irish, the Jewish, the Italian, the Asian rise up, depending on the stimulus or the image or the reference. Sometimes, of course, those elements may arrive through romantic or even negative stereotypes, or through the electronic media that has white children joking in the vernacular and the inflections of Gary Coleman on the one hand or, as Murray points out, certain black athletes appropriating the Midwestern accents of white sportscasters.

Fully aware of the intricate tangle of American experience, and far from afraid of his European literary influences, Murray provided much of what was needed from black writers in the last decade. For one thing, he was taken in by neither the simplistic versions of heritage nor protest that led to the political Zip Coon shows of LeRoi Jones, Eldridge Cleaver, and the like, both of whom have now repudiated their past in favor of mooning over Marx on one hand and marking time for Reverend Moon on the other. That Jones, who so consistently called for the murder of all Jews, could read not too long ago at the Naropa Institute, the Allen Ginsberg guru show, while Cleaver and Colson could share an early morning born-again Sunday praise-the-lord fest, are extreme examples of the kinds of mask-trading that Murray finds endemic, for both good and bad, in American culture.

"Unless," he says, "one can appreciate the wide paths that the human personality can cut in pursuit of safety, celebration, power, martyrdom, religious comfort, or whatever, the problems of art will forever exist in an unattainable province. That is my argument with all these guys who want to wall you into a dungeon with statistics and surveys and the glib terminology of the supposed social sciences—which change direction and application to fit the fashion of the day. That is exactly why they *aren't* sciences. Almost all of them are no more than new socio-intellectual dances on the make for best-seller royalties and a long line of clients.

Most of these so-called social thinkers would rather be celebrated on *Meet the Press* or some damn thing than make a real contribution to human understanding. Man, they can have all that crap. The finest art has always been better because it has always been concerned with what makes a people particular and universal—even if the creators of it were only trying to live up to the tradition they were faced with, which is to say a tradition that was sufficient to make universal statements."

Such were the concerns of his work when his books began to appear 10 years ago and his ideas started taking up more and more space in the conversation of black intellectuals and artists, as well as those whites who read beyond the best-seller lists. In a single decade he has published *The Omni-Americans* (1970), an increasingly important collection of social essays, reviews, and criticisms taken from magazines and anthologies, all of which form an attack on the numb fumbling in the areas of American racial and cultural evaluation; *South to a Very Old Place* (1971), a reinterpretation of the interwined culture and attitudes of the Southern experience that pins one-dimensional visions to the canvas; *The Hero and the Blues* (1973), a fine literary theory that interweaves social criticism, blues references, and speaks of the symbolic value of jazz musicians; *Train Whistle Guitar* (1974), a novel of great linguistic adventure; and *Stomping the Blues* (1976), the most eloquent book ever written about African-American music.

The range of experience and perception found in his work is reflected in the life the 63-year-old writer leads, which is full of investigation of the abundance of options available to the contemporary American. Recently, while he was at work on his current project, the autobiography of Count Basie, I called him at 8 p.m. to say that the World Saxophone Quartet, one of the finest realizations of the jazz avant-garde of the last twenty years, was playing their last show at the Public Theater at 10:30. He was there at 10:15 and was soon backstage joking with band member David Murray, having taken the subway from his Lenox Terrace apartment on 132nd Street. I know of no jazz critic who lives downtown who would have shown that interest on so short a notice, or who is so at ease with the players across the generations on their *own* terms.

You might also see him at the Strand, perusing a new book about Picasso, or at Books & Co. discussing a forthcoming show of Romare Bearden's with the painter himself as he prepares notes for the writing of its catalogue. On any day of the week he might be talking with Art Woods, a brilliant shade-tree jazz historian and ex-saxophonist who works at the collector's record shop on Twelfth and Broadway, in front of which he and Murray are whipping the air with switches of Harlem and Georgia wit. Holding the blues at bay as his apartment fills up with an ethnic stew of intellectuals, all of whom notice the kitchen pots and pans steaming up the windows with cuisine that leads back to the gutbucket and beyond, Murray's conversation might turn to the better cheese stores in the Village or a funny story from Duke Ellington's private stock. At his innovative book party for *Stomping the Blues,* not only was there a jam session featuring many jazz musicians of classic stature, but the audience was filled with friends that included Century Club members Ralph Ellison, Charles Collingwood, Russell Lynes, John Hammond, and musicians such as Ornette Coleman, resplendent in a white leather suit. Of course, he might also be seen at a dance concert talking with his daughter, Michelle, who toured with Alvin Ailey (for whom Murray has written program notes—such good ones in fact, that the master choreographer joked, "Now I understand better what I've been trying to do all these years!").

"What *I'm* trying to do," Murray says, "is lead a full life. For instance, when I was in the Air Force, we used to have a group of guys who were real collectors of Ellington records and all the other good stuff that was coming out then. We would take one of those planes, which you could do in those days, and fly a long ways as part of your training or keeping up your skill, and get the latest Ellington, say, and fly right back. Then, man, we'd sit back and listen to those fragile records which you had to take care of because they could break so easily. They were as valuable to me as the studying I was doing of Mann and Hemingway, who was not only writing novels but publishing good stuff in *Esquire*. Of course, everybody loading up his literary gun or wetting his literary reed was paying attention to old Wild Whicker Bill Faulkner, an absolute necessity."

It is that fullness of reference, insight, conception, and technique which led Walker Percy to write of Murray's first published volume, *The Omni-Americans,* that it "may well be the most important book on white-black relations in the United States, indeed on American culture, published in this generation." It is singular for its period in its easy acceptance of the multilayered ancestry, both cultural and genetic, of this country's Negro and national population. Taken to task are the Moynihan Report, the limited definitions of the blues, and the intellectual double standards of the literary world (which would have *one* black book tell the world what it means to be black in America, while no such thing would be said about a Wasp or Jewish work). Other targets are Eldridge Cleaver, black nationalism, the protest fiction of James Baldwin (who Murray brilliantly proves was the Harriet Beecher Stowe of the '60s), and the emphasis on degradation as the basic aspect of the African-American experience. Irresponsible and uninformed white jazz critics come under the gun, foreshadowing one of the themes of *Stomping the Blues,* just as his celebration of jazz masters and the broadness of the black American cultural milieu sets the reader up for *South to a Very Old Place, The Hero and the Blues,* and *Train Whistle Guitar.* It is an essential book for all who would better perceive the intricacies of national experience and provides quality rebuttal to all glib cultural evaluations. Nat Hentoff, who is himself drubbed in the book, nevertheless points out that *The Omni-Americans* should be required reading for all high school and college students.

Identity and the bittersweet tangle of relationship that make for the Southern heritage form the subject of *South to a Very Old Place*. That it is supposed to be a series of interviews and examinations of Southern people and places has little to do with it. It is mostly an autobiographical set of variations that use a structure similar to the dialogues in Faulkner's "The Bear," where what is supposed to be a romantic and even apologetic rendition of Southern history is constantly undercut by montages of blood-and-thunder complexity held together by wit both grotesque and ironic. For his purposes of investigation and image-making, Murray approaches each chapter as though it were a chorus in music. Like a composer, he builds layers of association that merge with his major themes— everything from literary theory to political examination—and can even bring about comparisons of the features of a person's face (like interviewee Robert Penn Warren) with some figure from his childhood.

Where Faulkner was wont to put thorns in the flowers of Southern rhetoric and pepper in the sweet water of its lyricism, Murray seeks and achieves an extension of that rhetoric into areas of syncopation the old redneck aristocrat would surely admire. Faulkner would also appreciate the literary knowledge which allows Murray to point out that *Absalom, Absalom!* is as much a variation on *Moby-Dick* as it is an examination of Southern bloodlines and motives through the tragedian chords of Greek drama and myth. Finally, an example of the kind of turnabouts this work puts on the aforementioned double standards: ". . . you can only wonder what happens to all that fancy Teacher College-plus-Bruno Bettelheim jive about the first few years of childhood being the most crucial, when the topic is the black mammy's relationship to the white child."

I mentioned to Murray in conversation that just as Ralph Ellison had rewritten Hawthorne's "Young Goodman Brown" for his own purposes in the "Battle Royal" sequence of *Invisible Man*, he himself had rewritten Ellison's vision of Tuskegee in one of the most exciting and hilarious parts of *South to a Very Old Place*.

"As I have often said, many statements are also counterstatements. For my purposes, as the book shows, Tuskegee prepared me in many ways for what I was to live. Since my childhood background fitted me with my boots and fitted me for my spurs, I went to Tuskegee and got those blue steel rowels! Shit. Some of those guys like old Jughead Hamilton were some of the most serious and perceptive intellectuals I ever met, and if that comes across to the reader in that Tuskegee section, then I have achieved my intentions."

Murray was himself to teach at Tuskegee not long after his graduation, from 1940 to 1943. His instructing career was interrupted by a three-year tour in the air force. Beginning in the fall of 1947, he began his graduate work at NYU, which was completed in June of 1948. While in New York, he regularly heard jazz.

"After my classes, I would study at the library on 42nd Street until closing time. Then I would make my way up to 52nd Street, the 3 Deuces, the Famous Door, and all those places. That's where I first heard Charlie Parker and Miles Davis in person. On weekends, as early as 9:30 in the morning, I might go to the Strand Theatre and catch old Lionel Hampton, or to the Paramount where Duke was holding forth. Talk about a Globe Theatre! You had the latest movies, which combined the technology of cinema and sound, comedians, dancers, and the very best in idiomatic American orchestras! I might hang out backstage with Duke and listen to his jokes or talk with Ray Nance, who was Ellington's combination of Puck and Burbage, trickster and joker as well as the loftiest of singers expressing deep human meaning and aspiration. Yet he did his best singing on the trumpet and the violin."

From the fall of 1948 to the summer of 1951, Murray again taught at Tuskegee. In 1950, he spent a very memorable summer in Europe. "Most of the time I was in Paris as the guest of H. J. Kaplan, who was writing the Paris Letter for *Partisan Review* and who was working at the American Embassy. That was where I met Romare Bearden, James Baldwin, and Saul Bellow. It was a very rich summer because everything was so close and there was so much available to learn. For instance, Michel Leiris, who had been with the Musée de l'Homme since 1934, and who was a close friend of Malraux's, one of my very favorite writers and men of culture, gave me a person-to-person tour of the African collection. He had become interested in African sculpture through the work of Picasso. I was just as interested in what Picasso was doing as everybody else, and how it was related to making use of the broadest range of stylistic possibilities. In fact, I went that very summer down to the Côte d'Azur, where the Maitesse museum was under construction; to Juan-les-Pins, where Sidney Bechet was playing; and to the Picasso exhibit at the Musée des Antibes."

Murray's next work, *The Hero and the Blues,* is a literary theory that counterstates the tendency in certain modern writers to genuflect before the social sciences and "scientific" political theories. Along the way, as with all literary theories and modern works of the multidimensional bent which he favors, Murray goes beyond conventional premises. He puts the ax to protest writing and shows that jazz musicians have not only appropriated the best in Western music for their own purposes but have developed means of extending the emotional and technical ranges of music-making in ways that parallel Shakespeare's high-handed reworkings of melodramas into fully rounded works of art (replete with enough vulgarity or farcical deflating to hold the interest and amuse both the rabble and the aristocrats). By the end of the book, the reader feels as compelled to know the work of Duke Ellington and Louis Armstrong as that of Ernest Hemingway and William Faulkner—another original contribution to the writing and thinking of our time.

Almost as though he were writing an introduction to his novel, *Train Whistle Guitar,* Murray wrote of Thomas Mann's Joseph that he can as easily be brought into the blues tradition as Moses was brought into the spirituals. Referring to Joseph as a "riff-style improviser," it is observed he so transcended his position of a slave that his story became "the sort of apocryphal cottonpatch-to-capital-city detail so typical of U.S. biography."

Scooter, the hero and narrator of the novel, gives us a whistle-stop tour of Gasoline Point, a small black town full of friends, enemies, liars, and killers, some of whom begin as individuals and move to mythic heights. Certain characters achieve this resonance by artistry, courage, wit, and fortitude; others by chilling the blood with the results of their rage. Like *Moby-Dick*, the novel displays enough concrete details to allow for literary leaps of imaginative association, but the purpose is to show how rich even the impoverished soil of the backwoods is with ambition and support of those who would realize the traditional and personal desires of *any people*. As with the best interviews of Louis Armstrong or anyone else who started at the bottom and became a grand national or international figure, over and over we are made to realize that it is all the result of spiritual homecooking. Memory, initiation, and the development of a mind and personality form a world as large as that of Stephen Dedalus, or Frederick Douglass for that matter. As full of daring and structural adventure as a long Sonny Rollins improvisation backed up by the subtle and boisterous textures of the Ellington Orchestra, the book allows the reader to experience a prose much closer to actual blues and jazz than just about anything claiming to make use of those rhythms and inflections.

It is unarguable that there has been good writing about jazz by some whites, but not much, especially not as much as good playing by white musicians. *Stomping the Blues,* the first real aesthetic theory of jazz, is a work of elegance, insight, and very fresh ideas. It dismissed much of the prep school Wasp jazz writing on the one hand, and unseated the Jewish riders of rickety and wooden socio-moralistic stallions on the other, and was vituperatively attacked by many members of both camps. Murray also pulled rank in the most intellectually responsible of ways and showed how limited were most of the ideas those men had propagated for years.

The work redefines blues as a music of confrontation more often than lamentation, illustrating that at its most artistic it is also a music of courtship and an unsentimental warning of the possible dues of unsuccessful romance. While white writers have long been bemoaning the term "race records," it had no derogatory meaning within the black community—on the contrary, the term was one of prideful celebration. The significance and value of dance and dance halls is made clear, and Murray goes on to show that the desire so many white writers have had for the music to leave those circumstances is no more than Europhile provincialism. Most terribly, as in chapter eight, when he makes it clear through wonderful memory-laden prose that he was *there,* the sting is most intense. Yet the secure person of whatever background will have no problem with the book, for the importance of the idiom within the human context of national and international art has never been stated as well.

After excitedly discussing the breakthroughs of the World Saxophone Quartet with Murray, as I watched the literary maestro youthfully stride for the subway, outside the Public Theater, I thought of what Duke Ellington had written for the dust jacket of *Train Whistle Guitar:* "Albert Murray is a man whose learning did not interfere with understanding. An authority on soul from the days of old, he is right on right back to back and commands respect. He doesn't have to look it up. He already knows. If you want to know, look him up. He is the unsquarest person I know."

7

OUR ORIENT
March 10, 1980

A California friend told me a very interesting story about two years ago. He had gone to a radio station to interview for a job as a jazz disc jockey. Tall, handsome, sharp as rat shit (that's sharp at both ends!), he found himself greeted by a white guy with long hair, T-shirt, ragged jeans, and bare feet propped up on a desk. After telling the man behind the desk that he was there to be interivewed for the position, he was told that he didn't appear to know much about the music.

"I blew up. This hippie-looking motherfucker thinks he can sit up there and tell me that! I told him my daddy was in a jazz band, I heard the music in my house from when I was a little kid. Just because I had on a suit and my shoes were polished, this punk's gonna try to talk down to me. I felt like kicking his ass."

But the problem is common and it has more to do with odd ideas about what constitutes being "middle-class" or "bourgeois" than ideas about race. For would-be bohemians, certain kinds of political activists, and people in search of an identity that contradicts the assumed shortcomings of their own backgrounds, the middle class has become something of an Orient in the terms Edward W. Said made clear in his book, *Orientalism.* Said writes, "The Orient is not only adjacent to Europe; it is also the place of Europe's greatest and richest and oldest colonies, the source of its civilizations and languages, its cultural contestant, and one of its deepest and most recurring images of the Other. In addition, the Orient has helped define Europe (or the West) as its contrasting image, idea, personality, experience."

If one looks back to the 1960s, particularly from the middle of the decade forward, it becomes clear that, from black radicals to hippies, the Orient to which nobody wanted to belong was the middle class. The conception was molded to a large extent in the Marxist universe in classical social terms: middle-class people or people trained in middle-class ways shouting down their backgrounds or dismissing the dreams of their parents. But, in addition, there was the contrived anti-intellectualism and willful vulgarity that goes back to the rise of American popular art in the 19th century, when rural lower-class whites came to the cities and commenced bumping heads with Europhile elitists as they demanded entertainment that recognized their existence. Unlike those rural whites who forced, by dint of numbers and sometimes riots, the creation of popular heroes (see Robert C. Toll's classic *Blacking Up*), many of the '60s people who baited, defined, and attacked the Orient of the bourgeoisie short of actual violence did so in middle-class terms. They researched, read books, listened to or gave involved analytical interpretations, discussed the significance or lack of significance of art, and spoke of the lower class in terms few of that class itself would understand (unless its members became surrogate middle-class through the luck of a fighting spirit that would seek out a good education if one were not available).

But the learning tools and approaches of the middle class were just as important to those who threatened to violently attack the society, drop out of it, or do violence to its standards through promiscuity, drugs, infrequent bathing, unclean or eccentric clothing, or a rowdiness of language and behavior. And however much persuasion people attribute to television and the social programs of rock and roll, certain books and films initially intended for a small or elite audience had the greatest impact on those who became the most influential, especially among activists. The tone and vision of LeRoi Jones's Black Arts Repertory Theater, his black nationalism and his essay "The Revolutionary Theater" were highly influenced by the Grove Press translations of Artaud's *The Theater and Its Double*, Genet's *The Blacks*, and Janheinz Jahn's *Muntu*. Just as important to the politics of the college activists of those years were two other Grove books, *The Autobiography of Malcolm X* and *The Wretched of the Earth*, without which I cannot imagine black nationalism, the canonization of Malcolm X, the emergence of the Black Panthers, the Yippies, the Weathermen, or the romance of the street thug (the *fellah* in Fanon's terms). Of course, rock criticism of the sort that can compare a rock singer to William Butler Yeats is far removed from whatever the popular sensibility might be, regardless of how mutually hot and bothered its writers and readers can get in the presence of spastic gyrations and amplification.

That the middle class became the target for most of the animosity of those years and still looms as a dragon of the Orient breathing good taste or less than abrasive deportment even now is pretty ironic. The worst upshot is the desperate mistaking of vandalism for avant-gardism or radical political statement simply because it seems to assert the bourgeois convention of the well-loved bad boy or *enfant terrible.* Such is the attraction of much punk rock, and there are still jazz musicians so studied in bohemian ways that they wear their hair like dirty pipe cleaners or step on bandstands looking as though they just came in from Men's Shelter—and have yet to figure out why their audience is almost totally white. That is as easy to understand as the problem my friend had at the radio station: The audience they have is still fighting our domestic Orient. The audience they would like to add is not. It is feeling the heat of another kind of dragon, and a trip to the Orient might be very refreshing.

ANOTHER MASTER
June 25–July 1, 1980

Few artists who would like their work to have political resonance can make important distinctions between the layered worlds where politics really work and the shorthand of slogans, placards, and sentimental characterizations. Senegalese screen writer and director Ousmane Sembene is a significant exception. An artist absolutely unsentimental in his depictions of historical and contemporary life in his country, Sembene successfully creates situations in which the primal and the intricate make for broad symbolism and meticulous nuance. There is no romantic vision of some traditional paradise destroyed or perverted by colonialism, modern ideas, communications, and instruments of war or luxury. Instead, he opts for an elevated sense of human dignity and responsibility that is hardedged and mythic.

That Africa contains both cities and bush villages, pretentious Europhiles and stubborn traditionalists, allows Sembene an exceptional scope of reference. He has at his disposal intrinsic themes of the sort that makers of the best Westerns have always had—a breadth of complicated and stark relationships that pivot on questions of land, the responsibility of the individual and the community, the poetry and flaws of primitive societies in conflict with sophisticated, eloquent, deceptive and often corrupt opposition, all woven together by the inexorable forces of history.

Three films of his which were recently shown at the Art Theater as part of a festival detailed his importance and showed up the failures of others with similar ambitions. The films were *Black Girl* (1966), which uses the classical theme of the proud and naïve country person shorn of all feathers in the city; *Xala* (1974), a satire of neocolonial politics; and *Ceddo* (1978), an intricate examination of the Islamic colonization of Senegal that also tugs at the rotten eyeteeth in the gleaming mouth of traditional court life.

Each of these films examines the interconnections of social and political relationships and achieves power through superbly nuanced expressions of arrogance, disillusionment, and rebellion in Sembene's characters. The central figures of the films finally confront their problems with personal choices that have ritualistic overtones, yet the shocking or humiliating results form only partial victories. Near the end of *Black Girl*, the illiterate but vain and giddy girl from the impoverished section of Dakar slashes her throat in the bath tub of the French couple for whom she has come to work during their vacation in Antibes, and by whom she has been reduced to an isolated and perpetually abused work animal. In *Xala*, a pompous and crooked member of a superficially independent Senegal is gradually shorn of his governmental position, his business and riches. In the final scene, his home is invaded by a group of cripples and beggars. In order to regain sexual powers lost through a curse imposed for his crookedness, the ex-minister must strip before his family and allow the invaders to spit on him. To a soundtrack of hawking and spewing, the frame freezes on the man, now slimy in absolute disgrace. *Ceddo* concludes with the revenge killing of a Muslim priest who has ascended to the throne of a 17th-century Senegalese village (its king had been murdered by members of his court who had converted to Islam). The priest is shot by the daughter of the murdered king who was kidnapped by a member of the village peasantry in protest against enforced religious conversion.

In heavier hands, these tales would be terribly sentimental when not obvious, but Sembene succeeds because all of the characters are both individuals and symbols; they have good or provincial ambitions, flaws and virtues, family joys and difficulties, as well as lovers. It is his interest in the intricacy of human relationships that makes his work so important. In *Black Girl* he is able to make both village life and romance as real and subtle as the problems the servant girl has with the bourgeois family. Through his fine direction of the performers, he builds great tension as the mistress of the house uses the girl as a buffer for her anger towards her own marriage and her lack of things to do. The tragedy is perfectly paced as the servant is transformed from a wigged and haughty young woman who does her work in the mistress's cast-off party dresses to a sullen and pained *native* girl slowly and rebelliously transcending her initial superficiality as she pads through the apartment on bare feet, fulfilling the image of a supposed savage. She is then as devoid of human feeling in the eyes of her employers as the African mask she had given them as a present.

Xala functions because Sembene so brilliantly brings together the contemporary and the primitive that one believes the modern world of Dakar, with Mercedes limousines and European luxury attained through corruption, can also contain witch doctors whose hexes are as accurate as precision engineering. A polygamist, the minister is cruel to his oldest and first wife, is henpecked by his second and younger, then cursed out by his third's mother, who returns his dowry when he cannot perform. His frantic searching for remedies provides for great comedy as his Mercedes carries him from fine homes and offices to dusty villages and medicine men. His loss of political position, money, and power doesn't gain him much sympathy, but when he must face the spittle of the deformed and impoverished in his living room, the man is transformed into a tragic-comic figure.

Had *Ceddo* been made and released for American audiences fifteen years ago, the romance of traditional Africa and Islam would probably have been very difficult for black nationalists to maintain. Sembene makes it clear that the slave trade was a three-sided affair comprised of African kings, Muslims, and Europeans. In the feudal village, there is a white man who calmly exchanges rifles and wine for slaves provided by the Africans themselves or the Muslims. Though the Muslims forbid the traditional worship of fetishes, there are many scenes in which they bow before the image of a star and crescent. The waning influence of Christianity is represented by a single Christian minister and his lone convert. As the story develops at a ceremonial tempo, all opposing forces fall before the Muslims, who sell the most rebellious into slavery and shoot the Christian minister. Though the kidnapped princess returns to kill the Muslim priest, it is clear that traditional society would eventually be overturned by the technology of Europe and the discipline and intellectual skills of Islam as illustrated by the craft of writing. Sembene seems to be saying that the role of African politicians and thinkers is to extract the best of all three, as much a problem now as then.

Given his skill at careful development of themes, characters, and situations, Sembene is an artist from whom many Americans could learn, for he seems interested in what one of his characters calls "the cruel sweet truth." That films like *Black Girl, Xala,* and *Ceddo* can stand as political statements that don't sell out artistry or the complexity of the human spirit makes them fine contributions to the expressive canon.

CRIME TIME:
DANGER AND ILLUSION IN HARLEM
March 31, 1980

The race-face changes the concerns as well as the game. When pointless or intentionally brutal crimes are committed by white people, they become "terrible comments on our society." If Harlem people commit them, they become comments on race. Such a problem exists in Manhattan today because the media and the hysteria connected with the fear of violence would lead one to think that the city is under attack by an army of young black toughs with blood in their eyes. That those young black people constitute far less than 1 percent of the black population is rarely mentioned, nor do many seem interested in the relationship of those youth crimes to cutbacks in both school and law enforcement budgets. The result is a group of young people who are, to quote a teacher who worked in three junior high schools in Harlem from 1972 to 1979, "bitter, vindictive, jealous, and dangerous." Left to handle them is a police force that is 90 percent white, on which the average cop is 39 years old. The young offender and the cop are performers in an intricately orchestrated drama. It is an interconnected social tragedy made up of drugs, boredom, unemployment, economics, blasé and corrupt attitudes in law enforcement, and immoderate emulation of bad boys in the worlds of entertainment and vice.

Veteran Harlem residents will tell you that there was always crime in Harlem, just as there was crime anywhere else in New York where people were poor. But they will tell you that the crimes were of a minor nature for the most part and rarely violent. What people are now concerned with is the sadistic nature of more and more crime, where even victims who don't resist are brutalized.

Those with a sharp eye for detail connect World War II and the influx of hard drugs with the creation of criminal situations and the kind of cynicism that can eventually lead to the coldest of crimes. As with all wars, substantial numbers of young men who might have been leaders and inspirational symbols of success were killed, others were wounded and crippled, while still others returned unable to adjust to what could be the humdrum of everyday life. If they had an itch for action, or a corrupt vision of adventure, the underworld could provide them with what they wanted. Too, the money was easy to accumulate and no honest occupation could compete with the amount one could make in so short a time. With the arrival of heroin crimes such as burglary, purse-snatching, or pocket-picking got rougher because junkies were in a big hurry and the degree of the panic they felt could define the violence of their actions. That violence arrived through a circuitous route that included jazz, the mafia, and gangs.

In the middle '40s, bebop was the new jazz music and it brought with it not only fresh ways of playing but its own slang and dress and the tragedy of heroin addiction. The last was responsible for destroying many of the greatest jazz musicians and reiterating the shady connections with the art that Ellington, Lunceford, Carter, and others had long fought to remove from discussion of the music, opting for images of class, taste, and discipline. Charlie Parker, however, was to change much of that and in terms he never intended.

Because Parker was such an extraordinary alto saxophonist at such an early age, many musicians took his use of heroin as a solution to the problem of playing as brilliantly as he did and thought he was trying to keep a secret from them when he tried to discourage their use of it. Parker's case was further complicated by his symbolizing the romanticized bad boy living by his own rules and counterstating the sterile or cowardly dimensions nice boys and girls—or Uncle Toms—could take on in so many minds. Just as the pre-radical chic Manhattan rich used to invite gangsters to their parties for the entertainment of hearing stories about taking people for rides, Parker's attractiveness to many young people had its roots in the black community's ironic twist on that love of law breakers. But among blacks it was an appreciation rooted in the heroic stature of those who had resisted racial repression or discrimination. That Parker's manner of supposed dissent only inspired many others to fuel the financial fires of the mafia was an even greater irony, for one musician pointed out to me that by the end of the '40s there were dope dealers all over Harlem, baiting the kids in. But it must also be pointed out that neither Parker nor the young men and women of his generation had the sobering benefit of seeing people destroyed by heroin. They didn't know what junkies were, only that heroin was the ultimate high and that it provided a perfect wall between the self and what one didn't like in the world.

Like prostitution and other forms of vice, drugs allowed gangsters to further develop domestic variations on colonial profit that general disinterest on the part of city government, law enforcement, and broad public opinion made possible in the black community. Quite a few people can detail the many funerals, almost on a weekly basis, of the musicians and teenagers found in kitchens, bathrooms, alleys, on staircases, in bedrooms. It was easy to observe that the way people lived in the community was fundamentally changed.

"In the old days," says a longtime Harlem resident, "if it was real hot, you could see people sleeping on the roof tops, on the fire escapes, or somebody would take a blanket or a quilt and sleep over in the park. Nobody would have the nerve to do that now."

As the drug trade increased, people began to wonder how a country so successful at combatting enemy sabotage during the war could be incapable of stemming the flow of drugs. Those people probably didn't know that the federal government had made a deal with Lucky Luciano to send out word from Alcatraz to the mob-controlled docks that they were to allow no sabotage in return for Luciano's release and deportation to Italy. Corruption notwithstanding, it seems easy then to understand how the same gangsters who could prevent sabotage could get drugs into New York.

But corruption created a new structure of graft and illusion over the years. Dope dealers were allowed almost absolute immunity if they informed on every new pusher who came into a particular territory. It would then appear that the police were penetrating the dope traffic, when in fact they were making it possible for a smaller group of people to garner even larger sums of money.

People with naïve visions of group responsibility are often shocked when they find out that the local dope dealers in the Harlems of America are black. But there are those who are not taken in by limited visions of good and bad, and who also understand that many criminals of certain sorts have generally similar backgrounds and aspirations.

"You see," says a man acquainted with street hustles for many years, "in the history of crime, dope people like Nicky Barnes, Frank Lucas, they're not that different from anybody else. They're not different at all. Different color, different street talk, but they're the same snakes in different wrappers. And they all come from gangs. All of your big gangsters, your big dealers, they come from gangs. Nicky was in the Turks, Lucas was in the Country Boys, just like Luciano, Costello, and all those guys came from gangs. Because there's *something* in the guy who'll go beyond a certain point in a gang. The guy who'll stomp somebody in the face when he's down, or after he's already been knocked out. The guy who'll go against what everybody else says and mug somebody, or push an old man around, even rape somebody's sister and dare her to tell anybody about it. These are the guys who become the dope dealers, the pimps, the strong arms, and the hit men. Everybody saw it coming, they just didn't know where it was going. And the crime game, it retards their minds. After a while, all these guys are good for is flash and cash—street slogans, slick cars and clothes, and big mouth dares backed up with big money. The minds of the people they're dealing with offer no challenges, no stimulation, and the paranoia they feel, it justifies anything they do. *Anything* they do. But the kids looking at those guys, they don't know they're looking at expensive talking coffins, with dead men inside."

The formulation of gangs and the emulation of street hustlers is the result of kids growing up in the streets, inferior education, and successful people leaving the community. "I'm 50 years old," says one person, "and I can remember when all those people were coming into Harlem from the South 40 years ago. They were poor, they had no education, they wanted to get up from under what the whiteys in the South were doing to them.

Often, both parents worked and got home late. The kids were out there in the street with no supervision. Remember, this isn't the South, there's a lot out in *these* streets, and the kids who weren't lucky enough to find their peers among those who were upwardly mobile—if only in their heads—they got involved with those who were upwardly mobile any way they could be upwardly mobile. Or they were taken in as kids can be by movies. When Alan Ladd knocked a guy down and started kicking him in *Lucky Jordan*, that because the big thing in the streets. Kicking a cat's ass, then stomping him. Gangs even started with names like the Jolly Stompers! Connect that attitude with the dope and you start seeing the development of vicious criminals. Add to that two and three generations on welfare and the only peers of theirs they see making money are the hustlers with the big cars, the fine bitches, and clothes, and you get a social womb out of which this stuff starts birthing. Besides, you see, if a gang's not full of potential murderers, it gives a kid a sense of belonging to something during the difficult years of adolescence. And since most gangs are made up of young guys who will eventually calm down and get jobs, they're not really that bad."

"Don't forget," says another guy, "when the musicians, the architects, the school teachers and what not, when they all lived uptown in *abundance,* the kids had other people to look up to and people who would give them pointers on careers they could respect themselves for having. But it's weird and sad that with the breakdown of discrimination, when those people *could* move down to Central Park West, that a lot of dreams moved down there with them."

"Plus," adds another, "you don't have the kind of dedication in the schools you used to have. All of us can read and write. A lot of kids 30 years younger than us are illiterate. And we're just average guys. We're not doctors or anything like that. When we were coming up, you had those teachers who were determined to make sure you *learned* stuff. They knew there was a war out here and that your education was your ammunition. They graduate youngsters today with all kinds of blanks in their guns. Those same kids come out of school with know-nothing diplomas and get frustrated real fast. Then they get mad, and when they mad, *look out!"*

"That's exactly true, exactly true," says the first guy. "The same thing with the police. They don't care either. A black cop, a friend of mine for years, told me this after the *Times* ran that story on Nicky Barnes. He says, 'Listen, man. Let me tell you something. The white cops in Harlem, they don't give a fuck about drugs. They don't give a fuck about nothing. They think maintaining order up here is a losing proposition. They think black people will *inevitably* kill or maim each other or tear up each other's property. But the black cops, we take it personal. Particularly when they try to make somebody like Nicky Barnes a goddam folk hero or some motherfucker tells you how dope provides jobs for the *downtrodden!* If they'll sell dope or help cut dope, they need to be down and *out.* If one of us black cops had had a chance, we would have taken Nicky Barnes some-where where nobody was looking and put two in his head. *Quick.*' That's the way he felt about it."

"I wish they had've killed him. I wish they'd killed all of them," adds one of the others, "because they not only sell dope, they're the ones the kids get this attitude of not giving a fuck about anybody else from. This is why kids beat up people after they already done gave up they wallet, or set somebody on fire. They probably think they're being cute, like one of these goddam hustlers beating one of his bitches in the street. He's proving to the world how *cold* he is. Now you got kids want to prove the same thing, or maybe they're just mad at the world. When you don't give a fuck, you'll do *anything*. People like that need to be behind bars or in the graveyard."

Of course, all black cops are not off the take and anxious to rid the community of known offenders, nor are all white cops blasé about black crime. But guilt can be assumed of a suspect where there is none, often to the tune of boxed ears or interrogations that reflect every insecurity within the cops' personalities and which may landslide a bevy of un-solved crimes into a brutalized suspect's lap. The confessed criminal, even the guilty one, will make a deal with the city to save time and money, and the credibility of the police will be maintained, though cyni-cism will be furthered among those in law enforcement. However, the cynicism goes further than the police force, to the very criminal elements which express their own versions. A dope dealer will point to the scandal over steel-belted radials to justify his trade, explaining that his customers, unlike the buyers of those tires, knew what they were getting into. An extension of that cynicism is the violence that sociologists call "expres-sive" crimes in which victims are shot, stabbed, or beaten even if they don't resist robbery or rape. The sociologists seem to think these kinds of crimes are new. I don't. We have come to recognize these kinds of point-less crimes from the Caligulas and de Sades of the world, for they were expressing through the license of political or economic power their out-rage with convention, boredom, and apparently meaningless lives. That these attitudes have filtered down to the lower classes is what is new. The poor seem to express both the anonymous freedom of the big cities and the anger with anonymous exclusion from its benefits. Apparently, this is the century in which we have the popular phenomenon of the most bitter of the poor emulating the worst aspects of big business morality, the decadence of the bored and dangerous, as well as the boldness of cellu-loid gangsters.

Of the young men who were robbing so many banks last year as though they were contemporary Dillingers, Baby Face Nelsons, and the rest in genetic black face, there are those who think they are the results of our depression known as inflation. Others are happy that they at least gave the more vulnerable people on the street a break. But no one seems to know where the guns used in so many crimes are coming from. Some claim to have heard they are being brought in through customs and the airports, but no one is sure. One thing they are clear on, though, is that the police don't have much to do with the proliferation of illegal firearms.

"Make no mistake about it, whatever the corruption is, all the money these cops get on the side for looking to the left when something's happening on the right, they don't know where those guns are coming from," a hanger-on in the hustling world says. "Whenever they *hear* somebody's got a gun, they'll tear a whole joint *up* to find it. They might not care how much dope some black man's got in his pocket, but you can bet they care about whether or not he's got a gun. That's one thing I'm sure they would stop if they could. Not because the black people might shoot other black people, but because they might shoot *them*. In fact, the kids believe the cops'll kill them anyway. What else should they believe? So many black youngsters get killed every year because the cops claim they *think* they have guns, you know what they'll do if they really have them. The saying among them these days is that they're not doing any time, they say they'll 'hold court in the street.' That's the way it is."

Given real estate strategies of gentrification, there might now be a *purpose* to the allowed continuance of flagrant crime in Harlem beyond the bilge of graft in which certain police officers, judges, and politicians float. It may have to do with the very restructuring of Manhattan.

Mayor Koch's statement a few months ago that if you can't afford to live in Manhattan why not move to Brooklyn, a fine community where *he* grew up, connects to a growing feeling that the crime that has developed over the years now has a social function: to drive black people out of Harlem. This would allow whites to "take back" Harlem so that gentrification plans can continue unimpeded. After all, as writer and Harlem dweller Larry Neal points out, "Harlem is full of incredible buildings. One guy showed me that Seventh Avenue is the widest boulevard in Manhattan and could be a potential Champs Elysee. People are very paranoid up here about the idea that the white people are trying to take this place over. They think that's what's behind a lot of the arson, too. It leaves fewer places for people to live in and empty lots for realtors to gobble up. Plus, if lots of white people start moving into Harlem, the schools will improve and so will the policing. They'll run all those dope dealers off 116th and Eight Avenue and the other boulevards."

Given the gas crisis and the fact that young, successful couples are moving into the city and looking for places to live, Harlem brownstones and refurbishable grand apartment houses concretized the grim sense of the observation. It would also add another irony to the many connected to this story, for it would mean that the criminals who have done so much damage to Harlem are now helping to change it even more. Where they once made whites afraid to go there, they might now be making it much easier for them to return.

Interestingly, Columbia University just bought three buildings at 145th and St. Nicholas, one of Harlem's most crime-infested blocks. The tenants have been removed and told they can come back. No one believes it. As the buildings are renovated, the word among the hustlers is: "It's time to clear out. They're getting ready to clean up this block."

THE FAILURE
OF TANTRUM POLITICS
August 27–September 1, 1980

I used to think of Miami as primarily a Mafia bastion and a Jewish burial ground in Deep South resort trappings, but it is actually a modern border town where black people live in an impoverished Southern past as the future takes place around them, and in ways for which they have no models. Due to massive Cuban immigration and the lucrative trade of running illegal aliens from Bimini for $500 a head, the city seems sprawled partially in the United States and partially in Latin America. It is now this country's major trade center for business with Latin America and the capital for cocaine smuggling which gives it a boom-town and violent flavor, just as it layers the black social struggle in Miami with the problem of learning Spanish. That is the big difference in the problems of that city's black people, for the Negro political struggles in other parts of America have not been complicated by immigration that necessitates learning another language to work in most of the public service and managerial positions fought for through so many boycotts and picket lines during the height of the Civil Rights Movement. However, the problems which are national in black communities also exist there and make even more difficult the handling of Miami's unique problems. Substandard education, police brutality, bad housing, unemployment, and a naïve disenchantment with local and state electoral politics in favor of presidential elections help prepare the way for continued intentional and unintentional victimization as well as disgruntlement and longing for charismatic leadership of the messianic bent. But more is needed in Miami than big daddy or big mama figures. Consequently, the May rioting and the Clockwork Orange violence of Liberty City's black youth in late July—which cost less in their $100 million than what one shipment of Colombian cocaine might be worth in the streets—were only the algae rising to the top of an intricate social pool.

The significance of language was the first thing I was to learn, when I arrived there with Jose Torres. It was two weeks after the May riot, Jimmy Carter's motorcade had yet to be pelted with rocks and bottles, and there was a deceptive calm in the tropical heat that did not suggest that there had been robbing and stonings of whites at red lights, police snipings, and the rest of the misbegotten violence of Liberty City black youth and seasoned criminals in late July. The plane landed late at night and the breadth of hues, textures, physical shapes, and clothing was customary for an airport. The air, however, was full of Spanish spoken at many tempos and with many inflections. The janitorial crews one usually sees in airports late at night were dominated by black people, some stoic and nettled, others laughing and joking or muttering. They all spoke English.

I was soon to become aware of the emotional complications one can experience when conversations swing back and forth between familiar and foreign languages, a feeling of moving from light to absolute darkness. As we rode to the Holiday Inn with a friend of Jose's, who was also from Puerto Rico, they would speak English only part of the time, breaking into Spanish when something important or emotional came up and to tell quick jokes. It irritated me not so much because I thought they were leaving me out of points in the discussion on purpose, but because I thought it was rude on the one hand and showed up my linguistic inadequacies on the other.

On the way to the Inn, we took 79th Street, a strip of which has been taken over by black hustlers and prostitutes, real women and those grotesque combinations of fantasy and medical technology that are transvestites. I felt as if I was looking at a hellish combination of a slave market, a dungeon, and a clearing house for the sly, the desperate, and the leeches who live under a truce of Constitutional rights and public disinterest, where dreams of vulgar luxury, constant intoxication, and sadomasochistic agreements of one sort or another coexist. Like all hustling sections, the visual atmosphere of illegality gave the feeling of secret missions taking place or being promised in public. Loud music periodically burst into the air and was cut off or muted as men and women in flamboyant dress, swaying invitation or rippling potential violence, entered the fast life-magnets of joints into which passersby could not see. An occasional police car would slow as its riders perused a group of men talking, all of whom would suddenly take on the look of blank meditation, contemplating a potential roust, then resume conversation in a street slang with which I was all too familiar, as the police car continued up the street. Recalling the hustling soldiers of fortune I'd watched quickly take over the Watts riots in 1965, I wondered how many of them had bootlegged political slogans as covers for their opportunism during Miami's May looting.

As we turned on Biscayne Boulevard, I began to notice businesses with Spanish names or island associations, such as Tropical Chevrolet, how neat they were, and the easeful atmosphere that counterpointed the tension of 79th Street. Within a few days, I was to become accustomed to the sometimes startling juxtapositions of the social worlds of Miami.

The desk of the Holiday Inn was manned by two Cubans, both olive-skinned, one large, elegantly officious, and jovial, the other slender with the look of a man who started each day by catching his foreskin in his zipper. There was a problem with the reservation and a dispute as to whether or not we would get rooms. Though the conversation began in English, Torres started explaining the problem in Spanish, and the tone immediately changed. While we were both somewhat condescended to initially, Torres suddenly became an insider, and I felt that old feeling a black person can sometimes have when in the company of a white man disputing with white men neither knows: the white guy is assumed the authority and you the sidekick. That Torres is dark and nappy-haired enough to pass as an African-American threw the race business out the door and made it about culture, a familiarity connected to language and the ability to relax other people by letting them speak the language in which they think. That he is also a celebrity in the Latin world helped just as much.

The next morning I found there was an all-Spanish station on television and that the children's programs on the other networks featured clever writing in which questions were asked in Spanish and answered in English, or vice versa. I became excited about the future of American literature and the challenges ahead, figuring that our most ambitious writers would begin mastering Spanish over the next decade, even our better newsmen, so as to address what Mexican novelist Carlos Fuentes calls our destiny of contradictions. As I walked around the hotel, Spanish words and phrases I'd learned 20 years ago began coming back to me. At the same time, I also became aware of the symbolic strata of Miami which was observable at the Inn. The menial jobs were handled by black Americans and Haitians, the first level of administration by Cubans, and the final authority was held by white Americans. It was a pattern I was to see repeated in many ways over the next week, for the blacks in Miami live in such an economic and political shadow that one is surprised when the occasional executive appears.

That shadow world is perpetuated by the failures of public education. In 1978, two-thirds of black high school kids in Miami failed a functional literacy test given when they entered the 12th grade. There have been vast improvements, however. Now only a third fail. Clearly, people with such a low quality of education are ill-prepared to deal with the sophistication and cosmopolitan tone of an increasingly bilingual city where Cuban immigration has bad effects on the black community that echo the arrival of European immigrants at the turn of the century. Cubans now constitute 50 percent of the city's population, while black residents make for but 13 percent, the country's smallest percentage in a major urban center.

Superficially, at least, the expanding circles of sophistication and strength exhibited by black Americans in politics, business, the arts and sciences over the past two decades would seem to exist in Miami. Since his election in 1973, Mayor Maurice Ferre, a Puerto Rican, has battled prejudicial police and fireman unions, gotten the justice department to prosecute state highway patrolman Willie Jones on charges of sexually assaulting an 11-year-old black girl, and decried the acquittal of the police officers who had beaten black insurance executive Arthur McDuffie to death as an example of judicial racism. The acquittal had sparked the May explosion and Ferre so incurred the wrath of the police union by calling officers "bums" who had written "looter" and "nigger" on parked cars they themselves vandalized during the rioting, that the Miami cops started circulating a petition demanding his recall. Under Ferre, more blacks have been involved with high-level city government than ever before, as city attorneys, commissioners, city managers, and so on. Yet for the majority of black Miami, segregation by law has been replaced with segregation by money, education, and language.

At the suggestion of Joe Oglesby, one of the *Miami Herald*'s two black reporters, I attended a Saturday morning breakfast at St. John's Baptist Church, where local leadership meets weekly. Since the Urban League office had been burned down the night before, I was prepared for fire-brand speeches and much posturing. There were those and more. In the meeting hall, a large bungalow with kitchen facilities and rows of tables pushed together, was a broad assemblage of black people and a few whites. Scrambled eggs with fried chicken, fish, and sausage were served, and what began as an old-fashioned church breakfast served by slow but militantly officious church women with gold-bordered teeth or their sassy daughters, quickly became a pathetic variation on the legislative scene from *Birth of a Nation*. Over a scratchy microphone, an Italian named Bogianni tried to speak about problems with the federal reserve. Few people paid attention, various groups talked loudly, some shouted at him, and a corpulent black man with a shirt pocket full of green cigars periodically rapped on a table with a pipe, chuckling and calling for order. The din rose and decayed with regularity. I was told by two women in attendance that the reason for lack of interest was because the speech had little relevance to the more obvious problems of Miami. Audible but unintelligible, Bogianni finally gave up in anger and brusquely collected pamphlets he'd passed out.

A large and middle-aged man of walnut complexion took the micro-phone and said that he was *not* going to speak, but that if he *did* speak, he would speak about *Jesus*, a man whose mighty suffering brought about great good and salvation. The crowd rumbled and roared him away from the podium. Father Gibson, a ripe cherry-dark Episcopalian minister, who is also a commissioner of Miami, grudgingly came to the front of the room after refusing to lead the assemblage in prayer. He started his talk by congratulating himself for saving some lives during the riot, for having served the community for 35 years, and accused the "new leadership" of having "star sessions" with the mayor to which Gibson wasn't invited. Gibson said they would get nothing but mayoral promises, mess things up, and have to come to him to straighten out their mistakes. "Don't forget," he shouted, one arm raised, index finger tickling the air, "I's got the vote! I's your representative to the City Commission. You all has got to learn to tango! You can't cuss out the white people and expect to get nothing." Then Father Gibson sat down, glowering.

Willie Logan, a tall, coffee-colored man in his early twenties who is the mayor of Opulaca, a small town just outside Miami, made the most sense at that point. Logan said that black people would have to improve the public schools by pressuring the school system, that they would have to pressure lawmakers and representatives through voter registration so that their needs and wishes could be heard through the ballot box, letters, and telephone calls. His brief address was not as well received as the speeches of those who referred to the riot as a rebellion, claimed that Vietnam veterans were responsible for its effectiveness, and predicted more violence if federal money wasn't gotten right away.

"We've never had a shortage of federal dollars here in Dade County," said a young woman who took the microphone. "The problem is how they're spent! We were promised 20,000 jobs last summer and 200 were produced. You so-called leaders had better realize that the '60s aren't over and that people are going to have to be organized on the grass-roots level so that we can get positive action, not looting and burning."

But positive action is hard to come by in Miami because of the obvious lack of insightful tactical vision on the part of the black leadership, which Mayor Ferre claims doesn't exist. This could be accounted for by the fact that those who are brightest within the black community tend to leave the city, complaining of white racism, the difficulty of getting small business loans, and the narrowing of the job market to those with a command of Spanish. Black Miami, therefore, finds itself with a very thin line of literate and articulate people capable of thorough analysis of the sort that would lead to precise though arduous social and political strategies.

What leadership remains has been accused of making deals with the right white people, state and local politicians, rather than organizing on the grass-roots level, which seems only partially true. A few years ago, community leaders urged black voters to support a transit bond issue that would account for almost a billion dollars in construction and jobs. The issue passed by only a few thousand votes and the black vote made the difference. Thus far, the jobs promised the black community have not surfaced, and disenchantment with electoral politics has grown as it seems white and Cuban firms will rake off most of the money, if not all of it. Black leadership, therefore, has to also contend with low voting turnouts by its constituency.

That kind of disenchantment is as tragic as the misbegotten violence. The upshot is that the tantrum politics of the late '60s have filtered down along with the belief that the American system resembles a detective story in which we need only find the smoke-filled room in which power is shaped or need only beat the bullrushes for a Moses who can shake and bake us out of our dilemmas. But, again, as Carlos Fuentes has pointed out, power in America is extremely diffuse, and its very diffusion demands more comprehension on the part of the populace and its politicians. And this is where the black leadership in Miami has failed, for it lacks the vision to push for mandatory bilingual public education and has been equally remiss in communicating the importance of voter registration and turnouts.

The Cubans will not forever vote in blocs, and a strong black vote could become a decisive factor in overall Miami politics just as it was in the transit issue. This is especially important because there is resentment towards the Cubans by whites who feel "like foreigners in your own home town," and who refer to Miami pejoratively as "Northern Havana," complaining that one must move north of Miami to return to the United States. Since whites are in the majority in Dade County and the Cubans have no impact on state politics due to gerrymandering and numbers, there has been talk of incorporating Miami into Dade County and dissolving it as a municipality, thereby doing away with elected officials, zoning boards, and its other present power. But, as Garth Reeves, editor of *The Miami Times,* says, "The black and Latin vote combined in ticket swapping could become an unbeatable force." Things like the differences in policy towards Cuban refugees and Haitians, who were neither welcomed in Miami nor adequately housed, have made the black community reluctant to form alliances with Latins. Yet, with the right leadership, such a combination could develop. Reeves also says, however, "Black folks had better wake up and learn Spanish if they want to live in Miami and survive. Now, they're resisting, saying they shouldn't have to learn Spanish to work in their own country. They had better realize their country is changing and they'd better change with it."

11

ATLANTA RECONSTRUCTED
April 29–May 5, 1981

In mass murder as in war, the great darkness of death can often inspire a sentimentality that distorts our perception of the intricate human struggles that preceded and will prevail beyond the body count. Such is the case of Atlanta, a city in which the grand ideals of democracy and the midnight oil necessary to achieve them have come together in ways which relate to the Civil Rights Movement in much the same way that Reconstruction relates to the Civil War. Yet the miscegenated identity of its political history, its culture, its alliances and antipathies are shrouded by the pain and terror felt locally and nationally each time the body of an adolescent black man is pulled freshly dead or in some stage of decomposition from a river or other hiding place.

But the texture of terror is not immediately experienced in Atlanta. What one first notices after traveling the interminable distance through the ugly Hartsfield Airport—the world's largest—is the spring air and the brightness of the sun. Then there are pine trees that seem primitive and gargantuan bottle brushes, slopes that give the city a roller coaster effect, many churches made of wood or stone, and more than a few fronted by Grecian columns, and finally the new office buildings and hotels and entertainments for conventioneers and locals that spread out from the center of town to impinge upon what classical American structures were left unharmed by the assault of Sherman's troops and the march of the modern age. There is a terror there, however, and it brutally counterpoints the city's typically Southern relaxation, eloquence, humor, and fatalistic sullenness. It is expressed in the somber understatement of a fine preacher quietly describing Satan, or it stutters the rhythm of speech like a loose fan belt. It is sometimes wrapped in a mystified outrage or dressed up like a grim Christmas tree with statistics of arrests, leads, time lags between disappearance and discoveries. Nothing, however, has led to a significant arrest or a solution to any of the killings.

I. THE HERITAGE OF RECONSTRUCTION

Atlanta is a city far more complex and far more segregated and given to bloody battles above and below the surface than most accounts allow us to see. The city proper consists of two counties, Fulton and DeKalb, and except for pine-filled woods and slopes, it is predominantly flat, 400 miles from the nearest mountain range and 300 from the ocean. Over the last

10 years, 102,000 white people have moved out of the city proper, while 27,000 black people have moved in, making the population of 450,000 65 percent black and leaving white Atlantans two-thirds removed from political control.

The fossils of classic segregation exist in streets that change names beyond certain points because, in the old days, whites didn't want to reside on streets with the same names as those where Negroes lived. Many neighborhood schools were built for black children following the desegregation ruling of 1954. Present segregation works, as it does in the North, by neighborhood. Most of the black population now lives in the south, southeast, and southwest ends of Atlanta, while most of the whites live in the north end, with midtown the most integrated. At the turn of the century, the well-to-do Negroes had lived on the southeast side of town, at the outskirts. Slowly they moved west, unavoidably leaving the poor behind. Presently, the more ambitious black business people are taking their trade to Campbellton Road, the main street of the southwest area, where the upwardly mobile Negroes have been buying houses as a result of white flight to the north and the suburbs (an interesting historical twist in that whites on the run from black political control now turn, as runaway slaves once did, to the north, albeit a local one).

The Atlanta University Center, because it has long provided the black braintrust of the city and the South as well, is largely responsible for making Atlanta so different from every other city in the South. Examples of those associated with that braintrust are: James Weldon Johnson, W. E. B. DuBois, Benjamin Mays, and Martin Luther King, Jr. Atlanta University, which was founded literally in a boxcar in 1867—18 years before Georgia Tech—was the first of the city's five black colleges, the others being Morehouse, Spelman, Morris Brown, and Clark (there are also the Interdenominational Theological Center and the Atlanta University Summer School, both cooperatives). The black colleges, in conjunction with the black churches, businesses, and social clubs, not only produced a developing intellectual and economic elite that inspired many Negroes to move to Atlanta but also built a network of social organizations designed to address the problems of relocation and community development. As Atlanta University's Dr. Edyth L. Ross wrote in the December 1976 issue of the college's review of race and culture, *Phylon:* "These organizations, varying in social structure from relatively amorphous social movements to highly formal voluntary associations, constitute a legacy which looms large in the structure of social welfare today."

Ross goes on to point out that the organizations expanded upon the settlement houses created as adjustment centers for European immigrants; these were full community efforts designed to provide everything from care for the aged to recreation for teenagers and homes for colored girls, from medical care and housing improvement to remedial reading and legal assistance. As early as 1873, 100 years before Maynard Jackson took office, a black church ran three health centers so successfully that the death rate among those it served was one-third less than that of the white population. It was this tradition of educational advance and social change that enabled the city's Negro community to continue the work of Reconstruction up through the election of Maynard Jackson. The colleges, churches, and businesses provided the city with theorists, researchers, organizers, sponsors, and, eventually, politicians who would parlay their growing strength in votes to a power position in the middle of city negotiations, not on the outskirts.

The long march from the first phase of Reconstruction to its present-manifestation has not come without enmities, for though Maynard Jackson's administration is predominantly black, Atlanta's economic power is almost completely white, with each side convinced that the opposition will only gain greater ground or maintain its strength at the other's expense. As an architect from an old Atlanta Jewish family says, "The financial strength *is* in the white community and it is being clutched more tightly than ever before because of the black political power. I think there needs to be a sharing of the financial power. But the mayor's interpretation of joint ventures has soured much of the white community because it sees the mayor's city government as serving a black constituency above all else. And the mayor's list of power positions in city government is quite considerable. The majority of the city council, the commissioner of public safety, the police chief, the president of the Atlanta Chamber of Commerce, and the chairman of the Fulton County Commission are all black. I don't care what the color of somebody is, but I *do* care about what they consider their constituency to be."

Yet except for its understandable suspicion of white people, that black constituency is far from monolithic and is given to considerable infighting, most of it based on color, class, and what part of the country one is from. It has also thrown its share of punches at Maynard Jackson and his staff, at his appointments and his firings. As with most light-skinned Negroes in positions of power, when Jackson does something the black community likes, the entire group takes credit for it; when mistakes or unpopular decisions come down, he is seen as a "high yellow" selling out blacks or working for whites. Writer Toni Cade will tell you that success in the city can depend on whether or not you're light-skinned and are part of the middle-class Morehouse-Spelman crowd to which Jackson and many of his appointees belong. Since Negroes from rural Georgia and just about every other place in the country now migrate to Atlanta seeking better lives, just as they did right after the Civil War, a television executive said that though he is successful, it took him almost four years to get local Negroes to see him as something other than part of a wave of black carpetbaggers come to take jobs away from the city's black, brown, beige, and bone sons and daughters. One of the mayor's appointees charged that jealousy is behind it all, that most of the native black Atlantans don't have enough drive and ambition to achieve success or prominence. Jackson's job then, is to balance his credibility in both racial groups while continuing the traditional involvement of Atlanta's black middle class with the greater black community. The two strata have always been close, because racism made it difficult, if not impossible, for a Negro to achieve a significant position outside the black community if he or she happened not to be an entertainer. Consequently, the city's black leaders in business, medicine, education, and religion achieved their prominence through the trade, the patients, the students, and the congregations provided by the bulk of the city's Negroes.

Because of Maynard Jackson's determination to better Atlanta, his administration has had to live up to its progressive heritage at the same time that it has been forced to scuffle with the riddles of black political power and the aforementioned white money, the complications of race and class, and the ills of poverty and crime that exist as appendages which bruise and wound a growing city that is still, for all the media talk of cosmopolitanism, an urban country town quite schizophrenic in its mix of eloquent sophistication and mumbling naïveté. As Janet Douglass, executive director of the Community Relations Commission and the Committee on the Status of Women says, "Sharing power never comes without pain." That pain, as well as a complex kind of pride, is felt on both sides, black and white. For certain whites, the pain results from Jackson's playing a kind of political hardball Negroes have never played in Atlanta; for lower-income Negroes the pain is connected to expectations that impose upon Jackson's leadership a messianic mantle that fits like a yoke; and for still others, both black and white, there is a pride in the fact that Atlanta has long been an oasis of relative political enlightenment surrounded by the redneck mandates of the rest of the state.

II. VARIETIES OF PATERNALISM

The versions of that political history are quite different if one is talking with an older white Atlantan as opposed to almost any black person who worked to break down segregation during the Civil Rights Movement. Those older whites will point with pride to William B. Hartsfield, the city's mayor from 1937 to 1960. As described by local white historian Franklin Garrett, Hartsfield was a man "who could be a hairshirt at times because of his quick temper but he could also be quite mannerable and genial. He discovered the charm of reading as a child and, though the son of a tinsmith and a man who came up the hard way, he got his law degree by reading law on his own. He wanted the city to become part of the aviation industry, which is why our airport is named after him. His desire was to see the city develop the standing it had as a transportation center which dates back to its significance as the most important railroad center in the Southeast with four major railroads by 1860, when Atlanta became the manufacturing hub of the Confederacy and turned out railroad ties and steel plates for the navy. He created the term, 'Atlanta, the city too busy to hate,' and realized that, with the Primus King Decision of 1946, which ruled that blacks couldn't be barred from local and general primaries, he could build a coalition since the city was 50-50 black and white, and had an educated class of blacks with which you could deal without a lot of loud rabble-rousing."

Hartsfield's coalition of upper-class whites and middle- and lower-class Negroes was formed to stave off the politics of redneck whites. This was a considerable achievement: On September 8, 1948, during the period when Hartsfield was integrating Atlanta's police force, Herman Talmadge gave his acceptance speech as governor of Georgia with Ku Klux Klan Grand Dragon Sam Green on the podium. Soon afterwards, Talmadge attacked the Atlanta Negro Voters League, of which Maynard Jackson's grandfather was a leader, and boasted that he'd keep primaries as white as possible. When asked if the black police would be allowed to arrest white people, Hartsfield is quoted as saying, "When somebody's breaking in your house and you yell, 'Police,' you don't care what color he is, all you want is for him to get 'that man out of your house." But these same policemen had to put on their uniforms at the black Butler Street YMCA because they weren't permitted to change in the station house.

Many black people saw Hartsfield as a benevolent dictator whose paternalistic politics used the black vote only to determine contests between white candidates. The same is said of his successor, Ivan Allen, a wealthy merchant prince who was mayor from 1961 to 1969. Lonnie King, one of the organizers of the desegregation protests during the Civil Rights era, says of Allen: "He was a paternalistic man whom some white people would say had noblesse oblige. Black folks know better, however. The best example is the Peyton Road wall which Allen had put up in the southwest when black people were getting ready to take advantage of other housing opportunities. It was a symbol that meant, 'Black people stop here. These homes aren't for you.' But Allen later took down the wall and went through a strange metamorphosis which led him to testify in Washington in support of the Civil Rights Bills of 1964 and 1965. He did it, by the way, against the advice of his affluent black supporters who had weaseled into a corner of the power structure. You know how some slaves look out for the master. But I think Allen saw beyond what they were telling him and realized the image of racism would, finally, do damage to the business interests of the city and discourage investors from coming to a town that might be constantly shaken by racial confrontation, which could mess up conventions, property, and profit."

Economics are pivotal, as usual. White businessman George Goodwin says, "In the late '40s, I wrote for the *Atlanta Journal* that the property tax digest was just up to what it was in 1860, when slaves were considered property. What is now Atlanta's First National Bank was started in 1865 and it was 10 years before it had $1 million on deposit and 1917 before it had $10 million. In 1929, mergers led to $100 million for a few days before the Great Crash. It was the late '30s before it got back to $100 million. After World War II, the pent-up buying power began and didn't really take off until the 1960s, which produced the array of office buildings you see in the city now. Though we were hit by the '70s depression, Atlanta is now a transportation center, wholesale center, retail center, financial and insurance center. In recent years, it's become a convention center, probably the third largest in the country. This provides jobs in hotels and services for visitors. The rest of the South may not be aware of it, but Atlanta knows we lost that Civil War. Sherman burned Atlanta because if he hadn't, it would have gone back to functioning in the same way for that time which it does now."

Following Allen was Sam Massell, a real estate man who was Atlanta's first Jewish mayor. Jews had been coming to Atlanta since before the Civil War and had often done well, but the city was hardly free of anti-Semitism, which was most brutally exhibited in the 1915 lynching of Leo Frank, who had been convicted of raping and murdering a young Christian woman on circumstantial evidence supplied by a black janitor. Atlanta Jews often supported progressive causes, but many blacks recall that Jewish merchants were no quicker to desegregate than anybody else in Atlanta's white power structure. Rich's, the city's largest department store, opened its lunchroom to blacks only when faced with the embarrassment of having to put Martin Luther King, Jr., in jail in his own too-busy-to-hate home town. To this day, there are clubs in Atlanta that Jews can't join and more than a few are bitter about it, just as some ruefully recall the bombing of a synagogue during the Civil Rights era.

Massell's appeals to the black community had been instrumental in his victory over an apparently more conservative opponent, Rodney King, who also lacked the New South image preferred by many affluent white voters. The flaps involved his brother, Howard, who had been accused by nightclub owners of traveling around in a police car to gather campaign funds with the promise that the city would become wide open if Massell were elected. Sam Massell claimed his brother's approaches were misinterpreted, only to watch him leave town for Miami after another scandal involving people with supposed connections to organized crime. Under Massell, the new police chief was John Inman. By 1973, Atlanta police led the nation in per capita police killings, with 29 civilians slain—27 black, 12 under the age of 14.

III. MAYNARD JACKSON'S NEW DESIGN

Maynard Jackson entered politics in 1968 by running against Herman Talmadge for U.S. senator. Jackson lost, but carried Atlanta by 6000 votes, and in 1969 was elected the city's first Negro vice mayor. Although expected to run again for vice mayor in 1973, he instead took on Massell and defeated him handily. Soon after he took office on January 7, 1974, Reconstruction returned to Atlanta. Prior to Jackson, the City Council was both administrative and legislative. In effect, the department heads ran the city, which gave it what George Goodwin calls a "weak mayor form." Jackson made all the committee heads responsible to him, which resulted in a "strong mayor form." This didn't sit well with entrenched whites, who no longer had the power to distribute jobs and money on the basis of friendship and familial connections. It also gave the mayor a more complicated job and made him less accessible to businessmen and others who had been accustomed to individually visiting the mayor's office. Even so, there are those who feel that Jackson is far less effective one-on-one than when addressing masses of people, which makes the very distance itself more comfortable to him.

Jackson's confrontation came with Chief Inman. Under Inman's predecessor, Herbert Jenkins, there had been a chosen few black officers, most of whom were disgruntled because they rarely got promotions. Inman eliminated promotions almost entirely by briefly assigning his favorite whites to acting or temporary positions and then, when time came to promote, pushing those whites into the slots, claiming that they had more experience than black officers who had been on the force longer.

Jackson initially moved to replace Inman with a white man named Clint Chasen. Inman confronted Chasen, eventually calling the SWAT squad into Chasen's office with guns drawn. Chasen decided that there were better jobs available in the world and Inman took his case to the State Supreme Court, claiming that he had an eight-year appointment through the former mayor and could not be fired, demoted, or replaced. The resentful legal staff with which Jackson was saddled is thought to have sold him out by botching the case. But Inman was unpopular with the District Attorney's Office, and a case in which Inman was obliquely involved set the stage for another approach. Inman had been living on the estate of pesticide tycoon Dilly Orkin, who attempted to get a police officer to kill the husband of a woman he was dating. The officer went to the district attorney's office and an out-of-state policeman was brought in for an undercover investigation which led to the jailing of Orkin. Inman wasn't specifically implicated in the conspiracy, but a lot of questions were raised about how and why Orkin came to believe he could get an Atlanta police officer to commit the murder.

Jackson's new city design included a commissioner of public safety, charged with administering the police and fire departments as well as civil defense. Reginald Eaves, a Bostonian who had gone to Morehouse with Jackson and participated in his campaign, was appointed to that slot even though he had no experience in police work. The white press in Atlanta, which immediately proved itself hostile to Jackson's designs, statements, and policies, dubbed the position "Super Chief." Inman was assigned to an office in a roach-infested basement and later left.

Eaves gained attention on his first work day by demoting 37 white policemen, and busting 14 more by the end of the week. Soon he became a villain in the white press and a hero in the black community. Even after it was revealed that Eaves's secretary had a heroin conviction in New York and that one of his relatives had gotten a CETA job, his popularity in the black community was undiminished, primarily because he announced that he would personally charge with murder any police officer who killed without reasonable cause. Police homicides ceased. Over a two-year period, Eaves got press by going on police raids, rigged to allow him to kick in doors and collar criminals for the cameras, much as J. Edgar Hoover had done in his day.

"Reggie," says another Jackson appointee, "took off in that job. Where he had kind of stood in Maynard's shadow before, he developed into an incredible speaker and was suddenly everywhere—at churches, picnics, socials, and everything in the community you could imagine. He was single, so the bitches liked him, and he took a hard line on crime, like Maynard did. He defined criminals as parasites within the community and let it be known he would give no quarter to a lawbreaker, regardless of color. He transferred cops with bad brutality records into jobs like guarding airplane runways and fire stations and made strong efforts to get the community to see the police as public servants, not trigger-happy parts of an occupying force. Quiet as it's kept, he was using the office to run for mayor and Maynard didn't know it. Then the shit hit the fan."

In the fall of 1977, Eaves was accused by officers within the department of supplying the answers to the civil service examination for the police force to black men he wanted to hire. Jackson was forced to call for an investigation that was handled by two private lawyers, one black, one white. The 300-page report proved that certain cops *had* memorized the tests beforehand since they gave the same sequence of answers when retested even though the questions were reordered. Eaves took a lie detector test that proved inconclusive. When the results were made public, 300 black people were gathered on the steps of city hall. For the cameras they asserted their belief in Eaves's innocence, but privately they said things like, "So what if he cheated? White folks have always been cheating." Some white liberals argued that there was no other way to balance the force.

Jackson had long taken the position that affirmative action was only a response to racist hiring practice, that it was neither a means of forcing the unqualified into jobs nor a form of reverse racism. But at the same time he was burdened with what those close to him consider his greatest weakness: an almost aristocratic sense of loyalty. Some kind of showdown was inevitable. Eaves was speaking in churches and at rallies, opening his statements with phrases like "Though my skin is dark and my lips are thick," implying that if he was removed it would have more to do with in-group color prejudice than a mishandling of authority. Cannon fodder from the University Center was hot to trot in support of Eaves and the press was making much of Jackson's deliberations. Eaves finally agreed behind closed doors to tender his resignation, promising it on a certain day, then another, then yet another. Jackson started getting angry at demands from the street that Eaves not be fired. "Maynard started saying," quotes one aide, "'I hired him and he carried out *my* policies, not his. Now these people want to act like *I* didn't have anything to do with bettering the police force.'" Finally, in the middle of the night, the resignation was delivered to Jackson's chief of staff, Gerri Elder. On the same night, much later, Eaves called Elder and said he'd changed his mind and would send his bodyguards to get it back. Elder, in a panic, called Jackson, who blew up and ordered her not to return anything, then sent his own bodyguard for the resignation.

The next day, in a cold, formal tone and in front of witnesses, Jackson called Eaves and told him his comment to the press was to be no comment and that he was to maintain a low profile. Eaves agreed, but in a matter of hours he was speaking to the press on television. "Maynard went through the roof," reports an appointee, "and called a press conference immediately at which he announced that Commissioner Eaves had been suspended. From that moment on, it was over because, you know Maynard's sister married a Nigerian, and he said, 'Even if my sister pickets me in Yoruba, Reggie Eaves is *gone!*'"

Jackson responded to continuing tension in the black community by appointing Lee Brown to replace Eaves and George Napper to take the slot vacated by Inman. Both were black and had doctorates in criminology. The resentment cooled.

Then there were the murders.

IV. EVERY MOTHER'S CHILD

I arrived in Atlanta the Friday before Reagan was shot and Timothy Hill's body was pulled from the Chattahoochee River. I checked in at the Hotel Georgian Terrace, a grand old midtown place with stone columns out front, plenty of marble in the lobby, and each of its first-floor wings given over to the hybrids only modernization can produce. To the left of the entrance is a 24-hour German deli and to the right is the bar, which has high ceilings and many potted plants, a few pinball and electronic space games, and a sound system that blurts out disco tunes at what seems the highest possible volume. After touring the city with newswoman Alexis Scott Reeves, I returned at early evening to find the lobby filled with black homosexual couples. Throughout the week, I was to find that the hotel was an evening meeting place not only for homosexuals but for certain integrated couples of whatever persuasion and that the midtown area had become the hub of the city's homosexual world. I also found out that Atlanta is the homosexual capital of the Deep South. Organized crime controls the city's homosexual bathhouses, discos, and gay bars, and as a result, the Atlanta Police Department's tough Organized Crime Division bumps heads with homosexuals as it moves to keep the mob from getting a toehold. The black female community, which some say outnumbers black men as much as nine to one, is hostile to both homosexuals and integrated heterosexual couples.

The next day I went on the search party for the then-missing children, which met at Ralph Abernathy's West Hunter Street Baptist Church, now a stone-columned structure on Gordon Street next door to the Wren's Nest, the home of Joel Chandler Harris, which was long controlled by a group of old white ladies who made it a segregated historical site until the 1960s. The search parties, of course, accept all comers, some of whom I was surprised to see that Saturday morning.

A light spring wind had set in, flipping Caucasian hair and that loose enough among the Negroes to move to so easy a touch. Green ribbons were in motion, tied to arms and the broom handles used for searching through bushes, or pinned to the fronts of coats, shirts, and blouses. The fancy patterns in which some of the ribbons were tied marked how long the searches had been going on, although personal style is never very far behind the establishment of insignias and symbols. Yet it seemed at first like a picnic gathering or preparation for an Easter egg hunt. This impression lasted only as long as it took to notice the search dogs and the ambience of sorrowful expectations casting an ambivalent mood in its wake, a mood that made the laughter and the jokes of those searchers who had become familiar with each other through the 25 weekends seem as much reactions to strain as expressions of humor or camaraderie.

The ironic flip-flops of history were also evident, for here were white men dressed in army surplus, sometimes driving panel trucks and sometimes possessing classic red necks, who had brought their dogs to work in combination with black men, women, and children to find the bodies of dead black children, not capture runaway slaves. Also ironic was the fact that more of the white girls wore what used to be considered exclusively black, even militant, hairdos as well as the gerri curl look favored by many of today's black men and women. Acknowledging the scavengers who gather around tragedies, a representative of the church's United Youth Adult Conference announced to the volunteers as they gathered in the cold gymnasium behind West Hunter Baptist, "We are here only to find the lost children and hope to God we find them alive. If you have any other reason than that, please don't go. We don't want anybody trying to convert anybody to be a Democrat, a Republican, a Black Nationalist, a Ku Klux Klan, or anything else."

The work for the day was going house-to-house within the lower- and lower-middle-class black community to find out if anyone had seen the most recent of the missing children, Timothy Hill and Joseph Bell, who had disappeared a few blocks from each other. Canvassers armed with photographs of the two boys boarded buses to work in areas of roughly 10 blocks. No one in the strip we covered, on and off a main thoroughfare called Simpson Street, had seen any of the children, but all communicated the dismay, the sorrow, the rage, and the wounded hope of those who had felt so much optimism since Jackson's election. The reports that Jackson, who had battled down a huge waistline, was gaining it back on ice cream binges in the wake of the crisis, were then understandable. The murders constituted a growing millstone that could sink the administration's achievements.

In fact, the computer technology and the task force directed by the relatively new commissioner of public safety, Lee Brown, seemed to increase the burden rather than ease the populace. Whenever anyone was asked if he or she thought the police were working as hard as they could, the response was disillusionment. "I hate to say so, but I really don't think so. No, not with all this time has passed. Seem like they would have come up with *something* by now. They got all the best equipment and plenty of money. No, sir, they can't be doing much as they can do."

That sentiment was expressed often that week, usually by people at the lower end of the economic ladder and those for whom literacy wasn't important or didn't have much to do with their daily lives. They were the black people who gathered most of their information and opinions from television and conversation. The upshot was that the television cop shows had created in them unrealistic expectations of the police. Unlike the television-show villain who announces himself at the start of the hour and is captured within 10 minutes of the next hour, the criminal or group working outside the established though fluid crime world is very difficult to capture, especially if he has even average intelligence, which is something most criminals don't possess. When a criminal or criminals work outside the underworld network, the effectiveness of bribes and rewards is limited. With $100,000 being offered, Atlantans can be sure the criminals of the city are on the lookout for the killers, as is everyone else who could use that kind of money. The lower-echelon criminal world is particularly concerned, according to Julian Bond, because the heavy presence of police during this period has greatly reduced the rapes, robberies, and car thefts that make Atlanta a typical urban center.

Atlanta is experiencing the paradoxes of success in the modern age and no one seems ready, the police no more than anybody else. Jackson's push for conventions, international investment, and the image of a cultured town—complete with dance troupes, jazz musicians, community theatre, and free citywide festivals—has attracted representatives of every one of Fortune's 500 to the city. It has also attracted Northern-style crime. Vern Smith of *Newsweek*, though observing that black-on-white crime can make headlines while black-on-black crime is rarely reported in the white press, adds that street crime in general is far less pervasive than what he saw when assigned to Detroit. "The crime Atlanta may have to worry about is drug traffic," observes Julian Bond, "because changes in vacationing patterns and the frequency of international visitors to the Southeast make for big profits in tourism and a lot of popping in and out of the airport. With any convention centers come vice, and there is now so much pressure on Miami dope smuggling that gangsters take advantage of the many little airports in Georgia that exist for private planes and quick jaunts by businessmen." Both black and white point out that the popularity of cocaine as an upper-middle-class drug results in grand profits for gangsters. Those who believe that the murders may involve the killing off of rival couriers in a dope war explain that in that world a $100,000 reward means very little.

During the first press tour of the task force office the question of homosexual killers was raised again and again. Commissioner Brown would only answer that there was no evidence of homosexual connections, though the investigation wasn't ruling out any possibilities. Local television, however, reported that, according to task force sources, two or three of the victims were thought or known to be guilty of petty theft or burglary, 10 of drug violations, and 10 of homosexual prostitution. A teacher interviewed on the show corroborated that at least three of the children were known to travel with adult homosexuals, and that the boy found the day Reagan was shot, Timothy Hill, had often been seen in their company. (This was also attested to by one of the cleaning women in the Hotel Georgian Terrace, who knew the boy and lived in the same neighborhood.) An FBI source I interviewed agreed that homosexual prostitution could be connected to some of the cases. He went on to say that the local police weren't experienced or sophisticated enough to handle this kind of big-city crime and were no further along than they were four or five months ago, adding that he knew federal agents who believed the obvious serial murders could be solved within two or three weeks. He observed that the initial belief that the killings were racially motivated may have cost many leads if, say, there is a black judas goat involved, which seems more probable by the day, and that the black community's ingrained distrust of police black or white had hampered the investigation. In all fairness, however, neither big-city police forces nor the F.B.I. always apprehend highly publicized killers or fugitives immediately, if at all. In San Francisco, the Zodiac Killer was never captured; the Boston Strangler remained at large for years; and the Weather Underground surrendered on its own schedule.

Since 1979, county prosecutor Hinson McAuliffe, in conjunction with Lieutenant F. L. Townley's organized crime unit, has closed down or run out of town 80 pornographic bookstores, 12 X-rated theatres, and all bathhouses, and is now moving on homosexual street prostitution. This has been a difficult and dangerous process. When Townley's unit began pressuring vice operations run by Tony Romano from Cleveland, he was subjected to death threats, a dead horse's head was put in his daughter's car, Xs were painted on his home's doors and windows, and a detective's car was blown up. Townley, a white man who has been on the force for 20 years, disparages charges of inefficiency that old Eaves supporters and other impatient citizens have leveled at Brown. "I think he's going to be the salvation of this city. He's a man's man; he's not afraid of anything, you can't buy him, and I feel more comfortable and have more confidence in him than anybody I've worked under in this department. If it hadn't been for him, I would have left here when those threats started. My wife and daughter were telling me to quit, officers in my unit were frightened for me, and Lee Brown stepped in, personally made sure my family was protected and backed me until we got Tony Romano, his wife, Virginia, and his son, Greg, in prison. They got it for prostitution escort services, bathhouses, bookmaking, pandering by compulsion, and communicating gambling information."

Townley couldn't corroborate the rumors that bitter white officers who had left the department after problems with black administrators were attempting to botch the investigation by leaking pertinent information they received from friends still on the force. He did say the leaking of plans for investigating organized crime was a problem within the department and there were other examples of corruption. He cited the recent arrests of a Fulton County officer for running a whore house, and an Atlanta officer found driving three stolen expensive cars when a $500,000 car-theft ring was broken. In response to the homosexual murder theories, Townley reported that a house of homosexual child prostitution had been smashed a few weeks earlier but the 40 boys were all white. Townley added that boy prostitution wasn't the problem it is in the North but that informants were close to the network in the black community, though no substantial leads had yet turned up. He concluded simply: "We know that whatever happens in the North eventually comes to Atlanta. The kind of money and resources these killings have brought in are *almost* what we need on a regular basis. If I had six more people in my unit, I could rotate them and be twice as effective, and we're not doing a bad job as it is. It's just we're overworked as hell."

However frustrated the police may be, the strain is obviously felt more deeply in the black community, with responses that range from habitual paranoia to irrational condemnation. The reduction in normal amiability is signaled by the questioning stares that arise when adult strangers enter black neighborhoods. The young restlessly resent the lack of mobility necessitated by the crisis; one parent, reporting a growing callousness in the children, repeated this comment by his 12-year-old son: "They found another one today. Bet they won't get me." The murders have taken on an obsessive quality for the mothers of the victims and for those who join search parties every weekend. But there's still no excuse for the black sentimentalists who complain that city officials take a business-as-usual attitude once they've publicly decried the horror of it all, as if the officials would have had any other choice were the dead children white—or as if the critics themselves have stopped the business of their own lives in the face of the present murders.

V. A CRISIS OF IMAGE

Those who criticize Jackson's concern that the killings mar the image of Atlanta his administration has worked so hard to create do not appreciate the nature of social and economic change in this society. They will dismiss local media claims about great improvements in public education with reports that the schools are terrible and frequently graduate illiterates, not realizing that improvement is impossible unless the tax base is increased, which means coaxing runaway whites back to the city. Blacks complain with considerable justice that a poverty level twice that of the nation, 23 percent, belies the image of a growing international metropolis. But the plight of Atlanta's poor doesn't move those affluent whites who believe their home town is now perceived as a black city, and who lend their voices to periodic rumblings about incorporating greater Atlanta's other 13 counties to bring about a resurgence of white political control.

"The entire population of all the counties is over two million and majority white," says Dr. Richard Long of Atlanta University. "But what black folk don't understand is that Jackson, even in face of certain bad and embarrassing appointments, didn't *have* to do what he did; he could have made some gestures like the improvement of police relations and gone on to placate the whites with money. His greatest achievement was the airport, which he demanded be a joint venture with both black and white contractors involved. Whites had never noticed when their competitors were white but they definitely did when they were black for the first time. Jackson also got 40 percent of the concessions—the shops, the duty-free businesses, and so on—for black entrepreneurs. This made the whites even madder. But black business here is, like every place else in the world, a joke. The *myth* of a successful black city does hazardous things to those Negroes who *think* they've been left out of the pot of gold. If there *is* a pot of gold, it's tin painted over. Almost every black in this city is on somebody else's payroll. But you know how susceptible blacks are to the myth of alchemy and always have been. At the same time, there is this image of an international city which Jackson has pushed very hard for by getting direct flights to and from London into the airport's schedule, foreign consulates to open offices here, and so on. This isn't liked much by the whites in or out of the press. They say he's the only mayor who has a foreign policy. Obviously, they've never heard of Ed Koch."

Though embattled and accused of arrogant sanctimoniousness by his detractors, criticized by his own staff for standing by bad appointees on sinking ships until the water reaches his nose, and convinced that his greatest victory was over the police department, Maynard Jackson's place in history will have most to do with what his supporters call "the politics of inclusion rather than exclusion." In the great tradition of Atlanta University Center and the many historic figures it has produced, he has not only striven for a contemporary vision of the full community efforts that date back to 1873 but has brought Negroes into positions of authority, involvement, and decision making that have not existed in the South since the first phase of Reconstruction and were nowhere near as comprehensive even then.

Eugene Duffy, Jackson's youngest appointee, says, "Maynard got them to bring that airport in under budget and early. The federal government can't do that with a Trident missile or a shuttle. He's marched with the striking garbage workers and has made sure that the black community gets exactly the same public services as the white people. He also plays hardball these white boys aren't used to from a black man. For instance, when Arrow Shirts wanted to move its factory outside Atlanta and sell the land to the Transit Authority for the subway route, Maynard knew it would cost the city 800 jobs and dwindle the tax base further. He called them and let them know if they tried to leave, he would inform the Transit Authority they would be denied a demolition permit. Arrow agreed to relocate inside Atlanta. Black folks don't appreciate that kind of stuff, unfortunately, because most don't know what high power politics is. Maynard does, though."

The city's cultural texture is, finally, much more subtle and complicated than the obvious struggles for political power and money initially reveal. It is as interwoven as the genetic histories of its people, histories affirmed by the broad range of features, hair textures, and miscegenated skin tones that also illustrate the failure of African-American representational painting. As one middle-aged white woman said, "I got Cherokee mixed in me and probably some other things. People brag about the Indian in them, but they's a whole lot of things they know and everybody else knows about the family blood that don't get talked too much about." That is just as true of the Negro community—'60s nationalism has influenced many younger, light-skinned Negroes, who frequently speak of racial matters so snottily that they seem to be suggesting they themselves are pure black, just as certain even lighter ones used to try and pass for pure white. Yet blacks and whites retain almost identical taste in foods, and their sense of humor is much the same. The good old boy, the gentleman, the belle, the orator, the scholar, the tale-spinner, and the fool-cutter also have idiomatic Southern variations on both sides. For all the huffing and puffing about who's got what, the geniality in more than a few integrated circumstances equals when it does not surpass that of almost all similar situations in the North.

The afternoon I left Atlanta was the 13th anniversary of Martin Luther King's assassination and there were funerals for the two black youths found dead that week, one of whom was in his early twenties and retarded. I thought of the inevitable sentimentality and the observation by State Representative Tyrone Brooks that the fund appeals had become "a pimp circus; all kinds of people pretending to be raising money for the mothers and putting it in their own pockets." By then, green ribbons symbolized moral pomposity and avarice as much as they did empathy.

As the cab traveled to the airport past the beautiful colors and trees and red clay in the gorgeous spring sun, I thought of Sherman's observation as his troops pulled out of the ravaged city: "We turned our horses'

heads to the east. Atlanta was soon lost behind a screen of trees, and became a thing of the past. Around it clings many a thought of desperate
battle, of hope and fear, that now seem the memory of a dream."

12

UP WITH CHARACTERS,
DOWN WITH MESSAGE
October 14–20, 1981

Black novelist John A. Williams has been fortunate enough to have two
of his works adapted for mass media: *Night Song*, a novel about a figure
much like Charlie Parker, and now Melvin Van Peebles's teleplay of Williams *The Junior Bachelor Society*, which was televised on NBC as *The
Sophisticated Gents* September 29 through October 1. Since *Night Song*
never got major distribution, limping through the art-house circuit over
10 years ago, *The Sophisticated Gents* was the writer's first big splash into
the mass audience. *Night Song* was important primarily because Dick
Gregory's performance as the lead character, Eagle, broke with the stodgy
acting styles that were so often imposed on black actors—either stiff images
of dignity who delivered messages with each turn of their heads or monu-
ments to cornball hipness. But where Gregory overshadowed a low-budget
production and amateurish performances by his fellow actors, *The Sophisticated Gents* was right on the mass-media money and opened some
doors it would do television well to push many other shows through.

The exceptionally broad range of characterization and the recognition
that the Negro American experience is not only epic but modal impressed
both television reviewers and the black people with whom I've talked. If
one were to go by the kinds of black images that sell well to audiences
across the board, one would think that black people have never traveled
much further than the other side of a pork chop, that economic motion
automatically results in comic or tragic soul drain, and that every relationship encapsulates in some way the nature of racial oppression in this
country. This popularization of buffoons and victims has downplayed the
complex victories many black Americans have achieved over the last 30
years, making it very difficult to produce anything vaguely related to
drama if black characters are the subject. That *The Sophisticated Gents*
went after drama, albeit in television fashion, made it an event.

Ironically, this near-breakthrough work was scripted by Melvin Van

Peebles, who invented the black exploitation film with *Sweet Sweetback's Badass Song*. That trend pulled Hollywood out of a slump, provided work for professional and amateur black actors, and then wrote its own walking papers, leaving many black actors embittered, feeling as though they had been used by the white man when he needed them and dropped when he didn't. Of course, many a successful white actor connected to a trend or a genre has had the same experience, although their tenure usually lasts longer. The dilemma facing Negro performers now is whether or not black drama or black subject matter can get the kinds of crossover audiences so captivated by science fiction, adventure, and horror films. Since *The Sophisticated Gents* did well on the first of its three nights but was drowned in an Irish soap saga its next two, it can be surmised that audiences like soap more than substance (nothing new in that) and that NBC didn't get behind it strongly enough.

It was also ironic that all of the leading men on the show had gained attention in black exploitation films—Ron O'Neal, Bernie Casey, Thalmus Rasulala, Robert Hooks, Raymond St. Jacques, Dick Anthony Williams, Rosey Grier, and Paul Winfield (the Charlton Heston of black genre films)—few of which gave them opportunities to show their real wares. With the exception of Van Peebles (who plays a pimp with a heart of gold, apparently his favorite image), all of the others got a chance to render complicated characters with complicated backgrounds.

The show dealt with the ambivalent taste of success and the nostalgia of middle age. The Sophisticated Gents are a group of men in their forties who are reunited to honor a coach who taught them valuable lessons as young men, lessons they all feel helped them top the barricades of racism and conquer their own weaknesses. The careers are quite varied— playwright, college professor, magazine editor, concert singer, housing commissioner, club owner, factory worker, and hustler. The suspenseful subtext gives the realism of the show a coating of the thriller. The pimp has killed a California vice cop and is, unknowingly, walking into a trap in his Northeastern home town where the reunion is held. The man stalking him is Albert Hall, the crooked black cop who resents and envies the fraternity of the Gents. But what makes the show so interesting is that it unapologetically looks at its characters' lives and avoids for the most part any speeches about human understanding showing up on the horizon someday. The problems of class and skin color within the Negro race are well rendered, the hostility many black women feel toward interracial marriages when the black men are *successful* is plainly stated, and the struggles for dignity and unsentimental self-awareness experienced by the more interesting black homosexuals are rendered with extraordinary richness and subtlety by Raymond St. Jacques, something of a first in itself. Not only are the scenes of interracial romance beyond the maudlin, but the Negro marriages offer more than the conventional brew of hambones- and-tenderness. Of the black actresses, Rosalind Cash's adulterous, cunning, and bitchy wife was the standout.

But it was comic, or even stereotypical, that all the white female lovers were nearly identical blondes, and it is unfortunate that more couldn't have been done with the problems of the housing commissioner who, in the book, fought fights for the black community which it didn't even know were going on and experienced the vise of animosity from both Negroes and whites. Still, for television, it was an advance, with almost every role played to a fare-thee-well. In fact, if there were an arena in which black villains were given sway, Albert Hall might become a star in the same fashion as Larry Hagman. His cop is performed with a cool viciousness and insecurity that is terrifying. Well, NBC, you provided television with a fine ball. Now the question is who will carry it.

NBC did, in fact, extend upon The Sophisticated Gents *with* Hill Street Blues, *the finest dramatic series ever to run on television. Its grand achievement was showing a variety of individual personalities, from high to low, in every ethnic group depicted. By doing that,* Hill Street Blues *brought a weekly show of an unprecedented American complexity into millions of American homes. Just as* The Sophisticated Gents *did in its time,* Hill Street Blues *stands alone, especially in its pulling on the hair shirt of adult decision and facing the problems of life in the United States with a sense of tragedy that has no sustained television parallel.*

BLUES IN THE CAPITAL
OF CAPITALISM
August 12–18, 1981

I. BLUES TO YOU

Like the South, the Southwest can delight with its warm vitality at the very same time that the sight and sound of constricting ignorance creates a sad, bitter repulsion. Such were my contrary responses in Houston as I attended a blues festival commemorating the 116th anniversary of June 19, 1865, when the Texas slaves were told that old master's world was a-moldering in the ground and they could go wherever the hell they pleased. As you might imagine, master didn't always initial this edict, but the proclamation gave birth to what became known among black people from Texas or nearabouts as "Juneteenth," not so much an African-American version of Passover as *done got over.*

The decision to celebrate that occasion with a blues festival was quite fitting, for good blues, with its boogie disposition, is as important to the personality of American music as the labor and folklore of the slaves were to the material development of the nation and its sense of life. A primitive shout documented with sophisticated tools; a mythology rich in archetypes; a form as rife with metaphor and fancy as it is full of erotic longing, celebration, and castigation; an idiom in which betrayal and bad luck are as basic as individual responsibility; an art in which geography is fate and motion a spiritual tonic. Blues is the music of the big feeling and the long memory, as John Lee Hooker and Muddy Waters say. It is also as much the music of *done been had* as of *done got over*.

But the national and international success of folk blues singers and players over the last 20 years or so is largely connected to young white enthusiasts, many of them Jewish, who have used those microtones to rail at middle-class convention just as the slaves used Moses and Samson to predict their liberation and the fall of the Philistines of the plantation system. The only difference is that the blues has often suffered in ways the biblical metaphor did not, partly because slavery produced a sense of rebellion far deeper and more substantial than adolescent discomfort with familial or class proprieties, and partly because most folk blues performers achieve artistry only through sensibility, not any sober aesthetic awareness. The upshot is that they have been as vulnerable to sociological theory as the cowboys of the Old West were to the conventions and styles created for them by Eastern writers and tailors. As Peter Guralnick has pointed out in *Feel Like Going Home*, a blues singer can be influenced to such an extent by white critics that he might nearly collapse on stage trying to live up to their impressions. Often too the bluesman will say ludicrous things just so white listeners will feel enough at home to hop up and down.

But the Juneteenth Blues Festival was about something else. It was an anachronism because two of the six concerts were presented in the black community, because thousands of black people turned out to them all, and because the whites who were almost nonexistent at certain performances and a distinct minority at the others got into the music with an authority and joy I have never witnessed in a Northern city. At the center of the difference was probably a sense of Southern tradition which eschewed the redneck racism that defines blues as "nigger shit." Before the last note was played and the last barbecue bone gnawed, I was to learn a lot about the continuing power of fine blues to communicate across ethnic lines as well as a lot about Houston's place in both the Sun Belt and the Dumb Belt.

II. TEXAS TEXTURE

Big gestures, bold and vulgar, define the Texan in the popular and intellectual imaginations. Adventurers and eccentrics, tycoons and cowboys,

Texans not only represent the freedom for good and evil that space allows but also suggest the difficult victories over distance, the great light cavalries of the Plains Indians, and the impersonal cruelties of nature. In a recent documentary about the Hunt family, Edwin Newman listed three basic tenets of the philosophy of the American West that the Hunts personify: think big, do it yourself, don't follow convention. That is the essence of many prominent white Texans, and it also explains Negro Jack Johnson quite well. Another Texan, Johnson became the first black heavyweight champion in 1910, whipping white men for a living and going out with white women for pleasure in an era when no black man could assume protection from white violence.

Yes, across ethnic and economic lines, Texans are people obsessed with the idea, pursuit, and maintenance of freedom both social and spiritual. They are prideful at all times and can be violent when they feel their dignity has been transgressed. And since (as David Dary points out in *Cowboy Culture*) so much of what led to the American West is rooted in the roping and riding techniques developed by Spanish, Indian, Negro, and Mestizo *vaqueros*, the cowboy actually represents both the Texan's mulatto heritage of heroism and the decadence of autonomous ritual. The cowboy style takes on a schizophrenic presence in our minds because it embodies our epic roots at one extreme and our capacity for meaningless, racist, and meretricious violence at the other. In Houston, that split is as obvious in the look and feel of the city as it is in behavior. And the black people who celebrate Juneteenth know it, if only through their skins.

The city proper, downtown at least, is a gaggle of skyscrapers and hotels, churches and businesses, with the streets torn apart, covered by boards, or narrowed for construction work. At the throat of downtown Houston is the impoverished black Fourth Ward, the fangs of which are slowly being removed as rich whites buy land for more large buildings or sandwich mansions between shacks. The swamp and bayous give a humidity to the air on hot days and one feels that if Houston were evacuated for only a short time the wilds would move forward until tropical creatures held court where humans had ruled only a few weeks before. For now, however, the refineries and chemical plants and industrial parks provide the intermittent stench refrigerated by the air conditioners in almost all cars and, as the city expands and more investors arrive, Houston seems to alternate between the erection of managerial citadels and those visually obnoxious structures where the raw materials of fuels and minerals are drawn and quartered.

Investors come to Houston because they know the laws and tax rates are tilted in favor of business. On the heels of the investors are people in flight from spavined job markets and the pressure of inflation. The political mood is shifting from conservative Democrat to conservative Republican, but large oil, insurance, banking, and development interests still control what is a colossal country town in nouveau-riche, jet-age Southwestern trappings. The conservative mood and the boom-town atmosphere help shape an aspect of the contemporary civil war between North and South. Today the word "humanism" has replaced communism as a catch-all term for what conservatives see as an imposed economic paternalism, in which government forces public support of what Ronald Reagan recently described as federal plantation slavery. Of course, in the old Civil War certain slaveowners argued that their chattels might someday be freed when they were elevated to the level where they could fend for themselves. Today that would be perceived as the humanism of affirmative action, while the abolitionist's position of every tub on its own bottom is the home-team song of the conservatives.

But philosophy aside, Houston business works like Texas business—with the private and the public sectors interwoven. While most of the voting population of Texas lives in metropolitan areas, many small towns supply state legislators, more than a few of whom are up for sale to the highest bidder. The Houston City Council is controlled by the local rich, even though the city continues to expand its boundaries, increase the number of council seats, and broaden its tax base. And in the city becoming known as "the capital of capitalism," the Chamber of Commerce is probably more important. In short, even though Houston is big enough to allow the enterprising to start successful businesses, freedom of choice and free enterprise have cutoff points. As a man who works for Mobil Oil says, "The plantation may grow bigger and become more sophisticated, but the ownership of the plantation remains the same."

The expansion of the plantation in Houston has some contradictory aspects, as does its xenophobic mood. According to Houston writer Harry Hurt, "Literally half the people in Houston weren't here 10 to 15 years ago and one could say that the arrival of Northern Republicans and Southern Democrats can have as much to do with the mood of the city as anybody born here." Even so, there is a hostility to outsiders that seems basic to Texas history—immigrants settling, becoming prideful, resenting fresh outside influences. The radio ad which refers to a firm as "a real Houston bank, not those people from Detroit trying to take your money," ignores how many Carnegie-Mellon dollars underwrote early Texas banks and how many people came down from industrial cities after the panic of 1907 to develop what would become oil companies as major as Texaco. Earlier, before Texas became independent from Mexico, Americans went there because the panic of 1819 (which followed the War of 1812) had forced up the prices of land within what was then the United States, while the Mexican government was giving away huge spreads, especially to those who promised to raise cattle. The development and defense of what became Texas culture was also dependent on technology from the North and the East, such as the mass production of barbed wire, ropes for cowboys, and Samuel Colt's Paterson, New Jersey, repeating pistol. But, like everybody else, Texans forget quickly, and the new immigrant has hell to tell the captain.

The immigrants who presently get the most static are Mexicans, many of whom are part of the illegal flood of one million Hispanics who enter the United States each year. There is animosity toward the illegals especially because they will work for low wages and cannot report bad treatment for fear of deportation, which means they get most of the entry-level jobs in construction and factory work that used to go to whites, Negroes, and Mexican-Americans. Since the black maid is dying at the hands of education and welfare, the majority of domestic workers and much of the servant help in public places in Houston are Mexican. Therefore, rich white women learn Spanish so they can give better cleaning instructions. Certain managers with an eye on the future are studying the language as well. Some realize that it is quite possible that, like Miami, Houston can benefit from the Latin American tourist trade, and the day may come when bilingual salesmen will be in demand.

Those resentful of Mexicans aren't actually any happier with skilled Northerners—white, black, or otherwise. As a black man who works in media and has been in Houston three years says, "At first, coming down here as a Northerner you were a curiosity and were looked up to for your knowledge and background. But as more people started coming down—anywhere from 5000 a month to 1000 a day—more and more people started saying, 'Hey, if this keeps going on, we won't have any jobs.'" This attitude is pervasive even though unemployment is half what it is in the rest of the country and the largest paper in the Southwest, *The Houston Chronicle*, prints 130 to 170 pages of job ads every Sunday.

The abundance of work available to the skilled and/or willing makes for a tempo in the career world that contrasts with Houston's generally tropical pace. As one newspaper man said, "Changes of position in personnel are where you see the speed in Houston. People can move from a counter job to a desk to a managerial slot sometimes in less than two years. If you've got the drive, they'll give it to you. It's funny. Even though the individual and aloof sensibility of the Texan—Lone Star State and all—creates animosity toward outsiders, they usually have respect for hard work."

The ease with which jobs are obtained provides what William Appleman Williams termed "an infinity of second chances," and may account for the slowpoke service so easy to come by in public places. It may also account for the shortness of tempers and some of the violence for which Houston is known. But there are those who explain the violence by saying, "Here everything is out in the open—actions and feelings. Individual style is all. But because of this people here also have a very limited tolerance for things they don't like and the rowdier ones *will* call you out."

If the rowdier ones don't, the Houston police might. Caught off-guard by the rapid growth of the city, some officers express bitterness as Northerners and minorities ascend to positions beyond their own. Four police chiefs have tried to bring the department up to modern levels of enforcement but have frequently been frustrated by the loss of good officers to the private sector, where they can get better-paying jobs and far less dangerous work in corporate security. Many of the officers who presently serve are part of what one newsman calls "a force within the force," spiritual carriers of the old, rugged, racist cross. These men have been known to be either vicious or downright lazy. They have been seen asleep in cars under bridges, drinking on duty, and ignoring private citizens guzzling beer as they drive. They are usually protected when they bend or break professional rules of conduct, although there has been controversy lately over some slayings by police that have had very dubious explanations. During the Juneteenth celebration itself, three black teenagers were arrested on marijuana charges and then drowned while in the custody of police officers; an autopsy found no traces of marijuana in two of the three. But though the victims are usually Mexican or Negro, more than a few whites admit to fearing the thin-skinned meanness of the local force. On one talk show, the host explained their quick tempers as the result of moonlighting, insufficient sleep, and "the pressure to get an expensive shotgun, a more expensive truck, and a bigger house." But some corporate executives feel that those police problems will decrease as Houston achieves more sophistication, affluent minorities develop, and the budding Hispanic political presence moves for power. In other words, those who steer the deals in Houston will make accommodations in the interest of business and the social order.

III. HEADQUARTERS

Shortly after arriving, I set up headquarters in the Fifth Ward, a black section dotted and patched by ditches and barely restrained swampland. The neighborhood can rise to almost middle-class comfort at the beginning of a block and dip all the way down into hideous poverty before the end. A well-kept home can be seen next to a hovel on the porch of which an oil drum barbecue pit seems a symbol of distant gusher dollars and down-home cuisine; the heaps of trash and broken bottles in yards are expressions of the apathetic *or* the ornery; and the heavy drinking, when not self-destructive celebration, is like a form of grieving in face of the day one was born. But such a neighborhood can also be great for a kid—the seesawing living standards come off as archetypes, the high grass provides a fine theatre for games of all sorts, the occasional abandoned house is a playing place and a subject for the imagination, while the crude discos and eateries that also function as bootleg liquor drops suggest the mysterious and exciting worlds where adults strut, primp, and show off their diamond rings and gold teeth, providing images of elegance as well as the forlorn decadence of extreme ignorance.

My mother, a former domestic worker and the first aristocrat I got to know, lives in the Fifth Ward with her fourth husband, a retired minister, and spends her days visiting friends, buying clothes, being genial and humorous, forever the celebrant. I associate her fierce self-esteem with my great-great-grandmother, Isabella Rose, whom I met when I was a small child in the early 1950s during a family visit from Los Angeles to Northeast Texas. A spry woman of over a hundred, she had been born in slavery but took great pride in the whip scars on her back, which she'd gotten when her owners tried to reprimand her for perpetual rebelliousness. When I think of Juneteenth, I see her sitting on her porch smoking a pipe or dipping snuff, the gray spinning top of a wasps' nest hanging from the edge of the roof.

IV. IF IT WASN'T FOR THE BLUES

I call myself the Kid and I come from Dallas
I fucked the Queen of England all over Buckingham
*   Palace*
My knees don't knock and my teeth don't rattle
I'll snatch the horns off a whole goddam herd of
*   cattle*
I jumped in the ocean and swallowed a whale
Handcuffed lightning and threw thunder's ass in
*   jail*
I walk through the graveyard with a bolt of
*   thunder*
Make the tombstones jump and put the dead on the
*   wonder*
I put fear in a gorilla and took the sting from a bee
You got to be an ignant, ignant motherfucker to
*   fuck with me!*

Though we missed the first concert, which took place a few days before I arrived, my mother, my sister, and I attended all of the others, the first of which we heard at Emancipation Park in the Fourth Ward. The performances—all professionally paced and supervised—were presented by SUM Concerts, a nonprofit organization that was founded in 1969 by Lanny Steele, a white man, Vivian Ayers, a black woman, and Bob Morgan, another white man. Ayers and Morgan have since left SUM, which is now directed artistically by Steele, a professional musician and assistant professor of music at Texas Southern University. SUM raises money to present everything from Stockhausen and Sun Ra to Arnett Cobb and Lightnin' Hopkins. They have been giving a free Juneteenth Blues Festival in conjunction with the city of Houston and private sponsors since 1977.

With each successive year, their festival has become a larger event, culminating in the presentation of an award from the mayor's office to a major blues artist on the final night. According to Steele, it is harder to raise money for the blues festival than for their fall jazz festival because the former music is regarded as black and the latter isn't. Given that Steele had to lobby heavily to get saxophonist Billy Harper into the famous

North Texas State Jazz Band as its first black player, this comes as no surprise. There was a great controversy the first year of the festival because it was feared that Miller Outdoor Theater would be destroyed by "thousands of undesirables" due to an incident involving the notorious professional redneck Jerry Jeff Walker. When Walker appeared there in a rock concert in 1977, he exhorted the white audience to drink up its Lone Star Beer and then throw the bottles at somebody. A riot broke out, the SWAT squad was sent in, a girl was raped in the dressing room, and two police cars were overturned.

There was no violence at any of the SUM concerts. But the gang was all there. The culture of poverty and the desperate, mumbling imbecility bred by near illiteracy would be juxtaposed against the jovial or sober dignity of those Negroes, both young and old, who carried themselves as if they knew they'd won a hard uphill battle on greasy ground. Whether the women I'd loved or the bitches I'd hated, the men I'd admired or the fools I'd despised, all were so committed to freedom that every one, regardless of personal warmth, was given to that distance individuality makes inevitable. These were the kinds of people who had produced the nameless cowboys and the famous black crooks of the Old West; these were the descendants of the 9th and 10th Cavalry, those Buffalo Soldiers black legend claims not only whipped many an Indian but chased Geronimo down into Mexico and brought him back, only to have the white officers push them out of the photograph. From this mix had come Henry Flipper, the first Negro to graduate from West Point and the first to be recognized as a professional engineer; Bill Pickett, the "dusky demon" who invented bulldogging; and Rube Foster, purportedly the first great black pitcher, definitely the first black manager of a professional team— the Texas Yellow Jackets—and also one of the founders of the Negro National League in 1920. Scott Joplin too was a Texan. But maybe in this context one should think most of Blind Lemon Jefferson, the down-home Homer and Aesop of the blues, whose "Prison Cell Blues" (Milestone Records) provides a straight line to the big-thinking, do-it-yourselfing, convention-be-damned genius of Ornette Coleman.

The soul substance of those Negroes made me think of my mother's parents, Lilborn and Matilda Ford, two Texans who often shocked both black and white people because "they acted like everybody was the same color." Their contrariness in face of indignities led to their being considered "crazy" by the whites of Northeast Texas. My mother's favorite story about her father is one in which she took him his lunch when he was working on a construction crew. A white worker asked, "Are you looking for somebody?" "I'm looking for Mr. Ford," she answered. "Ford," he called out, "there's a little nigger girl here looking for you." Pa Ford, as he was known among family, rushed up and grabbed the man by the neck. "When you speak to me, put a handle on my name. I'm *Mister* Ford and I don't have no niggers in my family. If you make that mistake again, I'll be in your ass up to my waist." He died in 1939, six years before I was born, but has—of course—remained a family hero. My grandmother lived until 1961, Matilda Ford was more than a Negro Calamity Jane or Belle Starr: she was a beacon of shit, grit, and mother wit, a personification of the frontier woman. With her strong eyes and high Choctaw cheekbones, she was small but powerful as a hand grenade, sweet as a fresh pineapple when her military willingness wasn't called into play. As a child, I watched her lord over a restaurant she owned in Bakersfield, California, where Negroes picked cotton all week, then drank wine and slashed or stabbed each other all weekend. Her self-reliance, discipline, humor, old wives' tales, confidence, and stoic sense of life gave gravity and distance to her presence. So did the .45 she wore beneath her apron as she took orders for chili. Everybody knew how tough she could be, so when those rough-and-tumble men entered the restaurant, a thick smoothness came over their voices and they were just as mannerable as could be.

But the violence, bitchiness, and stubbornness of which Texans are capable coexists with a courtliness especially evident in the rearing of children. Unlike the mannerless brats one becomes accustomed to in Northern middle-class, liberal, or bohemian households, the black children of Houston radiated a sense of individuality and community, for they were from a world where absolute lack of discipline or respect for adults didn't equal "freedom" or "creativity." It is that thorough awareness of individual style and communal responsibility that accounts for so many major jazz innovators being either literal Southerners or from the second-floor South of enclaves like black Philadelphia. It is the closeness to the slave experience and segregation that creates a willful individuality one is hard put to find in places like Manhattan, where fad and fashion are too often all.

Though Arkansas's Larry Davis played with an authoritative gutbucket lustre and Lightnin' Hopkins was well-received, the most impressive performance of the first few nights was that of James Cotton. Sandwiched between talented young Sherman Robertson and master of the erotic mantra John Lee Hooker, Cotton's group, with its control of tempos, nuance, and intensity and its amiable showboating, proved that there is a future for the blues in the hands of young black players. During Cotton's set, the sun went down and the night, full of people who had become three-dimensional shadows, was touched up by the rhythm of green phosphorescent loops spun to the four-on-the-floor beat of the drummer Ken Johnson. Something of an innovator in the idiom, Johnson knows all of the black rhythms and mixes jazz, latin, disco, skipping triplets, and surprising accents into the beat. The upshot is that the audience is captured by the tension and the release, the familiar and the exotic. Young lead guitarist Michael Coleman, tenor saxophonist Doug Fagan, rhythm guitarist John Watkins, and bassist Herman Applewhite were also quite fine. Cotton was definitely the leader, however, and a version of "Going Down Slow" was as moving as I've ever heard. During an encore, Cotton's harp quoted a Basie riff, Nat Adderley's "Work Song," and "When the Saints Go Marching In." While Cotton was reaching for a deeper groove, I overheard two black boys about 13 saying to each other as they swayed to the beat, "He's getting down now! He's getting down, man.'" I could never imagine that from Harlem boys. Finally, Cotton reached what he was looking for, that mood of a house party high on the wing of the night. At that point, spontaneous dancing had a domino effect and the audience reached that ritualistic level wherein all those hair styles, caps, cowboy hats, shapes, outfits, and colors connect in a deceptively imperishable moment of transcendence. The audience was ecstatic.

V. DOMESTIC CRUDE

The next day at my mother's home I met Tom Usselman of Luna Records, a small blues label. Usselman is from Pennsylvania and manages Sherman Robertson, who is a friend of my mother's and makes his living repairing cars in the Fifth Ward. Robertson had promised to give me a tour of the town but was unable to, so Usselman volunteered to provide me with what he termed "the grand dragon tour, where they drive around or sit in their pickups sipping their weasel piss."

Usselman is a small man of German descent who fell in love with blues when he was a kid and found himself traveling to black neighborhoods in order to buy the recordings, which were not sold in white areas then. As he told me that, I thought again how the world of black music was America's tropics. The bush was the Negro community, the sacred ivory a blues record. Young white kids were provided with adventure not so far from home and those who really got the blues bug eventually found themselves traveling to the Delta or some such place to meet the men and women who made the music. Some, like Usselman, ended up recording them. Others became experts on the natives in the blues bush.

"This is the most racist place I've ever been and I've been in every state in the union. Here they're nice to your face, polite, but they hate your guts and they'll do anything they can to stab you in the back. They hate four things and in this order—blacks first, then Mexicans, Jews, and Yankees. When I first got here a cop asked me why I moved to Houston and told me that he knew I came here to get away from the niggers. He said down here they walk the line or they get taught a lesson real fast. Just five miles from here is Pasadena, where they have the KKK headquarters. I moved there when I first got to town because I didn't know how they were. I was driving with a black man in the car and I got stopped by the police. I asked what I'd done and he said, 'I don't know yet.' Then he said, 'What you doing with a nigger in your car?' I said, 'I don't see a nigger *in* my car but I do see a redneck outside my car.' He put his hand on his gun then. I was lucky I was in my driveway and not on some isolated back road somewhere. I mean you can get run off the road because you have Northern license plates by these fuckers. They're gun-happy, they harass homosexuals, don't like to serve integrated couples, they're lazy, they never got to work on time, they're shiftless. They just don't give a shit.

"Women, white or black, are supposed to stay in their place. When they get drunk enough, they go home and they beat their wives and their kids. I saw a guy beating his daughter, backhand his wife when she tried to stop him, then go in the yard and feed his dog. Their most cherished possession, by the way, is their dog, and the dog gets fed first. Women are only good for a piece of ass, but these rednecks are too drunk to fuck most of the time."

By then we had traveled through most of the black sections of Houston and, at my request, were on our way to Pasadena, a town of over 50,000 in which one census gave the number of Negroes as 42. There the tract homes march motionlessly into mediocrity, dead cells of the imagination. Seething, Usselman told me, "Look, about two and a half years ago, Bobby Bland played a popular spot here called Gilley's and the place sold out because they didn't know who he was. When Bobby came on stage and they saw he was black, 75 percent of the audience got up and walked out. They're sick."

As an experiment, we stopped at a few places to test the service. Things went all right at a Burger King but were strange at a deli. When I asked for gum, the fat woman behind the counter said she didn't know about it because she didn't chew. Then a customer pointed at the gum rack, and the large woman feigned surprise. Usselman asked her what time it was and she said she didn't know. There was a clock right behind her head.

As we returned to Houston, we stopped at the San Jacinto monument, a tall edifice topped by a star which honors the April afternoon in 1836 when Sam Houston's army changed history in 18 minutes, surprising the Mexican army during siesta. The words chiseled into the monument clarify yet again the complexity of Texas history and heritage:

"Citizens of Texas and immigrant soldiers in the army of Texas at San Jacinto were natives of Alabama, Arkansas, Connecticut, Georgia, Illinois, Indiana, Kentucky, Louisiana, Maine, Maryland, Massachusetts, Michigan, Mississippi, Missouri, New Hampshire, New York, North Carolina, Ohio, Pennsylvania, Rhode Island, South Carolina, Tennessee, Texas, Vermont, Virginia, Austria, Canada, England, France, Germany, Ireland, Italy, Mexico, Poland, Portugal, and Scotland.

"Measured by the results, San Jacinto was one of the decisive battles of the world. The freedom of Texas from Mexico won here led to annexation and the Mexican War, resulting in the acquisition by the United States of the states of Texas, New Mexico, Arizona, Nevada, California, Utah, and parts of Colorado, Wyoming, Kansas, and Oklahoma, almost one-third of the present area of the American nation, nearly a million square miles of the territory changed sovereignty.

"The battle was won on April 21, 1836, Sam Houston in front of an international army, some of whom were Mexicans themselves."

About a mile from the San Jacinto monument is the battleship *Texas* and a small plaque which honors the men who went down with the *Sea Wolf,* which sank many enemy vessels during World War II and eventually went down itself. The names of most of the men who died on that ship are Hispanic.

On the road back to my mother's I noticed the intermittent sight of white couples in pickup trucks driving normally or wildly with two or three small children in the back, all of whom would have no protection if an accident occurred. In *Cowboy Culture* David Dary asks whether cowboy style is a way to avoid becoming a cog in the wheel of a machine. It seems to me that the question is also whether, in the process, certain people become nuts on the wheels of pickups.

VI. IT'S ALL RIGHT

On the evening of Juneteenth, I attended a party for SUM Concerts at the mansion formerly owned by the late Jesse Jones, who was a pivotal figure in developing the alliance between business and government in Texas. Jones was from Tennessee and is a mythic figure in the West. He conceived the idea of the ship channel which runs 40 miles inland and makes Houston a port city, now the third largest in the country. He started the Texas Commerce Bank, owned real estate, founded the Federal Loan Administration, and became Secretary of Commerce under Roosevelt's New Deal. Jones dispensed 50 billion dollars in federal funds and with a small group of associates ran the city of Houston from a room in the Laman Hotel that led to the term "the 8F Club" (also known as *the* card game in town). An important member of that club was George Brown, who received government contracts through his associations with Jones. Brown built NASA's Manned Spacecraft Center, the Mohole Project (to penetrate the earth's mantle), and the American facilities in Da Nang, which he sold for a rumored 37 million dollars.

Wandering through the late power broker's mansion that evening were blues singers and players, some of Houston's recent successes and arrivals, plus a bit of old Houston money. In that huge backyard, under those trees, while the Fifth Ward's Big Mama Thornton sat in a sullen stupor, James Cotton strolled about, amiable, chuckling, and talking about how much he'd liked playing for the black audiences in Houston and New Orleans. The members of his band were all authentic hambone Negroes. They bemoaned the fact that more younger black musicians weren't interested in blues but felt that this was slowly changing. The liquor flowed and the food was good.

A black corporate executive said something to me at the party that illuminated much of what I'd seen. "Whether people like it or not, the center of the drive for independent energy sources is in Texas, and the way Texas goes is the way the country is going to go as far as energy is concerned. There's no future in crude oil, but there's plenty of coal, shale oil, and in the Southwest in general all kinds of important minerals like uranium. That's where the Mexicans and the Indians come in. This could turn out to be another Oklahoma for Indians because a lot of those valuable minerals are on their reservations. The business people know it, the Indians know it, and so do the Mexicans. In fact, they're just beginning to talk about 'Mestizo Power,' you know. A coalition based on them being mixed up in each other's family lines. Now what the black people are going to have to do is stop being stupid and talking about dumb Mexicans and start trying to deal with those people politically, socially, and economically. If they don't, they won't need a blues festival cause they'll be singing the blues every goddam day."

The last shows were on Saturday, one in the afternoon, one at night. They started quite beautifully with Milton Larkin and His All Stars, featuring Arnett Cobb and Jimmy Ford. Larkin's set wasn't folk blues, it was hard jazz blues, including ballads and a disco tune he wrote for his great-great-grandchildren. From his metal crutches Arnett Cobb filled up the stage with his grand sound, and Jimmy Ford, veteran of Tadd Dameron's band, proved once more how much better Southern white players sound in jazz bands than their Northern counterparts. He was a perfect foil for the Texas tenor of Cobb, whipping out eloquent lines in Charlie Parker's language. Albert Collins played wonderfully at both concerts, with a weight to his guitar sound that made each note sound twice as thick as normal. The set began with rhythm and blues but moved into hard shuffle when Collins came on, so much so that an unidentified drunken Negro came on the stage and did a leg-wiggling dance as authentic as it was unexpected (and unwanted by the performers). Big Mama Thornton, butched up in cowboy hat and cowboy outfit, her clothes padded to give what she must think is an image close to her nickname, arrived at the festival in a dark blue Lincoln Continental which had "Big Mama" written on the right side of the windshield in gold sequins. Her entourage consisted of her sister and two militant, muscular Houston homosexuals with cowboy hats, sleeveless dark blue shirts, jeans, boots, and handlebar mustaches. Her set wasn't as interesting as her entrance, but she was in stronger voice than when I had heard her last.

By the time Eddie Cleanhead Vinson came on, people had been barbecuing for hours in the trees a few hundred yards from the bandstand, beer had been given away, and the crowd had sunk into the dark bliss of a hot summer evening. Vinson was suave and professional, teasing, and sophisticated in a way few of the previous performers had been. Here was a man who breathed the blues and its bebop extensions with such command his distracted appearance on the stage made his virtuosity even more apparent. Far more than Jimmy Ford, he showed how much range there is to the blues idiom and how many notes are now associated with the sensibility only because of the innovations of men like Charlie Parker.

Between Vinson's set and Clifton Chenier, one of the performers handed the other a beer, then lifted his own to toast.

"Cheers."

"What we got to cheer about? The white folks got all the money."

"Well, long as you living, you got a chance."

"I guess you right about that."

"How's that old knucklehead?"

"He's all right, but he ain't big enough to be a star and he ain't good enough to do nothing but play for the white folks. You know how they are: they like anything."

"Who you telling."

"But if you good enough, I mean all around good enough, you can play the blues all the goddam way from California to Calcutta."

"Well, you goddam right about that, too."

Clifton Chenier and his Red Hot Louisiana Band came on to excited applause. Chenier introduced his group by saying, "This here is what you call the real zydeco. I took the zydeco all the way from Opalusa, Louisiana, to Israel, Europe, and Africa." Playing his fancy new accordion and leading his group through a fiery set, Chenier's music rocked everyone within hearing distance. The ensemble, which includes electric guitar and bass, alto saxophone, trumpet, washboard, percussionist (bongos, scrapers, etc.), and trap drums, was the most exciting at the festival. The alto sound in the group achieves a color close to that of the harmonica and, in tandem with the accordion, provides extraordinary timbres. Synthesis is the essence of Chenier's achievement, for the music is protected from the sentimental by the heavy, rattling, scraping, thumping percussion that sets one foot in Africa and the other in the gutbucket. There are mock melodramatic ballads nearly country-and-western in feeling, Lester Young motifs, Louis Jordan alto spirals, sensual, pugnacious riffs, and barrelhouse boogie back home as the house farthest down in the swamp.

As Chenier went into "It's All Right," the entire audience had been transformed. No longer bothered by the heat or the mosquitos, the listeners became a huge polyrhythmic pulsation. The Mexicans did Hispanic steps, the whites clog-danced, and the Negroes, their identities deepened by so many miscegenations, were an encyclopdia of facial and body types, chanting voices and rhythms. As I looked at them I thought how prepared these descendants of mountain men, cowboys, frontier women, and daredevils seemed to be to move through the tragedy so basic to the black American story. For just as the Chicago bluesmen met the challenge of electronics and Clifton Chenier has transformed a polka pumper into a blues shouter, black Americans must conquer the frontier of the Information Society. As John Biggers, artist and teacher at Texas Southern University, says, "These black schools are falling apart. Desegregation has sent us all the bad white teachers and the dwindling budgets and the poor administrators. The white people found out the Civil Rights Movement came off these campuses and decided to destroy them. But now is the time for us to branch out and take over the big white institutions—not with bullshit, but with quality. A lot will be hurt and a lot will be left behind, but that's the way our history is. But the old people who came before us, the runaways and the rebels, that's the way they wanted it to be. They expected us to travel on. They just didn't want us to stumble into oblivion."

Texans, are, to use Octavio Paz's phrase, labyrinths of solitude, with cultural and ethnic pedigrees appropriate to human mazes. The Spaniards conquered the Indians of Mexico with Chinese gunpowder on horses and Moorish saddles, brought the architecture of the Alhambra to the country under a cover letter of vernacular Catholicism, introduced the big cattle-raising vision of the *rancho grande,* then created the mulatto race we know as Mexicans. They also brought African slaves whose ethnicity became part of an Afro-Indian race observed near the Rio Grande by the 1570s. Then came the white Americans and northern Europeans—hardy, self-righteous, and xenophobic Protestants. Like John Wayne's Ethan in *The Searchers,* they absorbed the severity, the flair, the fraternity, the pride, and the solitude of the region until, for all their connections to England, Scotland, Ireland, Wales, and Germany, they became akin—in spirit and often in blood—to their Indian and Mexican adversaries. So that in the end they were like the fellow in the Talmud who was spooked by an animal at night, only to realize it was a man as he came closer—and, finally, that the stranger was his brother.

STOP THE SOB SQUAD
September 16–22, 1981

At least since Burt Lancaster and Hume Cronyn did the antagonistic waltz in *Brute Force,* there have been those who sentimentally mantle convicts with qualities that would lead one to believe that the bulk of them are in prison for crimes of some political nature, and that prisons should cease being prisons and be transformed into homes away from home. Oh, there is no arguing that conditions in many prisons are terrible and that prisoners are sometimes the victims of racism and the sadism made possible by the circumstances (mean guards and the professional bone-breakers who evolve from enthusiastic bullies in street gangs mirror each other's bloodlusts and deserve each other). But the fact remains after the smoke clears (and the whites of liberal eyes have reddened) that the overwhelming majority of people behind bars arrived there because of their own selfishness: you have something and they take it because they think they should have it. They are dope peddlers, muggers, rapists, bank robbers, burglars, con men, and so on. They deserve much of what they get. For instance, the criminals with whom I grew up never expressed the slightest compunction about taking what they wanted from other people. Those outlaws could never have been deterred by sociological statistics or dictates of compassion. The impoverished, the infirm, the aged—all were seen democratically as potential victims—suckers and chumps.

That's only the first stage, however. Once they are in prison and hear a few militant speeches or read a few paragraphs of so-called radical literature, they turn, magically, into *political* prisoners. When pressed, though, a political prisoner is anyone who does something "the system" doesn't like. I'll give you an example. I used to teach literature inside Chino, a jumping-off place for convicts in California who have moved from maximum security all the way down to a farm on which they work while awaiting parole review. Every week I would hear something about political prisoners and how the black convicts were but examples of the racism of the country and the double standards in courts, what with "crime in the suites" being far less significant in terms of sentencing than "crime in the streets." Faced with this group of victims, all of whom were suffering fascist and racist repression, I once asked every one who was innocent of the crimes for which they were convicted to raise their hands. No one did. They then went on to say that they wouldn't be in there if they'd had the kind of money the rich white crooks had for better lawyers. I answered that the communities they had terrorized in one way or another were, in fact, lucky they hadn't had the money. I still think so.

I am opposed to almost all the cries from prisoners and their advocates for minimum wage, color television, and other creature comforts. Prisons were not built to make people comfortable or to acknowledge their ethnic cultures. Jews, Catholics, Muslims, and Hispanics were not put in prison for the appreciation of their cultural riches; they were incarcerated because they committed crimes, because they brutally or slyly broke the law. Distinctions are valuable only so far as they provide the information necessary for an arrest and conviction. If prisoners are fed slop, too bad. Lie on your back for weeks recovering from a mugging and get fed through your veins because both jawbones were broken and see how interested you become in the cuisine convicts get. It may sound cruel and callous, but my feeling is that what makes a criminal is a disposition toward cruelty, a laziness and impatience that leads to taking from others, and a cynicism that pretends there is a war going on, and that the victims are the result of a conflict somebody else started. As far as I'm concerned, chain gangs could be instituted in *every state* and those convicts could be put to more useful work—landscaping, cleaning up the streets, tearing down condemned buildings, etc. After all, they are supposed to be paying a debt to society; society is not supposed to pay them for being law-breakers.

I know the sob squad of white liberals will hate this, but they should spend some time talking to the victims of the Third World criminals they sympathize with so much. Dope dealers, muggers, burglars, car thieves are not seen within the black and Hispanic communities as rebels against an unjust society, courageous young men with a dream of liberation over the horizon. They are seen as the major threat to stability, a threat more ominous than inflation. At the same time, crime will be reduced in those communities when people start calling the police—*harassing the police!*—until something is done. If a person sees heroin sold on his or her stoop every day, for instance, and only complains to reporters, he or she is partially to blame. In fact, it seems as though the idea of the great white father who will either solve problems or ignore them has been accepted by too many people of color and has led to rampant destruction of their communities.

For people with histories of slavery and discrimination, it is easy to understand how the lawbreaker, the criminal, became a community hero. But chattel slavery ended with the Civil War and most of the racist laws that came forward at the end of Reconstruction have been knocked down. Now is the time for a sober look at what the cult of the criminal hero has done. It has left the black and Hispanic communities holding the ball. If the people of those communities want change, the conception of "the snitch" will have to be reworked until the person who fingers a community parasite is seen as a hero, not some kind of a traitor to a code founded totally in greed.

THE FAILURE OF BLACK POWER
November 1981

Ex-deputy mayor Haskell G. Ward was an embattled man during his 19 months in the Koch administration because he was the highest-ranking black person there and because his very position called into question certain basically wrong-headed ideas about political power and influence. However much they may be responses to peaceful or violent advocacy or dissent in the streets, the logistical nuts and bolts of policy come from the top, and those black people who find their ways to the top, in elected, appointed, or advisory positions, soon discover that being the only dark card in the game can inspire hostility, envy, or ambivalence. Such responses are especially characteristic of those black and white onlookers who believe that Negro Americans can never make any advances, never influence their fates, and can only achieve positions as tokens.

Things have now gotten so out of hand in certain quarters that the epithets of "racist" or "Uncle Tom" can be shouted at anyone who points out that the black and Hispanic communities in a place like New York constitutes a sleeping giant. The argument will be made that all problems within those communities are the fault of the system and responsibility of the system to solve. Slavery and discrimination produced self-destructive apathy; police malpractice discourages people in those communities from reporting daily criminal activity in their own blocks; the resistance to "white values" leads those most in need of good education to tear their schools apart; and the tight job market in tandem with hiring discrimination justify welfare cheating or the employment of welfare mothers to cut dope for dealers whose very trade is largely responsible for the destruction of the community. People who hold these ideas subscribe, perhaps unknowingly, to paternalism—benevolent or antagonistic—and ignore the fact that 45 percent of Manhattan makes for a potential of political and economic power (if only through boycott) that could easily equal the influence of white ethnic groups. It is the mobilization of that force which is the issue, not its helplessness, not its victimization.

Because he has no sympathy for that vision of helplessness, Haskell G. Ward is the kind of man who would very probably make the most farsighted activists of the '60s very proud. He understands quite well the ways in which political and economic changes actually come about and has systematically worked himself into positions where he has been able to observe and influence policy from within the citadels themselves, rather than theorizing from the outside, sentimentalizing bootlegged radical ideas that work better in parlors and periodicals than they do in the halls, offices, and limousines where policies are actually set. But black people like Ward are examples of changes at least 30 years in the making: since Ralph Bunche received the Nobel Peace Prize in 1950, there has been a swelling, unsentimental number of Amrican Negroes for whom the mechanics of domestic or international political power and influence, business technology and its applications, either hold no mystery or represent challenges they feel confident to meet.

Haskell Ward is a Negro-dark and handsome man who was born in Griffin, Georgia, in 1940, and his story is much like those of many talented Negro American musicians and athletes who came from nowhere to positions of status by dint of personality, drive, and ferocious ambition. In the tradition of the 19th-century success story, it is said that he had to start school late because there was no money to buy him shoes. He became a product of the influential brain trust in the Atlanta black universities when he graduated from Clark College, then went on to teach high school for two years in a Peace Corps program outside Addis Ababa. Though he had wanted to become a psychiatrist, Ward has said regarding his experience in Africa, "My concerns have always been with social justice, but I switched from the individual approach to the concern for groups." Upon returning from Ethiopia, Ward earned his masters in African Studies at UCLA and served as deputy director of Operation Crossroads Africa in Manhattan from 1967 to 1969. He then became a program officer in the Middle East and Africa Office of the Ford Foundation's International Division in Manhattan, also serving as an assistant representative of the foundation in its Lagos, Nigeria, office. After leaving the foundation, Ward first served as part of President Carter's transition team, then went to the State Department as a policy planner and specialist in African affairs, where he was quite influential in changing American policy toward Africa to favor a long view rather than what he calls "the mundane business of whether a country is presently run by Communists or not."

Ward first gained attention in New York when Mayor Koch appointed him to the task of cleaning up black and Hispanic poverty programs in which men like Ramon Velez, Hubert Irons, and Sam Wright had built what became known as plantations, corrupt entities given over to logrolling and graft, rather than laying community adversity low. But when Ward was initially offered the position of commissioner of the New York Community Development Agency, he turned it down, thinking that Koch wanted to use him not so much to improve things but to remove the mayor's political enemies so that patronage jobs could be handed out. He was eventually convinced otherwise by Koch himself, Andrew Young, and Percy Sutton. Ward left his position in the State Department and arrived in New York to rhetorical hoots and jeers from the local black politicians who resented an outsider's decision-making power.

They weren't wrong, at least if they wanted things to continue as they had been going. Steven Schlesinger reported in the October 22, 1978, *Post* that in Ward's first seven months he cut off funding to seven of the 26 agencies through which federal funds were supposed to get to the neighborhoods in East Harlem, East New York, the Lower East Side, Crown Heights, Morrisania, Hunt's Point, and Bedford Stuyvestant. The story went on to point out that Ward publicly condemned three of the agencies for fiscal irregularities and four others for maintaining illegal boards of directors, then called for a "ban in all projects on all individuals who have served in any governing capacity in any of the city's War on Poverty centers for five years or more." In that shutdown, 217 jobs were ended and $4.8 million in contracts was held back. In the process, Ward was threatened by phone and took police protection.

During those months, Ward was also attacked with stereotypical ideas that have their roots in the late 1960s, when large numbers of equally gullible young Negroes and whites were successfully convinced that discipline, planning, research, strategy, mastery of the English language, and sophisticated deportment were somehow exclusively white and irrelevant. Accused of not being a "real" black person, he was often called an *oreo* (white on the inside, black on the outside), which is but another way of telling those black people who can get the ears of the most powerful in the political and business worlds that they've stepped out of their correct places in society.

It also elevates inferior preparation to a position of purity. I have never heard anyone say, for instance, if John Connally is a real white man, then William Buckley is not, or that if Jane Fonda is a real white woman, then Loretta Lynn is not. Varieties of speech rhythm, diction, accent, taste, and style are fine for white people, but there must be a psychological and spiritual tub of tar a Negro should sit in each morning before facing the white day.

As Ward details that period, hard, internal muscle shows itself in his eyes, supplanting his geniality. "When I took that position, I was prepared to be attacked and called names. I was prepared to be attacked for taking jobs away from black people. I was prepared to be called misguided and so on. But politics is a tough business and if you aren't tough and can't stand the constant complexity of the pressures inherent in positions of administration and leadership, you shouldn't go into politics.

"You see, you have to be prepared to tell the truth. The poverty programs weren't working for blacks or Hispanics. They had become power bastions for black politicians and previous administrations had been content to leave them that way because of the racist idea that once you give blacks and Hispanics programs all they're going to do is steal anyway. But the interesting thing about it is that for all the noise from politicians and the intimations of racism and so on, when I was in the streets and having meetings with community people, I found out that people *knew* the programs weren't working; they knew they were corrupt. They knew that the purpose of the programs wasn't patronage but to better the conditions of their lives, which they weren't doing. They just weren't doing that. You see, crime and corruption have no color and you can seriously undermine community confidence in the long run if you protect somebody who's dishonest just because he's not white.

"In fact, for political seriousness and broadening of confidence, it is in our best interests when corruption by blacks is exposed by blacks. Then we lessen the disdain that blacks can often have for politicians and we can make it clear to *all* communities that we are working to protect the tax dollars of *everyone*, since everyone's tax dollars finance governmental programs. Whenever money is stolen or misused, every taxpayer, regardless of color, is having his or her investment in society undermined. You have to be able to say that. If you don't, you corroborate every stereotype we've been fighting all these years to knock down."

What was corroboration of a stereotype to whites was something very different within the minority communities. A naïve political disposition was fostered in the late 1960s through the professional adversary positions of many black leaders as political sophistication was upstaged by threat. The rhetoric that had once called for a commonality of American concern was replaced by one that set black Americans outside the mainstream of the country's experience. In the process, despite all the black tax dollars that go to the federal funding system, the government was seen as white and its funds as "the white man's money." Black corruption was then given a clever cover of ethnic nationalism and stealing was defended as a type of revenge for historical injustice. This was also justified by the proposition that whites were still racist and crooked, so that "getting over" on the white man was often given more significance than whether or not programs helped better our communities. The upshot was that a politics of exclusion created a vulnerability to exploitation by members of the race. Ward thinks that the only way out of this morass is to exhibit a fundamental sense of group responsibility that is sober, unsentimental, and pragmatic.

"My general sense is that we have not accepted the fact that we are responsible for the condition in which we live in this society. Because of the way we came to this country, we have had a greater feeling that somebody else is responsible for our condition, that somebody else did it to us. Until we take responsibility for our condition, we will never change that condition. We can shift the total perception of us when we acknowledge that we are responsible and don't intend to look to some-body else to do it for us. We will then align ourselves with people and institutions that address our interests. It may mean that we will be aligned with people who are seen as conservatives on one day and people who are seen as liberals on another day. It is not politically intelligent to automatically assume that a liberal solution is the best one for black people and a conservative solution is opposed to our interests. Unfortunately, we have been more inclined than most groups to stay locked in a position because of its ideological characteristics."

That statement is much more radical than it may appear—for it rejects the Marxist abstractions that have made for foolhardy black "leadership" in the past, just as it rejects the pity-ridden emphasis on the uniqueness of the black condition, an emphasis which led to social programs that usually created greater rather than lesser dependence on the government and liberal spirit.

Those social programs depended on economic prosperity in the nation at large, the moods of moral obligation and guilt, or, in the wake of the riots, fear. And though they did make it possible for a good many talented black Americans to break into citadels like the corporate world (which will have great significance by the end of this decade), the game plan made more of elaborate traction rather than getting the patient out of the hospital. The declining quality of public education was sidestepped by preferential programs in college admissions, the power of economic boy-cott was set aside in favor of demanding that the federal government redress prejudicial unions and the hiring practices of private businesses. In effect, the thrust and drive of the Civil Rights Movement was handed over to the government, and black leadership was able to duck the responsibility of more and more thorough community organization and the development of a political sophistication to parallel the fluidity of the social terrain.

As hard-nosed, astute black Americans have also been pointing out, less predictable political allegiances should make it more likely that both major political parties would compete energetically for the black vote and, I might add, given the burgeoning number of black millionaires, eventually, financial support.

Essentially, Haskell Ward recognizes that the terms of compromise have changed—not for a long time will access to mainstream American life come through laws intended to counter historical or present injustice. Solutions will result from deals or pressures based on self-interest, and the people most influential will be those who can best orchestrate self-interest and expand its applicability to include risk and sacrifice when necessary. If, for instance, private businesses are advised to finance training programs or other projects not immediately connected to profit, they must be made to understand that the only businesses that *really* profit from urban unrest, destruction, riots, or vandalism are insurance companies, which put it to businesses and residents with higher rates. What the poor must know is that when their communities are torn apart, the rates go so high that, especially in inflationary times like these, businesses are discouraged from opening or, if they do, the prices for goods will be adjusted to make profit *and* offset insurance overhead. It is, then, in the interest of poor and minority communities to develop images of law and order, which will clearly result in grueling and brutal battles with local parasites and overworked, lazy, corrupt, cynical, or apathetic police.

"We should have people down at City Hall saying that we don't like dirty streets. We should have people saying we want better housing, better schools, and the drugs off the streets in Harlem or Brownsville or wherever else in New York that they are illegally sold. One of the problems is that we don't say clearly to people who supposedly represent us that we don't like the way things are, so, those who govern assume that everything is okay with us.

"Another part of our problem is made particularly clear with the death of Roy Wilkins. He was prepared to associate with whomever he needed to if it meant he could get what he wanted—racist laws off the books and legislation that would meet the needs of black people and allow them full participation in this society. He was prepared to accommodate, to compromise, so that he could get where he wanted to go. We do not demonstrate often enough our political sense with respect to compromise in a range of areas so that we can associate with different groups. Wilkins was prepared to be vilified and to be called an 'Uncle Tom' because he knew this is the way you *can* get things done."

With that observation, Ward broaches the big question of sophistication in minority politics, something especially hard to come by because minority leadership has so long been media-dominated by those who address the political in melodramatic terms, reducing an extremely complicated arena to that of good and bad guys, not masters, journeymen, or fumblers in the art of compromise. Since the death of King, minority leadership has been long on homilies and short on organization and mobilization. It has invested too much in a kind of widow's mite politics wherein sincerity counts for more than substance, and too much in the voodoo politics of instant change, which makes of politicians only successful or failed magicians. This is in a political and economic vision so closely aligned to the ideas of the pure in heart and the quick fix that its offshoot has been community impatience or cynicism when confronted with the intricate relationships which must be orchestrated to bring about actual change. Ward, however, believes that the tendency to underestimate the power of compromise and the refusal to comprehend the rich variety of political approaches and ploys available is no more than a way of opting out of that process which must be learned and marshaled to actually gain the kind of political power that transcends parties and high officials.

Zionists have long been able to do that—American support of Israel has been maintained for the last two decades, under liberal and conservative, Democratic and Republican Presidents alike. The substance of that achievement was perhaps made most pointed in the, recently expressed support of Israel by Jerry Falwell, whose movement would almost automatically have been considered anti-Semitic if only on religious grounds, and the vote in the House of Representatives on the AWAC sale to Saudi Arabia. On this subject, Ward observed that Begin welcomed the support by saying that Israel had few friends and needed all she could get. "What we tend to do is criticize the Jewish community in New York because it has protected and promoted Israel's interests. That misses the point by a wide margin. What we ought to do is admire their ability to achieve their objective and sustain their position. What we do repeatedly is criticize the entire establishment as being against our interests. What we should be doing is moving in ways that will convince the establishment that it is in *its* interest to support us."

In terms of the present administration in Washington, Ward makes those observations specific.

"Politics is simply the art of the possible, and if you aren't addressing the possible, you aren't being political. You can't sit around saying Mr. Reagan is 100 percent wrong. Mr. Reagan is the President, and that has a certain dramatic reality to it. If we sit on the sidelines and wait until the next person comes in, whom we *hope* will think more highly of us, we will find ourselves left out of the entire political process. What if the next President doesn't seem to have our interests as major priorities? Will we sit through another administration and possibly another? I'm sure, deep down, we have more sense than that."

This goes against the grain among those who have become professional opponents of the government and who represent that wing of black politics in which what was once the brave power of the word has become the propensity to bore. Whereas once merely speaking out against injustice was itself an incendiary act that could bring violence or death to the speaker, over the last 20 years, or at least since Malcolm X, the gleeful or pompous haranguing of power has become a vocation. The image of the professional adversary has damaged the freedom black politicians have to make deals, to compromise, to really shape, influence, or wield power. Probably the worst effect of unrelenting rabble-rousing and the constant attempt to manipulate white Americans through the imposition of guilt was the destruction of the developing national identification with the problems of black Americans that had resulted from the efforts of civil rights leaders like Martin Luther King. In the wake of his death, telling white people off frequently became more important than changing power relationships. As usual, Ward looks at the matter strategically.

"It is no longer effective to call somebody a racist or to present our problems as exclusive and connected only to the condition of our color. By tending to define our problems as uniquely related to our blackness, we have made people who are not black feel as though those issues have nothing to do with them. But the fact of the matter is that whoever is in power is the person or group we have to deal with. We have to learn their language, their ideas, and shape our politics in a way that we can make it clear that our interests are the interests of *everyone*." That is not as great a leap as it might seem, especially since black Americans learned long ago that there were distinct differences between, say, Southern and Northern Democrats, something which the Republican party never took proper advantages of following the passage of the Voting Rights Bill. But, of course, Ward understands that such a statement can be seen as but an example of rank opportunism.

"I also want to make it clear that I'm not saying that we should simply make deals and not have any position or integrity. In fact, it would be hard to bring about better housing, better law enforcement, better education—all of them across the board—in an immoral fashion. I'm simply saying that we should *broaden* our constituency rather than narrow it, and that we cannot limit our constituency to only those who have historically agreed with us. In the process, we should also make it clear to the kind of black and Hispanic leaders who recently allowed their communities to get less New York representation by approving gerrymandering, that we won't allow them to barter away the interest of the minority communities in order to protect themselves."

Ward knows that problem well because he found himself in a position that called into question his own sense of bartering with community interests shortly after he set poverty program reforms into motion. Eleven months after he began working for the Koch administration, he was promoted to deputy mayor and his job was to oversee the cutting back of the municipal hospital structure. It was then that Ward found himself in the hottest waters. It was far easier, even for all the political opposition, to tighten up programs bloated with corruption than it was to make it clear to the community on one hand why certain hospitals should be closed, and to the mayor on another, why certain hospitals should stay open. The closing of Sydenham in Central Harlem evoked much outrage and demonstration; the mayor's determination to close Metropolitan led to Ward's resignation. Throughout, Ward learned a great deal about double-dealing and the fear many black politicians have of taking positions outside of charging insensitivity or racism. At least in public.

"Regardless of the protests, everybody in Central Harlem knew that if you had a problem with health care, you just simply wouldn't get it solved at Sydenham. Community residents who had the resources didn't go there. Now, if it wasn't good enough for those who had money, why should it be good enough for poor people? Hospitals are the end of the line anyway. The way to deal with health in a community is through preventive measures. You've got to be prepared to educate the people so that they know you're not depriving them of health care when you say that it would be better to establish health education programs, preventive programs, community health centers. You've got to be prepared to say that because, otherwise, you will be behaving dishonestly, which is what certain black politicians did. Behind closed doors, they supported Ed Koch on the closing of Sydenham, then said something else publicly. In fact, my experiences within the administration showed me quite clearly that blacks as a group could benefit far more from leaders who have the courage to tell the truth and take the heat for unpopular positions."

Ward took a great deal of heat as deputy mayor, reviled by columnists and activists alike. When he resigned, he was described as "burnt out" and disillusioned, even embittered. At this point, however, Ward denies those assertions.

"I knew what I was doing when I supported the closing of Sydenham and I knew what I was doing when I resigned. I knew it wasn't in the interest of the New York community, regardless of race, for us to be spending our total budget on hospitals. Yet when I opposed the closing of Metropolitan Hospital, I did so on the grounds that it would be depriving the community of needed health care and we were not presenting something to fill the gap in our alternative plan. I told the mayor in very clear terms that I could not support such a plan. That was my position and it was also the position of a number of other health professionals in the city. I also had to be prepared to say that.

"I left my position because I disagreed on that point and for that reason alone, not because some politician in the city thought I was misguided or that I had gotten off on the wrong political position. What they thought didn't matter to me or I would have done things in a way that would curry favor with local politicians. I wasn't interested in that. I was interested in serving the people of New York to the best of my abilities. I have a sense that that is also Ed Koch's objective, which is why I endorsed him for reelection. On the question of the hospital, however, we differed because I told him we were losing more money through management deficiencies in the Health and Hospital Corporation than we would save by closing Metropolitan. Those deficiencies were largely in the area of uncollected revenues due the Health and Hospital Corporation, which we were then losing in sums near $15 million a week. But we stood to save only $12 million or so by closing Metropolitan. When we were not able to accommodate those differences, I resigned."

Ward's support for Koch for reelection will automatically label him a reactionary to many. But the quality of his commitment to high political compromise is shown in his support of Brooklyn's Al Vann and Major Owens, both of whom have been strong critics of the mayor and are considered by Ward to be important leaders who need only to extend their constituencies across ethnic lines. Were he asked, he would also advise Koch on ways to extend his constituency in the black community.

"Ed Koch is truly not the issue in my opinion, even though he is an easy target since certain people tend to blame economic shifts and demographic changes on the figure in power, or the figure *of* power. The issue, in terms of this discussion, is what is going on in the black and Hispanic political evolution in this city. My own sense is that we're better served by having a mayor like Ed, who is prepared to play fairly and deal straight, say what he can do and what he can't do and say it openly. If he gives you his word, he will keep it.

"But the mayor should recognize that New York is unique in the extent to which minority groups as large as blacks and Hispanics are left out of the political process. Even though some black leaders have *double-crossed* him, he shouldn't give the impression that he is out to undermine black leadership per se. But I have enough questions about that leadership myself to know he shouldn't listen to them exclusively, however. He has to build more contacts in that community to inform his decisions. Ed should support full representation of the city's population on the governing councils. The mayor has to show precise concern about what our public school investment is producing in returns of functional people in our city, not just the improvement of reading scores by a few percentage points. We have become more and more of a service economy in New York City, but the educational system is producing people who are incapable of competing in the marketplace. They are being trained for unemployment and, as long as that continues, the public pays for inadequacy and suffers as a result of it. That is a basic and fundamental issue in this city."

Ward thinks it is of equal importance that the mayor bring together the best approaches developed by people who have worked in the black and

Hispanic areas in neighborhood self-improvement, so that neighborhood stabilization and redevelopment can be extended, which would produce jobs in cooperation with the private sector. The fact that the federal government lacks the massive funds necessary to rebuild the grotesque slums of the major cities isn't seen as a tragedy by Ward.

"This is not a hopeless condition. It's an enormous opportunity for the mayor to mobilize the resources of leadership within the public and private sectors that could, for instance, turn the situation around in Harlem very easily. Now that raises another question, because not everyone in Harlem wants an expanded development since that might suggest that whites will take over from blacks. I think we just have to be prepared to see a certain number of whites coming back into previously black and Hispanic areas and see that as encouragement for redevelopment."

In terms of black politics, Ward points out that the routes to political office and their strategies have drastically changed. The traditional elements have greatly declined in significance—the clubhouse, the patronage system, the boss system, and the party apparatus. So it is now possible to bypass the traditional routes to power and yet achieve it. He doesn't believe black politicians have taken enough note of those changes. Carter and, for instance, Reagan began more or less as independently promoted political figures who believed they could make a difference and stuck with that idea. But the kind of troops needed within the black political wing to bring change are scarce, a problem Ward has observed over the last decade.

"When I was working on President Carter's transition team, I noticed that the average young white of 25 or 30 years old was much more politically astute than the average black. Even though they were pursuing professional careers, they had been working in campaigns almost since they graduated from high school and they had the experience. We don't have many black professionals who will go out and work to *get* political experience so that they know how public policy is shaped, how things are done. In fact, large segments of that class who could make great headway for themselves, and blacks in general, look upon such work with disdain. But political experience is what ultimately shapes public policy. Through working in a campaign you get experience and a sense of the things necessary to develop policy issues, and you also get to know what the public will and will not support.

"Those areas of experience and judgment still constitute frontiers for us and, as we could see in the recent primary, black people will vote for a good candidate like David Dinkins, who made a strong showing against Stein. But he narrowed his chances of winning by gearing his campaign around the Board of Estimate. You can't go to an Italian, an Irishman, or a Jew and say, 'Vote for me so there'll be a black in that position.' It just won't work. But you can be sure that when blacks and Hispanics take their own fates into their hands and learn how to broaden their constituencies, we *will* see major changes in this city. If we had 70 to 85 percent registration in those communities and smart candidates, the ears at City Hall would open wide and they would listen very closely to what we want."

Ward is himself working on yet another frontier, that of liaison between private corporations in America and Third World countries such as Ghana, Nigeria, and Costa Rica. Since leaving the Koch administration in August 1979, he has formed a company called Haskell G. Ward Associates, which works in the areas of telecommunications, major construction, and the development of industry. His wife, an ex-vice president and general manager of Cartier, is a partner in the firm and assists companies in marketing and expanding plans. Ward sees very interesting similarities between underdeveloped countries and ethnic minorities within the United States.

In fact, he intends to pull together a nonpartisan civic and business group which will investigate the logistical problems of political and economic disaffiliation within Manhattan's minority communities. He points out that when he talks with his colleagues on the Trilateral Commission, for instance, he finds they have little experience with minorities and know less about their problems and how they are interwoven with those of the business community. His vision is that once those issues are presented clearly as dangers to the entire city of New York, those in power will see the importance of fair dealing to protect their own interests.

"What I have done is to take a look at what the needs of African and Third World countries are and translate them to American businesses. I'm not simply in this as a broker or to make money, I'm dealing with situations in which interests on both sides are most adequately met, with the maximum amount of fairness. Monumental readjustments in economic and market terms are taking place over the entire world and it is most in our interest to shape our future along the lines of enlightened policies rather than worry about mundane things like whether or not the Communists are in power. We should also be aware of the long-range dangers of computer colonization and the anti-American feeling that could mount if we were to use our technological advantages to deal unfairly with underdeveloped nations.

"It is also my feeling that just as economic realignment around the world takes precedence over race, racial history, or political history, the same problems exist in New York City. Local businesses should recognize the profound disaffection within the minority communities which parallels attitudes held about us in certain areas of the Third World. Quite simply, the absence of blacks and Hispanics from the economic and political alignment of this city is a greater threat to stability than the current fiscal crisis. That is the number one priority in this city. There is a built-in element of instability when almost 50 percent of the population is not able to realize its aspirations economically or politically. It has very serious racial implications with respect to peace and stability in the city. But I am not saying that issues should be organized or addressed solely around racial lines. What I am saying is that the task ahead is an economic and political one which could negatively manifest itself in racial terms if things continue as they are."

It is a profound indication of the significance of the multiracial makeup of America that its minorities are beginning to provide important business and political liaisons as the Third World emerges, and that those like Haskell Ward can make use of that experience to address the scar-tissued dilemmas of a place like New York. A very different future is looming.

16

ANIMATED COON SHOW
December 16–22, 1981

As the ultimate fantasy extensions of American comedy, cartoons provide a clearinghouse for popular impressions of the world—lampoon under celluloid. And since comedy in the slapstick tradition pivots on percussive climaxes, the animator's art allows for the surreal orchestration of the disappointments, conflicts, and brash surprises essential to the idiom. Crashes, accidents, explosions, and so on make the point of the tradition: who will get crunched? Will the hero or the villain be reduced to the status of buffoon by virtue of the humiliating act of violence? Characters rarely die, but the pompous, the arrogant, the malicious are pricked, punctured, or detonated at every opportunity.

When race enters the picture, things get much more surreal—a quality intensified when wartime propaganda changes the significance of the heroes and villians. "Sex, Violence, and Racism in Cartoons," the Eighth Street's midnight program of 11 animated shorts from the late 1930s and '40s, makes the connection clear between the provinces of the vituperative comic insult and the racial epithet from within or without.

Because of the stereotypes in much of this footage, many people may find the program more disgusting than funny or illuminating. Having grown up with cartoon events that were almost automatic, such as an explosion turning a white person or an animal character into a buckeyed pickaninny, I wasn't disgusted. But I was fascinated to see how little the comedy image of the Negro has changed and how incongruous that image was even then in light of the realities, say, of the sports world.

As with any ethnic group, there has always been an element of self-satire in most black American humor, a touch of the minstrel. But the irony of the grotesque reduction to sambo stereotype by white performers in blackface is that its popularity owed as much to the vitality it distorted as it did to the appeal of racism. Consequently, when cartoon characters are based on actual black entertainers like Fats Waller, the question becomes what it has been since Pigmeat Markham, Moms Mabley, Flip Wilson, or, for that matter, *The Jeffersons*. Where does the stereotype stop and the fun begin? Where do we draw the line between vernacular humor and cinematic slander? During the years when these cartoons were made, the shuffling, giggling, lazy, and stupid darkie was supposed to have represented black authenticity to white Americans. Maybe yes, maybe no. What, for instance, did white Americans think when they watched newsreels showing handsome Joe Louis whipping white men with very consistent regularity on programs that also featured Negroes running from sheets in films or personifying incompetence and abandon in cartoons? Perhaps it was simply more convenient to accept the stereotypes.

The cartoons in the Eighth Street series that deal directly with Negro American stereotypes are *Goldilox and the Jivin' Bears* (1944), *Clean Pastures* (1937), *Tin Pan Alley Cats* (1943), *All This and Rabbit Stew* (1941), and *Coal Black and de Sebben Dwarfs* (1942). In the first, we are given a version of the fairy tale told by a large, black piano player who trills blues or boogie-woogie figures between chuckles. The bears are Negro musicians and Goldilox (sic) is a vanilla-wafer tan sweetheart with a round backside, short dress, and high-heeled shoes of a sort that make the image extremely contemporary. When the big bad wolf commences chasing her, the bears fire up some music, and she dances him into sore-footed bad health. The scene seems a variation on Slim and Slam's appearance in *Hellzapoppin* and the kind of humor for which Waller was noted. And though it is sometimes amusing, one tires of its predictability, which is the bane of the stereotype.

Clean Pastures is really remarkable because it shows how much more attentive to skin tone cartoonists were than Broadway, and how pervasive Al Jolson's blackface image had become. In short, heaven—known at Pair-O-Dice—is in trouble because Harlem Negroes (all Negroes live in Harlem) are too busy singing and dancing to listen to the gospel. They will not be lured by promises of watermelon and so on. The brainstorm solution is that the angels will have to swing the colored people into Pair-O-Dice. Appropriately skin-toned caricatures of Cab Calloway, Waller, Louis Armstrong, and a blacked-up Jolson (!) are the Negro emissaries of heavenly butt-shaking. Of course, the Negroes—all anonymous Negroes are dark—go to Pair-O-Dice in droves.

Tin Pan Alley Cats makes it obvious how popular Waller must have been; a caricatured figure of the pianist is the hero of this very interesting cartoon in which good wins out over evil, *Guys and Dolls*-style. On the way to the Kit Kat Klub, our hero passes a street revival held by a group known as Uncle Tom Cats. He spurns their offer and goes into the club, where a series of hot notes sends him into a surreal netherworld in which he's assaulted by nightmare variations on stereotypic black American images. When he returns, the hero immediately joins the revivalists.

All This and Rabbit Stew finds Bugs Bunny pitted against a Fetchit-like hunter whom he finally triumphs over by pulling out a pair of dice and winning all of his possessions. *Coal Black and de Sebben Dwarfs* begins with a beautifully animated scene of a black mammy rocking a baby before a fireplace. It soon turns into a spoof of Disney's *Snow White* in which the evil queen is an FBI (fat, black, and indignant), and Prince Chammin is a zoot-suited spook with every tooth gold except for his two front ones, which are dice. Sometimes funny but usually contrived beyond the pale of sharp humor, it succeeds more as an example of eccentricity than anything else.

The program's other cartoons carve up the Germans and the Japanese or satirize sexual fantasies. Phallic symbols abound, and the symbolic erection and orgasm in *Plane Daffy* (1944) are brilliantly executed as Daffy Duck kisses the German spy Hata Mari. The duck's body goes horizontal and red hot as his lips touch hers; then he melts into a puddle of duck dripping down a flight of steps. *Russian Rhapsody* (1944) is extremely odd—because Hitler is wonderfully satirized as he gives a speech on "the New Odor," then replies to a question with a vernacular Jewish shrug and near-Yiddish inflection! *Bacall to Arms* (1946) is also quite fine in its parody of the moviegoer who loses all control when a sex symbol crosses the screen. *Scrap the Japs* (1942)—not a contemporary economic theory—stars Popeye, who defeats a whole ship of Japanese sailors single-handed. *Inki at the Circus* (1947) is in the same general league, except that it revolves around a single conceit—the hot pursuit by hungry dogs of a bone in the hair of an African circus boy.

I found the program both provocative and entertaining because of the accidental expression of the paradoxes that undergird so much of our culture. Once again, as with the technically brilliant openings of *Tin Pan Alley* and *Coal Black*, the invention bespeaks a level of human achievement that violently contrasts the xenophobic mocking which it was enlisted to articulate. And once again, vitality and vileness uneasily lay two heads upon a single pillow.

17

GAY PRIDE, GAY PREJUDICE
April 27, 1982

From the outside, a foreign world is much like a street covered by snow—unfamiliarity veils all the details, giving it a disguise in which variety is found mostly in shapes, until investigation melts away the mantle and reveals the details. So I had originally viewed the homosexual world. It had long been my opinion that black homosexuals had a kind of cultural access comparable to that of black servants and show people—that a commonality of style and demeanor based on sexual preference precluded problems of race and class. I was wrong. Extended conversations with writers John Rechy and Lionel Mitchell as well as other homosexuals have convinced me of how indelibly the cruelties of race and class texture a world already oppressed by real and ritual violence.

Initially, I had recognized that homosexuals, like all other officially ostracized groups, had their own versions of elite cliques from which they drew inspiration and occasional career assistance. They also had their own networks of influence—often in the worlds of art and design—and, again, as with other ostracized groups, the factor that made them a minority, their sexuality, usually garnered certain of them special places at social gatherings sponsored by the wealthy, whose supposed empathy masked an appetite for court entertainment. Their presence was also encouraged by the affection female patrons often have for the gay aesthetic blade, since those friendships have a built-in plantonic quality women find hard to come by with other men. Race complicates such dynamics because, in friendships with white women, black homosexuals can easily take on the roles of male mammies, confidants, and exotics with both ethnic and sexual twists.

In those circumstances, the black homosexual's interest in male flesh reinforces the white man's superior image of himself while allowing white women with racial sexual fantasies the freedom to play them out right in front of their husbands. The upshot is the most socially acceptable of all black men, at least as far as powerful white males are concerned: the Negro homosexual, eunuch by default in the heterosexual world. And since legend has it that a very famous Negro leader died from a caning he received when one of his white patrons discovered him in bed with his wife, it is also understandable why male patrons, whenever a choice has been available, have been partial to the talented young black homosexual. However much he might hang around, the daughter and the wife are always safe. What man could be more trustworthy?

At least since Harlem Renaissance power broker Alain Locke, there have been Negro homosexuals who have understood those dynamics. A notorious misogynist who eliminated women from his classes at Howard University by informing them in advance that their best possible grade was a C, Locke was never so impolitic in Manhattan, where he masterfully balanced the support of wealthy black and white women and never scandalized rich heterosexual men. With such support, he pushed many Negro artists, but he was partial to fellow homosexuals like Countee Cullen, Langston Hughes, and Richard Bruce Nugent. From those careers up through two of the most celebrated black writers of the 1960s and more than a few dancers, actors, and musicians, long- or short-term success has been spawned by two male heads on a pillow and the affection of patrons less threatened by homosexuality than heterosexuality. Patrons and the gargoyle minstrelsy of cocktail-party intrigue notwithstanding, the cultural influence of black homosexuals and bisexuals is undeniable—Jelly Roll Morton's mentor Tony Jackson, Duke Ellington's co-composer Billy Strayhorn, Ma Rainey, Bessie Smith, Billie Holiday, Cecil Taylor, and a closeted gaggle of others, including heroic symbols in church music, athletics, politics, and business. Their existence and the quality of their work say less about the innate abilities of homosexuals than about the potential of the entire species.

But homosexual elitists will tell you something else. Most members of scorned minority groups select one of three basic reactions to the greater society's contempt and the elitists choose the last of them; rather than accept inferior definitions of themselves or develop a stoic dream of equality, they draw up their own maps to the land of the aristocrats and define themselves as a chosen people suffering at the hands of insecure and sadistic barbarians. This probably accounts for the obsession so many homosexuals have with taste, art, style, and minute detail—in lieu of procreation, it allows association with the ageless greatness of human history. Ironically, however, the wing of militant contemporary homosexuality that claims to assault the conventions and brutishness of bourgeois mediocrity, morality, and sexual behavior upholds the traditions of race and class that have long stained Old Glory.

It's obvious, for instance, that there isn't much social involvement between black and white homosexuals in the West Village. What little there is, when not merely formal or regimentally cloned, often has a surrealistic quality symbolized for me by a couple I once saw: a black man with a three-day beard wearing a pistachio satin evening dress, complete with netted shawl, velvet pillbox hat, and red-roller skates as he traveled arm in arm with a handsome blond guy in a splendid tuxedo and patent leather shoes. And even the most ordinary relationships are so determined by traditional racism that a black homosexual can say of the Harvey Milk killing in San Francisco, "They could shoot them all because there's no difference between white faggots and any other rednecks. They are just as racist and they will use you and exclude you just as fast as anybody else white when they think they've gotten all you have to offer."

I. GUIDES TO THE SEX HUNT

John Rechy and Lionel Mitchell had a lot to say about the sources of such bitterness in a four-hour double interview during a New York visit of Rechy, who lives in Los Angeles, two summers ago. Since then, I have spoken with each of them many more times and collected overviews from other black and white homosexuals, both in conversation and on the printed page.

According to Edmund White, who introduced the writer at a reading two summers ago, John Rechy's best-selling first novel, *City of Night,* was "the first book to tell how we really live." Rechy's focus is the homosexual hustling world and the rituals of an erotic subsociety obsessed with emblematic fantasy symbols and anonymous private or public sex. His vision of that world is as harsh and critical as it is romantic, empathetic, and sentimental. *City of Night* reveals one of the best ears for speech patterns to appear in the last two decades. His most recent books, *The Sexual Outlaw* and *Rushes,* give quarter to neither heterosexual nor homosexual pieties and challenge both with equal rage. Lionel Mitchell's *Traveling Light,* a novel published in 1980, depicts a much broader social terrain, and, unlike most contemporary Negro fiction, conceives of black American life as part of a cultural complex that includes many races, religions, and folkways in Southern and Northern situations. Uneven, episodic, and loose-ended, it is nevertheless insightful, eloquent, finely observed, and orchestrated by both an ironic awareness of pretension and an irreverence that do fierce battle with the maudlin (although occasionally succumbing to it).

Rechy and Mitchell provide not only visual contrast but separate entries to extremity. Half Mexican, half Scottish, Rechy is a body builder of about 50 who seems to gain muscular bulk as he grows older, and his form is like that of Odysseus—huge trunk and short, small legs, the upper body looming and lightly heaving over the lower. His attire is the conventional tight-fitting, short-sleeved shirt, close-fitting jeans, wrist bands, and boots of a male hustler. Mitchell is ursine and endomorphic, a gourmand nearing 40 who carries 300 pounds on a big-boned mahogany frame five feet five inches tall. Usually unkempt, with pillow lint in hair and beard, stains on his shirts, sweaters, and pants, scuffed shoes, and long, semi-scrolled, lightish green and gray unlacquered nails that usually cover dark substances, Mitchell is the bulbous bohemian except on special occasions like his book party, where he appeared in a fine suit, perfectly groomed, to read from his work like the mandarin in charge.

Maybe because Rechy's body is the center of his performance, or his presentation, the speaking and reading voice is fluffy and modulated in

the tones of the homosexual radio announcer on the classical music station, while Mitchell's voice seems a compensation, a challenge, and an
onomatopoeia of experience. Fey and giddy one minute and pompous
the next, it can imitate the coos and kitchen diction of women, broaden
with the heavy sonority of the black church, or jumble sidewalk intona-
tions that stretch from New Orleans to Manhattan. Both men are witty
and narcissistic, Rechy about his body, his mind, and his work, Mitchell
about his intellect, the social terrain he's traversed, and his writing. But
both reveal a particular melancholy that bristles now and again through
their voices, eyes, and mannerisms, as each suffers from the pangs of
acute nostalgia and the obsessiveness that define what Rechy calls "the
sex hunt."

II. THE PREDATORY TRADITION

Almost as soon as the tape was turned on, Rechy wanted to make it clear
that every criticism he had of the homosexual world was also an indictment of heterosexual oppression, that homosexuals comprised the most
persecuted minority, in the world. "So much of our behavior is a response
to the relentless harassment through education, media, law, religion, and
the people who feel they have the right to attack us violently at will.
Furthermore, the more we pull away from self-criticism, the more our
problems grow. A lot of the dishonesties within the homosexual world
stem from the fear that if we admit to some things, the repressive machine
will roll over us. That was the fear behind the *Cruising* protests. We all
know that those places exist, but we were afraid that those kinds of images would be used against us."

Since then, Rechy himself has felt the effects of an increasing hostility
toward homosexuals which he attributes to the political climate created
by the Reagan administration. This climate has led to alliances between
homophobic police departments and minorities, specifically Negro and
Mexican thugs and gangs in California. This is not unlike the relationship
that was once the rule between racist troublemakers and local police in
the South, and that still pertains when white punks go after homosexuals
in almost any region. Street gangs, like any other predators, know the
difference between a difficult and an easy kill. If they are black or Hispanic, they learn very quickly that racism allows them to terrorize their
own, and that homosexuals of all colors and classes are the most vulnerable of all.

Verbal and physical assaults on homosexuals on Castro Street in San
Francisco by black, Hispanic, and redneck gangs have become a weekly
ritual parallel to the same aggressive acts by Mexicans in West Hollywood. Rechy has recently had some experiences that help one understand
the paranoia felt by growing numbers of homosexuals. He was in a bar
where a Mexican gang armed with lead pipes taunted and dared the
homosexuals to come out. Though called three times, the police never

arrived. On another occasion, the police stopped Rechy in an alley as he was about to have sex with another man. One of the officers was white but his partner was a female Negro who shouted, "Come out of there you goddamn queers or I'll blow your goddamn heads off!" Upon finding out that Rechy's partner was an Iranian, the female cop asked, "Don't you know that the ayatollah would have your head for this?" When a man in Rechy's company was bloodied by a metal bolt hurled with a slingshot, the police showed no interest in finding those guilty—"five scrunched-up, pimply-head Mexicans," as he describes them. All of these events and the growing calls for the repeal of homosexual rights laws are but variations on the hostile Sunday afternoon rituals Rechy witnessed as a child in El Paso, Texas. Right across the border in Juarez, Mexico, "the Mexican machos would ogle pretty girls and taunt effeminate men. Really brutal heckling. It's almost part of one's group manhood initiation in that culture—to overtly display hatred for male effeminate behavior. And if you didn't participate, you would become an outsider. For that and other reasons, I feel much more my identity as a homosexual than as a Mexican, while still feeling much concerned with all societal ills."

Mitchell is equally disturbed by the reports of intensified hostility, but his analysis is very different. Mitchell was reared by his grandmother in Pauline, Louisiana, about 30 miles from New Orleans. At the age of nine or ten, he was caught in his first homosexual act by his grandmother: "She went berserk, got the shotgun, and chased the boy all through the town. My world fell apart. Being an asthmatic, she beat me in relays— whenever she could catch her breath and whenever she thought about it." At one point, she threatened to cut off Mitchell's penis with a pair of shears; at another, she spread news of the incident throughout the town until it turned into a scandal. For about two weeks, adults and children neither spoke to nor played with him. But, he says, after that time the mood changed and he was accepted back into the fold. With the exception of a couple of merchants, the town was all black, and Mitchell says he never experienced the continual rejection homosexuals so often describe. In that rural setting, Mitchell had many clandestine love affairs with men he describes as "basically straight" who grew up to marry and have families. Like most homosexuals, he had to earn much of his acceptance: "I was always talented, I was always singing in the church or going off to some convention. I won awards. Black people have always pushed me and told me I had the mark of a special brightness."

When his grandmother died in March of 1956, he moved to Chicago to live with his father, who died in August of the same year. He was then sent to New Orleans where he lived with another part of the family and attended a school for gifted children. Mitchell attributes his not becoming "a drag queen or a mindless street faggot" to "the closet gays on the faculty who were very conscious of dignity, self-control, and discipline." With their educations, fine homes, and cars, "they instilled in me the fact that I would have to excel in something if I was going to lead a gay life.

By the time I graduated, however, I thought the worst thing my teachers had done was lead dishonest lives—getting married and having children. I have never been in any closet. Anywhere I've been, people have known they could burn me if they wanted to, but they had to take me as I was."

At that point in Mitchell's story, Rechy said, "Lionel, that sounds idyllic and wonderful, but how do you account for the hostility and the violence toward homosexuals in cruising areas and other places from blacks as well as Latins?"

Mitchell replied, "No one, especially those referred to as 'the underclass,' respects what they consider illegitimate power. If they feel you're not contributing anything, that you also have the fine apartment or the brownstone, and you're not good for anything other than the pursuit of your own interest, you might be in danger. Like those West Coast people's idea of the gay community—the only people they help are gays, the only people they're interested in are gays. I think this is a tactical blunder and a very bad error. You have this business of people trying to impose the gay experience on children. What should stop me from wanting to protect children from being molested just because I'm gay? What should stop me, because I'm gay, from wanting to see children get the best education? If I saw a faggot trying to mislead one of my friend's children who call me 'Uncle Lionel,' no more terrible force would she have to deal with than myself. Yet you have the West Coast gays telling you this is an issue and talking about breeders and nonbreeders. And now they're playing right along with gentrification, buying up neighborhoods and supplanting the heterosexual population.

"Those are uses of advocacy that are threatening. It's using gay as a club to hit straights over the head with and is becoming so *irrationally* challenging that it begets nothing but paranoia, which is the same criticism I had of black militants in the late '60s. They helped alienate America from the correctness of the civil rights demands. The gays have to recreate the image of their movement so that they are not trying to separate from straight society but become a part of it."

When Rechy told Mitchell that he had a very conservative vision, the latter replied, "If the white gay movement would bother to canvass more black gays, they would probably find that black homosexuals are much more conservative than they are." He went on to say that since the black community is beleaguered, it cannot countenance complete disregard of respectable romantic conduct, and added that he felt white homosexuals tended to have "ugly American" attitudes which disdained the codes of given communities so that their sexuality was seen as a contemptuous affront. "If you want to change society," he continued, "then you form a political effort. A sexual effort doesn't really qualify as a political effort."

Rechy responded: "The heterosexual laws against homosexual acts of some kind in all but 23 states make homosexuality political, just as the laws of segregation made ordering a sandwich in a public restaurant political."

III. CLASS STRUGGLE VS. ASS STRUGGLE

It seemed to me that the hostility of minorities toward homosexuals was more complex than either had suggested up to that point. Though minorities do tend to be conservative, their attitudes are rooted in the American character. Americans have long gritted their teeth at aristocrats and those who "put on airs." Fey behavior, contrived accents, and dandified snobbery, all often perceived as innate characteristics of homosexuals, are rejected as virulently as unconventional sexual practices. There is also the question of counterfeit. Many heterosexuals, no matter what homosexual activists tell them, perceive men who sleep with men as imitation women, and define drag queens or transsexuals as either ultimate examples of a misbegotten Mardi Gras, or as Frankensteinian symbols of gender science fiction. And since most people believe that quality ought to be hard to come by, the clone getup, for all its loose parallels to the standardized dress of Wall Street, the military, or even the sports world, is as symbolic of sexual availability to outsiders as the dress of prostitutes. Meanwhile, the leather faction not only triggers aversions to sadomasochism, but neatly connects to the famous murders committed or instigated by homosexuals or bisexuals like Leopold and Loeb, Charles Manson, Dean Coryl, John Wayne Gacy, or the champion of them all, Reverend Jim Jones. And however easily it can be proven that there is no direct relationship between homosexuality and the demonic deeds of the psychopath or the sociopath, it is also quite clear that every homosexual (like every woman) who lives promiscuously and invites strangers home is risking his life or health just as surely as a policeman does the moment he goes to work. (Perhaps this, as much as anything else, explains why so much homosexual sex takes place within the confines of bars and baths.)

At the rawest end there is the question of economics and the images of humiliating homosexual imposition all lower-class minority adolescents get from friends who have been in penal institutions. As William Burroughs points out: "You know, homosexuality is a worldwide economic fact. In poor countries—like Morocco and parts of Italy—it's one of the big industries, one of the main ways in which a young boy can get somewhere. If he's lucky and gets a rich lover, he can then go on and get rich himself. Naturally, the homosexual is taking advantage of the fact that people are poor. But in view of the situation that exists, why not? It's not in my power to change the economy of Morocco or other poor countries." Perhaps so, but as a result impoverished young men who sell themselves to homosexuals often hate them for taking advantage of economic privilege, while those who become fag-bashers express a violence minority men also reserve for white johns in whom they see vice layered with ethnic and economic exploitation. There is also much to Edmund White's observation: "Straight teens want many of the same things gay adult men already have—glamorous cars, sporty clothes, memberships in the best discos, sexual license, lots of spending money, access to drugs. It's not that the kids want to be gay, far from it. Indeed, the kids are disturbed precisely because the gay way of life is too close to the one they'd like to lead. Heterosexual adults—married, a bit staid, not up on the latest fads—seem less attractive as models. Gay men are attractive in every area except the crucial one of sexual orientation: the conjunction of so many admirable attributes with a despised sexuality turns gays into natural targets for adolescent fag-baiting." It is also likely that adolescent young men, who tend to travel in groups and dress alike, may feel the pressure to distinguish themselves from homosexuals with verbal abuse or physical violence. Finally, the threat of homosexual assault in penal institutions looms in the minds of young men as the most nightmarish form of degradation.

Of assaults by homosexuals in prisons, Rechy said: "That is minuscule. It exists, but it is minuscule. The majority of men who pick up young hustlers on the street are not homosexuals, they are heterosexual men, most of whom are married and most of whom have children. They have problems with women and the boys they pick up are effeminate boys. The acts they perform will come as close as possible to turning that boy into a female—even visually. These men will not be found in a homosexual bar or any cruising area. They will just come in from the suburbs for the purpose of picking up an androgynous boy. He is not a homosexual but is in some way a closet heterosexual, a man who, because of his difficulties with women—impotence or whatever—can be turned on by drag, long hair, or the younger boy before the sexuality has been defined. So, regardless of the myths about prison and hustling, the exploiter is not a homosexual, but a heterosexual with problems concerning women.

"Though there are situations where homosexuals do exploit, there are also the situations where a homosexual with money will be murdered. In essence, it involves a great deal of mutual contempt: the hustler feels you can get me only if you pay and the client feels that after he pays you have to stay in his nice apartment for a short time before you go back into an unpredictable world. But there is an aspect of the economic situation that should be discussed: a willing thirteen-year-old who knows what he is doing and what he is going to get paid for is not being exploited by that person but by the system that does not allow him to do other than that. If he chooses to do it, fine, but if he thinks it is a necessity, then his exploitation is the result of his education and social background—the limitations imposed by this system."

Mitchell concurred: "He's right. That young disco freak has to hustle faggots in order to get the money to go out! Those outfits, those big radios, the admission to get in the discos—how can they afford it? Straight people hate them because they think they can't give a dance without the kids fighting. So, they don't and the churches don't either. There are no places to go besides the discos except to the faggot who'll let him and his girlfriend neck—or fuck—in his apartment while he's gone. Straight society's hatred of young people has pushed them into the arms of the faggots. Those designer jeans and the commercials on television put everybody's ass—male and female—at a premium of sexual interest. And since I have had many stormy, Rimbaud-like affairs with the teenagers of the Lower East Side—though I don't select all my lovers from them—let me tell you that the kids know it. They know what's going on and their anger at their economic limitations can boil over on the faggot because he's the most vulnerable and the least respected. Who cares if a faggot is murdered? Almost nobody except others like the victim."

That kind of victimization can be more complicated. As one black homosexual who traffics in teenage boys said: "At first, they might act strange or haughty, like they're doing you a favor. Then you start baiting them in. They get used to having that pocket money; they get used to being able to buy things or get the new pair of pants, the latest outfit. That's where the real strength comes in because, once they find out they're dependent on you for the finer things of life, they try to assert themselves. But I don't care how streetwise a seventeen-year-old thinks he is, he can't stand up to a thirty-five- or forty-year-old man. He hasn't the resources or the experience. He can easily be overpowered because basically he is still a child. The boy comes to learn, sometimes bitterly, that the submissiveness you exhibit is only part of a sexual ritual. Outside of bed, things are very different."

Even so, many homosexuals are victimized by the very standards of quality they set for themselves, especially since so much revolves around an idealization of youth. An inclination to a highly charged nostalgia develops and the tyranny of appearances manifests itself in rejection— rejection of age, class, and race.

Of this problem, Rechy says: "One of the greatest sins I've committed in the homosexual world is not having become a mess—extending my sexuality beyond all boundaries brings about attacks. It's the movie-star syndrome: a movie star ages three years to the average person's one. So they're waiting out there for me to fall apart so they can ridicule me."

When I asked Rechy if that was an element of the legendary "faggot bitchiness," Mitchell interjected, "How many gays aren't bitchy, anyway? Two percent? The bitchiness is actually faggot macho, *our* way of manifesting manhood."

Rechy didn't entirely agree, but he did say: "A certain group of homosexuals have elevated bitchiness to an art form, albeit a negative one. I don't mean the wit of the survivors, I mean the self-destructive attacks you get from the Fire Island school of homosexuals, the doggedly chic types. Unfortunately, the Fire Island columnist has also taken over the homosexual voice with the languid-sounding bar gossip, which is like Proust on poppers, so precious and effete. At the same time, it's now out of style to be effeminate, which is why there is such a macho stance and why so many of us walk so stiffly—as if we're afraid the hip might swing out."

Rechy observed that the fear of assaults from the outside has largely

resulted in homosexual publications opting for a cult of silence, an avoidance of the problems he sees as most acute—age, race, dissipation, and
sadomasochism. "One of the inescapable problems facing us is rampant
ageism. My novel, *Rushes,* deals with that as well as s&m. Now you've
got to be a certain type of macho and you've got to have a certain type of
beauty. Increasingly, there are signs, especially in California, which say,
'No Fats, No Thins, No Over 35s.' Along with those signs, there is a tacit
understanding that ethnic minorities will be excluded—blacks, Mexicans,
and, most of all, Orientals. To avoid suits, there are no explicit signs, but
when ethnic gays appear at the doors of chic gathering places, they will
be told there is no more room, then some pretty blond boy will be
allowed in. If it is not done that way, ethnic homosexuals will be excluded
by making places private clubs one can enter only with a membership
card. As you might imagine, only whites get cards."

IV. EPIDEMIC DISHONESTIES

Mitchell was quite aware of the depth of racism and class prejudice as
they affected black homosexuals. Over 20 years ago, he was told by a
white homosexual in New Orleans that "the idea of a nigger sissy was
absolutely ridiculous because niggers were too crude to be sissies, that
sissydom was the exclusive preserve of the high culture of white men."
In 1964, when Mitchell was in the company of "a gorgeous white sailor,"
a drunken white homosexual pulled the sailor to the side and asked him
what he was doing associating with his social and cultural inferiors.
Every Negro homosexual I talked with had similar recent tales; some
even pointed out that terms like "dinge queen" and "coal miner" were
pejoratives white homosexuals used to dismiss an attractive white homosexual in the company of a black man. They also reported that service for
Negroes in gay bars could be very slow, that black bartenders were almost nonexistent, and that white homosexuals usually admired Negro
"soul" in a limited and primitive sense because they didn't believe black
men capable of "elevated" sensibilities.

Racial stereotyping isn't exclusive to white homosexuals. There are
black homosexuals who assume that if a white guy is involved with a
Negro he is available to all black men, who are interested only in white
men, who will accept homeliness in white men that they would reject in
other Negroes, and those who, to quote one black homosexual, "have to
be shown that they can't run that loud, phony street shit they use to
intimidate white queens." It also invades the world of male prostitution.
According to Mitchell, some hustlers "will usually pass up a black person
in favor of a white person because they figure he will pay more money.
The white queens play upon that and they will not hesitate to use their
economic advantages and attempt to take a handsome man away from
you at the slightest opportunity. And since white queens think they
should get the best of everything, they can't quite understand why a

poor, black gay might not let go, or the boy that they offered the money might have enough self-respect to tell them to fuck off."

Recy added, "Economics and class are very important to racism in the homosexual world. So many of the chic homosexual leaders and rich homosexuals come from a class that is taught to oppress by the universities they can attend and the clubs they can join. Therefore, as an element of preparation, racism is endemic to that particular class."

"It still remains a mystery to me," Mitchell replied, "how, even though black transvestites struck the first blows at Stonewall, the movement suddenly became white. Only lately has there been an effort to develop black gay chapters. You see, 'Miss Thing' with her black unruly ass became nothing more than cannon fodder—the Crispus Attucks story in drag. They gave people like Dave McReynolds another chance since the blacks didn't want the old left or the new left anymore and the antiwar thing had died out. The post-Stonewall era gave them a chance at continuation. Continuation of what? White control of radical leadership. It was a new manifestation of the classical patterns of whites pushing blacks to the side and ripping off the driver's seat rather than sharing it.

"That we prefer not to deal with these things illustrate the many, many dishonesties in the homosexual world," Rechy said. "Symbols of the epidemic dishonesty are all these love and joy books, all the new journals with statements like the things we look for in sex partners are, firstly, hygiene, secondly, good personality. That's bullshit. Appearance is number one. Further, there is the problem of alcoholism, which is hitting our young people so early. Why, at a time of so-called liberation, are so many of our young men staggering around drunk at 5 o'clock in the morning? But the day after, if they're interviewed, they'll say how wonderful it is to be gay and how they wouldn't change anything. And however unpopular it is to say this, the main problem on the homosexual interior is sadomasochism. It is increasing in everything from the discos to the piers and the leather has nothing to do with it, for leather is only the tip of the iceberg."

In discussion of sadomasochism, I asked whether the creaking and rattling leather-and-chain getups might be part of an attempt to handle the obsession with youth when one went over the hill of 25 or 30. Mitchell answered, "Certainly when you see them in the daylight, you see that the sun is not their forte. It brings out all the wrinkles, the hanging arms, and what have you." He went on to connect it to the flagellation gangs of the European Middle Ages, reasoning that it was primarily a European phenomenon and that, since black homosexuality came from a warmer climate and culture, Negroes didn't tend to enter that group too often. Mitchell also felt that, given the black experience, identification with men who dressed in Nazi garb was "ahistorical." Rechy explained that the leather faction had racist inclinations but, even so, black involvement in sadomasochism seemed on the rise, and said that though he found fantasy costumes—sailors, cowboys, and such—"terrific," he thought the leather and the chains symbolized the executioner—"the murder and mourning of sex"—and rituals of humiliating self-hatred. "Unclothing the body was the first movement away from puritanism, as sex is associated with unclothing, displaying beauty, and so forth. Sadomasochism in its extreme cannot be seen in this way because there is a total clothing of the body. The naked body is almost taboo now. It is the costume, not the person, that does the attracting. There are the hoods, the leather gloves, the face is hidden, and, quite often, many of the acts have nothing to do with sex. A thousand Anita Bryants cannot do the devastation we are committing upon ourselves by substituting the fist, which is the most powerful symbol of aggression we have, for the penis. The act is a symbolic assault. There are no sexual sensations in that and there is no sexual response. With fist-fucking there is always a soft cock. There are very few hard cocks in the orgy room. There are mind experiences and experiences of degradation. In fact, I've often said that in a homosexual s&m ritual, there is only one sadist—the invisible heterosexual whose hatred we're ritualistically duplicating. But I'm not speaking from a moralistic point of view. I participate in sadomasochistic rituals still. I'm not free of that. At one time that was what I desired more than anything else. I still go to the Mine Shaft. But I need it less and less and less, and if I can clarify any little edge for a kid who's just come in the city, then my experience has been worth it. He will not have to do the same."

Though neither agreed with me, I speculated that sadomasochism probably had the added attraction of solving the problem of intensity in sexual relations. The infliction of pain immediately guarantees the kind of immediate intensity normally achieved through mutual chemistry and the discovery of individual hot spots. Mitchell's concerns were with the backlash anarchic or destructive behavior could bring down on homosexuals uninterested in such practices: "Public knowledge of this stuff will invariably play into the hands of the faggot-haters. And the fact that we would romanticize something like fist-fucking is even worse."

There was a heated disagreement between Rechy and Mitchell over the issue of anonymous promiscuity and public sex, which Rechy supports and Mitchell abhors. Rechy argued that, after 8000 sexual experiences, he would say that some of the most exciting took place with men he would never see again. He argued further that anonymity might be one of the richnesses of the homosexual world which is beyond heterosexuals. But it was by advocating public sex as a form of protest that Rechy most infuriated Mitchell, who sees public sex as debilitating, one of the reasons there is such an astronomical amount of venereal disease among homosexuals—*The Gay Health Guide* reports that homosexuals contract nine times as much as heterosexuals. Rechy countered that because homosexuals are more sexually aware, perhaps they just go to their doctors more quickly. (I didn't go for that one either.)

I then said to Rechy, "You have also pointed out that there are a range of physical disorders that result from fist-fucking and other sadomasochistic rituals that are suppressed by the homosexual press."

"I wasn't referring only to fist-fucking. I was talking about sadomasochism in general. Yes, that's true. But with few exceptions, s&m in the homosexual world is predetermined and it is a charade of raging violence. It is consensual."

"But if society is a witness," Mitchell interjected, "what you do to your body has a psychological effect on me. That is why suicides aren't allowed. That's why they're restrained and I think they should be."

"That's totalitarianism," Rechy charged.

"No, it's ultimate humanism. It's what Christian humanism is based on. We *all* must carry our image at a certain acceptable level. That's why I say s&m is ultimately aimed at the jugular vein of society and society does have the right to regulate it and to defend itself against it."

"Though I will speak out against sadomasochism," Rechy said, "I would rage against its being legislated against. I would never legislate against suicide. My belief in freedom goes so far as to consensual murder. Suicide is the ultimate art form. If one lives one's life as good art, then the ideal is to end art at the top. One should have the right to end one's life when and at the time one chooses."

"But now you're idealizing," Mitchell responded. "We talk about ideas when we have the capacity to communicate ideas via satellite to a hundred million people. But the majority of people who would use these ideas, misconstrue these ideas, have no discriminating intellectual background. I know teenagers who haven't even lived who kill themselves for the stupidest of reasons. We're dealing with people who are on the fringe of Western civilization, and they aren't prepared for all the ideas we intellectuals would advocate."

"Though I'm a socialist, I really do dislike humanity, I must say," Rechy sighed.

"I try to love humanity. It's difficult. I have no illusions about that."

"Lionel, you do too much emphasizing on the word 'love.' The word makes me terribly uncomfortable because it's been tossed around so much. Gore Vidal says that whenever anybody mentions the word love, he reaches for his wallet because he expects to be robbed."

I then asked Rechy why there was such a persistently moon-junish tone to homosexual writing about romance. I also observed that the love objects were often ignorant and abusive brats. After all, heterosexual men who chase after or idealize teenage girls are assumed immature until proven otherwise.

"I would agree that our literature largely reflects that problem. You'll get no argument from me. But at its best, I would say that the homosexual sensibility has greater depth, primarily because of the duality which is at work, the role-playing, the writing in drag, or the macho. We can go deeper, we dare to go deeper, if only because we live a life of risks. Yet your point is a true one: for all of the talent some of us have, we tend to deal with subjects that are not worthy of our talent. And even though it is connected not so much to homosexuality as to the age-old problem of the intellectual figure being fascinated by someone like the woman in the *Blue Angel*, we must also remember that it could be an aspect of our greater freedom to indulge in fantasy, escapades, and episodes since we do not marry and do not have children—if we're not living in closets. The danger is that our only real children—the next generation—will not receive the images of increased enrichment as one grows older."

"But by the same token, there are some really beautiful old men. I know people who only sleep with old men. Spencer Tracy, for instance, he was just as fine as he wanted to be with all that white hair."

"Yes, Lionel, but at the Ramrod Bar, by last call, Spencer Tracy would find himself alone and everybody would leave the bar saying how gorgeous an old man he was."

Even so, Rechy said, "I go out hustling about once a month just to reassure myself that I have been able to survive in a very hard world and because I get enormous pleasure from the offers, from the fact that they are still willing to pay. It's a rush. But it does become increasingly difficult because now I get recognized and it takes the whole pleasure out of it. People ask for autographs, which I find very embarrassing and I pretend not to be myself, not to be a writer." When asked how he handles the possibilities of rejection, Rechy continued, "I let my muscles take over. Where youth is a premium, one can carry it off with other attractions. As they say in the profession, 'a gimmick.'"

V. LIBERATIONS

It struck me that there is a built-in sadomasochism to the standards of beauty and the obsession with youth that pervade the homosexual world. Perhaps the terrible treatment so many older homosexuals accept from their young sexual hirelings parallels the observations Susan Sontag has made about women and their lovers: "Notoriously, women tolerate qualities in a lover—moodiness, selfishness, unreliability, brutality—that they would never countenance in a husband, in return for excitement, an infusion of intense feeling." As one homosexual said, "Since so much of the gay experience is based in fantasy, you don't mind going through these things with these young boys because they give you that fire older men no longer have and you get so much status from the other queens. You have a mouth-watering fantasy lover unencumbered by the responsibilities that impinge on the sexual drive of mature men, and all the other queens would just *die* to be with him. In those cases, darling, you wear their envy and their stares that could kill like medals of honor." But sooner or later, that fantasy lover will have to face the passage of time and can become the victim of the standards and insecurities that once gave him so much power. After all, Rechy has pointed out the high suicide rate among ex-hustlers, just as Edmund White has reported a higher incidence of alcoholism and suicide among homosexuals in general. The fear and disappointments that come with the furious risings and settings of the sun may have a great deal to do with such self-destructiveness.

Given the increasing self-criticism spurred by such problems within homosexual society, perhaps what Mitchell calls "an across-the-board liberation movement" is necessary. In *Christopher Street* recently, Neil Alan Marks attacked the guarded spiritual hollowness of clone behavior, then criticized the basic antipathy that exists between lesbians and homosexuals, an antipathy rooted in the worship of vaginas by one group and the worship of penises by the other. The issue of pornography is beginning to damage alliances between homosexuals and feminists, who are floundering in the contemporary version of the temperance movement that sidetracked women's suffrage early in the century. At the center of that problem is the objectification of sex objects, something as rife in the homosexual press as the heterosexual, and something which invites anonymous sex of the sort women find unattractive (quite obviously, this is an expression of the adolescent male vision of sex wherein orgasm without human string attached is the ultimate goal, and a goal that perpetuates the panting promiscuity of radical homosexuality). Mitchell thinks that homosexuals should get involved with other oppressed groups, and should take part in community improvement beyond gentrification and remodeling homes—charities, clothing drives, and whatever makes it obvious that there is more to them than promiscuity and the pursuit of the latest fads. They are, regardless of whom it gladdens or maddens, always joined to the greater community if only because they're the single minority that doesn't reproduce itself and whose continued existence—even in isolation—would be dependent on procreative foreign aid.

If homosexuals make the political moves Mitchell proposes, they may come as responses to the deepening dangers inherent in their separatist way of living. There is an urge to rein in the rage to ramble because of diseases like the new strain of gonorrhea that resists penicillin and the even more ominous frequency of physical assault, from within and without. At the last session, Mitchell, who had arrived in a depressed and brooding mood, finally exploded, filling the room with his noisy anger at the discovery he had made shortly before. An old friend of his, a dancer who was supporting a Puerto Rican boy, had been awakened by the boy's attempt to stab him to death. The friend's face and neck had been so mutilated that his carrer was jeopardized. It had triggered the memory Mitchell had of another performer, an actor, who had been doused with gasoline and set afire by a man he had brought home. The actor had survived and had gotten the best available treatment, but was still so disfigured that he had to leave his profession. In retrospect, the lesson is clear: what seems a simple farewell can be final if the friend is a homosexual, promiscuous, and given to bringing home strangers or taking in impoverished kids. For all the paranoia most men may have about violence in the streets, nobody has ever said of a woman he brought home what a brilliant and elfish homosexual friend told me: "I was just about to get down with this big muscle-bound guy when he turned around and said to me, 'What if I murdered you?'" Whatever the meaning of homosexual liberation, it must, finally, answer that question.

WILL THE REAL MAN STAND?
August 24, 1982

Excepting black Americans from what we know of human behavior and human history makes it possible for misbegotten ideas to hold sway longer than logic would assume. I am particularly interested in a cliché that has fluctuated in popularity over the last 20 years—the one that upbraids or pities the black man for his historical lack of courage, his inability to be a man, to defend family, home, and, in the process, exhibit dignity. That idea became equally popular among those Negroes eager to don the martyr's garment on the way to the podium or the boudoir, and those whites quick to bemoan the trampled manhood of the colored guys and lick their salted wounds. The result was that the trauma of thwarted male potential became an explanation for everything from wife-beating to loud clothes to ostentatious behavior. The colored man's brain was frying in the molten grease of defeat. White racism had turned his knees into castanets and his very presence brought with it a funeral atmosphere of bereavement, for here was a man who had never had a chance to be a man.

Had that conception been popular only in misdirected political circles, it would probably have gone the way of most shallow theories. Unfortunately, those with an appetite for the apocryphal have chosen to propagate it, even in an era when the dominant symbols of conventional manhood in the world of sports are African-American. In a raft of poems, plays, fiction, and essays, there is, for instance, the persistent image of the white man raping the black woman at will, an abstraction for the ages. Gullible black men have beaten each other over the head with this picture, while those equally misguided black women who haven't depicted the Negro male as the bogeyman on the doorstep of the night have been nearly hysterical in their rage at the supposed fact that he didn't die rather than let that happen to his woman. This is closer to mythology than truth, especially because it's so removed from the basic questions of power that permeate all societies. Surely, some black women were coerced into bed with white men (none, of course, was ever attracted to them), whether through force or the promise of favor, but that seems more in the tradition of sexual harassment on the job and the casting couch than the exclusive mark of racial oppression so often asserted. It is also obvious that if as many were raped and impregnated as ideologues claim, African-Americans would be a race of predominantly yellow-skinned people.

This, however, is as far from the truth as the idea that any time a white man found himself bothered with an errant erection all he had to do was stroll into "the quarter of the Negroes," as Langston Hughes called it, tear off some darkie poontang, then saunter back home, ringing with release and completely free of any responsibility. That happened far less during slavery than many would have us believe, and there were even fewer instances following the Civil War (though conquering Union officers dressed the prettier and more willing slave girls up in the clothes of the plantation mistresses and treated them like valued concubines, probably resulting in a number of mulattoes). Further, those who would eternally trumpet the terrors of exclusive oppression have little to say about the white wives who have lain in many an uncomfortable bed to garner promotions for their spouses, a recurrent theme in depictions of careers far removed from the cotton fields back home. In the film *Lenny*, for instance, when the older, established, and powerful comedian fondles the legs of Lenny Bruce's wife right in front of the hero, Valerie Perrine should have leaped up and said to Dustin Hoffman, "How dare you allow this! Don't let this tan confuse you!"

Yet the persistent implication is that Negro males have often been cardboard men, while Caucasians have set the standards for the real thing, always ready to fight for what was theirs, literally or figuratively. Hollywood, however, has made billions propagating the opposite interpretation of white men in two of its most popular genres, the Western and the gangster film, where the quality of individual heroism is so frequently measured by the timidity of the male mass. Over and over we have seen the average town of white men allow powerful range barons to take their land, rowdy cowboys to shoot up their businesses, and a handful of professional killers to make the streets unsafe for women and children. Hence the hired gunfighter who, were he compared to a civil rights worker 20 years ago, would have been considered "an outside agitator," especially when developing deputies and posses. The gangster film has proposed that the overwhelming majority of white men would rather pay protection so that they could safely run their businesses than go to the police. And now, when courageous efforts of African-Americans have cost the Ku Klux Klan and the various white citizens' councils all controlling influence, with black men running up the highest body counts, it is still easily observable how much influence through intimidation the Mafia has in New York, Philadelphia, Atlantic City, Boston, Miami, New Orleans, Detroit, Chicago, Las Vegas, and San Francisco. We needn't even mention the trade unions of the roughest of white men—truck drivers and the like. After all, how many organizations formed in the interest of black people have been taken over by rednecks? How many black Southerners ever paid rednecks for the right to be sharecroppers? I rest my case.

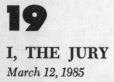

I, THE JURY
March 12, 1985

The Bernhard Goetz affair is but part of a remarkable confluence of events, all of which illustrate the rage, indifference, corruption, arrogance, and hysteria surrounding crime in this city and this nation. This clairvoyant shootist has been called the father of a new rainbow coalition, since his support initially dissolved racial lines. Legislators report that a multibillion-dollar crime bill expiring on its knees in Washington was snatched to its feet by the elevation of Goetz to heroic status. One television interviewer was assigned to learn what he had for breakfast, and though we have yet to find out his shoe size or whether he wears any bawdy tattoos, we do have the word of the impeccably public-minded Myra Friedman that she heard Goetz say at a community meeting: "The only way we're going to clean up this street is to get rid of the spics and niggers."

When it first got out that a blond man in glasses had shot four black teenagers on the subway, Goetz received broad sympathy in the Negro community, even though there was still heat in the air over the Bumpurs shooting. Many agreed with Roy Innis, who had lost one son to street violence and had seen another wounded: The man was right in defending himself. Perhaps this would teach some of those kids a lesson; maybe it would discourage those emboldened by the vulnerability of the subway rider and the lack of support most victims fear if attacked. Race was one thing, crime another. It was no longer second nature for black people to take the side of the impoverished colored teenager who created so many of their own problems: "The thing is you start hating these young people out here today. They don't have any respect for anybody. They curse around anybody, play those goddamn boxes loud as they can, write that dumb graffiti all over everything—their own building, a subway car, whatever. They don't care. Then they knock people in the head, too."

This Harlemite was clearly describing teenagers like two from Bedford-Stuyvesant I overheard as they sat behind me on a bus and discussed the world in which they live, a world so savage it seemed a universe of tall tales. They were traveling upstate to a correctional camp where they were supposed to study and get away from bad influences. They spoke sometimes at the tops of their voices, cursing and giggling as they reminded each other of the violent deeds they had brought off as a team or independently: robberies, rapes, beatings, shootings. Both young men detailed how street-crime fads had changed over the years. "Yo, you remember when it was them sheepskin coats, then it was boxes, then it was running shoes, gold chains, and now these sunglass frames?" When I later asked them if they thought there was any racial connection, one said, "Hell no. Jealousy, man. You see a motherfucker with something you ain't got and you get mad. You start thinking, 'Now, why *he* got it? How come I can't have it?' So you get your tool and you stick it in his face. He gives it up. It can happen to you, too. At school, I was in the hall with my sheepskin, you know? So the next thing I know is this nigger got his tool in my face and I'm trying to look and see if he has bullets in the chambers or if he's bluffing but the light was in my eyes. It wasn't cocked so the chamber has to move for the bullet to get under the hammer. If it was empty on both sides, he was bullshitting, but I couldn't see. So I let him have it, but like a fool he didn't search me, just took my coat. Then I pulled my tool on him but I cocked it. You ever seen," he laughed, "the way a motherfucker will stop when he hears that sound? He thought I was going to kill him. All I wanted was my coat back. Plus I had another gun. His."

Young men like that create understandable reactions. Linda, married with two small children, lives on Edgecombe Avenue in a building once famous for its celebrities. There are still show-business legends behind the multilocked doors but for all the wonderful living spaces no contemporary stars have joined them; today, 160th Street is perilous. As he returned home one evening, Linda's husband, a carpenter and painter, found himself staring into the barrel of a pistol held by a burglar who promised to blow his head off if he spoke or moved. This did not make Linda, who comes from an affluent Philadelphia family, feel any safer. So her routine became even more careful.

When she prepares to leave home for work in the morning, Linda opens the door slowly and looks both ways, making sure there is no one she doesn't know in the hall. At the elevator, she stands so that she can see the entire inside of the car. If there is an unfamiliar man in the elevator, Linda says she's going up if he's going down, down if he's going up. Inside the car, she is ever prepared to leap out and start screaming if someone tries to trap her. On the way to the subway, she walks close to the curb so she can jump into the street and start shouting for help if necessary. At the train station, Linda doesn't stand near the tracks for fear of being pushed and always looks for an escape route or space to struggle in. Once on the train, she makes sure that she is situated near a door, since it is so easy to get rolled or intimidated in between, where the only exit would be a window.

But the feeling of being cut off from a vandalized environment, unsafe in crowds, and ignored by public institutions funded to protect society was replaced with something different the first few days after Goetz shot his way into the news. "When I first heard about the shooting," Linda says, "I was glad. I thought it served them right. I was actually happy for a few days, and the mood in the subway cars was a kind of camaraderie I had never felt before. Everybody seemed closer. It was like we all had won one. Nobody said anything, but you could feel it. It didn't have anything at all to do with race. Everybody was in agreement: Goetz had done something for *all* of us."

Goetz seemed to focus the perhaps unprecedented public anger, cynicism, and sense of victimization that results from what Dr. Willard Gaylin, author of *The Rage Within,* calls "the vulgarization and destruction of the public space." In 1940, says Gaylin, a citizen of New York had only a one-in-ten chance of witnessing a serious crime; 30 years later he or she had a one-in-ten chance of *not* seeing one.

As further details came to light, Goetz seemed both more and less than what he was touted as. Blue-collar Caucasians saluted him on talk shows, white intellectuals analyzed his expression of urban frustration, the Guardian Angels praised him. But soon the literal writing on the walls conveyed meanings that seemed to belie those first few days of subway closeness. "Goetz was wrong" is answered on the bathroom wall of a Sheridan Square coffee shop by "Why don't you baboons go back to the South Bronx where you belong!" *Voice* writer Carol Cooper noticed pickpocket warnings on the subway with a note written next to the illustration of the thief's fingers—"The hand should be black." A *Voice* messenger was stopped on Central Park West by police one night and told to leave the neighborhood because he looked like a mugger. They didn't go into detail about what they meant, but he guessed.

Clearly, there was more to Goetz's support than tabloid attention, more than admiration for a person who had stood up to danger. The Hawkins family in Los Angeles had been much more heroic, holding off gangs that attacked its home with pistols and Molotov cocktails in 1982. Quite recently, an elderly man in Chicago shot and killed an attacker bent on robbing him. He spent one night in jail and was released. When asked if he would so defend himself again if necessary, the old fellow said he would and was forgotten. There was even the grandmother from the South who scared off a pack of muggers when she pulled her pistol in the Port Authority Building a couple of years ago. Her story made the papers for a day or two, but soon she went on to line bird cages and cat boxes with the rest of the briefly famous. But Bernhard Goetz hasn't been briefly famous, because, unlike those others, he is white. Goetz seems to have become the Gerry Cooney of urban America, the white hope on whose shoulders rest the burdens of contemporary Caucasian uneasiness.

That mood entails a selective process focused on class and color. Obviously the white people who helped make *The Cosby Show* the most popular television program, who bought so many Michael Jackson records, who were thrilled by the performances of black athletes at last year's Olympics, and so on, aren't troubled by Negroes per se. Their nemesis is the violent criminal who is too often construed as emblematic of the black underclass. I would suggest that their anger isn't so different from that of anyone humiliated by a person inferior in every way other than his ruthless willingness to intimidate or assault. So the white person in the city feels like an easy kill for an impoverished, illiterate brute with his hat turned sideways, his mouth full of vulgar epithets, his running shoes canvas-and-rubber cushions for quick getaways. Then Bernhard Goetz steps forward, looking for all the world like a piece of meat ready for the predator's platter. But not Bernhard! The wimp who would save the world, Goetz is transformed with a few bullets into Clark Kent, the mild-mannered bachelor ready to shoot a mugger before he makes a single bound.

Given the new information about Goetz, most recently revelations of how callously Goetz fired twice at one of his victims, his smallest swallow of judicial castor oil should have been four counts of attempted manslaughter as well as the illegal weapons charge. But his case converges with the indictment of Sullivan for the Bumpurs shooting, the indictment of six transit cops in the Michael Stewart case, and allegations that medical examiner Elliot Gross falsified autopsies in favor of the police. Individual and bureaucratic immorality intensify the crisis of public morale—the emotional dues of anxiety, disgust, and uncertainty that go with the streets, the dilapidated subways, and the quick claw of robbery. Already as impatient as anyone else with courts that seem to favor criminals, black people feel even deeper ambivalence toward those in public service when thousands of police gather in the Bronx to support Sullivan and one sign reads: "If Goetz is a hero, Sullivan is a saint."

Videotape notwithstanding, the Goetz grand jury was not so different from others, according to Queens district attorney John Santucci. On February 3, he told ABC's Milton Lewis that in many cases a store owner had shot a robber with an unregistered gun and the grand jury refused to indict even for illegal possession of a firearm. Though the grand jury was consistent, I doubt that if a black man, say, bus driver Willie Turks, had shot those white guys who had attacked and killed him then skedaddled home, the Queens police would have left a polite note under Turk's door requesting that he come in for questioning as the Manhattan division did in the Goetz case. This double standard erodes whatever confidence black people might have in the police. But the confidence of the entire city should have been shaken when Philip Caruso, president of the Patrolmen's Benevolent Association, explained to Gabe Pressman on NBC on February 10 that he thought citizens shouldn't be allowed to decide cases involving purported infractions by officers in the line of duty because laymen are incapable of evaluating subtle points of law. This becomes even more disturbing when the police make statements implying that the word of Sullivan and a few of his co-workers should take precedence over the findings of an autopsy. The fact that Michael Baden, who was drummed out of the coroner's office and replaced by Gross, is the man who faced down the Rockefeller regime's explanation of the hostage killings at Attica, makes the importance of the Gross case even clearer. Caruso's belief that people who decide so many other complex cases should stay out of police affairs is as close to the call for a police state as anyone could imagine a contemporary official making. And though I feel the term "police state," like "fascism," has been beaten past pulp to liquification since the '60s, it is difficult to find a better explanation for Caruso's vision.

Ironically, the metaphor of victimization is now so well circulated that it is used to explain everybody's predicament: the teenagers wounded by Goetz were victims of poverty and barren social services; Goetz was the pawn of frustration in face of threat, flagrant dope dealing, and the justice system's revolving door; Bumpurs was victimized by police callousness or racism; Sullivan suffered as fall guy for the failures of the society and District Attorney Mario Merola's antipathy toward the police; while he was apparently defacing public property, Michael Stewart became a casualty of color prejudice; the six transit cops were wrongly charged because of the hysteria whipped up by the media; and our poor boy down among the corpses, Elliot Gross, is the target of professional enemies. Such a sweeping sense of victimization implies that the idea of individual responsibility has fallen by the wayside and no one, purported mugger or clairvoyant shootist, policeman or casualty, coroner or grand juror, is truly accountable for his or her actions. Human beings are no more than silly putty pulled and shaped by forces beyond their control. That might be meat for a Marxist or behaviorist analysis in which human beings are piano keys that go out of pitch when the weather is inclement and need only a master tuner to get them in order, but such explanations are the antithesis of civilization, brought into battle by so many different parties in these cases because they have worked so well for criminals—prompting even police to use them!

Such developments could intensify the cynicism tantamount to fatalism that neither this city nor this nation can afford. The only way solutions can be reached is for people to stop acting as though America is a monarchy—this *is* a democracy, and the responsibility for bird-dogging elected officials is theirs. This is especially important in terms of the black community. As playwright Charles Fuller says, "We have to take back the streets. Us. Black people. We have to involve ourselves in the workings of society and play our role in what is not only good for us but good for the general society. There is no truly segregated reality in America. All we have is different styles. Crime is the same for all of us. Fear is the same to all of us. Education and safety are equally important to all of us. We cannot abrogate our role as participants in American life."

Nor can black people ignore the truth. Less than 1 percent of the people in the most dire economic conditions deface public property, commit violent crimes, or frighten residents from the streets of their own communities after dark. Those who do are by and large black teenagers and the children of teenage mothers. As Dorothy I. Height, president of the National Council of Negro Women, points out in the March 1985 *Ebony:* "We find that in 1950 only about 18 percent of all black infants were born out of wedlock, and only about 36 percent of all black infants born to teenage mothers were born to unmarried women. In 1981, 65 percent of all births to black women were out of wedlock. Among black women under 20 the proportion was over 86 percent. The fastest growing black family formation today is that headed by teenaged mothers." From these households come many of the violent criminals who lord over the night. As one resident of 152nd Street reports, "You see these kids throw a cat on the tracks and watch it get run over. They have no compassion because they've never felt any. It has never happened to them—the feeling of love, I'm talking about. All they know is life on an animal level. They're only conscious of their needs; they lack the capacity for self-conscious awareness of right and wrong. Right is what you can get away with; wrong is the mistake that keeps you from getting away. That's all they know. They're beasts. Savages. Capital punishment, hard, *hard* labor, and long sentences in the penitentiary are the only things that will straighten them out."

You hear the word savages quite often, though it never comes trippingly off the tongue. It is usually uttered with a combination of pity and bitterness, knowledge of how dangerous things become when teenaged mothers discover that parenthood is at least a 20-year sentence and become abusive. In too many cases the male children deflect that abuse onto the society itself. One man I know threatened to take his daughter to court and fight for the custody of her son if she didn't stop letting his buttocks become raw because the cost of changing the boy's Pampers would cut into her nickel bags. She had married too early, gotten tired of motherhood, and treated her son with a malicious indifference. "She has no sense of sacrifice," he says. "She thinks that if she doesn't come first something is wrong. I told her she was a barbarian, and when I heard her try to read, I was convinced of it. Illiterate, selfish, and incapable of comprehending any kind of subtle ideas. Her mother was ignorant, my mistake was getting her pregnant and letting her raise the girl on welfare. But I'm not going to let my grandson be destroyed like his mother was."

According to Ulysses S. Kilgore III of the Bedford Stuyvesant Family Health Center, 40 percent of the mothers of these girls with teenage pregnancies don't know the most fertile time of the month themselves. "These children are surrounded by ignorance and the only thing that is going to change the situation is rolling up our sleeves and putting aside the textbook rhetoric for a while—a long, long while," he says. Kilgore understands that black people themselves must act to solve this problem; what he terms "textbook rhetoric" is no more than the defeatist sneering at destiny rather than wrestling with it. That the cases under discussion rise from the subway to an eviction, descend from the grand jury to the morgue, accentuate the need for accountability from law enforcement agencies and call into question the quality of urban life and the necessary support systems that define it, suggests that Fuller's observation about the need for Negro participation in the workings of American life is absolutely on the mark. It is only through participation that the social morale of both the black community and the nation at large can be raised. "It all has to come from us," says Kilgore. "If we make the thrust, roll up our sleeves and *work* at fighting the things that hamper the progress of black people, others will follow. But now, I think we have to make the first move and the second and however many more are necessary to get something going."

Getting something going is obviously a big job that calls for a new vision of social action from Negroes, not as outsiders but as voters, taxpayers, and sober thinkers. All civilized societies know that unless what is largely the sexual energy of adolescent men is channeled, anarchic behavior is almost automatic. Unless people get education sufficient to compete in the world, they will either become criminals or welfare leeches draining off funds that could be used to better life rather than sustain dead-end poverty. Unless there is a reciprocal respect between citizens and law enforcement agencies, an adversary relationship develops that creates mutual contempt and paranoia. Unless young women learn that this is the best time in history for them to take on careers and explore their talents, they will continue to give birth to children with dubious futures. The history of Negro Americans, for all its heartbreak and tragedy, is also one of extraordinary accomplishment in face of ruthless resistance. If all the shootings and the controversies serve to alert both Negroes and the society at large to a grander struggle, none of the shock and despair will have been in vain.

20

CHARLES JOHNSON: FREE AT LAST!
July 19, 1983

Since most contemporary novels involving race are scandals of contrivance, unwheeled wagons hitched to cardboard horses, it's a particular pleasure to read Charles Johnson's *Oxherding Tale*. This is his second novel and, being a long ball past his first, *Faith and the Good Thing* (1974), it separates him even further from conventional sensibilities. In

Faith, Johnson told the tall tale of a black girl's search for meaning—What is the good life? What is good?—and soaked it through with skills he had developed as a cartoonist, television writer, journalist, and student of philosophy. This time out, he has written a novel made important by his artful use of the slave narrative's structure to examine the narrator's developing consciousness, a consciousness that must painfully evaluate both the master and slave cultures.

The primary theme is freedom and the responsibility that comes with it. Given the time of the novel, 1838 to 1860, one would expect such a theme, but Johnson makes it clear in the most human—and often hilarious—terms that the question of freedom in a democratic society is essentially moral, and that social revolution pivots on an expanding redefinition of citizenry and its relationship to law. The adventure of escape only partially prepares Andrew Hawkins, the narrator, for the courage and commitment that come with moral comprehension. Andrew's growth is thrilling because Johnson skillfully avoids melodramatic platitudes while creating suspense and comedy, pathos and nostalgia. In the process, he invents a fresh set of variations on questions about race, sex, and freedom.

Though only 176 pages, *Oxherding Tale* is so rich that Johnson's contrapuntal developments of character and theme gain epic resonance. He expands his tale with adventures of style that span the work of Melville and Ellison, Twain and Bradbury, opting for everything from the facetious philosopical treatise to a variation on *The Illustrated Man.* Like a jazz musicians' high-handed use of harmony, Johnson's prose pivots between the language of the novel's time and terms from contemporary slang, regional vernacular, folklore, the blues, academia, and Madison Avenue. The technique recalls American film comedians' pushing the talk and attitudes of the day into period situations, lampooning the conventions of the past and the present. But Johnson is essentially a gallows humorist who manipulates microscopic realism to sober and control the reader's response, just as he takes narrative liberties to create an echoing, circular tension in which characters and dangers rhyme and contrast.

Johnson models his book on the work of Frederick Douglass, especially *Narrative of the Life of Frederick Douglass, An American Slave,* published in 1845. Douglass was an epic hero if there ever was one, and his work spans experience that moves from slavery to partial freedom to escape and eventual celebrity. His greatest importance to Johnson, however, is that he took Hawthorne's assault on New England hypocrisy south. In order to assert his humanity, Douglass questioned the Southern social order and everything that upheld it, from force to compliance, superstition to imposed illiteracy. He continually attacked the amoral sexual practices of the slaveholders and the distortions of American ideals caused by their defense of the chattel system. Douglass's native intelligence allowed for insights that only our finest novelists have been able to extend—the often dangerous nature of personal responsibility, the mutual infantilization of master and slave, the roles of religion and folklore, music and humor, risk and victory. In effect, Douglass is the figure who provides the moral passageway between Hawthorne and Melville and supplies the foundation for *Huckleberry Finn*.

By using Douglass's achievement as a model, Johnson perforates the lays of canvas-thick clichés that block our access to the human realities of American slavery. He also creates a successful metaphor for the 1960s, when black militants and intellectuals (students mostly) rejected Christianity and capitalism, and collided head-on with elements of black culture as basic as food (familial conflicts between emulation of Islam's disdain for pork and the hippie concern with health foods are symbolized by Andrew's embracing vegetarianism in imitation of his first white guru). The metaphor's impact comes from Johnson's sense of the play among history, cultural convention, and the assertion of identity in personal and ethnic terms.

Like Douglass, Andrew Hawkins is a mulatto. Unlike Douglass, he can pass for white, a fact that adds complexity to the moral choices he must make when he becomes a runaway. That fact also places him between what seem only two worlds but are actually many, and it adds the texture of an espionage tale in which "passing" is essential to suspense and victory. To thicken the plot, Johnson introduces a transcendentalist who supplies Andrew with a set of Eastern references and a pursuit of "The Whole"—though all systems of thought the hero encounters are satirized mercilessly. These devices allow Johnson to undercut Andrew's theorizing with concrete summonings of the worlds through which he passes—even inserting, as Melville might, a two-page treatise on the nature of slave narratives!

Johnson's ironic humor resounds at the novel's beginning as he pushes the master's wife into the position of slave woman by proxy. Just as "Benito Cereno" explained the behavior of slaves by reversing the situation, showing white men acting strangely—often "childlike"—because of their slaves' disguised rebellion, Johnson creates a bumbling Kingfish and a sullen, desexualized Sapphire in the master's house. As the novel opens, a drinking session is in progress. Jonathan Polkinghorne, master of Cripplegate, and his butler, George Hawkins, who is also his favorite slave, are indulging in a distinctly male camaraderie that seems to transcend their races and stations—each catches hell from his spouse when he comes home drunk. Literally inebriated with power, Jonathan proposes that they exchange wives for the evening in order to avoid static in the bedroom. George follows orders after the master makes it clear that he intends for them to be carried out.

Wobbling from the effects of wine and anticipation, George crosses the territory of *Invisible Man* and *The Odyssey*. In Ellison's novel, the narrator is upbraided and expelled from a Southern Negro college for following orders rather than pretending to, for not knowing he should give white people what they *want*, rather than what they ask for. George makes a parallel mistake and proves himself an even bigger fool by revealing his identity. As he makes love to Anna Polkinghorne in the darkness, she yowls with delight, calling him "Jonathan," but George can't resist telling her who's doing the satisfying, just as Odysseus couldn't resist shouting his name to the Cyclops. Like Odysseus, George is humbled by losing almost everything: as Anna swells, pregnant with George's child, his social position diminishes. He falls to the position of field hand—oxherd—outcast and laughing-stock of the slave quarters, given his comeuppance for ever having felt secure and superior to his follow slaves. Though George's wife, Mattie, accepts Andrew as her own after Anna refuses to see him, she is forever fighting with George, a mad battle in which their mutual needs are persistently camouflaged by complaint and derision.

Faced with Anna's hatred of being treated like a slave—a beast of the field to whom mates can be assigned—Jonathan's explanation includes the popular justification for rape: "Anna, you wanted George, not me, to be there, didn't you?" Like Benito Cereno, Anna is forever changed by experiencing the other side of slavery and becomes a variation on the now standard black shrew who rejects her husband for what he has "let" happen to her. As if writing an improvisation on Cleaver's "Allegory of the Black Eunuch," Johnson describes her transformation:

> What had been a comfortable, cushiony marriage with only minor flare-ups, easily fixed by flowers or Anna's favorite chocolates, was now a truce with his wife denying him access to the common room, top floors, and dining area (he slept in his study); what was once a beautiful woman whose voice sang as lovely as any in this world when she sat at the black, boatlike piano in the parlor, one foot gently vibrating on the sostenuto pedal, was now an irascible old woman who haunted the place like a dead man demanding justice. . . .

Jonathan is estranged from Anna because of the immoral nature of the order he gave George, and because he is a victim of a system in which immoral power choices can also ricochet. George's problems with Mattie stem from something only he knows—that his action could be explained as the result of many things, including cowardice, but when he felt lust for Anna and rationalized his act as an expression of God's will, he was using the order for his own purposes, embracing the slaveholder's self-justifications, and was culpable. Just as Jonathan and George mirror and provide contrast to each other, so do Anna and Mattie. Anna rejects Andrew because he complicates her identity in a way she finds repulsive, while Mattie, however embittered, saves her outrage for the men responsible and loves the child. While Mattie becomes more contentious, Anna becomes a voluntary spinster whose desexualization by slavery will be echoed by Minty, Andrew's first love and the daughter of a womanizing mulatto slave. Minty is introduced with a naïve but fearful lyricism:

> . . . I saw her eyes—eyes green as icy mountain meltwater, with a hint of blue shadow and a drowse of sensuality that made her seem

voluptuously sleepy, distant, as though she had been lifted long ago
from a melancholy African landscape overrich with the colors and
warm smells of autumn—a sad, out-of-season beauty of autumn—a
sad, out-of-season beauty suddenly precious to me because it was im-
perfect and perhaps illusory like moonlight on pond water, sensuously
alive, but delivering itself over, as if in sacrifice, to inevitable slow
death in the fields.

Minty is seen a few years later, after Andrew has escaped and is passing
himself off as a white man at a slave auction.

> . . . I stood trying to recognize something of the girl in Cripplegate,
> in whom the world once chose to concretize its possibilities in the
> casements of her skin. . . . If you looked, without sentiment, you
> could see that her dress was too small and crawled up when she
> moved, flashing work-scorched stretches of skin and a latticework of
> whipmarks. Her belly pushed forward. From the cholesterol-high,
> nutritionless diet of the quarters, or a child, I could not tell. She was
> unlovely, drudgelike, sexless, the farm tool squeezed . . . for every
> ounce of surplus value, then put on sale for whatever price she could
> bring. She was, like my stepmother, perhaps doubly denied—in both
> caste and gender—and driven to Christ (she wore a cross) as the
> only decent man who would have her.

The road to that hideous epiphany is a long one, taking Andrew
through continual redefinitions of his identity and the nature of his surroundings. When Anna demands that Andrew be sent away because he
symbolizes her humiliation, Jonathan refuses and makes provisions for
his education. From Ezekiel William Sykes-Withers, Andrew gets a
classical education expanded to include the teachings of the Eastern
philosophers and mystics. Andrew embraces the idea of the universe as
the Great Mother, becomes an intellectual fop, and makes pompous
evaluations of the problems of man. Ezekiel, with his head ever in the
clouds, and George, with his pushed into the earth, give Andrew anti-
thetical perspectives experience will allow him to synthesize. George's
bitterness at his fall from grace shapes an overview that defines anything
connected with white people as bad:

> Too much imagination, he decided, was unwholesome. And white. If
> you were George Hawkins, you were coldly courteous to a Master who
> banished you to the bleakest life possible, a life spent among animals,
> away from the center of culture at Cripplegate; but wasn't his exile a
> blessing? Didn't it prove that whites were not, morally, Nature's last
> word on Man? They were, George swore after three fingers' worth of
> stump liquor—his eyes like torches—Devils or, worse, derived in
> some way he couldn't explain from Africans, who were a practical,
> down-to-earth people.

That homemade ethnic nationalism is the spiritual tragedy of Andrew's
father, a man who sustains his hurt and sands down the universe to fit

his disappointment: "Grief was the grillwork—the emotional grid—through which George Hawkins sifted and sorted events, simplified a world so overrich in sense it outstripped him. . . ." George had no knowledge of the threat that education and imagination posed.

Andrew's schooling will later make it possible for him to read and forge documents, to make language work for him, just as the slaves had made Christianity function as religion, self-expression, style, political editorial, and code of revolt. And because of his learning, Andrew, for all his naïveté, comes to realize he must ask for his freedom: "Consider the fact: Like a man who had fallen or been rudely flung into the world, I owned nothing. My knowledge, my clothes, my language, even, were shamefully second-hand, made by, and perhaps for, other men. . . . My argument was: Whatever my origin, I would be wholly responsible for the shape I gave myself in the future, for shirting myself handsomely with a new life that called me like a siren to possibilities that were real but forever out of reach."

The oblique references to Caliban and Odysseus are apt: the runaway slave that Andrew will soon become is a man whose knowledge must be used to free him from teachers as he looks for home—except that the home for which slaves felt nostalgia was more the dream of freedom than an actual place. But before Andrew chooses to pursue freedom in concrete geographical terms, he floats along in the philosophical clouds he shares with Ezekiel. Too mystical to trust sensuality, Ezekiel longs for a system that will explain everything and sends Karl Marx the money to visit America. Johnson brilliantly satirizes the relationship between a revolutionary's self-obsession and his theories: "As of late, political affairs affected Marx physically. When he felt a headcold coming on, a toothache, he looked immediately for its social cause. A new tax law had cost Marx a molar. Nearby at a button factory a strike that failed brought on an attack of asthma. These things were dialectical."

Marx's appearance signals Andrew's first awareness that ideas have human sources or targets, Marx, a jolly family man and sensualist, has as his credo. "Everything I've vritten has been for a voman—is *one* vay to view Socialism, no?" Marx's boredom inspires Andrew to look more closely at the stern Ezekiel: "Abruptly, I saw my tutor through his eyes: a lonely, unsocial creature unused to visitors, awkward with people as a recluse. Not a Socialist, as he fancied himself. No, his rejection of society, his radicalism, was not, as he thought, due to some rareness of the soul. It was stinginess. Resentment for the richness of things. A smoke screen for his own social shortcomings." What Andrew had thought the opposite of George's vision was substantially the same—a world view created out of bitterness. Yet Andrew, the pampered mulatto, has still to taste the sourness and terror of slavery, the black world beyond abstraction. His decision to ask for his freedom will bring him cheek to jowl with sexual decadence, drugs, and death.

Andrew's second white mentor is Flo Hatfield, a ruthless voluptuary on whose plantation Andrew expects to earn money that will buy freedom for George, Mattie, and Minty. Middle-aged and beautiful, Flo Hatfield has been infantilized by her power over others, but Johnson makes her as sympathetic as she is repulsive, self-obsessed, and petulant. Good at business and something of a feminist, Hatfield's resentment of male privilege becomes a justification for her appetites. She dresses her lovers, all of whom are slaves, as gigolos; when she tires of them, they're sent to work in her mines, where death is certain. Though she seems sexually free at first, a cosmopolitan upper-class white woman beyond the erotic provincialism of Negro women, she is actually so much a slave to sensation that Andrew's job as sexual servant results in addiction to opium, her favorite aphrodisiac. When Johnson writes that her lovers had "died and gone to Heaven, you might say," he is playing on the black dictum: "A colored man with a white woman is a Negro who has died and gone to heaven," but he is also creating a metaphor for the inevitable fall that follows the spiritual death of decadence.

No more than a tool of Hatfield's narcissism, Andrew falls for her hedonistic heaven when he strikes her in anger after she refuses to allow him to earn his freedom. Andrew is sent to the Yellow Dog Mine, where the landscape echoes Bessie Smith: "Wild country so tough the hootowls all sang bass." With him is Reb, his second father figure. En route, Andrew asserts his white features and they escape, pretending to be master and slave. In the process, they must outwit the Soul-catcher, Horace Bannon, a man who psychologically *becomes* a slave, then goes where slaves would hide. Bannon's technique is close to the one Reb preaches—a slave must learn exactly how masters think so that he can control their relationship as much as possible. Bannon is a psychopath whose "collage of features" suggests mixed ancestry and whose bloodlust is allowed free rein by the constant flight of slaves. Perhaps the greatest condemnation of the chattel system is that it instituted sadistic behavior for the maintenance of injustice. From Reb, Andrew learns what historian Forrest G. Wood meant when he said that what had been endured by the vast majority of Negro slaves exceeded the suffering of even the most oppressed white group. A captured African slave whose name has been changed twice by different masters, Reb is himself a harsh lesson in the stoicism born of tragedy. He no longer dreams of Africa, where Islam was as much an imposition of slavery as Christianity was in America. Reb faces his fate, raising his fists in his own way.

All that Andrew has learned, both intellectual and moral, is put to the test when he decides to marry a white woman—or she decides for him. Once Andrew enters that world, the theme of espionage, of assumed identity that allows for information about the opposition, also allows for a fantastic parody of the liberal wing of the town. One of the bridesmaids at Andrew's marriage comments, "*My* problem is that whenever someone gives me a quick feel in a crowded room, I wheel round, naturally, and slug him, then I realize he's Indian, black, or Mexican, and I feel simply dreadful for the rest of the day because I've hurt someone disadvantaged." From there, Johnson moves to a climax remarkable for its brutality and humbling tenderness; Andrew must dive into the briar patch of his identity and risk destruction in order to express his humanity.

That a work of such courage and compassion, virtuosity and intelligence, has been published by a university press is further proof that commercial houses have a very circumscribed notion of African-American writing. But then, any black writer who chooses human nature over platitudes, opportunism, or trends faces probable rejection. Charles Johnson has enriched contemporary American fiction as few young writers can, and it is difficult to imagine that such a talented artist will forever miss the big time that is equal to his gifts.

TOTE THAT JUNGLE
December 14, 1982

It is no news that information and liberation, ignorance and slavery, are intertwined. Information is what inspires us to question stereotypes and to refine the pluralistic definition of human value that is the greatest event of the age. And as a society learns to accept the range of its own citizenry, it is ultimately forced to accept the variety beyond its borders and its laws. But social responsibility is stymied when in guilt over imperial history we further exploit the former exotics by encouraging or accepting barbaric practices in the name of cultural relativity.

I bring this up because a couple of recent events illustrate the depth of the problem. One is the controversy in Europe over African workers performing clitoridectomies on their daughters. The French have prosecuted the Malinese for performing this operation, sometimes with a pocket knife. The retort is that the tradition is neither European nor the European's business, that its practice should be a right guaranteed the foreign workers, is traditionalism at its cruelest, since female circumcision is destructive regardless of how long it's been ritualized. And here is the obvious twist: though it has been outlawed in Norway, Sweden, and Denmark, there is no legislation against it in England, where, according to *Newsweek*, "private doctors on London's Harley Street acknowledge that they perform clitoridectomies for immigrant women at fees as high as $1700."

So the literal price of that barbarism is twofold—an irreversible disfigurement that forever limits sensual satisfaction at the same time that it allows exploitation as callous as any during colonialism. This time, though, the native demands the right to be had. There is also the strong possibility that an infant girl who is victimized by her parents' ignorance or self-righteous provincialism will grow to hate her culture in ways the most chauvinistic missionary would have had to struggle to inspire. And if there is a right those who advocate female circumcision should have outside their own countries, it is that of adult women to have those operations if they wish—the same privilege to be mutilated for money that transsexuals enjoy.

A related phenomenon reverses the missionary impulse, often expressed in impassioned whining over the decline of primitive life in the wake of modernization. In Les Blank's *Burden of Dreams,* for instance, Werner Herzog bemoans the clearing of the Amazon jungle while he films *Fitzcarraldo*. Though Herzog had to provide his Indian extras with prostitutes and be careful that rival tribes didn't kill them, though the Indians would pay $2 apiece for Polaroid pictures of themselves or become near-violent when their soccer ball was deflated, the German director goes on and on about allowing them to maintain their own ways in a world that is constantly becoming more and more the same, with so little of the primitive and the pure remaining—the entire globe succumbing to commercial culture. The narrow world of superstition and tribal violence we see the Indians living in doesn't make them less human, but it is quite clear that few viewers would want to live in their twilight universe of pervasive ignorance. This as much as anything else accounts for what romantics call "cultural imperialism": though initially startled or intimidated by the light that hits his savage world, the primitive will move toward it if given the chance. Ironically, those who dismiss the term savage by pointing at imperialist atrocities fail to understand that they are but the latest critics in a tradition at least as old as that of Samuel Johnson, who toasted slave rebellions and the work of American abolitionists. It is possible to argue for the perpetuation of savage life on its own terms only because Western culture provides a context so large that we can appreciate and be moved by the universal human attempts to translate experience into art, dance, religion, oral literature. We must realize, however, that the choices those societies provide are very limited. No people in the modern age will forever escape the trauma that results from change, which is basic to the history of science and democratic thought in conflict with religious dogma and inherited political power. Civilization costs us the absolutes of religion and leadership through bloodline.

So the ultimate issue here is what provides the greatest storehouse of information for a higher quality of life. After the last rattle has been shaken, the last drumbeat sounded, the last greased and feathered leg danced on, no amount of traditional African medicine, for instance, will give anyone a clue as to what sickle cell anemia is in concrete terms;

that information came with the microscope. And now some European-trained African doctors are trying to build medical approaches that take the facts gathered from abroad and mate them with those domestic techniques that work, whether in ritual or herbal form. Unlike those so guilty over the history of colonialism that they ratify almost anything that preceded the arrival of the slave trade and the colonies, those doctors are concerned with one thing—not cultural nostalgia but the best possible health programs they can build. As a young Nigerian I met in Amsterdam said to me in 1977, "What I do not understand about the American black man is the same thing I do not understand about the American and the European white man: why do they want us to still live in the bush? They think African culture should remain in the same place so they can get the good tourist entertainment when they come there. When I go to France, the French take you on a tour of the caves where the prehistoric men painted the walls, but they do not live in the caves—even though the walls are so beautiful. The British do the same thing with Stonehenge: nobody British lives there. But all of these people love the Africa they think they destroyed. I love the Africa that we Africans are now building—the Africa that maintains what is good and best for the people, and the Africa that borrows what will help it do these things."

He is obviously right. But there is one more thing. When a vanishing way of life is romanticized by those who have grown up in a more advanced world, their very power can intensify the feeling of anguish in the primitives, adding to the inevitable pain a disposition of militant self-pity. The humane approach is to make the transition as easy as possible, not glamorize the warm mud from which they must arise, sooner or later.

AFRICAN QUEEN
June 12, 1984

From the time I arrived in British East Africa at the indifferent age of four and went through the barefoot stage of early youth hunting wild pig with the Nandi, later training race-horses for a living, and still later scouting Tanganyika and the waterless bush country between the Tana and Athi rivers, by aeroplane, for elephant, I remained so happily provincial I was unable to discuss the boredom of being alive with any intelligence until I had gone to London and lived there a year. Boredom, like hookworm, is endemic.

I have lifted my plane from Nairobi airport for perhaps a thousand flights and I have never felt her wheels glide from the earth into the air without knowing the uncertainty and the exhilaration of firstborn adventure.

Beryl Markham, the author of those words, is a mulatto by culture instead of blood, a woman of action equally formed by the dictates of the bush and the heritage of Western sophistication and technology. She became famous by making the first east to west flight across the Atlantic, from England, in 1936; her *West with the Night*, originally published in 1942 and recently reissued, selectively covers the 30 years of her development that led to the historic flight. Markham spent those years on a colonial frontier that provided her with a richer range of racial mentors than she would have had in England, and was able to mature with relatively unbound ambition because necessity dictated that the best person for the job got it, regardless of sex. Of the Africa she knew, Markham wrote, "It is as ruthless as any sea, more uncompromising than its own deserts. It is without temperance in its harshness or in its favours. It yields nothing, offering much to men of all races." But her position as a white European woman in Africa offered her a freedom enjoyed neither by white women in Europe nor by the native black women.

Markham's vision is unsentimental and complex—the bush is wonderful but filled with threats to human and animal life; her father's farm is beautiful yet it lessens the beauty of the wilderness; horses are magnificent creatures but a trainer can be crippled or killed trying to tame one; the Nandi warriors are men of great courage, skill, and tenderness, but were she a Nandi girl, she wouldn't be allowed to hunt with them; the experience of flying is breathtaking but the loneliness can be almost overwhelming. She re-creates the splendid textures of a life at once inside and outside the universes of the black African, the Indian, the white settler, the farmer, the horse breeder, the aviator, and the white hunter. Whether bushmen or pilots, pursued beasts or hunting dogs and racehorses, they populate a spiritual epic in which the writer puts a big enough narrative spin on the meaning of cosmopolitan to make the work some sort of modernist classic.

Markham was born in England in 1902, the daughter of Sandhurst graduate Captain Charles Clutterbuck, who brought her to what is now Kenya in 1906, separating from his wife and leaving her with a son. (Markham refers to Clutterbuck only as "my father"; her mother and brother are not mentioned.) Her father built the first important sawmill in British East Africa, pushed back the wilderness with his large farm, raised horses, but lost all to drought and moved to Peru when Markham was 17. She remained, hired herself out as a horse trainer, got interested in flying, and was a free-lance aviator from 1931 to 1936, "the only professional woman pilot in Africa at the time," delivering mail, people, medicine, and supplies, and scouting elephants for safaris. After she made her trans-Atlantic flight, she rode through the confetti blizzard of a New

York ticker-tape parade, had an audience with LaGuardia, and told a newspaper reporter, "Flying is my job. This flight is part of it. It is not a romantic venture, but a hard job of work. I believe in the future of the Atlantic air service. I want to be in at the beginning." She eventually went to Hollywood, where she worked on flying sequences for films. After World War II kicked off, her third husband, screenwriter Raoul Schumacher, was drafted, and Markham recently told a reporter that she wrote her only book to keep boredom from her door. She dedicated the work to her father.

The book so excited Hemingway that in August of 1942 he wrote to Maxwell Perkins, "This girl who is, to my knowledge, very unpleasant . . . can write rings around all of us who consider ourselves as writers. The only parts of it that I know about personally, on account of having been there at the time and heard the other people's stories, are absolutely true. So, you have to take as truth the early stuff about when she was a child which is absolutely superb. . . . I wish you would get it and read it because it is really a bloody, wonderful book." Even so, it soon went out of print.

In 1981 George Gutekunst, owner of Sausalito, California's famous restaurant Ondine, bought a copy of Hemingway's recently published *Selected Letters* at the suggestion of the writer's son, John. Gutekunst was shocked by the great man's enthusiasm for an obscure book. Using the Marin County computer, a librarian friend of his found a single copy in the San Rafael Library that had been checked out only seven times since 1942. Gutekunst caught the fever and lent the book to novelist Evan Connell, who spread the little epidemic to his own publishers at North Point Press. They discovered that Markham was alive and well training horses in Kenya and happy to make *West with the Night* available.

Such complex connections through time zones, mail service, publishers, posthumous letters, computers, and so on correspond to the intricacies of Markham's life—a life that exemplifies the link between an evolving technology and the social evolution of the modern woman. (During those years, aviation was an open field in which many women proved themselves equal to the best fliers.) But the book is important primarily because of Markham's world-class literary skills and her willingness to play with form while holding on to facts, anticipating—as did *Green Hills of Africa*—what some now call "the nonfiction novel." Like Hemingway, Markham created a work that could compete with that of the imagination, but she had an enviable edge on the master: her tale took place during three decades instead of a single safari, and included more interesting characters, more opportunities for toying with time, and infinitely more exciting events.

Had she wanted to, Markham could have appropriated Hemingway's foreword to *Green Hills:* "Any one not finding sufficient love interest is at liberty, while reading it, to insert whatever love interest he or she may have at the time." Though set between 1906 and 1936, the book mentions neither her first marriage around 1920 to Jock Purves nor her second around 1928 to Mansfield Markham. (Their omission might be explained by her belief that "all great characters come back to life if you call them.") While she eulogizes Isak Dinesen's lover, Denys Finch-Hatton, who died in a 1931 plane crash, her rumored affair with him is never discussed. Judith Thurman's biography of Dinesen contains a description of Markham in the late 1920s when she started rattling the Danish lady's nerves: "She was tall, broad-shouldered, and fair, resembling Greta Garbo both in her features and in a restless, pantherine grace of movement. Her private life was the subject of endless gossip and speculation, and to the common imagination Beryl was a sort of Circe." But *West with the Night* isn't aimed at or produced by a common imagination.

The book opens on June 16, 1935, when Markham is flying on a dual mission—to try and find an airman who has disappeared and deliver a tank of oxygen for a sick man to a mining camp. The work ends 18 months later, after she has made aviation history, while the bulk of the narrative flows in flashbacks, flash-forwards, and asides that create suspense and enrich the story line. As she pretends to muse, a word, phrase, or event will elicit a memory that prepares the way for an upcoming insight or dramatic moment. Within a few pages, her double vision emerges. Though she loves Africa unequivocally, and shows great respect for hard-working settlers, she also has a deep reserve of contempt for the condescension and bullying that made empire so abominable. "What upstart race," she writes in the first chapter, "sprung from some recent, callow century to arm itself with steel and boastfulness, can match in purity the blood of a single Masai Murani whose heritage may have stemmed not far from Eden? . . . Racial purity, true aristocracy, devolve not from edict, nor from rote, but from the preservation of a kinship with the elemental forces and purposes of life whose understanding is not farther beyond the mind of a Native shepherd than beyond the cultured fumblings of a mortar-board intelligence."

However offensive that might sound to those who hate the idea of any kind of elite, I find Markham's hierarchy acceptable because it is based on human quality instead of race or station. Quite consciously, she recalls the similarity and consistency of information about life and duty that she gleaned from mentors as superficially removed from one another as a bushman discussing spear-throwing and a pilot talking about the shortcomings of the plane's instrument board. The description of a childhood friend who later comes to work for her sums up that vision: "Arab Ruta is a Nandi, anthropologically a member of a Nilotic tribe, humanly a member of a smaller tribe, a more elect tribe, the tribe composed of those too few, precisely sensitive, but altogether indomitable individuals contributed by each race, exclusively by none."

To give her world view experiential weight, Markham wrote a book that is primarily a spiritual autobiography; it explains the initiations that gave her the heart to do everything she did. She revives those initiations with a series of compelling memories that develop into lyric and gritty parables. The purpose of the tales is to celebrate her mentors, detail her world, and protest limited or contrived visions of human beings—not by squawking but by focusing on her central concerns: courage, skill, discipline, humor, and compassion. They depict a broad range of experience; Markham brings the precise eye of a hunter to a world in transition, an Africa moving from the prehistory of the hut, the spear, and the oral tradition to the 20th century of the city, the rifle, the book, the railroad, the airplane, the telegraph wire. In a sense, her story is the story of that move, because she knew the world of the black African from the inside.

Captain Clutterbuck obviously ignored the colonial dictum expressed in Henry Owen Weller's *Kenya Without Prejudice*(!): "As children grow up they must be kept from familiarity with Africans. Girls must never be left alone with male natives. At boarding school this matter receives careful attention. To neglect it at home would be asking for trouble." Clutterbuck's neglect allowed Markham to make a remarkable life in which her self-confidence grew with each successive testing of her talent. The excellence with which she eventually did everything, from spearing African warthogs to breaking horses to flying blind through black night, defines a heroic human being rather than a person limited by her sex. All the people who teach her how to pursue her talents are men, but they have "the kindness not to show tolerance"; they treat her as a potential equal and understand, as her flying teacher Tom Black says, "I could have warned you—but you shouldn't be robbed of your right to make mistakes." When she learns to hunt as a child, the Africans prepare her for the rigors and dangers of the bush, "Here! Bend down and look. See how this leaf is crushed. Feel the wetness of this dung. Bend down so that you may learn!" Arab Maina is Markham's most admired childhood model other than her Spartan father. Brave but never foolhardy, a great strategist of the hunt, and the surest hurler of the steel-pointed spear, "He believed in duty and in the kind of justice that he knew, and in all the things that were of the earth—like the voice of the forest, the right of a lion to kill a buck, the right of a buck to eat grass, and the right of a man to fight."

When Markham ditches school to join Maina for the hunt, the Murani warriors accept her with great affection. They allow her the position of proxy boy, not because Nandi society is free of sexual restrictions, but because she is European and poses no threat to their social order. Markham tells us this subtly, through the questions of Jebbta, the African girl, who is puzzled by the lanky blond girl skipping class to participate, Masai spear in hand, fighting dog at her side. "Where do you find the strength and the daring to hunt with them, my sister?" Markham has no answer. "Your body is like mine; it is no stronger," Jebbta says, before turning away to avoid the eyes of the men, as is customary.

Markham's friendship with the Nandi boy Kibii, as she learns the tribal games, makes her status even clearer: "One of the games was jumping, because the Nandi said that a boy or a man must be able to jump as high as himself to be any good at all, and Kibii and I were determined to be good. When I left Njoro, at last, I could still jump higher than my head. I could wrestle too, the Nandi way." (As usual, Markham also shows the sour side of her sweet life. Besting one Nandi boy leads to a fight in which he slashes her with his father's sword. She bops him behind the ear with a knobkerrie, the same weapon she later uses to kill a baboon who loves her father but hates and attacks her.) Markham also learns to shoot with a bow and arrow and observes the Kikuyu tribal dances with Kibii beneath the full moon. But not all her instruction is physical. She says of a game Kibii taught her that it took months to learn and "the mental arithmetic required was more than I have since used in 20 years," a strong statement from a person who had to master the mechanics of aviation to get her flying license.

World War I is a recurrent symbol of modern life and modern problems encroaching on Markham's elemental paradise. Recruits from the city and the bush gather, ragtag as all get-out, in front of Nairobi House, "looking at best like revolutionists" who had "predecessors once in America." The big war's somber mystery hovers over Markham and Kibii, who "did what children do when there are things abroad too big to understand; we stayed close to each other and played games that made no noise." After the war is over and her father has lost his farm, Markham moves to Molo to train horses and again meets Kibii, who has been tribally initiated as an adult and given the name Arab Ruta. When he calls her "Memsahib," the writer responds by thinking "this stilted word that ends my youth and reminds me always of its ending." At that point, her anger at colonial society explodes:

> What a child does not know and does not want to know of race and colour and class, he learns soon enough as he grows to see each man flipped inexorably into some predestined groove like a penny or a sovereign in a banker's rack. Kibii, the Nandi boy, was my good friend. Arab Ruta, who sits before me, is my good friend, but the handclasp will be shorter, the smile will not be so eager on his lips, and though the path is for a while the same, he will walk behind me now, when once, in the simplicity of our nonage, we walked together.
>
> No, my friend, I have not learned more than this. Nor in all these years have I met many who have learned as much.

The obvious irony is that were it not for the colonial frontier, she would never have had the freedom to know Arab Ruta, nor would she have learned to respect the world from which he came. But as he works for her, first helping train racehorses, and later taking care of her plane, Markham makes it clear that service is not the same thing as subservience. Ruta remains proud and brings to his work an almost intimidating confidence, something those who define triumph or degradation only in material terms can't understand. In his way, he comes off as an African version of those extraordinary porters on the old railroads who carried themselves with the dignity of agile and humorous judges. While preparing for a race that will test Markham's reputation as a trainer, Ruta grooms her filly, Wise Child, then spits with contempt as he addresses the opposition: " 'Wrack—I warn you! You are a colt, but God has given our filly the blade of a Nandi spear for a heart, and put the will of the wind in her lungs. You cannot win, Wrack. I, Arab Ruta, say so!' He turns to me. He is solemn. 'It is settled, Memsahib. Wrack will lose.' "

The section on horse training and the race itself show an important aspect of Markham's personality; she never takes the advice of those she most admires if it will limit her ambition. As Markham prepares to leave for Molo, her father tells her that she is only a girl and not to expect too much. But she has the will to contest, even when her age and sex draw smirks: "Trainers big-chested, trainers flat-chested. . . . All of them men. All of them older than my eighteen years, full of being men, confident, cocksure, perhaps offhand. They have a right to be. They know what they know—some of which I have still to learn, but not much, I think. Not much, I hope. We shall see, we shall see." Her self-confidence is tested when Wrack, the colt she has trained, is taken away from her 12 weeks short of the big Nairobi race. Wrack's owner accepts the word of a male trainer that he, not an inexperienced girl, is best for the colt. But the owner of Wise Child, a filly with weak shanks, brings his horse to Markham, confident the young trainer can do enough with her in three months to challenge Wrack's supremacy at Nairobi. In one of the best descriptions of a horse race I've ever read, Markham implies a symbolic battle of the sexes, not for supremacy but for respect, and the suspense intensifies as the narrator's heart goes back and forth between two superb animals she respects equally.

Markham gives up horse training to learn flying from Tom Black, whom she first meets when he is repairing his car. "The automobile so sharp sketched against this simple canvas was an intrusion; it was as if a child had pasted the picture of a foolish toy over a painting you had known for years." The painting is the African landscape, which will change into "a land that is unknown to the rest of the world and only vaguely known to the African" once she sees it from the air. And when the writer explains aviation in Africa, her references are those of the cultural mulatto: "Everywhere in the world, highways had come first—and then the landing fields. Only not there, for much of Kenya's future was already the past of other places. New things that shone with the ingenuity of modern times were super-imposed upon an old order, contrasting against it like a chromium clock against a rawhide shield."

Markham frequently reverses the convention of describing urban life with similes and metaphors from the wild. She compares the awe a zebra foal shows for an eccentric and beautiful thoroughbred filly with the dazzled eyes of a London urchin she once saw "enraptured to the point of tears at the sight of a lovely lady swathed in sables stepping from her car to the curb." Or she writes of a looming bull elephant bent on crushing her and her party to death, "He paused, listened, and swung round with the slow irresistibility of a bank-vault door." Such images come easily to a writer who observed the conflict between the wild and Western technology from childhood: "Often a herd of giraffe found it expedient to cross the railroad tracks, but would not condescend to bow to the elevated strands that proclaimed the White Man's mandate over their feeding grounds. As a result, many telegrams enroute from Mombasa to Kisumu, or the other way around, were intercepted, their cryptic dots and dashes frozen in a festoon of golden wire dangling from one or another of the longest necks in Africa." Aviation is the ultimate expression of that conflict, and the same world war that costs Arab Maina his life and ends Markham's hunts in the bush makes Black a pilot. Though at first reluctant to enter the vortex of technological innovation, Markham gets curious about flying when she observes Black returning from a mission with the ashes of a cremated hunter in a biscuit tin. Flying is her final step into the modern age.

When Markham starts to fly, she comes in contact with the threat of death every time her plane takes off—a threat that has been crucial to the narrative from the beginning. In the second chapter, when Markham delivers the tank of oxygen to the mining camp, she is asked to speak with a man dying from blackwater, the color of urine in fatal malaria. She toys with the word, letting it scratch the reader's curiosity before telling what it means, and flashes back to a plague during her childhood. Before she can entertain the dying man with small talk about Nairobi, the writer has to "fight back an impulse to throw open the door and bolt across the runway into the protecting cockpit of my plane."

Further on, Markham writes of dangerous confrontations with animals, usually lions. As she flies over the Serengeti Plains, searching for a lost flier, she observes that the only similarity between lions and house cats is their whiskers, as those emboldened by a lion's ease in front of a camera will find out if they get too close. The next section takes place over 20 years earlier, when Markham visits a neighboring farm with her father. The slim young heroine runs for the woods rather than join Clutterbuck and his friends for high tea ("evidence of the double debt England owes to ancient China for her two gifts that made expansion possible—tea and gunpowder"). As Markham runs she sees Paddy, the hosts' supposedly tame lion, preparing to attack her. Just before he moves, Markham restokes the image of a house cat: "He was rusty-red, and soft, like a strokable cat." Though knocked down and clawed, Markham is saved just in time. Too aware of natural law to be bitter, she says that the lion is a wild thing, and "I cannot begrudge him his moment."

A few chapters later, she describes a standoff between the Murani with whom she hunts and a lion at his prey: "Smears of blood were fresh on his forelegs, his jowls, and his chest. He was a lone hunter—an individualist—a solitary marauder. His tail had stopped swinging. His great head turned exactly in ratio to the speed of our stride. The full force of his lion-smell, meaty, pungent, almost indescribable, struck our nostrils." Another battle, with wild pig, is as exciting as it is bloody. Markham's dog, his coat already scarred from battles with warthogs and leopards, is ripped open. The boar "charges once more with magnificent courage, and I sidestep and plunge my spear into his heart." Much later, we see why she mentioned cameras in her first observation about lions. The ashes in Tom Black's biscuit can are those of a hunter who foolishly tried to photograph a lion he and his partner had mortally wounded. Echoing her statement about Paddy, the lion who forgot he was tamed, the writer says, "Death will have his moment, however he comes along, and no matter upon what living thing he lays his hand."

During Markham's teenage years, for all the poetic compression of memory, death is always close, whether the end she almost suffers while trying to break a proud stallion or the shooting of marauding lions and leopards come to kill farm animals. The idea for her eventual career, scouting game from the air, is Denys Finch-Hatton's, but his fatal crash occurs before he can try it. Tom Black tries to discourage her because of the danger, but Markham ignores his advice. "Elephant! Safari! Hunting! Denys Finch-Hatton had left me a legacy of excitement—a release from routine, a passport to adventure."

There is adventure all right; Markham and the white hunter Bror Blixen (Isak Dinesen's former husband) are nearly trampled by elephants. But Markham admires the upper-class crowd she works for no more than she does colonialism: "The essence of elephant-hunting is discomfort in such lavish proportions that only the wealthy can afford it." Among the local rich is John Carberry, a sadist and one of the nuts James Fox describes in *White Mischief,* his investigation of murder and upper-class decadent doings in Kenya. Markham deftly implies the violence and hysteria of Carberry's circle by describing it as "a company of characters snatched from an unfinished novel originally drafted by H. Rider Haggard and written by Scott Fitzgerald with James M. Cain looking over his shoulder." Though Markham chose to discuss those characters only in code, she obviously expected someone like Fox to fill out the story.

In March 1936, Markham decides to leave Africa, looking for more to do with her life, and takes Blixen to Europe. On the way, they encounter the Italian army in Ethiopia and the looming shadow of World War II. The Italians evoke the ominous hilarity of Keystone Fascists and symbolize the worst aspects of bureaucracy gone mad: "the arrival of a foreign plane afforded them the opportunity of surrounding its passengers and holding them captive beyond the sights of a battery of snub-nosed rubber stamps." In Libya, Blixen sees a man's severed head in the streets and they meet a prostitute whom Markham renders with a superb combination of rage and compassion.

In England, Carberry, described as "a man who snickers when circumstances pointedly indicate the propriety of a shudder," and who once chortled while contemplating some very dangerous weather Markham would have to fly through, accepts the suggestion that he finance the female ace. Carberry proposes, with an "almost ghoulish grin," that she fly across the Atlantic, west with the night, from England. Perhaps the idea of her crashing thrilled him as much as the prospect of her making it to New York. The narrative echoes its first image of death, blackwater malaria, when Carberry says, "I wouldn't tackle it for a million. Think of all that black water! Think of how cold it is!"

Markham decides to risk death because, of all the record flights, "none had been made by amateurs, nor by novices, nor by men or women less than hardened to failure, or less than masters of their trade. None of these was false. They were a company that simple respect and simple ambition made it worth more than an effort to follow." In her suspenseful account of the flight, Markham makes clear once again that heroic action has more to do with will than with fearlessness. She describes how she feels when the plane seems about to crash: "It has all happened a hundred times in my mind, in my sleep, so that now I am not really caught in terror; I recognize a familiar scene, a familiar story with its climax dulled by too much telling."

Though the hero's welcome given Markham in New York, then a page or two in aviation history, is now no more than old photographs and newspaper stories of the 1930s, *West with the Night* will prove a more enduring achievement. Sooner or later, someone, male or female, would have crossed the Atlantic from England. But no one else has written a book like this one. Hemingway pointed out in "Monologue to the Maestro" that Thomas Mann would have been a greater writer if he had produced no more than *Buddenbrooks*. He could have just as easily been talking about Beryl Markham.

LIONEL MITCHELL, 1942–1984

October 23, 1984

As he lay in a coma at Bellevue, Lionel Hampton Mitchell died last week at 42 of pneumonia propelled by AIDS. For something under a year, his 300-pound bulk had been shrinking. At first, I thought he was giving his heart and his system a break, since Lionel was a diabetic prone to ruthless consumption of sweets. But now and then he would abstractedly say, as though to himself, "I hope it isn't AIDS." As he got smaller, I began to worry about him. An odd sort of stoicism had come into his demeanor and the once wonderful voice, capable of filling city blocks with the width of his anger, had begun to lose its power. The clever eyes so rich with ideas and worlds, wit and information, seemed to cast less light. He appeared forever tired and a bewildered sadness I had never seen in him replaced the pugnacious spirit that could be as compelling as it was overwhelming when the barbs in his bloodstream took to the air for a vituperative attack. Then I would ask him if he was ill and Lionel would answer that he was losing weight at the advice of his doctor after a mild stroke. I now think that Lionel knew what was happening to him and, as some have suggested, chose to face his end in secret.

I had first met Lionel at the Bini Bon, a cheap Lower East Side restaurant where struggling artists of one kind or another came for the heavy-duty breakfasts. I was talking with David Murray when this rotund Negro in a nappy sweater started expounding on the nature of New York, sometimes sniffing and barely sneering as he explained the interwoven corruption of Manhattan. As I got to know him better I found out that he was a writer working on a book about lower Manhattan called *Traveling Light*. I saw an hilarious essay he wrote and began to encounter him on Second Avenue. When he was in a public place, Lionel would usually find someone to make the butt of a joke or the object, if not the subject, of a long lecture about some point in military history, literature, social origins, or whatever. Once, he stood up as he argued with someone, saying, "You don't know anything about black culture. Have you ever been in the Baptist church? Can you preach, you understand what I mean? *Preach!*" Lionel then summoned an enormous baritone and commenced to chant about the camel going through the eye of the needle, using "you got to bend down" as a kick phrase. All the while he was moving for the exit, and a jaunty step came into his hulking stride as he reached for the doorknob, still preaching, his words now hot with biblical references and that combination of flower and sweat so basic to the near-song of the Negro pulpit style. Lionel knew all heads had turned in his direction and he made a theatrical dip as he raised one finger in the air, reiterated his kick phrase—"Whoa, you got to bend down, you got to *bend* down!"—and went into the street.

But Lionel Mitchell wasn't only a character. He was a man of the mind who knew the streets, the overt and covert actions of human beings, the illegal or subterranean lives of those on the social and sexual outskirts of conventional society. His early life in New Orleans had taught him many things about the distances between appearances and secret facts, about the intricate crossings of bloodlines and cultures, histories and monies. And like any serious student of military history, Lionel knew the opposition in detail. Lionel could analyze white southerners by class, physical type, and point of European origin, and explain their social evolution. His account would begin with their getting off the boats, move on to the development of an economy based on slave labor and poor white trash, then detail its destruction by the irresistible innovations of the Union Army. He understood the gloomy empire of segregation and violence that rose in the wake of Reconstruction and the importance of Negro colleges in preparing the way for most of the major movers in Negro American political history. "Yes, it was in those lowly little backwater nigger colleges that the intellectual ammunition necessary to take these crackers on was smelted and poured *boiling hot* into those thick wooly skulls."

It was because Lionel knew so much that he was a refreshing answer to simplifications about racial history. "House niggers? What are these fools talking about? I submit that Toussaint L'Ouverture was the greatest house nigger in history! These little fake nigger intellectuals better read. They better sit down with Mr. Frederick Douglass, with Mr. William Faulkner, with a whole lot of goddam books so they can cover their asses with some *facts*."

In his 1980 novel, *Traveling Light*, Mitchell showed just what his potential was. I still think, as I once wrote, that it, "unlike most contemporary Negro fiction, conceives of black American life as part of a cultural complex that includes many races, religions, and folkways in Southern and Northern situations. Uneven, episodic, and loose-ended, it is nevertheless insightful, eloquent, finely observed, and orchestrated by both an ironic awareness of pretension and an irreverence that do fierce battle with the maudlin (although occasionally succumbing to it)." The book never went anywhere and was soon remaindered, though Lionel lived at the peak of a dream while it was hot off the presses. His boasting led to a confrontation with one of the slew of empty-headed Puerto Rican street boys he paid for their favors, often pretending that he was giving them spiritual and intellectual guidance. The boy, tired of Lionel's patting himself on the back, struck the writer twice over the head with the heavy metal springs of a bull-worker. But Lionel, who had no dog in him, got out his knife and nearly gutted the boy. "All I ever want is the strength to take one with me. I know it's dangerous messing around with these boys. I would have to be a fool not to know it. Right next to my bed I have a knife soaking in garlic juice. If they come for me, all I say is, 'Lord, don't let me die *alone*.'"

Well, he did die alone, fighting something no knife could stop. I had last seen him about eight weeks ago in the *Voice* office, sitting dejected with his belt all the way over to the last hole and his pants bunched and slipping down beneath the loops. It was then he told me he had had a mild stroke and asked if I could loan him five dollars for some food. I did and walked him out of the office. From what I have been able to gather, Lionel soon got more and more down. Henry LaFarge, a long-time friend from New Orleans, remembers visiting him in the last days. The usually unkempt apartment on 11th and Second Avenue, which had been a clearing house for boy prostitutes, was absolutely filthy. Roaches covered the floor and the walls, cans of cat food were opened and thrown about, the cat box hadn't been emptied for weeks, and all of Lionel's plants were dead. He was soon evicted and began staying with friends, usually leaving because he had lost control of his bodily functions, filthying himself and their homes. At one point, he traveled north near the Connecticut border to try and stay in a monastery. Rejected, he was later arrested for defecating in the park, then sent back to New York, where he finally went to Bellevue. There they pushed tubes down one end and up the other, through his nose, and fixed one for urination. He was incapable of speech when people visited him, sometimes turning in bed until the machines went crazy, which led to his hands being tied. Soon, he was dead.

I don't know if Lionel's story qualifies as a cautionary tale; I don't know if anyone's does. He was much more than the horror of his end, than the obsession with young boys, than the willingness to roar above it all at any time. He was his own man, conflicted, complex, compassionate. I have known few as individual, and I know his like has railed through this life only once.

MISSISSIPPI BLUES
December 25, 1984

Martha Lacy Hall's *Music Lesson* contains some of the best short fiction around. When she gets up on her beat, Hall brings together a fine eye and an invincible ear for the sweep and intricacy of life in Sweet Bay, Mississippi. She knows all the modernist tricks that make for speed of allusion, manipulation of time, and dramatic contrast, and almost always uses them to bring down big game; she doesn't disturb the silence to shoot at an empty horizon. *Music Lesson* is her *Dubliners:* it's the "moral history" of a society, investigating the possibilities of "spiritual liberation," and detailing the problem of "paralysis." What William York Tindall wrote of Joyce's stories could just as easily describe Hall's: "His stories, faithful to his intention, betray impotence, frustration, and death. . . . The paralysis of Joyce's Dubliners is moral, intellectual, and spiritual." In Hall's fiction, the paralysis—or the struggle against it—occurs within the eroding conventions of a society that is part racist, part nostalgic, and given to violence in unexpected situations.

Hall shows imposing skill at delivering the stings and satisfactions, the revelations and horrors of life as they appear at different plateaus of experience. Her small children are as complete as her adolescents, her college girls as naïve and feisty as her middle-aged parents are steady and mature, while the older women who visit their erstwhile teachers in rest homes or attend the funerals of their relatives have appropriately seasoned souls. Hall shows the sibling jealousies and animosities that sometimes influence relationships long after childhood has passed. At the bottom of it all, she has a sophisticated, humorous, and tragic sense of life in which bravery and terror, violence and inertia function in a moral context. Compassion is at the center of her canon, and she makes clear how important it is to understand the nature of another's life before judging. But death, dissolution, and change snip at her characters and their world.

Hall is concerned with the ways in which children, adolescents, middle-aged and older people face or flee their fates, learn or refuse to learn about life's scarification. The emotional complexities of family dynamics over the years, the ever-present influence of the Negro on Southern white life, the changes in individual consciousness, the evaporation of eras into memory, and the inevitable unfairness of human fate are her basic themes. She does not describe; she brings to life. Just as a musical instrument contains a universe of dormant sounds, her stories compress whole sweeps of detail and feeling that envelop you after a few paragraphs. Hall's vision is heroic as well as intimate; the dragons her people face are fire-breathing demons of the soul, when not provincial attitudes and habits that impair apprehension of the humanity in others. Hall knows that when one limits other people's possibilities, the circumscribed vision also shackles one's own life to a contrived image. And since she is talking about the South, she shows how a romantic nostalgia for a universe that never really existed can put a character out of step with the world. But what brings a loud cheer to the front of the reader's spirit is Hall's awareness that we are often handed grand batons by example and that they aid us in the race to meet the carnivore of time.

Six of Hall's stories are told in the first person, four in the third. With one exception, her central characters are female, girls or women of various backgrounds with distinctly different personalities and perspectives. Some are reticent, others prideful, a few melancholy or bitter, and a number given to empathetic wit and philosophical overviews that never deny the measure of tragedy. Visits are used in a variety of ways, with the central characters going into worlds usually counterpointed by recall or expectation.

The masterful "Joanna" does it all. It contains superbly manipulated recollections of a once great and arrogant beauty who became an alcoholic, reared her children, dropped dead, and lay on her kitchen floor for four days before the corpse was discovered. Virginia, Joanna's younger sister, goes to pay her last respects, driving alone from New Orleans to their old hometown in Mississippi, reflecting on how Joanna had always hated her for being born last and taking away the title of baby daughter. The tragedy of Joanna's life is balanced by memories of her autocratic sassiness and the joy she brought before her soul was swallowed by drink.

To achieve her effects, Hall uses the interplay between past and present, emotion and technology, that's essential to modern writing. She describes it this way as Virginia drives to Mississippi:

> She looked in the rearview mirror to see what she looked like, reciting childhood verse on her way to her sister's funeral. Dr. Foster was part of a shift into the past that began yesterday, almost the moment her brother called. As they talked, it was as though someone kept switching television channels from the evening news to an old movie.

Besides confidently appropriating an image from McLuhan's *The Medium Is the Massage,* which showed the rearview mirror of a car containing the image of a covered wagon, Hall embraces film as a metaphor for experience rather than a threat to literature.

But that old movie often arrives in montage or brief recapitulations of time, place, and emotion that have the kind of impact Hemingway begat in the italicized intermissions between the tales of *In Our Time:*

> When Joanna's freewheeling ebullience persisted after she was "adult" and married to Kip, who went next door to kiss his mother goodnight every night until she died just before he did, old heads nodded over Joanna and watched impatiently for her to settle down to behavior prescribed for young wives in Sweet Bay. But she continued, as a married woman, to wear short shorts and bounce with the rhythm of her baby grand as she beat out jazz and swing. She chain smoked, learned to drink bourbon with Kip and his friends, and developed a laugh you could hear a block away. She was just too much, they sighed. She was also as sensitive as a fresh wound. Nobody ever seemed to catch onto that. If the gypsies who used to camp every spring out in the Heaslips' pasture had stolen Joanna, what a life she could have lived.

This is writing that combines colloquial with formal and brings the scope of the epic to a single paragraph. It contains the texture of actual life, of an individual bending local convention, awareness of the pain beneath an apparently cavalier personality, anger at the fact that Joanna's spirit was never understood, and at the whimsical way people often put things in place by imagining that the damaged goods of the heart might have escaped a sorrowful fate had the mythical freedom of a group like the gypsies intruded. But no. Joanna, also known as Red McCall, was doomed:

> Joanna's laughter lost its mirth. At thirty she was an alcoholic, by forty an eccentric recluse, and at fifty a widow. She would have been sixty had she lived another month. For years she had been one of the town's many drunks. She had locked her doors, literally, against her family, sometimes even her own grown sons. She locked Mama out— Mama now long dead of her own heart attack. She locked Daddy out, who lived twenty years a widower, but not before she made off with some of his favorite possessions—furniture, odds and ends. He had

disinherited her before he put out his last Pall Mall and hacked his final emphysemic cough. He spent his last decade in bitterness, glad to be steadfastly furious enough with his child to "cut her out—a disgrace to us all." As he railed against Joanna he never evoked one recognizable image of her. She had become a monster, foreign, his fascinating, red-headed McCall child.

In fifteen pages, Hall executes so many things with a commanding grasp of vitality, heartbreak, and the details of nature, fashion, utensils, and architecture that not only does the life of Joanna stand up on the page and roar out its humanity, but the personalities and fates of an entire family and town emerge with equal force. There are no vague supporting characters. There are also no happy endings. All of the people are now old and either in bad health or pretending to be. Virginia, whose own husband's face and pace have been changed by a stroke, feels melancholy and disappointed with her surviving brothers and sisters, not one of whom attends Joanna's funeral. Nelda, the eldest sister, is a hypochondriac who has chosen to remain "ill" so that the role of pampered belle sequestered from the rude world by her rich husband can be made to fit the present-day South. Nelda has no intention of going to the funeral, though her husband, Frank, will drive Virginia.

> "Francis is much more upset over this than I am. It came as no surprise to me. I've been expecting it for years. Joanna withdrew from family and all society years ago. I knew that sooner or later this very thing would happen. Now it has. The last time she came here—two or three years ago—she went straight to the bar—it was ten o'clock in the morning—and she revisited it several times before she left— about noon. She didn't seem intoxicated. I've been interviewing a woman—a maid."
> "Oh. Are you going to hire her?"
> "I am not."
> "Oh?"
> "When they walk in here like that—I've been through all this too often—they're all ruined. The Roosevelts started it. You can't remember all that."
> "Nor the defeat of the Armada. Nor Appomattox."
> "What?"
> "Has Hattie quit?"
> "No, but she can't be here every hour of every day. I've got to have somebody to fill in, Virginia. I'm an invalid. I seldom go downstairs. Nobody realizes how bad my health is. . . . Francis traipses from clinic to clinic with me, he doesn't know how bad I feel—or care."

It is obvious that Nelda, like Joanna, removed herself from society years ago. She has the brat's self-pity, snootiness, and ease in the face of her own ignorance. Without a doubt, she personifies all that was horrible in the more genteel wings of the old South, just as she symbolizes the self-destruction inherent in choosing a gilded cage over the shifts of sky and weather.

As the story moves toward the grating blues of Joanna's funeral, Hall recreates the Mississippi of the 1930s and '40s. We get the feel of the Depression, the pieties and proprieties, the breathlessness of holidays, the shape and smell of the gardens, the photographs of movie stars, and the joy that fuses with awe and admiration when a free spirit blasts its Roman candle light through the sky. There is a touching placelessness to the feeling of the funeral as Virginia finds herself among people who appear from out of the past, worn and reshaped by time into different faces and bodies, capable of no more than trivial comments that increase the feeling of loss.

"The Visit" is another extraordinary story. In 1943, Marianne, a girl from Chicago who has come South, is invited for a weekend's entertainment to the home of Betsy Cameron, one of her classmates. But the community is heated up over the impending execution of a Negro who has killed a white man. Again, Hall gives life with imagery:

> But now here we were, uniform, in our box-pleated skirts, saddle oxfords, and baggy sweaters, peter pan dickies, and pearls (mine "simulated," of course), sitting three abreast, tootling down the highway in Marcy's little blue '38 Chevrolet coupé, singing "I Don't Want to Set the World on Fire" ("I just want to start a flame in your heart").

Marianne enters World War II Mississippi as an outsider from the lower-middle class who experiences the culture of what looks like the unchallenged domain of Southern whites. It isn't simple for her to grasp, though she learns very quickly that "everything seemed to date from the Civil War, seventy-eight years after Appomattox." At college, Negro women cleaned the dorms, sang in the kitchen "like in the movies," laughed and clapped as the white girls "jitterbugged to records in the spacious end of Winifred Weatherby Dining Hall before dinner," took care of the students' clothes for extra money, and carried names like Iceophene, whose accent demanded translation. But as the tale progresses, those Negroes expand into figures both on and off stage who have much more impact on the lives of the whites than their positions of servitude would suggest.

As Marianne "becomes" a Southerner, Hall subtly sneaks in the effect on her diction: she has the Chicago girl tell us, "Betsy cut her eyes toward me"—a verb nobody from her background would normally use. Marianne becomes a Mississippian because she is taken by the feeling of warmth and ease that radiates from the Cameron home. "I saw it all as with the click of a camera," Marianne tells us. Then with startling artistry, Hall builds houses, fills closets, prints magazines and comic books, knits coasters for bottles of Coke, and gives the characters voices that contain within their vocabularies and rhythms not only their social places, but their aspirations, values, and senses of humor.

The paternalism of Judge Cameron and his family toward the impoverished and uneducated Negroes isn't denied, nor is the moral influence exerted on the Camerons by Lily, the black servant who makes no bones about believing the judge should call the governor and plead for a stay of execution.

> "Lily's after me again. Abaloyd's mother is about to drive her crazy. I can't help them. If intervention were indicated, I'd intervene, or try to, but it's all over and done with. And the governor wouldn't listen to me under any circumstances. He can't forgive me for not supporting him. And he knows that if he runs for the Senate, I won't support him for that."

Hall knows that this kind of moral pressure set the stage for many of the changes that took place in the South, however many howls were heard when more was demanded than paternalistic kindness. It is quite easy for Mrs. Cameron to call the killer Abaloyd a boy and the dead white fellow a man, just as she can easily say, "He has a wife and a houseful of little pickaninnies, of course." There is no avoiding the human context of the matter, though, and we are shown that even the sense of entitlement underlying paternalism doesn't make it any easier for Mrs. Cameron to stop worrying about her own son's fate in the forthcoming invasion of Italy, than it is for the offstage mother of Abaloyd as she awaits his execution.

Marianne comes to see the communal nature of experience that transcends race. Hall builds the elements with great skill and brings off a lyric conclusion that could easily have sunk to a mushy bottom. Marianne goes with the family to the railroad station and watches as the arrival of a troop train shows yet again how the wages of war are the same for all, regardless of segregated cars.

> Then we saw a pine box, a coffin, being brought through the wide baggage-car opening. A spic-and-span colored soldier was shaking hands with several people; then he helped some men move the box down our way and onto the back of a flatbed truck.
>
> Mrs. Cameron leaned forward to look. "Some colored boy," she said. We could see people come and stand close to the back of the truck. A woman was weeping, having to be supported. The soldier turned to her and removed his cap and laid his hand on her shoulder, and she looked up at him, her face twisted in soft brown lumps of sorrow.

As the story continues, Mrs. Cameron identifies with the mother of the dead soldier, obviously wondering if she, too, will await a coffin, and is brought around only through one of her daughter's loud and laughable whistles, summoning Judge Cameron back to the car for the trip home. The story concludes as Betsy raises her arm and waves to "a plump, middle-aged waiter" in the dining car. He is not described as Negro, though we know he must be. By this time, Hall's people are free to see the humanity first, if only for a few moments.

But the old South without terror is no South at all, and Hall proves that with "The Peaceful Eye." It is a tale about violence inspired by the brutal god of racial purity, a tale that grows to a horrifying conclusion as each paragraph moves further and further away from what initially seems an idyllic and mysterious adventure. When young Mary, the story's heroine, first expresses revulsion at having to go visit Miss Emma's house, we think it is no more than a child's problem with an older person's eccentricities. As Mary dutifully performs the errand for her school teacher, Miss Scott, Hall again manages to create the breadth and feel of a community's life:

> Miss Scott wasn't Miss Scott anymore. She was Mrs. Fite. Last year she had married Billy Fite, a fat little meatcutter who cried and called his mother when it lightninged. Everyone in town knew about that. Billy was a butcher—a butcher! Everyone called him a meatcutter. It somehow sounded better—almost artistic. Billy wore a bloody apron, and Mary had watched him cleave the largest joint of a cow with one blow of that great axe-like knife. It was a splendid and terrifying performance, and Mary knew that Billy put his heart and soul into that blow. Afterward he would strike the surface of his square block of a tree that was his table and leave his meat axe vibrating while he wiped his hands on his blood-browned apron. He had a sweet shy smile.

Once more Hall's narrative combines the feeling of a young girl looking at something and the consciousness of a grown woman remembering, the diction flowing back and forth between the language of youth and adulthood. It also sets up a distinction between the lack of sentimentality toward killing animals for food and the reaction to slaughtering them for unforgivable reasons. The unforgiveable act is committed by Miss Emma.

> . . . Mary used to spend hours in Miss Emma's porch swing, her toes barely scraping the clean gray-painted floor. As she swung gently back and forth, her fingers would travel up and down the links of chain, and she and Miss Emma talked about all sorts of things. The porch faced east and was lovely and shaded in the afternoons—in the spring fragrant with wisteria and magnolia fuscatas humming with bumblebees. . . . But all of this ended for Mary months ago.

We come to learn that there is something more than casually significant to the fact that "Miss Emma's yard was surrounded by hedges—low boxwood up near the house but an eight-foot privet down by the cedar, to screen off the Negro quarter which started right across the street." Miss Emma, we're told, "loved Silky better than anyone or anything. She brushed her and fussed over her and never let her run with the other dogs in the neighborhood. Last spring when it was discovered that Silky was going to have puppies, Mary thought Miss Emma might go crazy over it, she was so upset." Miss Emma does go crazy, and what she decides to do brings all the racial hatred up to the top within a symbolic context that, attempted by a lesser talent, would probably hit the canvas face forward as Roberto Duran did in his fateful meeting with Tommy Hearns, the Motor City Cobra. But Hall is a mongoose if there ever was one, and the power with which she attacks her subject is as uplifting as it is horrifying. It is, like "Joanna" and "The Visit," probably some kind of recent classic, but this time out, a moral diving bell that explores the connection between racism, genocide, and ecological disaster.

Yet Hall's world isn't without humor or jauntiness. "Just a Little Sore Throat" is a very funny story about how the woman with the biggest bustline in the town must reveal herself when examined by the new doctor, all of the events observed by the young girl who goes to the office with her. "Lucky Lafe" is told by a man in his sixties who recounts the adventures and losses of a much-admired friend; Hall shapes his talk perfectly, taking the occasion to strut the brusque precision of her ear. "The Man Who Gave Brother Double Pneumonia" captures sibling rivalry again, this time as an older sister is sentenced to have her hair cut— yet again—at the barbershop with her little brother and fumes as she becomes the butt of jokes about looking like a boy. "Privacy" is a sweet and witty tale told by an eavesdropper. She overhears an older woman being castigated by her sister for wasting her life on a husband who was once a high school athletic star but has been an embarrassing and shiftless—though elegantly dressed—town drunk for many years. At the conclusion, we discover that the drunk's wife is no victim at all: she has a clandestine love affair with a man who has worshiped her for decades. I didn't like the other stories as much, though that doesn't matter when a writer can create the kinds of successes Hall does if everything is working for her. That a writer of her talent is published by a university press when so many books from the major houses these days are filled with tales soggy at their centers is *truly* ironic. But what's important is that Hall's work will be around as long as readers wish to learn more about the vagaries of the human soul.

NATIONALISM OF FOOLS
October 29, 1985

There again were the black suits and red ties, the bodyguards in blue uniforms, the women in white, the aloof cast of the eyes and the earthy manner: the Nation of Islam. Twenty-five years ago it was Malcolm X's show, though he could never have filled Madison Square Garden. On October 7, 25,000 people turned out to hear Louis Farrakhan.

They queued up outside—the poor and the young, the unemployed and the gang members, the middle-class Negroes. They were anxious to get in and hear someone attack the people they felt were responsible for their positions in the burgeoning illiterate mass; or they were there out of curiosity, intent on hearing for themselves what Farrakhan was about. Many came because they were happy to support a black man the "white-controlled" media unanimously hated. Or because Mayor Koch had called Farrakhan "the devil," usurping the Muslims' term for the white enemy—if Koch hated him, he might be lovable, an understandable reaction given the long-standing antipathy between the mayor and New York's black community. I also think many were there, especially the young, because they had never been to a mass black rally to hear a speaker who didn't appear to care what white people thought of him, a man who seemed to think their ears were more important than those of Caucasians.

The atmosphere at Madison Square Garden was unusual. Though the speeches started two and a half hours late, the audience was patient, partly out of respect and partly out of awareness that the Fruit of Islam doesn't play. A fool and his seat would soon have parted. I overheard one young black man saying that he could look at the Muslims with their neatness and their discipline, their sense of confidence and their disdain for white privilege, and understand their appeal: "They look like the last thing they ever think about is kissing some white boody." After repeatedly telling a blond female photographer that she couldn't sit in the aisle, one of the FOI said, to the joy of the black people listening, "Miss, I asked you three times to *please* not sit in the aisle. Now you will either get your behind over or you will get your behind *out*." And there was something else. As one woman put it, "Well, what can you say? Nobody looks better than a black man in a uniform. Look at all those handsome black men. I know I wouldn't want to be in the Nation, but I wouldn't mind it if they lived on *my* block. I bet there wouldn't be any mugging and dope dealing and all of *that*." From the outside, at least, Farrakhan's group projects a vision of restraint and morality. It's about smoothing things out, upholding the family, respecting the woman, doing an honest day's work, avoiding dissipation, and defining the difference between the path of the righteous and the way of the wicked. At one point the commander of the FOI came to the microphone and said that he could smell reefer smoke. He asked that anyone who saw those guilty parties report them to "the nearest brother." Wherever the puffing was going on, it stopped.

Beginning in 1959, when the press started bird-dogging Malcolm X, the Muslims' disdain for white people seared through the networks, eventually influencing the tone, the philosophy, and the tactics of black politics. The Nation of Islam offered a rageful revision that would soon have far more assenters than converts. Though it seemed at first only a fanatical cult committed to a bizarre version of Islam, Elijah Muhammad's home-made Nation was far from an aberration. The Nation fit perfectly in a century we might appropriately call "The Age of Redefinition." Its public emergence coincided with the assault on Western convention, middle-class values, and second-class citizenship that shaped the '60s in America. The whole question of what constituted civilized behavior and civilized tradition was being answered in a variety of wild ways. So Elijah Muhammad's sect was part of the motion that presaged transcendental meditation, sexual revolution, LSD, cultural nationalism, black power, the Black Panther Party, the anti-Vietnam War movement, feminism, and other trends that surely appalled the Muslims as thoroughly as the Nation did its roughest critics. As much as anything else, those angry home-grown Muslims foretold the spirit of what was later known as "the counterculture."

But Elijah Muhammad's counterculture was black. Where others explained the world's problems with complex theories ranging from economic exploitation to sexism, Muhammad simply pinned the tail on the white man. In his view, black integrationists were only asking for membership in hell, since the white man was a devil "grafted" from black people in an evil genetic experiment by a mad, pumpkin-headed scientist named Yacub. That experiment took place 6000 years ago. Now the white man was doomed, sentenced to destruction by Allah. If "so-called American Negroes" separated themselves from the imposed values of white culture, then moved into their own land, black suffering would cease. In calling for five or six states as "back payment for slavery," Muhammad reiterated a Negro Zionism rooted in the "back to Africa" schemes of the middle 19th century, which had last fizzled under the leadership of Marcus Garvey.

In the context of prevailing media images and public racial struggle, this was all new. Here were Negroes who considered *themselves* the chosen people. They proclaimed that the black man was the original man, the angel, and that since the first devils to roll off Yacub's assembly line were the Jews, the idea of *their* being the chosen was a lot of baloney. By embracing Muhammad's version of Islam, his followers stepped outside of Judeo-Christian civilization, asserting their African roots at exactly the same time Africans were coming out from under colonialism and remarkable shifts in world power were in the offing. They declared the white man a thief and a murderer: he had ripped off the secrets of science from Africa. (Muhammad's ministers taught that Egypt was an acronym for "he gypped you.") Using the Africans' information, the blue-eyed devil went on to steal land all over the world, including America from the Indian. The Muslims "exposed" Christianity as no more than a tool to enslave black people, a way of getting them to deny their origins and worship a "white Jesus" (when the Savior was described in Revelations as having skin the color of burnished brass and hair akin to pure lamb's wool). They spoke of dark skin and thick lips as beautiful, charging that the mulatto look of light skin, thin lips, and "good" hair was the mark of shame, of rape on the plantation. In attacking the Caucasian standard of beauty, the Muslims foreshadowed the "black is beautiful" buttons and revisionist images of race and gender we would soon hear from all quarters.

Though most of what they said was no further out than the mythological tales of biblical heroes, their explanations lacked poetic grandeur. But their exotic integrity made that irrelevant. Just as there is a beauty in a well-made club or knife or rifle, there is a beauty in those who yield to nothing but their own ideals and the discipline necessary to achieve them. The Muslims had that kind of attraction, particularly for those who had known the chaos of drug addiction, prostitution, loneliness, abject poverty. Suddenly here were all these clean-cut, well-dressed young men and women men, mostly. You recognized them from the neighborhood. They had been pests or vandals, thieves or gangsters. Now they were back from jail or prison and their hair was cut close, their skin was smooth, they no longer cursed blue streaks, and the intensity in their eyes remade their faces. They were "in the Nation" and that meant that new men were in front of you, men who greeted each other in Arabic, who were aloof, confident, and intent on living differently than they had. Now the mention of a cool slice of ham on bread with mayonnaise and lettuce disgusted them. Consuming the pig was forbidden and food was eaten once a day because a single throe of digestion "preserved the intestines." Members didn't smoke, drink, use drugs, dance, go to movies or sports events.

The Muslims' vision of black unity, economic independence, and "a true knowledge of self" influenced the spirit of black organization as the Civil Rights Movement waned. Few took notice that it was much easier to call white people names and sneer at voter registration drives from podiums in the North than to face the cattle prods, the bombings, and the murders in the South. Since the destruction of America was preordained, the Muslims scorned efforts to change the system. Theirs was the world of what the French call "the total no."

Though they were well mannered and reliable, the Muslims were too provincial and conservative to attract the kind of mass following that would pose a real political threat. Yet as chief black heckler of the Civil Rights Movement, Malcolm X began to penetrate the consciousness of young black people, mostly in the North. While his platform was impossible, a cockeyed racial vision of history that precluded any insights into human nature, young Negroes loved to watch him upset white people, shocking them no end with his attacks on their religion, their history, their morality, their political system, and their sense of superiority. He described nonviolence as nonsense. And he said it all with an aggressive, contemptuous tone that had never been heard from a black man on the air. What we witnessed was the birth of black saber rattling.

Malcolm quickly became what is now called a cult hero. But for all the heated, revisionist allusions to history and exploitation, Malcolm X's vision was far more conventional than King's. Where the Southern Christian Leadership Council and the Student Non-Violent Coordinating Committee were making use of the most modern forms of boycott, media pressure, and psychological combat, revealing the werewolf of segregation under a full moon, Malcolm X brought the philosophy of the cowboy movie into Negro politics: characters who turned the other cheek were either naïve or cowardly. The Civil War had cost 622,500 lives; the Civil Rights Movement had brought about enormous change against violent opposition without losing 100 troops. But you could never have told that listening to Malcolm X, who made each casualty sound like 100,000. He talked like one of those gunfighters determined to organize the farmers against the violent, vicious cattlemen. One of his last speeches was even called "The Bullet or the Ballot." Hollywood had been there first.

In the wake of Malcolm X's assassination and canonization came the costume balls of cultural nationalism and the loudest saber rattlers of them all, the Black Panther Party. Both persuasions rose from the ashes of the urban riots, each dominated by egomaniacs who brooked no criticism, defining all skeptics as Uncle Toms. They gathered thunder as the Civil Rights Movement floundered. The remarkable Bob Moses of SNCC abdicated following the murders of Schwerner, Goodman, and Chaney. The organization became a shambles as white support was driven out. Stokely Carmichael and Rap Brown devoted their efforts to inflammatory rabble rousing, encouraging the anarchy of urban "revolts." King was felled in Memphis. America then endured the spectacles of Ron Karenga and LeRoi Jones, Eldridge Cleaver and Huey Newton. Hollywood didn't miss the point: it turned pulp politics into pulp films. Black exploitation movies saved a few studios as Negro heroes moved from scene to scene beating up white villains, usually gangsters, in chocolate-coated James Bond thrillers. It all wore thin as would-be radical black youth discovered that romanticizing Africa and wearing robes or calling for the violent overthrow of the American government led to little more than pretentious exotica and the discovery that the police weren't paper tigers.

When Elijah Muhammad died in 1975, Louis Farrakhan was a member of the Nation's upper echelon. He had seen the organization survive Malcolm X's defection in 1964. So it must have been rough on him when Muhammad's son Wallace repudiated his father's teachings, opting for regulation Islam. Suddenly, Farrakhan was back in the world without a filter. Elijah Muhammad's vision had created an extended family of believers destined to come out in front when Allah gave the word and evil was struck down. Now Wallace was spurning seclusion from society and the guarantees that come with apocalyptic prophecy. And there was another problem. Elijah Muhammad had explicitly aimed his teachings at the downtrodden black man in America, not Muslims in their own countries. When charged with distorting Islam, he had explained that this was a special medicine for a special case, a people who had "no knowledge of self." Submitting to conventional Islam meant giving Middle Eastern Muslims the inside lane. But Louis Farrakhan wasn't about to become just another one of millions of Muslims. The Charmer, as he was known when he was a singer, wanted to lead. And he did: he broke with Wallace to carry on Elijah Muhammad's teachings.

Now, after 30 years of watching others chased by reporters and interviewed on national television, Farrakhan has his moment. Malcolm X is dead, King is dead, the Panthers have been declawed, Eldridge Cleaver is born again, Ron Karenga and LeRoi Jones are college professors, and the factions devoted to urban guerrilla warfare have been either snuffed out or chased into hiding. Now it is all his, the mantle of extreme militance, and the media hang on his words, no matter what they make of him. He is a national, if not an international, figure, a man who can draw turn-away crowds, get $5 million from Qaddafi, and surround himself with a surprising array of supporters.

The appearance of Louis Farrakhan at this time seems a comment on the failures of black, liberal, and conservative politics since the Nixon era, when cultural nationalists started putting on suits and Marxist revolutionaries sought the great leap forward of tenured professorships. Though black mayors were elected in more and more cities, and many millions were spent to eradicate obstacles to Negro American success, the thrust of these attempts at social change was no more accurate than Chester Himes's blind man with the pistol. The epidemic proportions of illiteracy, teenage pregnancy, and crime in Negro communities across the nation tell us what went wrong. The schools became worse and worse, the salaries for teachers less and less; there were no serious efforts (including welfare cutbacks) to discourage teenage parenthood; and the courts were absurdly lenient with criminals. The result is a black lower class perhaps more despairing and cynical than we have ever seen.

But conservative programs have been equally deadly. While the administration chips away at the voting rights of black Southerners and panders to religious fundamentalists, it ignores human nature by deregulating the business sphere with such vengeance that the profits of stockholders take precedence over the environment. In this atmosphere,

Farrakhan's broad attacks are political rock and roll—loved more for the irritation they create than for their substance.

The guests who filled the podium gave the impression that Farrakhan had a broader base than assumed. They included Christian ministers, American Indians, Palestinians, Stokely Carmichael, and Chaka Khan. Of Khan's presence, one young man said, "She shouldn't have done that. Her record sales are going to go down. Those Jews ain't going to like that. She might be through." I wasn't so sure of that, but if black people were in equivalent positions in the record business, I doubt they would think lightly of a white star sitting on a podium with the Ku Klux Klan.

When things finally kicked off, a Christian choir opened with a song and Stokely Carmichael spoke first. He bobbed and flailed, often pushing his head past the microphone. The sound went up and down; some sentences came through clearly, others were half-heard. He attacked Zionism, calling for war against Israel and recognition of the "sacredness" of Africa, where Moses and Jesus were protected when in trouble. The intensity was so immediate and Carmichael got carried away so quickly that the address seemed more a high-powered act than anything else. In his white robe and white hair the lean and tall West Indian looked much like the ghost of Pan-African nationalism past. As Kwame Touré, he carried the names of fallen idols, African leaders who resorted to dictatorial control when things didn't go the way they wanted, whether that meant throttling the press or subjecting the opposition to the infamous "black diet." But then much of what Carmichael has had to say since the black power years has been itself a black diet, a form of intellectual starvation in which the intricacies of international politics are reduced to inflammatory tribalism.

A Palestinian, Said Arafat, attacked Zionism as "a cancer" and called for "the total liberation of Palestine." Russell Means, one of the founders of the American Indian Movement, gave a predictable address about an Indian taking his tomahawk to an insulting white man. Then a golem popped out of his bandana: "When we were in Los Angeles the Jews did a number on Mr. Farrakhan." He concluded by saying, "I want you all to remember that Hollywood has denigrated and debased every race of people, but there are no plays or movies denigrating the Jewish people." (Half right, half wrong. As J. Hoberman points out, many movies with Jewish stereotypes were made during the silent era, but the moguls backed off when sound came in, yielding to community pressure. And though Hollywood's contribution to "negative images" of ethnic groups is unarguable, it is also true that revisionist Westerns such as the classic *Fort Apache* started appearing long before AIM was founded.)

All the speeches were short and made their points. Then the featured attraction was introduced. The audience rose to its feet and burst forth with a heroic sound, filling the Garden with a gigantic chord of collected voices. Very soon, Farrakhan proved his shrewdness, highhandedly using the rhetoric of social movements he would have opposed 25 years ago. When the applause ended, Farrakhan called attention to the female bodyguards who surrounded him and claimed that Elijah Muhammad was the first black leader to liberate the woman. Point of fact, the Muslims used to say, "The black woman is the field in which the black man sows his nation." But after all, the past is silly putty to men like Farrakhan, who used the subject of women as the first of many themes he would pass through or over. "The world is in the condition it is," he said, "because it doesn't respect women." Growing bolder, Farrakhan attacked the separation of the sexes in traditional Islam, saying women should be allowed into the mosque. That will no doubt be quite a revelation in the Middle East, when Farrakhan goes on his promised Third World tour.

Farrakhan went on to be consistently incoherent for three hours, embodying the phrase "Didn't he ramble?" He circled many topics, always ending on his favorite subject: Louis Farrakhan. He talked about how good he looked, how he should be compared to Jesus, how the Jews were after him, how he was on a divine mission, how he would go to the Southwest and die with the Indians if necessary, how "examples" should be made of black leaders who criticized men like him, how black people needn't worry if they were called upon to go to war with America, since Allah would do for them what he did for David when the boy fought Goliath. He piled his points in Dagwood sandwiches of contradiction, moving from the "fact" that whites were invented devils to the observation that if America is hell, then those who run it must be devils; then obliquely referring to the *Annacalyptus,* an occult history, with the remark that we have never seen races evolve from light to dark, further proof that the "Asiatic black man" must be the father of all races. To finish off that run, Farrakhan dug out the anthropological findings in East Africa, which suggest that man originated there. Rounding the bases of absurdity, metaphor, and the occult, he hook-slid into science.

When Farrakhan wasn't talking about himself, he most frequently baited Jews. When he does that, Farrakhan plumbs the battles that have gone on between black people and Jews for almost 20 years. He speaks to (though not for) those who have fought with Jews over affirmative action, or have felt locked out of discussions about Middle East policy by Jews as willing to bully and deflect criticism with the term "anti-Semite" as black people were with "racist" 20 years ago. I'm sure he scores points with those who argue that Jewish media executives are biased in favor of Israel; who say that films like *Exodus,* TV movies about Entebbe, Golda Meir, Sadat, the stream of documentaries, docudramas, and miniseries given over to "the final solution" are all part of a justification for Zionism; who were angry when Hollywood saluted Israel's 30th anniversary with a television special, and cynically wondered if "those Hollywood Jews" would salute any other country's birth.

I don't know of any other country Hollywood has saluted, but a propaganda ploy by a few executives does not a conspiracy of six million Jewish

Americans make. (You can hear them whispering into the phone at your nearest deli, "Hey, Murray, I just got word we'll have another special coming up; spread the word in your block. But make sure no goyim are listening.") If such a conspiracy exists, how has it allowed South Africa, Israel's ally, to get such an overwhelming amount of bad press?

Of course, Israel's relationship to South Africa complicates the question. For all its moral proclamations, the Israelis supply arms to Botha's gang and refuse to cooperate with sanctions. This convinces certain quarters that Israel and its sympathizers support racial injustice and antidemocratic regimes, angering those who had a sense of international black struggle hammered into their minds by Malcolm X and his emulators. That sense of collective black effort was a sort of political evangelism, bent on saving the Third World from white savagery and exploitation, a racial variation on international revolutionary Marxism. (It was this sense of foreign destiny that inspired the back-to-Africa movements, which eventually led to the founding of Liberia, Israel's true forerunner—a country begun for free ex-slaves to the resentment of the 60 local tribes. One wonders how much Herzl and associates knew about Liberia and whether or not they were inspired by its example.) At present, however, it seems to put more emphasis on the interests of a foreign country than on the conditions of black Americans, a tendency I doubt we would see in the Jewish community if it had the same degree of social, educational, and economic problems that burden millions of Negroes.

But screwed-up priorities are nothing new to black politics, nor, unfortunately, are anti-Semitic attacks loosely using that most dangerous article of speech: "the." Those three letters fan conspiracy theories and push us back to the 1960s, when LeRoi Jones brought a grotesque refinement to anti-white sentiment by reading poetry that baited Jews on college campus after college campus, to the cheers of black students. Such tours probably had had more than a little to do with intensifying the Zionist fervor of many Jews who had been told to get out of civil rights organizations.

The failure of Jones, Karenga, and other black nationalists to realize their separatist dreams made for a jealousy that floats to the surface in the speeches of Louis Farrakhan, their heir. When Farrakhan makes references to Reagan "punking out" to the Jews or the Zionist lobby having "a stranglehold on the government of the United States," he is projecting the kind of power *he* wants onto the American-Israeli Public Affairs Committee, commonly called the Zionist lobby. In his version, however, Farrakhan feels free to make threats on the lives of black reporters, politicians, and anyone else who criticizes him.

The envy of AIPAC's influence reflects a nostalgia for the days when so much of the national dialogue was given over to the racial question and the quality of black life in the country was an issue at the front of the political bus. During those years, desegregation and racial double standards were the primary concerns. There was little room for anti-Jewish or anti-

Zionist feeling, regardless of how deep they might have run in black nationalist circles. Now the judas goat of Jewish conspiracy is trotted out again as an explanation for the loss of concentrated attention on black problems.

Yet it would make more sense to emulate the efforts of activist Jews that have made AIPAC, as Paul Findley's *They Dare to Speak Out* documents, such a force on Capitol Hill. Obviously, black leaders have failed to create a comparable force to lobby for the interests of Negro Americans. The nationalist rhetoric backfired and made black problems seem more those of a group in a self-segregated world than central to the country at large. As one black woman, infuriated by Farrakhan, said, "We should be putting our feet in the pants of these politicians. Get this dope out of here. Get these schools working. Clean up these neighborhoods. Do what we need done." The Jews who work in Israel's interest know the secret: hard work, fund-raising, monitoring voting patterns, petitioning, telephoning, writing to elected officials. It's difficult and laborious work, but it can get results. As that angered black woman concluded, "We can get all this up off our backs if we want to do something besides listen to some fool who hates ham talk like he's bad enough to exterminate somebody."

But for all his muddled convolutions, Farrakhan's vision isn't small. He wants it all. The world. Who else would feel free to promise that he would tell the Muslims of the Middle East how they had distorted Islam? Who else would claim to be single-handedly raising a people from the death of ignorance and self-hatred?

Though Farrakhan's address was supposed to reveal his economic program, his ideas about black-produced mouthwash, toothpaste, and sanitary napkins took up only 10 or 15 of his 180-minute montage of misconceptions. They were cheered now and again, as was almost everything he said. I doubt, however, that the black people there rising to their feet, screaming themselves hoarse, roaring as though he was scoring baskets as he bounced his ideas off their heads, followed his content. What clarity there was had little connection to a black American point of view. Though his look and his podium style owe much to the black church, his ideas were dominated by a bent Islamic fundamentalism that might get him more money from Arabs. But whatever the underlying goals, Farrakhan's cosmology has little chance of overthrowing the strong tradition of Negro culture, custom, and thought improvised in the "wilderness of North America," as Elijah Muhammad might say. Few black people will ever believe that Farrakhan is so divinely significant that if the Jews try to touch him Allah will bring down the blood of the righteous on America and they will all be killed outright. As a guy sitting near my row pointed out, "Anybody who uses the first person pronoun as much as he does can't be saying anything. If they were, they would just say it, not keep telling you how great the one who is *about* to say it is."

But Farrakhan isn't just your garden-variety megalomaniac. "Louis Farrakhan," said one woman editor who lives in Harlem, "is a creep. He is a fascist and has nothing to say. Whenever people try to defend him by saying he's speaking out, I always wonder what the hell they mean. He has nothing to offer but half-truths, he tries to intimidate the black press into a cheering squad or a bunch of silent lampposts. His exterior is clean and neat, but his insides are dirty and his talk is pure sloppiness. How can educated people like him? It's just laziness. All they want is to anger some white people, or pretend he's angering them in any way serious enough to warrant the attention he's getting. Nowadays if you try to bring up a serious topic in a lot of middle-class black circles, people want to change the subject and treat you like you're causing trouble. This kind of thing is crazy."

The real deal is that few intellectually sophisticated black people are ever seen on television discussing issues. Reporters seem to prefer men like Louis Farrakhan and Jesse Jackson over genuine thinkers and scholars. Farrakhan obviously reads little that gives him any substantive information, and Jackson admitted in his *Playboy* interview that he hates to read. As Playthell Benjamin, one of Harlem's finest minds, says, "There is a ban on black intellectuals in the media. As the '60s proved, if we were allowed back into the area of discussion, the nature of the social vision would be radically changed, from politics to art. There are all kinds of men like Maynard Jackson, David Levering Lewis, Albert Murray, and others who could bring this sophistry and nonsense to a halt. They could make the dialogue more sophisticated." Benjamin is absolutely on the money. We rarely get to hear the ideas of black people who have spent many years studying and thinking and assessing their American experience and the policies of this country around the world.

By and large, those were not the kinds of people who came to hear Louis Farrakhan, roaring and cheering until the evening was finished off by an overripe Chaka Khan singing, strangely, a song called "Freedom," a cappella and quite beautifully. Beyond the podium and not far from Farrakhan's white limousine were the young women bodyguards, who had stood through the entire three-hour address, hardly moving and constantly scanning the crowd for assassins. They were hugging each other and crying, releasing the tension that had percolated through the long watch. Some were thanking Allah that their leader hadn't been harmed. All of them were brown and their skin had a luxuriant smoothness, their eyes the clarity of those who don't dissipate, and behind what I'm sure was experience in martial arts, was the same tenderness a man always notices when women feel deep affection.

Yet one image remained in the front of my mind: this light-skinned young man wearing a camouflage shirt and pants, brown fringe sewn across the shoulders, studded black leather covering his forearms. Whenever Farrakhan said something about "the Jews," that young man screamed or shouted, pushing both fists into the air, frequently leaping to his feet.

Near the end of the evening, when I had moved down toward the stage and was preparing to leave, I looked up and saw him once again. The front of his eight-inch-wide black belt bore a large Star of David formed in studs.

26

DAMNING ADMISSIONS
February 14, 1984

The Negro is still at the moral center of American writing, because the history of the African-American has been consistently interwoven with the issues that determine the fight to realize the Constitution. In *Open Admissions,* an incredibly important impediment to the right to life, liberty, and the pursuit of happiness is examined with a pen often transformed into a flamethrower. Playwright Shirley Lauro sees the decline of public education and its neglect, masked in academic jargon, as yet another form of disenfranchisement. With characterizations that rarely blunder into rants, Lauro successfully proves that urban public-school teaching is a profession on the moral frontier of our culture, since ignorance has been both a justification for discrimination and a determining factor in the individual's perspective on himself and his chances for success. But she fails by avoiding an element of complexity and culpability that I will come to later.

The action takes place on a wonderfully designed set that shows two households and gives way to a drab city college. The households are those of the hero, Calvin Jefferson, the poor black student, and Ginny Carlsen, the middle-class white teacher. Supported by his toilet-cleaning sister, Calvin is in his third year at college, can read at only a fifth-grade level, yet has received "Bs" throughout his freshman and sophomore years. Ginny, the woman from whom he will learn how he has been victimized, is married to a compulsive gambler and caught in an economic vise. She has conned herself into believing that he will someday get a job and she will finish out her doctorate. Meanwhile, she teaches day and night, passing semiliterate, illiterate, and inept students. By showing the students give speeches and interpretations as comic as they are terrible, then letting the viewer know how high their grades are, Lauro makes the horror of public education overwhelming. She is also smart enough to make it clear that ethnic pride has been turned on its head. Ginny's Korean, Italian, Hispanic, and black students need only identify with Shakespeare through the most superficial and ludicrous references to their own backgrounds and they will be patted on the back and sent on as ignorant as they were when they entered her classes.

In the lead, Calvin Levels gives one of the best characterizations of a young black man who is ignorant but not stupid that I have ever seen. He may not have yet the powers of visceral orchestration that Giancarlo Esposito brought to *Zoo Man and the Sign,* but his range of vocal timbre, accent, and body rhythm brings him close; he expresses frustration, disillusionment, rage, bitterness, and pathos with a clarity that lifts him far above agitprop to the truly tragic. Marlyn Rockafellow's Ginny is also superbly done.

It is to the playwright's credit that she shows that the stereotype of the hard-working black woman and the no-count black man can also be true in the middle-class household of a white Midwestern family. To push it home, Ginny argues with her husband and turns racial slurs back on him, telling the gambling man who has subtly pimped her that *he* is the nigger—lazy, shiftless, and wagering away the family's money. As Ginny's husband, Kevin Tighe is all guile and manipulation, an excellent villain, while one of the most rounded performances is that of Sloane Shelton, the tenured professor and divorcée who sluffs off all responsibility to her students and reveals the loneliness of her own life in a poignant final scene. I found Nan-Lynn Nelson as Calvin's sister good but thought her part too pat an annal of degradation, just as I thought the other ethnic types in the classroom were too close to stereotypes. But the children, portrayed by Pam Potillo and Maura Erin Sullivan, were perfectly written and perfectly done.

The conclusion of the show, which stumbles into the *Miracle Worker,* was a disappointment, but there is a bigger problem. Lauro's decision to make the condition of the public schools appear only the fault of the whites is like laying the problem of slavery only on the doorsteps of the buyers because the sellers were eventually colonized. The result is a play less bold than it initially appears to be, one that is brilliant when good but fundamentally weakened by its failure of nerve. None of the black theorists who thought that a lowering of standards would somehow lessen the problems of competition are ever seen or heard, nor are any of their black opponents, those who knew that the championing of "black English" and "black style" at the expense of actual skills would only result in intensified despair when those students entered the world of work. The cynicism and naïveté that convinced a large segment of poorly prepared black students that a college education was no more than "a piece of paper" are never addressed. Had they been, what is still an extremely important play would have completed the circle of moral riddles and confrontations that it only partially closes. Even so, it is a work that should be heard by everyone concerned with the future of the country. I would pay $500 to see it in a seat between Ron and Nancy Reagan.

27

YEAR OF THE DRAGON:
GENRES REORCHESTRATED
Summer 1985, unpublished

Year of the Dragon has inspired more rage from movie critics than anything we've seen recently. The jury has been almost unanimous in its hatred of the film and of Michael Cimino, its director. The most caustic reviews fuse the movie and the director, drubbing him for being so egotistical, almost as though the critical community has chosen to defend the moguls, fighting their cause against the recalcitrant employee. All of the stories about Cimino's highhandedness and back-stabbing during the filming of *Heaven's Gate* help fuel the attacks, though it doesn't really matter much if Hollywood loses now and then, nor should it startle anyone that a director would feel such contempt for his backers, trying every trick he could to force them not only to go his way but to unknowingly pay him for things they didn't even know he was selling. Over and over, one reads how Cimino's hero, Stanley White, obviously symbolizes the director and his fights with Hollywood. Even if that were true, which no one can prove until Cimino confesses, the things that make *Year of the Dragon* very good have been missed altogether. But that isn't hard to understand since it has also been picketed by outraged Asians and by feminists, charging that it is both racist and sexist: The villains who get the most footage are Chinese, and the beauteous Chinese anchor woman falls for the loutish white hero.

I think all of those people are wrong, the critics, the picketers, and the feminists. The critics are less important in their opinions than the picketers, and the feminists are as predictable as ever. The picketers are part of what a black filmmaker and I once decided should be called the PIT, the Positive Image Tribe, those minority members who feel that any complexity or corruption that doesn't clearly function as some sort of a Madison Avenue ethnic massage fuels stereotypes and promotes racism. On one level, those kinds of people might be right, but what they consider alternatives are usually sentimental and dull. In the case of the Chinese, they have a peculiar problem: Unlike white actors, they play only Asians and are part of a group that the country at large doesn't seem very interested in seeing on the screen. But who knows what the country at large will want to see until it has a chance? Given their intensity, the picketers of *Year of the Dragon* were probably concerned about the limited work available to Asian actors, about the creation of a new Asian villain convention if the film made money, and about the dislike of Asians that has begun to show itself in people as different as academics and blue-collar workers.

The growing numbers of Asians on college campuses have alarmed those who want to limit their attendance because they are considered clannish and boring, all too often majoring in math and science, disciplines dominated by the least interesting students. Asians apparently come to college for the purpose of mastering their areas of study, not to join fraternities and sororities, not to become cheerleaders or party-givers and -goers. They clearly miss the point of higher education. But their obsessive willingness to work hard is what *really* irritates most of their critics. I remember a teacher at Juilliard once chuckling that the terrors at the music school weren't Jews anymore, "They're those goddam Asians. They will practice longer and harder than *anybody*. When Asian students come in classes, people roll their eyes to the ceiling. They know they're in for a lot of work if they intend to keep up."

Then there is the violent animosity toward Asians that has developed since Japan emerged as a world economic force: A couple of Chinese men killed in Detroit by irate auto workers who thought they were Japanese; Vietnamese run out of neighborhoods in Washington state or literally fighting for their lives with rival fishermen in Texas; and Asians attacked in Boston, that up-South cradle of redneck rage. In such an atmosphere, *Year of the Dragon* is especially unnerving, given its message: All Chinese aren't hard-working and honest; some are crooked and use their distance from mainstream identification to get away with exploiting their own people. Perhaps a Chinese filmmaker could say that, but PIT Asians don't like it coming from Cimino, who doesn't stop there. As a Chinese doctor from California told me in Grand Rapids, "They know it is true that you have these gangs, sweatshops, and these drug smugglers in Chinatown, but they want the world to believe that the Chinese are only hard-working and honest. They would like the world to believe they are perfect. It's not true, but's it's a nice idea." Whether or not they want the world to think they are perfect, there is no doubt that they don't want outsiders to spend much time thinking about the gangster element. But Cimino is thinking about more than just that.

Year of the Dragon is far from a masterpiece but it is a very good movie that cleverly mixes Western, detective thriller, and monster genres. *Dragon* is mythic and calls for a morality that disdains cultural justifications for minority criminals, and it makes brilliant visual use of Chinese mythology, improvising on it as loosely as Joyce did on Homer's *Odyssey* for Bloom's epic day. And Cimino's action directing is perhaps the best since the excitement and tragic horror at the center of Sam Peckinpah's finest work—who else could equal his shoot-out and chase that begins in a bathroom, moves onto a disco floor, continues through it and a boxing gym to conclude in the street?

The use of Chinese mythology at the opening is obvious, since the pounding drums precede war. But the war is internal and external, among the Chinese themselves and with the Italians who run the drug market. Chalk-haired police captain Stanley White, for all his references to himself as a Polack, is a variation on the snow-feathered fighting cocks of Chinese legend. Their crowing announcements of sunrise chase away ghosts and they "discourage demons from making themselves known," according to *Things Chinese*, a book the hero holds up in a restaurant as a clue. The cock symbolizes literary genius, a vicious contender in close combat, courage, benevolence, and one who "never loses track of time." White brags about being the most decorated captain on the police, "I'm talking combat decoration," and, when he bursts in on Chinese gangsters meeting after the murder of one their inner circle, he will hear no excuses for extortion as part of Chinese tradition "thousands of years old." White responds by saying he's tired of "Chinese this and Chinese that," telling them that they are no more above the law than the Puerto Ricans or the Polacks. "This is America and it's 200 years old. You better get your clocks fixed."

The point is that one of the worst aspects of racism is that it can allow the lower elements of a group to freely exploit their own, using segregation as a guard against law enforcement, a theme the best black writers have been examining for a long time. There is also the implication that people come to America to get away from the sourest elements of their own cultures, whether foot-binding or slavery, tribalism or repression; and that what, finally, makes them American is their increased freedom, which allows them to influence the United States at large. As long as they are denied their rights, they are only partial Americans.

In their reviews many complained of the racial slurs in the dialogue and the crude character of the hero, missing the point. Mickey Rourke's Stanley White is a combination of the bruising, bullish American hero and lover Lincoln Kirstein first defined when reviewing *Public Enemy*, but he is also closely related to the arrogant, obsessive Ethan of *The Searchers*. What makes him a hero is his ability to perform heroic action, not his manners, his language, his attitudes toward women, or his penchant for ethnic slurs. He is, again, a fighting cock, a killer equal to the opposition. In that sense, he is also much like those he opposes. The crucial difference is that he, like Peckinpah's Pat Garrett, is "sitting there with all that law crammed inside [and] just bustin' to get out." Even the continual bursting through doors in the movie is connected to Chinese mythology, T'ang Yin's poem describing the rooster in *Things Chinese:* "It struts, its body covered in snow white feathers. / All of its life it dares make few utterances, / But when it crows, ten thousand doors bursts open."

Perhaps the most impressive use of mythological transferring is found in the character of Joey Tai, performed with extraordinary skill and range by John Lone. Lone is remarkable, using his voice and his body for different meanings in almost every scene. His Tai is always conscious of how he looks and how he sounds, ever the wily king who will not be upstaged. From his suave and murderous style comes the meaning of the title for

Cimino, which is again explained in *Things Chinese*. The dragon was appropriated as an imperial image by Chinese rulers. "The only harmful variety of the dragon is the *chiao* which is scaly and resides in the marshes high in the mountains. For its strength, the dragon is always shown pursuing a pearl, which is called the Pearl of Potentiality. If lost, the pearl leaves the dragon helpless and incapable of action."

All of the Chinese crime bosses are dragons, living like their mythological counterparts in the heaven of their offices above the streets and in the muddy underground of ruthless corruption. When the bodies of two hired Chinese killers are found dead in the vats of a soy-sauce factory, the camera travels through the wet murk of a world where Chinese laborers are sweatshop exploited, if not by the crime dragons, then by others who know how much they can get away with, given segregation. As White steps into one of the vats, he enters the filth of the dragons' world (the same law applies when he stomps into the bathtub of Tracy Tzu, the Chinese television reporter, Mandarin by heritage, descendant of rulers, but a good dragon).

Joey Tai is truly a dangerous dragon whose "junior hit men" in punk attire are but the vicious counterparts of the workers in the soy-sauce factory. When he travels to Thailand to make a heroin deal with a communist crime lord, Joey is seen stepping into a river before he is taken to his meeting, where he bargains for a cut in the price of the kilos, which are called dragon pearl. After he is beaten up by White, Tai isn't made to look needlessly silly as one reviewer thought. Instead, the monstrous underside of his character is shown and he closely resembles the five-fingered dragon on the cover of *Things Chinese*, a look that is intensified by close-ups through the windshield of his Mercedes as he is chased by the hysterical White in the next to last scene.

As David Denby saw so clearly in his *New York* review of the movie, there is a class joke rooted in *The French Connection* that runs throughout the movie: the elite criminals have the best manners and the best taste in clothes, all gloss and guile. White is unkempt, loud-mouthed, obnoxious, and driven, a manic counterpoint to the smooth dragons. But it seems that White successfully convinces them that he is all crowing and strutting, which allows him to get a wire into their offices, the interpreting done by British and Chinese nuns, as sly a reference to imperial history as the fact that Joey Tai represents the reversal of the function that drugs had in the Far East, when the British used opium as a tool of political and economic control. Now the Third World figures make fortunes from illegal drug smuggling, whether straight-out crooks like Joey Tai or political leaders, 20th-century variations on European pirates and colonizers. Grim but accurate ironies.

Overall, the film is grim and the hero moves from arrogant self-congratulation to panic, focused only by his desire to put Joey Tai in jail, or kill him. But that is what makes it as much a Western and a monster movie as a detective thriller. Early on White announces to the Chinese gangsters that he is the new marshal in town; there is a following scene in which his superiors laugh at the idea of a Chinese mafia as the authorities always do in monster films; and there is a classic, high-noon shoot out at the end, where all the genres come together for a superb moment of dragon killing. The criticisms of his quarrels with his wife, of his affair with the Chinese reporter, and of his arrogance seem misdirected. An egomaniac like Stanley White could probably only love a woman who submitted to him, which the Chinese woman does and his Polish wife doesn't. That a wild man who flaunts his barbaric manners and goes out of his way to empty spittoons on convention would appeal to Tracy Tzu isn't any more surprising than the making of rock brutes into heartthrobs, itself a stylization of the attraction upper-class women of certain types have always had to louts (her falling for a man who throws around racial epithets shouldn't startle those who witnessed all the Vassar types going with black nationalists during the '60s).

Some of the dialogue is dull, even insipid, but I think the reviewers missed the fact that White, in all his pomposity and would-be poetic insight, would say something like "I've got scar tissue on my soul" and would try to analyze television negatively in order to put the woman he's trying to bed on the defensive. But, for all its clinkers, *Year of the Dragon* is an imposing work, a film about war in which there is no line between combatants and noncombatants. Cimino's virtuosity is rivaled by few and his attempt at a bigger-than-average morality is brave. He is right in the end, knowing that American law is supposed to protect everybody and put everybody in jail who belongs there. The struggle toward that goal will always break conventions. Joey Tai, assuming the face of the indignant victim of racism when the television microphone is pushed his way, suggests that reporters should address "positive things." He understands where he is and how easily the noose can be slipped when a dragon knows how to handle liberal pieties. So does Michael Cimino.

FORTUNE DANE'S
MIND/BODY PROBLEM
April 15, 1986

In the ratings-routed *Fortune Dane*, black actor Carl Weathers hoped to capture the television audience that loves Tom Selleck. The opening MTV-style montage showed this undercover troubleshooter exercising a substantial amount of beefcake; but it soon became obvious that his character was an all-American hero, and much more akin to Odysseus than to Mr. T. He was athletic, handsome, attractive to women, capable of handling himself in a scrape, and quick-witted. But this Saturday night series had to compete with the geriatric gunk of *The Golden Girls* and the cornpone Negroisms of *227*, neither of which offered any challenge to conventional television. *Fortune Dane* came in third, garnering a 15 percent share in its time slot. After a few episodes, ABC sent Weathers's vehicle to the burial ground of shows that try to achieve the unprecedented.

As a series, *Dane* was neither too good nor especially bad. Yet it had the makings of something that could have been very interesting, given the time to smooth out its kinks with the pomade and stocking cap of better plots and stronger acting from the lead. Weathers was asked to deliver lines like "A man without ambition is like a car without a carburetor," and was too often given to self-righteous smirks. In a sense, his character was a contemporary incarnation of the starched dignity Sidney Poitier thought an appropriate rejoinder to Stepin Fetchit.

What made *Dane* unique was its attempt to take new territory. It strayed from every other depiction of Negroes on television—including the best: *Hill Street Blues* and *The Cosby Show*, each of which is indispensable because of the variety of insights that inform its racial and ethnic characterization. *Fortune Dane* wasn't rich, unvarnished drama like *Hill Street*, and it was by no means an intentional comedy, however absurd some of its lines may have seemed. Its desire to appropriate the terrain of the weekly thriller built around a heroic figure suggested a fresh thematic moxie for popular entertainment. Given the fact that black athletes have been supplying the nation with an increasing line of disciplined heroes—drug controversies aside—since the snipping of the color line in professional sports, the idea wasn't so far-out. And since Mr. T moved to a position of prominence after his success with Stallone, why couldn't Weathers, who had appeared as Apollo Creed in all four of the *Rocky* films?

But Weathers, who had a hand in formulating the show, was after something beyond the image of a muscle-bound boob with no brain but a big heart that Mr. T is famous for. Because the thirty-eight-year-old Weathers had wanted to perform since he saw *The Defiant Ones* as a child, and had begun studying for an acting career at the age of eighteen, his ambitions were more substantial. Even if Weathers's character sometimes wore those dumb short jackets with the huge pockets in the front, there were no earrings, no strange haircuts, no gold chains, no barely literate muttering. Fortune Dane was a muscle man with the ability to deduce answers and outthink his opposition, regardless of their sophistication.

The adopted son of a southern bank president (Adolph Caesar), Dane quits the police force and leaves his hometown in the first episode when he discovers that his father and the local officials are busy covering up a money-laundering scandal. In Bay City, Dane is hired by the female mayor (Penny Fuller) to head up a troubleshooting team intent on crushing city corruption. Dane's subordinates are a white man and a white woman (Joe Dallesandro and Daphney Ashbrook).

What made the show different can be seen in its near-precedents. We can remember Greg Morris as the technician in *Mission Impossible,* a rejoinder to the illiterate Uncle Remus figure. (Though the avuncular types played by Wallace Berry and Spencer Tracy are not much different from that stereotype, they're hardly the only way white men are portrayed.) But Morris, like Cosby in *I Spy* was largely a eunuch. In Cosby's case, the situation became so ludicrous that Nancy Wilson was drafted into one episode so that Cosby didn't have to, once again, stand invisibly holding his johnson as Robert Culp walked off with another beauty. Viewing Culp's inevitable success with the white women who turned up in episode after episode was like watching Cosby charm them by proxy, a palatable proposition for the time. Culp's blatant co-opting of Cosby's speech rhythms and gestures was like the history of jazz or rock and roll transformed into a TV thriller. It was the kind of racism that the Rolling Stones weren't afraid to discuss as central to their success when they first toured America.

That hasn't changed much, at least as far as interracial situations are concerned. Though black couples abound on everything from thrillers to soaps, integrated couples don't. The white man with the black wife on *The Jeffersons* was the beginning of a one-sided miscegenation ball that has maintained itself, extending even to MTV, that bastion of white male fantasies. Now on *Dynasty,* we can see Diahann Carroll pursued by white men and not even blink, but when the female district attorney in the first episode of *Fortune Dane* offered to drop her drawers if he solved a case, we were into another arena. That she would later greet him at her home in silk underpants and camisole was a bit much, so much that Dane's refusal to acknowledge what was readily available seemed oddly realistic. Clearly, this black man had met many women, white or otherwise, who felt they could get him to do what they wanted by offering entrance into the great divide.

The implication was of a reality television consistently avoids, preferring asexual Negro men or those who rut only in their own racial roost. Dane's decision to take a job as a troubleshooter for a woman mayor connected his unusual image to that of a female wielding greater power than any other on el tubo. That very partnership called into question conventions of characterization within and without Hollywood, conventions that say a great deal about the layers of symbols and meaning that come with race, sex, and religion in America.

We Americans have long been better at comedy than tragedy, at melodrama than drama, at thriller than subtle characterization. So it is understandable that few works in which "outsiders" are central to the telling of the tale have had any human resonance. However hard it is to point at dramatic achievements in which black characters are fundamental to the narrative, it is equally hard to find such works in which Jewish characters are essential. Since the enormous influence of show-business Jews on Hollywood is undeniable, the fact that there are so few works as well done as *Save the Tiger* suggests that either the public or the moguls themselves have concluded that if one is to risk money on movies with ethnic figures in the lead, they had better have sentimental overlays that pump the audience for pity, or violence. Or they had better be bent on provoking convulsions of laughter.

For those reasons, the once verboten image of the violent Negro has become marketable. Twenty years ago, visiting a Watts theater group, Bill Cosby said of his role *I Spy:* "I'm the first black man they gave a gun and let him shoot whitey." Many white man have fallen since then, including all those offed during the high tide of black B movies that pulled Hollywood out of the red. The cardboard heroes of those films are nearly interchangeable with the ludicrous heroes of '60s agitprop black nationalist plays, works unknowingly rooted in the traditions of minstrelsy—the arrogant and deceptive slave Jasper Jack who debunked, tricked, and sometimes physically assaulted his white masters.

. Where Hollywood envisioned dollars, nationalists saw the chance to convert, and equally simplistic ideas about Negro men seeking their "manhood" dominated both camps. One saw heavy-handed rejections of the *Birth of a Nation* stereotypes and shiftless darkie buffoons. Griffith's murderous, raping black cossacks didn't last long in film, but the Negro who would do anything to escape work or who could be shaken to his core by the flapping of a sheet on a clothesline held on for quite some time, functioning, perhaps, as a rejoinder to flesh-and-blood men like Jack Johnson and Joe Louis. Just as homespun white everymen slipped banana peels under the feet of the pretentious in 19th-century American theatre, film Negroes sneered at "oreos" as they moved to physically right Caucasian wrongs. The so-called "street brother" was elevated over the Negro intellectual, as though a command of the English language and a comprehension of the complexities of history and society meant submission to a foreign order. In short, real Negroes were inarticulate, semiliterate, and quick to finish debate by physical means. Except for their willingness to fight, they weren't very different from the traditional image that evolved in the minstrel shows and took on celluloid wings in Hollywood.

Those conventions still exist, and *Fortune Dane* dared to buck them. This is the age when black performers such as Mr. T and Eddie Murphy have made successes for themselves playing the roles of noble or ignoble savages, big-hearted brutes, or wise-cracking corner boys. Yet there is still no range of characterization for Negroes comparable to that which stretches from John Wayne to Cary Grant. Body and brain have yet to meld. Perhaps Carl Weathers and his colleagues were defeated in their effort by the kind of mentality that now urges white sports commentators to say of black basketball performance, "Don't forget, this isn't a thinking man's game." But that doesn't mean that such ambition won't eventually succeed. Since we have seen the asinine *Jeffersons* supplanted by *The Cosby Show*, it is reasonable to assume that the American audience will rise to appreciate better material. *Fortune Dane*, though only a thriller, attempted to raise the ante, which suggests that some such show will succeed, opening the way, perhaps, for a black dramatic series as good as *Hill Street Blues*.

METEOR IN A BLACK HAT
December 2, 1986

In the Greenwich Village section of Rome known as Trastevere stands Number 9 Piazza de San Calisto, the building in which the painter Bob Thompson died in 1966. It is a large place, the outside a dried red mud color, then burnt sienna, then near-beige, then red mud battling with sienna for the next level, the top floor sandy and ocher, giving way to the roof, itself an orange, like rust or dried blood. Number 9 is across from an arch that opens to a statue of Pius XI, built in 1936 by the fascists, the same year that Charlie Parker decided to become a serious saxophonist and sank into the quicksand of heroin addiction. Tragically enraptured by the romance of erosive dissipation, Thompson died not far from a pagan church where the Virgin Mary wears a wedding dress, and silver purses hang from her outstretched arms. Such meretricious sects begat the outrage that foamed into Protestantism, just as the genuflecting before sensation that defined too much of the bebop era inspired the sobriety of the contemporary generation of jazzmen, many of whom neither drink nor smoke. Thompson knew no such disdain for chemical bliss. Though he saw the hill of corpses left by the pit bulls of self-destruction, Robert Louis Thompson chose to roll up his sleeve, push in a needle, and climb to the top of the pile.

I. WHERE AND WHEN

I first became aware of Bob Thompson through a 1967 Archie Shepp recording that included a piece entitled "A Portrait of Robert Thompson as a Young Man." It was wild, full of group improvisation, crashing drums, squeaks, honks, and marching-band interludes; then there was a sensuous and melancholy line close to the blues. I wondered who this Thompson was but didn't find out until I saw a painting of his on a Steve Lacy album cover, which had a photograph on the back of Lacy and a large Negro with a hat crouched over in a corner. When I moved to New York in 1975, I began seeing small Thompson paintings on the Lower East Side, works he had given friends. In 1978, there was a show at Harlem's Studio Museum, where Thompson's identity whirled and roared from the walls.

Thompson was a spiritual muckraker whose shocking, erotic, satiric, and mystical paintings were intricate fusings of classical and American themes, methods, and images. Symbols, designs, taboos, and stereotypical figures were interwoven with subtle African patterns and religious suggestions. Sexuality was celebrated and teased in some works, while other paintings illuminated its mysteries and terrors; the literal and metaphoric implications of violence, horror, transcendence, and apocalyptic destructions were confronted and probed.

The black identity in Thompson's world is part of a boiling gumbo. Heroes and demons, angels and villains, come from everywhere, and the victim reverses his role—usually in intimate situations—to become the monster or join the gargoyles. Adoration intertwines with cannibalism; love, narcissism, and dependency descend to a revolting and devouring gluttony. Like blues, the work often evokes the reverberations, hooks, joys, and sorrows of intimate romance. The complicated interminglings of passion to the brink of ambivalence and beyond to terror are always there. An angular, wild, comic, and threatening universe broods, sulks, dances, parodies, celebrates, crushes, and eats. Black men are usually cast as satyrs and white women as nymphs, which led some to dismiss his art as imitative for its classical sources and self-denigrating for its apparent content.

Thompson also toyed with the image of the black person in Western art, from classic to political and commercial. The onlooking black servant of Manet's *Olympia* or so many other paintings, the grinning, subservient, criminal, or ignorant coon of racist placards, pamphlets, cartoons, advertisements, and films is dismissed in favor of a black-hatted voyeur. Reminiscent of and perhaps inspired by the ominous, onlooking specter of plate 57 from Goya's *Caprichos,* Thompson's personal symbol often spies perverse circumstances that parallel the spiritual horror stories told by many domestic workers. But there is no pomposity there, for the very same black-hatted figure is just as often the leader of the desperate death dance himself. The sacrifice, redemption, and revelation that course through the violent ecstasy of so much Christian imagery are transposed to an orgiastic underworld. Union between light and dark, man and woman, races and cultures pervade Thompson's relentless variations on the many, many levels of miscegenation. Though cryptic in his interviews,

Thompson obviously had a confident grasp of Ralph Ellison's observation that miscegenation in this country produced "a complexity of bloodlines and physical characteristics that have much to do with the white American's reluctance to differentiate between race and culture, African and American, and are the source of our general confusion over American identity." Perhaps that general confusion explains the art world's failure to give Thompson's themes their due, to see the difference between the simplistic politics that engenders so much poor art and the broad aesthetic possibilities of racial subject matter as universal metaphor. As Thompson himself said to Jeanne Siegel in June of 1965: "I think painting should be the format or the foundation . . . should be like the theatre, a representation of something. Not only to expose the ability of the artist, but also for the viewer. To relate, like the painters in the Middle Ages, and the Renaissance . . . painters were employed to educate the people . . . they could walk into a cathedral, look at the wall, and see what was happening. . . . I am not specifically trying to do that. . . . I have much more freedom, but in a certain way, I am trying to show what's happening, what's going on . . . in my own private way." Thompson improvised the world he knew onto his canvases, creating a mulatto art rich with rowdy, seditious humor.

II. WHAT WENT ON: LIVING IN DOUBLES

There was more overt racial hostility in the East Village, Bob Thompson's home base between 1959 and 1966, than is generally acknowledged. The few black men and interracial couples then living there might be called names, have things thrown out of windows at them, or find themselves facing gangs of Polish, Ukrainian, or Italian ruffians. But if they avoided certain streets and neighborhoods, they could find a community where race was played down or satirized in favor of aesthetic agreements and a concerted struggle against convention. Rationality was dismissed by some and replaced by a stylized anarchy; moderation and taking care of oneself were displaced by a romanticized intensity that could include long, long bouts of heavy drinking, dope, and interracial, homoerotic, and collective sexual experiments.

Within that world, Bob Thompson thrived. His behavior, aesthetic achievements, and career successes amused, shocked, entertained, scandalized, inspired, made jealous, and awed. Some describe his exoticism as contrived, his high-powered, loud, and rowdy behavior as no more than a ploy. Well over six feet and more than 200 pounds, he was known for taking over places when he arrived, for dressing like a thug—huge overcoat, hat pulled down over his eyes—and for charming his way through situations where racial animosity bucked against a short leash. Thompson is recalled by some as an innocent, a big kid run down on the fast track he traveled. He is also described as a fine thief when broke and an excellent con man. But all the contradictory tales corroborate his enormous creative output, constant study, and preoccupation with painting, wherever in the world he happened to be.

Saxophonist Jackie McLean caroused with Thompson in Paris and was shocked when the painter took him to a windswept studio and showed the musician what appeared to be hundreds of paintings. "They were stacked up one on top of another, rolled up like rugs. There were big ones, little ones, paintings on wood and masonite. I didn't believe it, because whenever I saw him, which was often, he was drinking wine in the cafés, hanging out, and listening to jazz. But whenever he did it, he definitely did it. And even though I didn't know anything about painting, his work grabbed me, because it was so strong. It pushed out at you and made you look at it."

LeRoi Jones remembers him as a man he saw in the Village with a huge Abrams art book under his arm spring, summer, fall, winter. "He was *always* excited about something he was studying—Tintoretto, Poussin, or whomever—and he would open the book and start pointing things out to you. Bob would take you over to his studio and show you his work, or trace out the structure of a master painting and tell you what colors he was going to paint things, how he was going to change it. Sometimes he would be laughing, because the way he was changing it was funny to him. But the demons weren't, and they would usually be there, too, lurking around, waiting for something to suck up or haunt."

Fellow painter Emilio Cruz met Thompson in 1957. Thompson was then twenty years old and an abstractionist studying at the University of Louisville, where he had work in all the campus shows. Though he spent his childhood in Elizabethtown, Kentucky, about 40 miles from Louisville, Bob Thompson was no hayseed. He was from the middle class, his family had a fine home, and his knowledge of etiquette, food, art, and culture was a surprise to Cruz when he finally found out about it. "At first," Cruz says, "he appeared to be a loud, brilliant, lower-class man." Thompson's father had died when the painter was a teenager and his mother, who was a stickler for formality, taught school and was on the Board of Education.

Thompson underplayed his background, disdained what he considered empty intellectual posturing, and devoted most of his energy to painting, studying, and thrill-seeking. But there was gloom beneath the revels and the panty-chasing. During the summer of 1958 in Provincetown, Massachusetts, Thompson complained to Cruz of a drug problem and an overwhelming sexual appetite that fed off each other. He was drinking great quantities of black rum to stave off the desire for heroin, and was asking almost every attractive woman with whom he had an extended conversation to marry him, claiming he would die if she didn't. "You never knew," Cruz laughs, "if Bob was serious or if he had just come up with another technique for sexual success. But it is highly possible that he was serious."

At Provincetown, Thompson and Cruz met Dodie Muller and Red Grooms, who were part of a movement rising in reaction against Abstract Expressionism. Figurative images that took advantage of expressionism's freedom from photographic reality were the center of an inclusive aesthetic. Thompson and Cruz were immediately influenced. For the next few years, they were to work closely and discuss many different kinds of painters and paintings. The Provincetown ideas gave Thompson the conception necessary to translate his passion for and identification with the art of the masters into his own mythology. The bright colors of much Renaissance painting, the dark worlds of Goya, the geometric masterpieces of della Francesca, Van Gogh's carnivorous plants and *Starry Night* skies, the cartoon, graffiti, and willfully primitive abstraction could meet, transfuse, or collide.

Canceling his formal studies, Thompson came to New York in 1959, almost eager, it appears, to become the fluid of Joyce's observation: "Hot fresh blood they prescribe for decline. Blood always needed. Insidious. Lick it up, smoking hot, thick, sugary. Famished ghosts." He was studying black culture and history in Harlem, consuming and emitting images come upon in books or in the city's museums, crossing all manner of class, cultural, and ethnic lines. Traveling at a meteoric velocity, Thompson quickly produced a number of paintings and erected his own spotlight in the art world of the East Village.

Thompson's appetites led one man who knew him to say, "He lived in doubles. Whatever anybody else had, he had it double. Double brandies, two vodkas, two scotches, two women, three women. It always felt like that around him. He projected this burning energy whenever he came in the room. You could feel him in a room if you didn't see him, if you had your back turned."

A typical Thompson day began with a double vodka, then breakfast and a trip to a bar, where he perused the faces of derelicts as he studied an art book. Leaving the bar, Thompson went to Harlem because a $3 bag of uptown heroin contained three times as much dope as a $10 Lower East Side bag and might have triple the potency. If he felt safe uptown, Thompson used the drugs there; if not, he took a train home and shot up. Now even more jovial and humorous, he visited a rich collector to study a painting or sell one. Money in his pocket and hungry for dinner, Thompson went home to his wife, Carol. After wolfing down food, he went to work, painting from the evening into the early morning, ambidextrously wielding his brushes with the speed of a fencer. Satisfied, he then headed for the Five Spot, or a party, or an erotic occasion.

Carol Thompson observes that even with his drug problem and his constant partying and nightclubbing, the artist always got his art supplies, his pigments, brushes, and canvases, with plenty to spare. He sometimes worked for two or three days straight, resting now and then from a big canvas by knocking off a small painting on wood, or drawing with pencil and crayon. People were invited over so that he could turn his work into a performance. The many yellow women with scarlet hair began to appear after his redheaded Caucasian wife came down with hepatitis.

Bob Thompson's ability to assimilate ideas and techniques quickly, produce a large amount of work in a short time, and win important friends was clear in the summer of 1958, and that ability functioned well for him in New York. When his direction changed in Provincetown, Thompson became buddy-buddy with the rebels against abstract expressionism and exhibited thirteen paintings with them at the Provincetown Art Festival; Walter P. Chrysler, his first collector, bought them all. So when Thompson arrived in Manhattan, he already had allies who helped him get his first shows and introduced him to the intricacies of the big city.

Though known for his generosity, Thompson was also a charmer and a manipulator, a thorough and quick reader of character who could always don the necessary mask. The painter radiated charisma in two worlds by juxtaposing cultural references—springing existentialist concepts on his pool-room buddies, then trumpeting *motherfuckers* and *bitches* among Caucasian aesthetes and bohemians hungry for social spice. Or some lunkhead he hung around with to the despair of his friends would turn out to be the son of a rich collector whom Thompson was stalking.

Thompson's awareness of the vagaries of human, racial, and class conduct must surely have alienated him, must have accounted for some of the terror, disgust, gloom, and rebellious carnality in his work. As an avant-garde artist, as an intellectual, Thompson was automatically alienated from the Negro community, where neither the well-off nor the lower classes had—or have—cultivated enough of an appreciation of the depths of the Afro-American aesthetic tradition—or any other—to get beyond the commonplace in visual art, or writing, or any expression other than religious and secular music, athletic grace, and social dance. He also came to early manhood during the bohemian fascination with existentialism, the emergence of Ingmar Bergman and Samuel Beckett, and the harrowing revelations of Southern racism through the televised protests of the Civil Rights Movement. His alienation was deepened by the hostility between his school of painting and that of the Abstract Expressionists, by his interracial marriage, and by excesses that were terrifying to his friends.

Emilio Cruz recounts once arguing with Thompson about his use of drugs in such large, even record, proportions. "We went around and around, and I asked him if he was scared and he kept coming back with these evasions and clever arguments and satires he could use to make your position seem silly. But, in the end, he told me that damn right he was scared, and that life was bullshit anyway. He also told me something that I just could not handle at the time, which was that he was in this automobile accident when he was thirteen and saw his father killed right before his eyes. After that, he said that he had this recurring image of his father's death. Of course, Bob always told people that he was going to die early himself. I think he was caught up in the romance of Charlie Parker and that whole thing. But, in many ways, I think heroin acted as a sedative for Bob; it calmed him down and made it possible for him to paint and remove himself from his nightmares, even though they turned up on the canvases all the time. In fact, Bob produced so much work—seven or eight paintings a week—that you couldn't argue that the dope was getting in the way."

Carol Thompson's version of the accident is an example of how the painter could revise reality to protect himself. "Bob probably did feel some guilt for his father's death, but he wasn't in the accident. He had asked his father, who was dead tired from a hard day's work, to come see him play in a basketball game that night. His father agreed, had an accident on the way to the game, and died of a heart attack."

Thompson's renown rose quickly in New York. After one-man and group shows at Red Grooms's Delancey Street Museum and the Zabriskie Gallery in 1960, critic Meyer Schapiro took notice of the painter's work. Thompson's art and his personality began to attract collectors. But Carol Thompson doubts that he liked New York much, since he seemed so relieved upon receiving a grant that provided him with the funds to leave Manhattan for Europe in March 1961. The Thompsons and collector Steven Pepper made the trip together, crossing the Atlantic by boat.

III. SHEDDING ON THE SEINE

When Thompson arrived in London, he had his wife take him to meet saxophonist Jackie McLean, who was performing in *The Connection*. The painter was out of drugs and starting to suffer from withdrawal, which was especially terrible for him because he had a very low tolerance for pain. McLean's tolerance was also very low, and he sympathetically shared his own stash with Thompson until he was able to set the painter up with a doctor who took care of addicted musicians. It was the beginning of a close friendship. Thompson had no money but Pepper provided for him and his wife until they got to Paris. There fellow painter Christopher Lane helped the couple get a studio in Glaciere for about $35 a month.

The Thompsons, Lane, and a sculptor named Larenzo Hale used to pool money for food Carol Thompson cooked. Funds were very short and the painter's wife remembers the landlord turning off the heat and electricity in the winter. Undaunted, Bob Thompson placed candles on top of his easel, put on gloves, sweaters, and an overcoat, and continued working at night. Lane remembers him always working to music, dance-shuffling and hunched over the canvas, tongue inside his lower lip, stroking with either hand, powerfully and swiftly, scrubbing the pigments into the canvas, following the rhythms of the music, answering it with shapes, colors, and abrupt angles. Thompson's zeal resulted in many paintings, some of which were sold to collectors sent to him by friends in the United States.

Upon coming to Paris, Jackie McLean saw Thompson every morning. After getting high the two regularly went to watch a woman masturbate over the heat of a manhole. McLean would then ascend a balcony and address the passersby in a nonsense imitation of the sound and rhythm of German that made Parisians gawk and often laid Thompson on the sidewalk. Daily they traveled through the city looking at buildings, studying faces, visiting museums, joking or making fun of their surroundings.

"They say this city is supposed to be beautiful," the painter once remarked to the saxophonist, "but everything here is gray. Look at that building over there. What is that building saying to you?"

"How the hell do I know what a goddamn building is saying? What is that building saying to *you*?"

"That building over there is saying, 'Motherfucker, don't look at me: I'm UGLY!' "

Like other black artists, musicians, and writers who came to Paris, Thompson was largely free from the pressures of race, but a photographer who knew the painter in France remembers him as an angry young man all too aware of how black artists in America were rarely recognized beyond the fringes of the art world. Perhaps that anger helped deepen his resolve to gain as much from his trip to Europe as possible, so much artistic power that the forces he had to fight would find him difficult to stop. In Paris, Thompson studied the sweep of European and African art, strengthening his technique and clarifying the intellectual conceptions that underlay a visual force some mistakenly believed was sincere but naïve. Thompson's capacity for emblematic intensity, for the transfusion of emotional muscularity into design, made him a primitive in style, not thought. His attraction to the superficially simple reflected his profound understanding of abstraction—communication achieved through the intensification of every aspect of painting, the single stroke, image, or color endowed with a provocative velocity of association. Where the realistic painting accumulates meaning through detail, the abstraction suggests multitudinous detail through its force and rhythms. Both provide a dialogue with the past that fills in what is left out.

Thompson's sensibility synthesized styles. His barbaric strokes functioned like Goya's, expressing the world of nightmares, the cannibalistic violence at the center of mammalian life, and a disdain for any form of lyricism that avoided the bitter tenderness and pity of mourning, even mourning for the sweet moment that will soon dissolve into the muddle of memory. Like Picasso, Thompson wasn't reluctant to display his autobiographical boudoir obsessions, and his bristling rhythms, though usually less angular than the Spaniard's, were kindred. The Negro American painter shared with the Matisse of *The Dance* (1910) and *Music* (1910) a belief in an elemental world that precedes the artifice of civilization, the congestion of grandeur, subtlety, mediocrity, and garbage that constitutes modern life. He was inspired by della Francesca's visual orchestration and by the somber isolation that surrounds so many of the Renaissance master's figures. In a college essay, Thompson observed that della Francesca's geometric command nearly obviated the faces of his figures. For his own orchestral purposes, Thompson apppropriated the silhouette, leaving all particulars except hair and genitals behind and turning bodies into melodic motifs or dance figures in musical or choreographic ritual forms. The many miscegenations that created the gene pool of world culture were being brought into the Louisville tale-spinner's grasp.

Where the Cubists were sophisticates inspired by the distortions and rhythmic power of primitive art, exploiting it for decorative purposes or for fresher and more powerful expression, Thompson's decision to shoot primitive energy through the classical models that attracted him reversed this process. The gall of it was that Thompson placed his own work next to that of the masters he loved most, encouraging comparison with the greatest painters of all time. Classical paintings were his song forms, the "standards" on which he improvised his identity. Like a jazzman, he felt free to impose his identity on established material, only instead of elevating pop tunes he asserted himself through recognized classics. In 1965, he told Jeanne Siegel that his Paris experience made him wonder why contemporary artists spent so much time trying to be original. All that was necessary was to be oneself.

His attraction to jazz meant that Thompson didn't just copy—he bent, twisted, extended, and remade. No situation, theme, shape, or creature appearing or recurring in the work has a single definition or function. There is constant flux. Emilio Cruz points out the dynamic animism, the anthropomorphic surge of Thompson's landscapes. Primary colors dominate many of the canvases, with red an organizing principal that makes the traditional suggestions of fire, passion, anguish, and destruction. The birds, angels, and halos of classical painting fuse into combined images of black hats and flying creatures. Birds themselves represent force and flight—weapons, liberators, vultures, methods of escape. Most of the situations and actions in the paintings take place outdoors or within caves; the architectural and technological hand of man is almost always absent.

Like jazzmen who based their own tunes on the first sixteen bars of "I Got Rhythm" and the middle eight of "Honeysuckle Rose," Thompson frequently combined classical designs as he weaved his variations. In his diptych *Expulsion and Nativity*, Thompson sets an improvisation on Masaccio's *Adam and Eve Cast Out of Paradise* on the left side of the canvas and his personalization of della Francesca's *Nativity* on the right. Thompson telescopes art history, demonstrating how the earlier painter's aesthetic was elaborated upon by the latter. But the left panel also summons the stark expressionism of Munch's *The Scream*, which Munch said expressed a scream traveling through nature: The clouds were like real blood, and the colors themselves were supposed to scream. What feeling could better evoke the day Adam and Eve got the bum's rush? Thompson takes Munch's tormented figure as a visual chord, then fuses the eaters of forbidden fruit into an emotion of loss, the bodies once separated in joy and companionship now united in anguish, an armless grotesque with three legs. The tree under which Adam and Eve walk extends into the right panel, Thompson's reiteration of the belief that the need for a savior was set in motion by their original sin. But della Francesca's angels in Renaissance dress are transformed into nude white women carrying birds instead of lutes, the white baby on the blue cloth is now a blue baby on a white cloth, the Madonna is a large, purple, Negroid woman with red hair on her head and her crotch. Joseph is a brown abstraction and one of the shepherds has become a red woman who points to the huge bird figure standing behind them all, some savage power in nature that was a building in the original *Nativity*. The patches of dark earth from della Francesca's landscape now form a quilt that develops into an orange, brown, and green landscape. In harmonic design, the sky on the right of the diptych echoes the sky on the left. In perfect Thompson terms, the complex and the primitive, the historical and the arrogantly inventive come together.

Thompson changed convention thematically as well as structurally. He never backed off from depicting the interracial bacchanal that existed in Lower Manhattan, an island paradise the opposite of that familiar one where the white man becomes king of a tropic joyland, surrounded by entranced brown or red or golden girls. Bob Thompson, like many black men who lived in the East Village, knew the abundant passion of willing white women in flight from the middle class, seeking "heroes they could believe in," as John Gruen reports in *The New Bohemians*. Whether they were actually attracted to the black men they pursued or were fumbling through fantasies made no difference to the painter; Thompson consistently spread what he knew on the canvas.

Thompson's delight in showing black men as satyrs and white women as nymphs vaunted a commitment to sexual freedom that existed in neither the black nor white world, but found expression among the kinds of people the painter knew and among the college students who were reading Miller and Lawrence and experimenting with approaches to pleasure that might have shocked their parents. Contrary to racial myths, Negroes were neither promiscuous nor less repulsed by certain sexual delights—or "unnatural acts"—than the white middle class. But just as European experience during World War II began to change the sexual expectations of black men, so did the domestic experience with adventurous white women. As I heard a Negro woman say to a "consciousness-raising" class for black college girls in 1968, "These white women are taking our men from us because they will do all those things we used to think only whores did—*anything*. This is not Victorian England, and if we want to get them back we have to be ready to sexually liberate ourselves from thinking of normal adult acts as *nasty*." Jump to no conclusions: in that era, black males' erotic sophistication tended to stop at the receiving end.

Yet Thompson, for all his warm, even tender, paintings of interracial couples and his playful or comic orgies, knew there was more to those unions than transcendent love or big fun. *Tree* is an example. Its sources are Goya's *Caprichos,* plates 61 and 62, "Gone for Good" and "Who Would Believe It?" In the first plate, Goya expressed his jealousy by symbolically crucifying a lover in a floating nowhere with three bedraggled bullfighters clutching clouds beneath her feet. In the second, two semi-human grotesques battle in an equally placeless darkness as a demon claws at their struggle from below while another rises above them. In Thompson's painting, as a red-haired angel uproots a tree, she scornfully watches an orgy in which two demon figures—one red and the other red-eyed, yellow, and black (strongly suggesting an African mask)—receive fellatio from pinkish-white sections of bodies, while a brown figure with terrified red eyes and mouth appears to be entering a woman from the rear or stuck within her. On the right side of the canvas, a red figure's hand is being eaten by a white creature with blue hair and red eyes as a monster claws at both of them and a red-flecked brown demon floats over their heads.

Another extremely rich improvisation is *St. Matthew's Description of the End of the World,* owned by the Museum of Modern Art and presently tucked away in a warehouse for the insides of wrappers to enjoy. Its source is *The Final Trumpets* from Michelangelo's *The Last Judgment.* The situation has been changed from a gathering in the sky to an apparent combination of a voodoo ritual and a cockfight. The powerful central angel no longer rests his right leg on a mound of cloud, extending his left leg forward and pushing his left arm back into empty air as he blows the long trumpet pointed downward and held with his right hand. He is now a dancing brown man with vague features and orange hair, shaking a red bird in front of him and slapping away a yellow, red-haired woman. The book of evil deeds on the right of the canvas is now a magenta bird with a three-peaked wing that outlines pink breasts pointed in the manner of African sculpture. Colors have been changed or function differently than in the source, though the skin tones of some this ritual's participants are close to the colors of the robes worn by the angels. A simple interpretation would infer the painter's harsh refusal to step back from his nearly pagan pursuit of sensation, but the meaning is finally so ambiguous that the painting truly approaches the province of music and dance, with its figures given brutal vibrance by the colors and the rhythms. Perhaps it is much like Baudelaire's description of Goya, expressing "a love of the ungraspable, a feeling for violent contrasts, for the blank horrors of nature and for human countenances weirdly animalized by circumstances."

IV. WE WANT BOB!

When the Thompsons returned from London, Paris, and Spain in the fall of 1963, the painter made his greatest career leap: At the age of twenty-six, he got a one-man show at the prestigious Martha Jackson Gallery and became the black *enfant terrible* of the art world, a mantle he wore uneasily, arriving at the opening very late as an overflow crowd chanted, "We want Bob! We want Bob!" To one painter Thompson appeared very frightened and very high.

Harold Hart, then director of the Martha Jackson Gallery, told me, "I had never seen an opening like that one. It was amazing. There were so many people there from so many walks of life and did they love Bob Thompson! But it wasn't hard to love him, because he gave off such positive feeling, such warmth and goodness. When you met him, you felt as though you had known him for a very long time. He was a wonderful man.

"I'm also convinced that Bob Thompson was a genius and that if he had been white, he would have been much more successful. His color definitely held him back, but the racism in the art world is very, very subtle. Black painters are usually given the runaround—not that white painters aren't, too—and there is a hesitance about taking them on, about having too many, and wondering whether or not their shows will be reviewed. The reviewers, collectors, and galleries will respond very differently to a piece of work once they know that the painter is black. But if they didn't know they might like it more, be less unbending, pay more money for it, or so many other things. It is a very complex issue, but I think Bob Thompson handled himself very well in his situation, always making friends. I remember when we got word in the gallery that he had died in Rome, spontaneously everyone started crying. He was that well-liked."

Hart's observations notwithstanding, Thompson's success brought the usual resentment, a substantial amount of it from black artists, whether out of aesthetic disagreement or disdain for the tricks of his climbing game. In addition, most black artists were afraid that when the "presentation spook" was selected, no more need apply. The anger of certain black painters toward Bob Thompson is worth recording, if only because we can better understand the complex of hostility that knows no racial limitations.

"If Bob had been white," said one, "he would have been dismissed as a primitive and never shown. He didn't have any problems with white people and he didn't present any challenges in his art, because all of his forms came from the European masters. That made white people comfortable."

"At a time when most black painters were scuffling," another observed, "Bob Thompson had a big loft, paint and canvases, brushes, all the materials he needed, plus a habit and money to waste on dope. He was no more than a bourgeois junkie in blackface. Actually, he was one of the luckiest people I have ever known."

"Painters," fumed still another, "don't mature until they're at least 35. People are just trying to make a legend out of that guy. He was just an overrated painter whose technical limitations were excused because of the coon show he put on downtown."

Doubtless, Thompson knew what he was doing, but what sculptor Mel Edwards says about him is clearly more to the point: "Bob Thompson did a lot for black artists in that he showed it was possible to get your ideas out there as they were coming into existence, which was, and still is, very unusual for one of us these many years later."

V. DEATH WAS THE LIMIT

Back in the United States in 1964, Bob Thompson once again felt racial pressure. But the pressure was different from what it had been when he left America. Black nationalism was the rise, its spokesmen contemptuously attacking the vision of racial coalition and social ease at the center of the Civil Rights Movement. Though LeRoi Jones recalls discussing the inevitable decline and failure of nonviolence with the painter, Thompson had been caught off guard by the focus on ethnic identity and fate that was seeping into bohemia, which contradicted his own dedication to individuality and to the metaphorical protests of art. Yet Thompson responded to the violence of his era in ways that revealed the delicacy within his durable exterior. Jones was out with Thompson the day John Kennedy was assassinated in Dallas. The painter stumbled into the gutter and began sobbing, a response he was to repeat upon hearing that a bum he knew died, just as he wept and had to be consoled by Jackie McLean when his landlord expired, and by both LeRoi Jones and his wife Hettie after Carol Thompson had an operation in 1963 for cancer of the uterus.

According to LeRoi Jones, 1964 was an especially difficult year for black artists living in the East Village: "It seemed as though each person was being forced into a political or philosophical position, whether or not that person was formally involved with an organization." Four months after Kennedy's assassination, James Baldwin's *Blues for Mr. Charlie* opened and the whole question of nonviolence was put in another perspective. As one reviewer pointed out, violence in pursuit of liberation is very different from violence that sustains oppression, though the carnage is the same. In April, Jones's *Dutchman* began its performances, filling the air with threats, disavowing any white understanding of black alienation, art, or motive. Then Harlem rioted in July.

By that summer, Bob Thompson's habit had so depleted his veins that he was forced to push the needles into his hands, the swollen and tracked fingers of which he hid beneath heavy woolen mittens as he walked the humid Manhattan streets in his overcoat. Thompson would try cures, but he always returned to heroin, sometimes prolonging his avoidance with alcohol.

Often during his last months in New York Thompson would pick Jackie McLean up from his house and take him to a bar, pointing out derelicts' faces with awe. "Look at that motherfucker with the crushed up face and bloody lip. Can you imagine what he must have seen? Now this is *really*

America down here. There ain't no color, just suffering. I want to express some of that in my paintings, tell these motherfuckers how it feels out here. Now let's go uptown for some stuff."

One of the last memories McLean has of Thompson is his getting up out of his bed, leg broken, hobbling down the stairs on crutches, and going out into the winter of early 1965 to catch a cab that took him to a pusher who wouldn't sell anything to McLean because he didn't know him. The habit was then demanding that much of Thompson.

On February 21, 1965, Malcolm X was assassinated and six months later Watts rioted. By this time, one of Thompson's friends was with him when it took the painter two hours of exploratory jabbing and pricking to find a vein for his fix. By then, Thompson's heavy Austrian World War I overcoat was hanging more loosely around him, though he painted and partied with the same fervor, broadening his style and reflecting the period with apocalyptic visions that abstracted the events of the era to metaphors of torturers and victims. Thompson had his say through Sambo figures looking helplessly on as demons flayed or mutilated a captive.

On September 21, 1965, Thompson broke all attendance records at a second one-man Martha Jackson show. Following his success, Thompson asked Jackson to send him to Rome for a year, promising he would come back after studying the masters with some fine, fine paintings. Jackson agreed, and in November Bob and Carol Thompson left for Rome.

In Italy, Thompson's greatest dream was fulfilled: He finally saw the Arezzo frescoes of Piero della Francesca. Musician Richard Teitelbaum was there when Thompson first looked upon the work of the Italian master. "It was very inspirational, because I had never seen anyone respond to art with so much intensity. It was the most visceral experience I had ever witnessed. He was awed, angered, and challenged. He loved the work, it intimidated him, and he vowed to equal what he saw. It was beyond shaking one's fist at fate; Thompson was shaking his fist at the weight of history, art history, a history he understood intimately and clearly, so well that his responses to it were physical and vocal. It was almost frightening to watch."

Though he wasn't looking very well, Thompson was studying and dissipating with his usual fervor. He did a lot of work by anyone's standards but his own. His paints and canvases, brushes and easels, were held up in transit somehow and didn't arrive in time for him to use them. Most of his art from those last days is in crayon, ink, or pencil.

In March, Carol Thompson rushed her husband to the hospital. Doubled over with pain, Thompson was told by a doctor that if he had an operation on his gall bladder he could eat and drink anything he wanted. Carol Thompson disagreed. "I told him that if he wanted to have an operation, he should have it in New York, not in Italy. He wouldn't listen to anything I might tell him. But he could be convinced by a father figure, a priest or a doctor, who could be a complete stranger." Bob Thompson consented to have the operation.

The surgery left Thompson in so much pain that he rued having given his permission. Upon leaving the hospital in April, the painter was told that he couldn't drink or use drugs, and his tragedy was given its final downward thrust. Troubled, depressed, and confused, he separated from his wife, sending her to Greece with her sister, where they remained for four weeks. He would be dead when she returned to Rome.

The last four weeks of Bob Thompson's life were spent as he had lived the previous eight years. He stayed in the streets, ate very little, and took a lot of drugs. One musician who saw him at the time recalls, "Oh, yeah, Bob was shooting a lot of dope, but everybody did. Those were very self-destructive days and you found out what was enough when it killed you. Death was the limit."

In Thompson's final days some musician friends arrived in Rome with a supply of very potent black heroin, which they used in small quantities. Thompson was told that he couldn't have any and that he should get some rest. At that point, Thompson was stirring up heroin and Quaaludes in Coca-Cola, drinking the mixture, and going to sleep. He went to a party with the musicians the night before he died. Vibraphonist Karl Berger was staying with Thompson at the time and thought he was quite strong, since the painter had brought a woman over to his apartment and spent the day in bed with her a few days earlier. When Thompson arrived home after the party, he awakened Berger and showed him a family album. "He told me all about his life, stories from his childhood and his career. It went on for quite a while, as if he wanted to make sure someone knew who he was. Since he had awakened me at the time, I didn't make much of it, though there was a real urgency to what he was saying. The next morning, I went to wake Bob up and he was dead. I think now that perhaps he knew he was going to die and chose to tell me his story before he did." Thompson's lungs had flooded, dousing the fire that had become legendary in the interracial bacchanal he detailed with such primitive zest and sophisticated terror.

VI. CODA

Though Bob Thompson died across the square from a Catholic priest who martyred his way to sainthood by hurling himself out of a window, the painter's importance to us now, two full decades after his body could no longer hold destruction at bay, is not defined by the way he paved to his grave. No artist whose clarity of sensibility produces a parallel technical triumph is a martyr. While Bob Thompson lived he stood up to the demands of his gifts, and to the history of visual art, and to those painters he most admired, using it all to tell a spiritually gory tale of love and glory. The painter knew himself well enough to realize that the flag of sensation under which he campaigned against his body was impossible to carry beyond his early years. Physically, Bob Thompson loved the things that destroyed him; artistically, he summoned the will that gives emotion such a timeless form that passion transcends the circumstances of initial inspiration and becomes emblematic of human experience. No one needs talent to die from drink and drugs; but only Robert Louis Thompson could have left us those paintings.

FLOGGING THE WEST
October 14, 1986

Controversy rages over *The Africans, A Triple Heritage,* a nine-part series that begins Thursday, at 9 p.m., on WNET. Lynne V. Cheney, chairman of the National Endowment for the Humanities, flipped out when she saw the series her agency helped underwrite for public television, demanding that the NEH's name be struck from the funding credits. Cheney called the series "anti-Western," accused the producers of duping the government, and sneered at the script for lacking scholarly objectivity.

Given the show's dubious ideology, I can easily understand Cheney's outrage. But it seems to me that she might better have proposed half-hour discussions following each episode. That way of examining a subject has often been used on public television, allowing for disputes while the audience has all the points fresh in mind. Then the viewer would get a bigger frame of interpretation than *The Africans* itself provides.

When I first became aware of this series, I thought it might have been done by, or in conjunction with, David Lamb, whose book, *The Africans,* is the strongest and most honest contemporary reporting I've read on the subject. Lamb documents insipid American foreign policy, African complicity in the slave trade, Soviet racism, Western arrogance and brutality, one military dictator bloodily rising after another, catastrophic economic policies, and so on, playing no favorites and ultimately concluding that it might be wrongheaded to impose any Western economic structure—capitalist or Marxist—on postcolonial countries at such primitive levels of development.

But this series isn't Lamb's work, nor is it informed by the unsentimental intellectual rigor we need in an age when so much human complexity is obscured by trickle-down moral posturing from the right or left. The four episodes I screened are largely devoted to what Middle East scholar Edward Said terms "a politics of blame." The script is given to unconvincing, barely veiled rants about the victimization of Africa and the demonic influence of the Western world. Obviously, a balanced analysis would be impossible without a list of physical and economic atrocities, but balance isn't important to Ali A. Mazrui, a Kenyan scholar who wrote and narrates the series.

The Africans purports to discuss three sources of the continent's cultural and economic identity: tribal, Arab, and Western influences. Instead, Mazrui apologizes for almost any intrinsically African evil in order to flog the West as often as possible. Though he rails against the hypocrisy of Christianity, he goes pretty easy on Islam, never really jumping on the Arabs for their imperialism. Unlike the Ousmane Sembene film, *Ceddo*, Mazrui talks as though he's never heard of the Islamic sweep of the African continent that made one either a believer who couldn't be enslaved or an infidel who could. He is quick to talk about how badly Africa came out in its business dealings with Europeans, but chooses to ignore the effects Arab oil prices have had on black African countries, and he completely avoids the colonization of African votes against Israel in the U.N. with petrol dollars. He claims that the industrial revolution begot a higher morality, and turned England from the biggest investor in slave ships and their cargoes during the 18th century into the prime abolitionist government in the 19th. Was there a comparable abolitionist movement in any Arab state; was there an Islamic underground railroad? I have no idea, and I didn't find out from *The Africans*.

The way Mazrui floats over African involvement in the slave trade, raids on other tribes, marches through the bush, sales of human beings for rum, red cloth, umbrellas, trinkets, and rifles is shockingly dishonest. Oh, we had our slavery, too, he admits. Standing in a fortress cell where slaves captured and sold by other Africans were kept, Mazrui has some sense of what a Jew feels in a death camp. Does he now? Then he contends that "the slave trade rapidly transformed Africans into the most humiliated race in human history." The American Indians might contest that claim, as might the Jews, the Cambodians, the Ukrainians, and others.

His reference to Karl Marx as the last great Jewish prophet may explain why Mazrui doesn't really push Marxist African dictators like Sekou Toure up against their atrocities, preferring to focus on those ruthless men supported by Western democracies. He does come down hard on the persistence of military coups with statements such as, "The barracks and the military college have replaced the colonial prison as a university for future leaders." But that observation is tempered by an absurd claim that denies the long African history of ruthless relationships to power: "By weakening Africa's ancient institutions and creating modern armies, colonialism has left the continent threatened by two forces—the danger of anarchy in the sense of too little government, and the peril of tyranny when there is too much."

Such apologies abound in *The Africans*, and logic is crushed by defensiveness. Even so, there are great moments in this series, such as a satire of military incompetence performed in Nigeria. There is a compelling presence that comes through whenever Africans enter the frame. To see them straddling or synthesizing the old and new has an intriguing excitement, suggesting fresh versions of modern life as opposed to any loss of identity. Watch *The Africans* if you wish, but read David Lamb if you want real information, and even pick up Mazrui's book that accompanies the series; it is given to much more thorough thinking.

AUNT MEDEA
October 19, 1987

Much of the Afro-American fiction written over the last 25 years derives from a vision set down by James Baldwin, who described the downtrodden as saintly. According to Baldwin, those who had suffered most knew life best; they had more to tell the world. Though Negroes had been taught to hate themselves, though they were emasculated, driven mad, or driven to drink or to drugs, Baldwin insisted that somewhere in the souls of those black folk were truths that might set everyone free:

> I do not mean to be sentimental about suffering—enough is certainly as good as a feast—but people who cannot suffer can never grow up, can never discover who they are. That man who is forced each day to snatch his manhood, his identity out of the fire of human cruelty that rages to destroy it knows, if he survives his effort, and even if he does not survive it, something about himself and human life that no school on earth—and, indeed, no church—can teach. He achieves his own authority, and that is unshakable. This is because, in order to save his life, he is forced to look beneath appearances, to take nothing for granted, to hear the meaning behind the words. If one is continually surviving the worst that life can bring, one eventually ceases to be controlled by a fear of what life can bring; whatever it brings must be borne. And at this level of experience one's bitterness begins to be palatable, and hatred becomes too heavy a sack to carry.

Baldwin's success as the voice of the racially oppressed proved that something had changed in American entertainment. The United States had no sense of tragedy because Americans hate losers, William Carlos Williams observed in his emotionally brambled *In the American Grain;* but with Baldwin the claim to martyrdom, real or merely asserted, began to take on value. One no longer had to fear the charge of self-pity when detailing the suffering of one's group. Catastrophic experience was elevated. Race became an industry. It spawned careers, studies, experts, college departments, films, laws, hairdos, name changes, federal programs, and so many *books*. Blessed are the victims, the new catechism taught, for their suffering has illuminated them, and they shall lead us to the light, even as they provide magnets for our guilt.

Toni Morrison's new novel is another patch in that quilt, the most recent proof of the course of racial letters since Baldwin. It was not long before feminist ideology brought its own list of atrocities to the discussion: The horrors wrought by the priapic demon of sexism. Men and their obsession with manhood, with conquest, with violence, with the subjugation of the opposite sex and even the environment itself, were the problem. They had made things so bad that some feminists felt comfortable saying that "woman is the nigger of the universe," usurping a term of insult, and opening the way for those black women who would rise to contend for the martyr's belt that had been worn so long by the black man.

The influence of feminism on writing by black women led to work that was charged with corroborating the stereotypes of bestial black men. Zip Coon, the dangerous darkie whose pedigree stretched back to the minstrel show, became a stock character in black feminist writing. Old Zip replaced Uncle Tom as the lowest form of black life. In various manifestations he threw his children out the window, abused his wife until she murdered him, raped his daughter and drove her mad, or made intimate life so harsh and insensitive that lesbianism was the only human alternative. A pip-squeak in the world, he was hell on wheels at home. As Diane Johnson, writing on Toni Morrison and Gayle Jones, noted:

> In a demoralized subculture, everyone is a victim, but women, especially girls, are actually the most defenseless. . . . Morrison and Jones present them also as cleverer, more interesting, and eventually more homicidal than men; men are childlike, barely sentient, and predatory. Nearly all the women characters in these works have been sexually abused and exploited, usually as children.

Baldwin, Malcolm X, Eldridge Cleaver, and others had sung the same song, but now the circle of culprits was expanded. White America was still racist, violent, spiritually deficient, and exploiting, but the venom formerly reserved for Caucasians was spewed far enough to drench black men as well. Though black men clearly experienced racism, the worst of them were not above taking advantage of patriarchal conventions and brutally lording over their families—in the same way Southern white trash had used racism as an instrument of release whenever they were frustrated and Negroes were available to absorb the shocks of their passions. What might have begun as rightful indignation quickly decayed to a self-righteous, bullying whine and, went the claim, was turned inward, on one's own.

Black feminist writing was especially resented by those black men who had enjoyed the social, political, and sexual benefits resulting from the smug cartoonish version of "black manhood" promoted by radical organizations. That stylized image supposedly restored the patriarchal privilege denied by bondage and racism. Black feminists challenged the predictability of protest writing by black men, and the idiot cards of "positive black images," criticizing the plots and portraits as incomplete, as failing to tell the entire story and avoiding the problems of personal responsibility. The majority of black male writers had been content to see the difficulties experienced by black women at the hands of black men as no more than the byproducts of racism, but Negro feminists protested something different. As Johnson observed, "Undoubtedly, white society is the ultimate oppressor, and not just of blacks, but, as Morrison and Jones show, the black person must first deal with the oppressor in the next room, or in the same bed, or no farther away than across the street."

So the martyr's belt hadn't been worn very well by the self-declared champ. But exposing the shortcomings in protest writing by black men didn't automatically make writing by black women any better. Writers like Alice Walker revealed little more than their own inclinations to melodrama, militant self-pity, guilt-mongering, and pretensions to mystic wisdom. What the Walkers really achieved was a position parallel to the one held by Uncle Remus in *Song of the South:* the ex-slave supplies the white children and the white adults with insights into human nature and the complexity of the world through his tales of Brer Rabbit. Better, these black women writers took over the role played by the black maids in so many old films: when poor little white missy is at a loss, she is given guidance by an Aunt Jemima look-alike.

Toni Morrison gained more from these changes in black literary fashion than anybody else. As an editor at Random House, she was one of the most powerful people in the New York literary world. With *Song of Solomon,* which appeared in 1979, she became a best-selling novelist too, proving that the combination of poorly digested folk materials, feminist rhetoric, and a labored use of magic realism could pay off. Shrewdly Morrison separated herself from the speeches and writing produced in the middle to late '60s by Stokely Carmichael, LeRoi Jones, Eldridge Cleaver, and H. Rap Brown, but avoided any serious criticism of their views. She told an interviewer that "those books and political slogans about power were addressed to white men, trying to explain or prove something to them. The fight was between men, for the king of the hill." Yet none of the black women whom Morrison proceeded to celebrate— Toni Cade Bambara, Gayle Jones, Alice Walker—took any significant positions of their own against the wrongheadedness of a black politics that mixed a romanticized African past with separatist ideas, virulent anti-white racism, and threats to overthrow the government of the United States "by any means necessary." Morrison didn't either.

What Morrison did do was consolidate her position as a literary conjure woman. Consider, for example, Mary Gordon's fantasy about her. It provides a generous taste of the spiritual and intellectual status that Morrison assumed in the dream world of white women:

> I once dreamed that she bought a huge old Victorian mansion. It would one day be beautiful, but now it was a wreck, with cobwebs, broken windows, mice, rats, and vermin everywhere. I asked her how she was going to deal with all that mess. She simply said, "No problem," and waved her arms in the air. Immediately the rats and roaches disappeared and the house was beautiful.

Hoo doo to you too.

Beloved, Morrison's fourth novel, explains black behavior in terms of social conditioning, as if listing atrocities solves the mystery of human motive and behavior. It is designed to placate sentimental feminist ideology, and to make sure that the vision of black woman as the most scorned and rebuked of the victims doesn't weaken. Yet perhaps it is best understood by its italicized inscription: *"Sixty Million and More."* Morrison recently told *Newsweek* that the reference was to all the captured Africans who died coming across the Atlantic. But sixty is ten times six, of course. This is very important to remember. For *Beloved,* above all else, is a blackface holocaust novel. It seems to have been written in order to enter American slavery into the big-time martyr ratings contest, a contest usually won by references to, and works about, the experience of Jews at the hands of Nazis. As a holocaust novel, it includes disfranchisement, brutal transport, sadistic guards, failed and successful escapes, murder, liberals among the oppressors, a big war, underground cells, separation of family members, losses of loved ones to the violence of the mad order, and characters who, like the Jew in *The Pawnbroker,* have been made emotionally catatonic by the past.

That Morrison chose to set the Afro-American experience in the framework of collective tragedy is fine, of course. But she lacks a true sense of the tragic. Such a sense is stark, but it is never simple-minded. For all the memory within this book, including recollections of the trip across the Atlantic and the slave trading in the Caribbean, no one ever recalls how the Africans were captured. That would have complicated matters. It would have demanded that the Africans who raided the villages of their enemies to sell them for guns, drink, and trinkets be included in the equation of injustice, something far too many Afro-Americans are loath to do—including Toni Morrison. In *Beloved* Morrison only asks that her readers tally up the sins committed against the darker people and feel sorry for them, not experience the horrors of slavery as they do.

Morrison, unlike Alice Walker, has real talent, an ability to organize her novel in a musical structure, deftly using images as motifs; but she perpetually interrupts her narrative with maudlin ideological commercials. Though there are a number of isolated passages of first-class writing, and though secondary characters such as Stamp Paid and Lady Jones are superbly drawn, Morrison rarely gives the impression that her people exist for any purpose other than to deliver a message. *Beloved* fails to rise to tragedy because it shows no sense of the timeless and unpredictable manifestations of evil that preceded and followed American slavery, of the gruesome ditches in the human spirit that prefigure all injustice. Instead, the novel is done in the pulp style that has dominated so many renditions of Afro-American life since *Native Son.*

As in all protest pulp fiction, everything is locked into its own time, and is ever the result of external social forces. We learn little about the souls of human beings, we are only told what will happen if they are treated very badly. The world exists in a purple haze of overstatement, of false voices, of strained homilies; nothing very subtle is ever really tried. *Beloved* reads largely like a melodrama lashed to the structural conceits of the miniseries. Were *Beloved* adapted for television (which would suit the crass obviousness that wins out over Morrison's literary gift at every significant turn) the trailer might go like this:

"Meet Sethe, an ex-slave woman who harbors a deep and terrible secret that has brought terror into her home. [Adolescent sons are shown fleeing.] Meet Paul D, who had a passion for Sethe when they were both slaves, but lost her to another. [Sethe shown walking with first husband Halle, smiling as Paul D looks on longingly.] During slavery they had been treated as human beings at Sweet Home in Kentucky by the Garners. [Garners waving to their slaves, who read books, carry guns into the woods, seem very happy.] That was before the master died, the mistress took sick, and schoolteacher, the cruel overseer, took over. [Master Garner on deathbed, Mrs. Garner enfeebled, schoolteacher being cruel.] No longer treated like human beings, reduced to the condition of work animals, the slaves of Sweet Home plot to escape. [Slaves planning escape around a fire.] Sethe, swollen with child, bravely makes her way to Ohio, determined to see that the child is born free! [Sethe trudging along with great determination.] And there, in Ohio, the terrible deed takes place. [Slave catchers dismounting and Sethe running into a barn with her children.] Sethe's home is ruled by the angry spirit of an innocent child, until Paul D returns to her life. [House shaking, Paul D holding onto table as he shouts.]

"Now they are together, but the weight of the past will not let them live in the freedom they always dreamed of. Then the mysterious Beloved appears and becomes part of the family, charming Denver, Sethe's only remaining child, and the horrible past begins to come clear. [Scenes of Africans in the holds of ships.] Relive some of America's most painful moments—slavery, the Civil War, the efforts made by ex-slaves to experience freedom in a world that was stacked against them from the moment they were sold as work animals. But, most of all, thrill to a love story about the kinds of Americans who struggled to make this country great. [Sethe, Paul D, and Denver walking hand-in-hand.]"

Beloved means to prove that Afro-Americans are the result of a cruel determinism:

> . . . [that's] what Baby Suggs died of, what Ella knew, what Stamp saw and what made Paul D tremble. That anybody white could take your whole self for anything that came to mind. Not just work, kill, or maim you, but dirty you. . . . Dirty you so bad you forgot who you were and couldn't think it up.

This determinism is also responsible for the character of Sethe, the earth mother heroine who might be called Aunt Medea. Mistakenly thinking that they will be sent back to slavery, Sethe gathers her four children for slaughter, and kills one daughter before she is stopped. When the novel opens, it is 1873. The ghost of the dead daughter has been haunting Sethe's home for years, frightening off neighbors, shaking, rattling, and rolling the house.

The book's beginning clanks out its themes. Aunt Medea's two sons have been scared off: There is the theme of black women facing the harsh world alone. Later on in the novel, Morrison stages the obligatory moment of transcendent female solidarity, featuring a runaway indentured white girl, Amy Denver, who aids pregnant Sethe in her time of need:

> A pateroller passing would have sniggered to see two throwaway people, two lawless outlaws—a slave and a barefoot whitewoman with unpinned hair—wrapping a ten-minute-old baby in the rags they wore. But no pateroller came and no preacher. The water sucked and swallowed itself beneath them. There was nothing to disturb them at their work. So they did it appropriately and well.

Woman to woman, out in nature, freed of patriarchal domination and economic exploitation, they deliver baby Denver. (Amy is also good for homilies. While massaging Sethe's feet, she says, "Anything dead coming back to life hurts." When Sethe quotes the girl as she tells Amy's namesake the story of her birth, Morrison writes, "A truth for all times, thought Denver." As if that weren't gooey enough, there's the fade-out: "Sethe felt herself falling into a sleep she knew would be deep. On the lip of it, just before going under, she thought, 'That's pretty. Denver. Real pretty.'")

Then there is the sexual exploitation theme, introduced in a flashback in the opening pages: for ten minutes of sex, the impoverished Sethe gets the name "Beloved" put on the gravestone. This theme in particular is given many variations. One of the clumsiest comes in an amateurishly conceived flashback designed to reveal that even Sethe's mother had a touch of Medea:

> Nighttime. Nan holding her with her good arm, waving the stump of the other in the air. "Telling you. I am telling you, small girl Sethe," and she did that. She told Sethe that her mother and Nan were to-

gether from the sea. Both were taken up many times by the crew. "She threw them all away but you. The one from the crew she threw away on the island. The others from more whites she also threw away. Without names, she threw them. You she gave the name of the black man. She put her arms around him. The others she did not put her arms around. Never. Never. Telling you. I am telling you, small girl Sethe."

It doesn't get much worse, or the diction any more counterfeit.

Baby Suggs, Sethe's mother-in-law, is philosophical about the house ghost, and introduces the stoicism theme when it is suggested that they move away. "Not a house in the country ain't packed to its rafters with some dead Negro's grief. We lucky this ghost is a baby," she tells Sethe. "My husband's spirit was to come back in here? or yours? Don't talk to me. You lucky. You got three left. Three pulling at your skirts and just one raising hell from the other side. Be thankful, why don't you? I had eight. Every one of them gone away from me. Four taken, four chased, and all, I expect, worrying somebody's house into evil." Through Baby Suggs we will eventually learn how right Paul D is to conclude that "for a used to-be-slave woman to love . . . that much was dangerous, especially if it was her children she had settled on to love. The best thing, he knew, was to love just a little bit; everything, just a little bit, so when they broke its back, or shoved it in a croaker sack, well, maybe you'd have a little love left over for the next one."

Morrison is best at clear, simple description, and occasionally she can give an account of the casualties of war and slavery that is free of false lyricism or stylized stoicism:

> Sethe took a little spit from the tip of her tongue with her forefinger. Quickly, lightly she touched the stove. Then she trailed her fingers through the flour, parting, separating small hills and ridges of it, looking for mites. Finding none, she poured soda and salt into the crease of her folded hand and tossed both into the flour. Then she reached into a can and scooped half a handful of lard. Deftly she squeezed the flour through it, then with her left hand sprinkling water, she formed the dough.

Or Paul D remembering the people he saw on the road after making his escape from slavery, people

> who, like him, had hidden in caves and fought owls for food; who, like him, stole from pigs; who, like him, slept in trees in the day and walked by night; who, like him, had buried themselves in slop and jumped in wells to avoid regulators, raiders, paterollers, veterans, hill men, posses, and merrymakers. Once he met a Negro fourteen years old who lived by himself in the woods and said he couldn't remember living anywhere else. He saw a witless coloredwoman jailed and hanged for stealing ducks she believed were her own babies.

But Morrison almost always loses control. She can't resist the temptation of the trite or the sentimental. There is the usual scene in which the black woman is assaulted by white men while her man looks on; Halle, Sethe's husband, goes mad at the sight. Sixo, a slave who is captured trying to escape, is burned alive but doesn't scream: he sings "Seven-o" over and over, because his woman has escaped and is pregnant. But nothing is more contrived than the figure of Beloved herself, who is the reincarnated force of the malevolent ghost that was chased from the house. Beloved's revenge—she takes over the house, turns her mother into a servant manipulated by guilt, and becomes more and more vicious—unfolds as portentous melodrama. When Beloved finally threatens to kill Sethe, thirty black women come to the rescue. At the fence of the haunted property, one of them shouts, and we are given this: "Instantly the kneelers and the standers joined her. They stopped praying and took a step back to the beginning. In the beginning there were no words. In the beginning was the sound, and they all knew what that sound sounded like."

Too many such attempts at biblical grandeur, run through by Negro folk rhythms, stymie a book that might have been important. Had Morrison higher intentions when she appropriated the conventions of a holocaust tale, *Beloved* might stand next to, or outdistance, Ernest Gaines's *The Autobiography of Miss Jane Pittman* and Charles Johnson's *Oxherding Tale*, neither of which submits to the contrived, post-Baldwin vision of Afro-American experience. Clearly the subject is far from exhausted, the epic intricacies apparently unlimited. Yet to render slavery with aesthetic authority demands not only talent but the courage to face the ambiguities of the human soul, which transcend race. Had Toni Morrison that kind of courage, had she the passion necessary to liberate her work from the failure of feeling that is sentimentality, there is much that she could achieve. But why should she try to achieve anything? The position of literary conjure woman has paid off quite well. At last year's PEN Congress she announced that she had never considered herself American, but with *Beloved* she proves that she is as American as P. T. Barnum.

MAN IN THE MIRROR
November 17, 1987

Because Afro-Americans have presented challenges to one order or another almost as long as they have been here, fear and contempt have frequently influenced the way black behavior is assessed. The controversy over Michael Jackson is the most recent example, resulting in a good number of jokes, articles in this periodical and others, and even the barely arctiulate letter by the singer himself that was published in *People*. Jackson has inspired debate over his cosmetic decisions because the residue of '60s black nationalism and the condescension of those who would pity or mock black Americans have met over the issue of his face, his skin tone, his hair.

Since the '60s, there has been a tendency among a substantial number of Afro-Americans to promulgate a recipe for the model black person. That model has taken many forms, but all of them are based on presumptions of cultural segregation between black and white Americans. The symbols of that purported segregation were supposed to permeate the ways in which black people lived, dressed, wore their hair, ate, thought, voted, walked, talked, and addressed their African heritage. And though the grip of such nationalism weakened over the years, it continues to influence even those who were lucky enough not to have been adolescents during its period of dominance.

Greg Tate is clearly one who has been taken in, and his recent article on Jackson illustrates the provincialism inherent in such thinking. Jackson alarms Tate, who sees the singer's experience under the scalpel as proof of self-hatred. The trouble with Tate's vision is that it ignores the substance of the American dream and the inevitabilities of a free society. Though no one other than Jackson could know what he seeks, to automatically assume that the pop star's cosmetic surgery was solely intended to eradicate Negroid features in order to "look white" seems far too simple, ignoring both African and American cultural elements.

Présence Africaine published some 20 years ago a compendium of papers delivered in Senegal at the World Festival of Negro Arts. One of the lecturers made note of the fact that a number of African tribes considered the lighter-skinned the more attractive. This vision of beauty was free of colonial influence and probably had more to do with the quality of exoticism that is as central to magnetism as to repulsion. Further, Jackson could just as easily be opting for the mulatto look—if not that of the Latin lover and dandy—that has resulted from the collusion of gene pools whenever light and dark folk have coupled on the Basin Streets of history. Or could he be taken by the keen noses and "refined" features of Ethopians?

The fact that Michael Jackson not only is a person of African descent but is also an American should never be excluded from a discussion of his behavior. The American dream is actually the idea that an identity can be improvised and can function socially if it doesn't intrude upon the freedom of anyone else. With that freedom comes eccentric behavior as well as the upward mobility resulting from talent, discipline, and good fortune—*and* the downward mobility observed in *some* of those who inhabit the skid rows of this country because they *prefer* the world of poverty and alcoholism to the middle-, upper-middle-, or upper-class backgrounds they grew up in. As one bum who had obviously seen better days said to a waiter as he was being ushered out of the now defunct Tin Palace for panhandling, "People come from all over the world to be bums on the Bowery. Why should I deny myself that right?"

Tate should easily understand this since he is from a well-to-do black family in Washington, D.C., but has chosen to wear dreadlocks in a hairdo that crosses the Rasta world with that of the mohawk and, eschewing the conservative dress of his background, looks as often as not like a borderline homeless person. That Tate is a bohemian by choice rather than birth means that he has plotted out an identity he prefers to that of his social origins and has found the costumes that he feels most appropriate for his personal theatre piece. Though it is much easier for Tate to get another haircut and change his dress than it would be for Jackson to return to his "African physiognomy," each reflects the willingness to opt for imagery that repudiates some aspect of the past.

That sense of improvising an identity shouldn't be thought of as separate from the American—and universal—love of masks. Nor should it be seen as at all separate from the "African retentions" Afro-American cultural nationalists and social anthropologists refer to so frequently. The love of masks, of makeup, and of costumes is often much more than the pursuit of high fashion or the adherence to ritual convention; it is also the expression of that freedom to invent the self and of the literal *fun* Americans have often gotten from scandalizing expectations.

As Constance Rourke observed and as Albert Murray reminds us in his invaluable *The Omni-Americans*, those colonial rebels dressed up as Indians for the Boston Tea Party might have enjoyed the masquerade itself as much as they did dumping the cargo in the ocean. Considered within the spectrum of the happy to hostile masquerade that has since evolved, Michael Jackson's affection for his mirror image veering off from what nature intended places him right in the center of one of the whirlpools of national sensibility.

One needs only to look at any book of photographs from the '60s to see how the connection between protest politics and the love of masks was most broadly played out—SNCC workers donned overalls; hippies took to long hair and tie-dyed outfits; black nationalists wore Figi haircuts and robes; and self-styled Afro-American revolutionaries put on black berets, black leather jackets, black shirts, pants, and shoes, or appropriated the combat dress of Third World military men. And no one who looks at the various costumes worn today, from dotted, yellow "power ties" to gargoyle punk fashions, should have any problem seeing their connection to the masking inclinations rooted in the joy of assumed identities. That love is still so embedded in the national personality that the people of New Orleans are admired as much for the costumes and false faces of Mardi Gras as for their cuisine and their music. And those of us in New York know how much pleasure the greasepaint, sequins, feathers, and satins of the Labor Day parade in Brooklyn bring to spectators and participants.

As far as further African retentions are concerned, it could easily be argued that Michael Jackson is much more in line with the well-documented argument many primitive African cultures have had with the dictates of nature. Have the people of any other cultures so perfectly prefigured plastic surgery or been more willing to accept the pain of traditionally approved mutilation? It is doubtful. In photograph after photograph, Africans are shown wearing plates in their lips to extend them, rings around their necks to lengthen them, plopping red mud in their hair for homemade conks that emulate the manes of lions, filing their teeth, and suffering through the slashes and the rubbed-in ashes that result in spectacular scarification. Whatever one wants to say about "different standards of beauty" and so forth, to conclude that such cultures are at all concerned with "being natural" is to actually reveal one's refusal to see things as they are.

That willingness to suffer under the tribal knife is obviously addressed with much greater technical sophistication in the world of plastic surgery. In fact, the so-called self-hatred of black Americans, whenever it *does* exist, is perhaps no more than a racial variation on the national attitude that has made the beauty industry so successful. In those offices and in those operating rooms where plans are made and carried out that result in millions of dollars in profit, the supposed self-hatred of black Americans has little to do with the wealth earned by plastic surgeons. Far and away, the bulk of their clients are Caucasians in flight from the evidence of age, Caucasians dissatisfied with their profiles, their eyes, their ears, their chins, their necks, their breasts, the fat around their knees, their waists, their thighs, and so forth. Nipped, tucked, carrying implants, and vacuumed free of fat, they face their mirrors with glee.

Where there is so much talk about Afro-Americans fawning over the lighter-skinned among them, what is one to make of all the bottle blondes this country contains and all of those who make themselves sometimes look orange by using lotions for counterfeit tans? It is a certainty that if some Negro American genius were to invent a marketable procedure that would result in harmlessly emitting the desired levels of melanin for those Caucasians enthralled by tans so that they could remain as dark as they wished throughout the year, his or her riches would surpass those of Bill Cosby. Would this imaginary genius be exploiting Caucasian self-hatred?

Then there is the problem some have with Jackson's apparent softness, his supposed effeminacy. That, too, has a precedent within Afro-American culture itself. The late writer Lionel Mitchell once pointed out that certain black men were bothered about the black church because they were made uncomfortable by those choir directors and pretty-boy lead singers who wore glistening marcelled hair and were obviously homosexual. A friend of Mitchell's extended the writer's position by observing that those very gospel songs were just as often masks through which homosexual romance was crooned. "What do you think is going through their minds when the songs talk about being held close to *His* bosom?" (What a variation on the ways slaves secretly signaled each other through spirituals, planning flight or rebellion!) This is not to say that every homosexual gospel singer thought of things more secular than spiritual when chirping those songs in which love is felt for and from an almighty He or Him, but it is to say that those who feel Jackson has somehow sold out his masculine duties have not looked as closely at their own tradition as perhaps they should.

There is also the fact that Jackson, both as androgynous performer and surgical veteran purportedly seeking to look like Diana Ross, has precursors in the minstrel shows of the middle 19th century. It is there that the tradition of the romantic balladeer actually begins, at least as a phenomenon of mass entertainment. As Robert C. Toll observes in *Blacking Up*, white minstrels became very popular with women because they were able to publicly express tender emotion through the convention of burnt cork and were sometimes able to become national stars for their performances as giddy mulatto beauties. "Female impersonators excited more interest than any other minstrel specialist," writes Toll. "Men in the audience probably were titillated by the alluring stage characters whom they were momentarily drawn to, and they probably got equal pleasure from mocking and laughing at them. . . . At a time when anxiety about social roles was intense, the female impersonator, who actually changed roles, fascinated the public. As a model of properly 'giddy' femininity, he could reassure men that women were in their places while at the same time showing women how to behave without competing with them. Thus, in some ways, he functioned like the blackface 'fool' who educated audiences while also reassuring them that he was their inferior. Neither man nor woman, the female impersonator threatened no one."

Jackson quite clearly bothers more than a few, from Eddie Murphy to the rappers interviewed by Guy Trebay in the article that accompanied Greg Tate's. The pit bull of Murphy's paranoia over pansies has often been unleashed on Jackson and the fact that the rappers were disturbed by Jackson's persona suggests something other than what it seems. Perhaps what bothers them most is that the singer's roots in minstrelsy are so different from their own. As Harry Allen revealed not so long ago, more than a few rappers are actually middle-class Negroes acting out their version of a "gangster aesthetic." Instead of minstrel mugging, you have counterfeit thugging, more than a tad in line with the faddish cracker sensibility of acting bad to bust the ass of the middle class on the rack of rock and roll.

Yet the actual sorrow and the pity of the Michael Jackson story is that he has had to carry the cross of an imposed significance far beyond what his music merits. Jackson comes from rhythm and blues, which is itself a dilution of blues, a descent from the profound emotion of America's first truly adult secular music. As a pop star, Jackson's fame and riches have come from the expression of adolescent passion, but he is also the product of an era in which profundity has been forced on music actually intended to function as no more than the soundtrack for teenage romance and the backbeat for the bouts of self-pity young people suffer while assaulted by their hormones. Rock criticism changed all of that, bootlegging the rhetoric of aesthetic evaluation to elevate the symbols of adolescent frenzy and influencing the way pop stars viewed themselves. So when a man's power is found in an adolescent form, time impinges upon his vitality. If sufficiently spooked, he might be moved to invent a world for himself in which all evidence that he was ever born a particular person at a particular time is removed. That removal might itself become the strongest comment upon the inevitable gloom that comes not of having been given too much too soon but of having been convinced that one is important only so long as he or she is not too old.

INTO AFRICA
December 17, 1985

Africa is one of the centerpieces of fantasy in our time. Its ambiguity and variety have always challenged the imagination, partly through dark and brutal acts, partly through a vitality that interweaves the subtle and the sizzling. Though Africa's cooperation fueled the Atlantic slave trade, though its conquest stands as a repulsive record of colonial misjudgments and excesses, and though its periodic coups are usually the work of blue-ribbon brutes, the continent's people constitute a startling and inspiring catalogue of languages, customs, and physical types.

When I was there two summers ago, traveling in quick stopovers from Dakar to Monrovia to Lagos and then spanning the continent to Nairobi, where I remained for two weeks, it was easy to see that if you want to know where the heat comes from, Africa will set you straight. If you have a passion for the scorching rendition of the human story by drums and percussively elastic dancing, Africa will run rhythmic rings through your nose and teach you new stanzas of the poetry of the pelvis. Not that there isn't abysmal poverty reminiscent of Belzoni, Mississippi, in Shauri Moyo, which means "You Are Hot," not that there isn't a gloom as wide as the waist of an elephant standing on its hind legs. But you see and feel a will intent on reducing the hold of ignorance, filth, and imprecision, intent on fusing African poetry and Western fact into a fresh interpretation of modern life.

So Africa is moving through the mist of its—and our—misunderstandings. If history is benevolent, the wounds suffered from within and without, from the worst of colonial history and contemporary African corruption, greed, and gangster politics, will all someday become no more than the ritual scars of an initiation into world status. We see only the forehead of Africa now, but it is levitating through the steam of its own heat.

I. MIDDLE PASSAGE REVERSE

On the plane I sat with a couple of Nigerians, one a tall, maple-syrup-brown student studying in Chicago, the other reddish beige, stocky, and recently graduated into the world of computer software. The student was comical, his accent and look that of a young trend-addicted Texan—a leather tie around the collar of a red shirt, that shirt covered by a black suit, his nappy hair oiled and a small suitcase of Jheri curl solution to keep those kinks under control once home and to provide friends and family entry to the circle of black American style. Both were aware of the Buhari takeover, which felled a democracy, albeit a corrupt one, and wondered whether or not the new (and since deposed) leader's submission to Islam would make much difference. It was concluded that tribal roots were deeper and thicker than religion or politics. "In our country, it is not who you know but who you are related to that makes the difference between being in the jail or out on the street, begging for your money or getting the very good job. That is how we are. But this Buhari guy, he might try to be honest. That is very dangerous in Africa, however."

The software African, an Ibo who as a child had been a terrified witness to the Biafran war of 1967–70, sat in front of me. As soon as he mentioned the war, I remembered the photograph of an Ibo mother gone mad, her huge breasts black and flaccid, her embraced baby starved dead, her hand filled with a rotted chicken she swung to taunt the hungry. He spoke softly because the other Nigerian was a Hausa, a member of the once largely ignorant tribe that the educated Ibos meant to free themselves from when they seceded. But all of that was past and he became disgruntled about other business as the flight progressed. "Look at this plane. It is filthy. I wonder if this plane is so dirty because it is going to Africa." He wrote a note to the stewardess on a napkin: *I hate you Pan Am. You have no respect for the African. You think all we deserve is dirt.* But since he wanted a second helping of food—"I am really hungry, miss"—he chose not to hand it over. I joked with him that I would give her the napkin and they would never let him fly Pan Am again. Except on the wing. Of course, when he was asked why his people weren't interested in planes, one African witch doctor answered, "We fly in our minds."

When the plane landed in Dakar and I was on the land of Africa for the first time, I didn't experience any special excitement because the greens and the low trees and the milky brown earth reminded me of the arid parts of the American Southwest. But on the low hills that surrounded the airport like a badly tattered sombrero brim, five or six long, nilotic bodies were moving in a percussive gait akin to dancing, their robes shifting position in the dry air as if measuring the wind. As we lay over, I left the plane and walked across the field, passing first a shed in which automobiles were being repaired, then a guard near the wire gate that opened to the dirt road running parallel to the landing strip. There were lots of Peugeots and Africans whose small body types counterpointed those so tall they seemed to balance the sky and the clouds on their shoulders. The wind was a hot glove, thick with invisible fur covering your every movement. But as more clouds gathered, the air cooled and the light changed, transforming the milling Senegalese in the distance into shadows in robes. I had now become accustomed once again to the African smell I'd first encountered 20 years before in college, that scent reminiscent of grease and condiments that sometimes becomes a smooth stench. And there was also the somber pride that inhabits the eyes of many and that appeared by the end of the trip to be the most universal aspect of African people, cutting across the whirlpool of religions, languages, and historical enmities.

Senegal was the land of Ousmane Sembene, that muckraking Marxist and sardonic weaver of celluloid tragedies; and the land of Léopold Senghor, whose 1930s poetry of negritude had saluted Duke Ellington's "Solitude" as a salve for the lonely African blues in Paris, but whose regime, for all his stanzas' pandering to the Baudelairean appetite for ersatz savagery, had been largely a flight from the bush to the Louvre. Here, according to the films of Sembene, the African was tied to the ground more by tribal custom, Islam, and corruption than by the oft-criticized attraction to French elegance. After all, it was the work of European scholars and explorers that informed provincial tribes which knew little of each other that there were not only more varieties of culture than they could imagine but that there was, in fact, an African *continent*. Yes, for all the huffing and puffing, for all the black kingdoms that decayed mysteriously back into prehistory, Africa is largely a European idea, the result of bigger maps and the will to knowledge as well as the desire to exploit labor and raw materials. A huge woman I saw hobbling under her blubber, a babushka spun around her head and her body covered with a print dress of smoldering color, gave me a feeling of the easeful warmth I forever associate with the American South, while the passing men who seemed formed of flesh and stilts had an effortless grace that presaged the African basketball I would see in Kenya. As the plane rose from the airstrip and headed for Liberia, an odd melancholy melted down through my skin as I sensed the long, hard march Africans would have to make. A steaming road of asphalt caked with blood lay before so many of them, just as the monstrous records of dictatorships lay immediately behind them. The mood was perfect for a sky ride to the next domain.

Monrovia was very different from Dakar. Its greenness was sweet to the eye and its air a smooth and warm rejoinder to the droning noise of the airstrip. In the airport, the shine boys were on it, after dollars, their almond eyes and high cheekbones capable of instant pathos or entrancing smiles. There was warm beer for sale, and the customary picture of the president in every shop revealed a nearly comical severity much like that of Sapphire's photograph in the old Amos and Andy television show. Except that there was little comic to it when you thought of the blood let to destroy one order and push Dr. Samuel K. Doe up to the top. The army men who walked about with the vicious arrogance of pit bulls left no question as to how power was maintained in this country. What we have read of the Reign of Terror is almost always a few seconds away in Africa, the distance only as far as the gathering of enough guns to wrest control.

In 1980, Doe had brought off a coup, storming the palace with fewer than twenty men, who gouged out the eye of the former president and disemboweled him, after which their leader called for public executions. The doomed were wounded as many times as possible before a shell bit off the top of a head or plowed fatally into a body. Perhaps that was the cost of a tradition in which the 60 local tribes had been living for over 130 years under the condescending weight of a regime begun by freed American slaves. Thinking of themselves as black pioneers, they took the land with America's military backing and formed the first African republic in 1847. Those colonizing Negroes saw their African cousins—"brothers" and "sisters" has always been an absurdly maudlin exaggeration—as no more than savage labor sources. Some think they emulated the antebellum ways of the whites they knew in America, yet in a way they were really no more than an intrusive "tribe" anticipating a monstrous aspect of Africa's political future. And they would probably have reacted in much the same way had they been put in command of droves of illiterate black Americans, given the fact that some ruthless ex-slaves had chattels themselves when they could afford them.

In the airport I met a black American businessman getting a shoeshine who had been working deals in Africa since 1976. He immediately pointed out what he considered the differences between the aggressive Monrovian shine boys and young U.S. Negroes. "If they had half the hustle these kids have got, we could get this goddamn welfare and all that crap up off our backs. Work is the only solution to our trouble." He had become well acquainted with West Africa and laughed at the local newspaper. "I buy these things to cop a giggle. They're ridiculous. 'Today the president looked out the window. Today the president put his pants on. Today the president wiped his ass with his left hand. Today the president blinked twice before sunrise.' They're all on that level. News is an unknown commodity in Africa. But one thing is sure: there are big bucks to be made over here. Big bucks. So far, the fattest deal I've done was 20 million, but that's not the top. It's our time over here—those who got their stuff together and can handle the funny ways you got to deal with these Africans. You can offend your way out of a million dollars in five minutes. No telling what the man with money looks like. He can be a dirty, nasty, greasy-looking sonofabitch. He can be in a robe or a suit with raggedy sandals and his hair hasn't been washed in only the crystal ball knows how long. But this guy can be sitting on some money, buddy. You've got to be cool. You can't look down on anybody. It's always a mystery. And the most interesting thing about it is that they *prefer* dealing with *us,* not white folks. Same thing with the Japanese. They choose spooks, too. It's our time. But it ain't going to be about the niggers in that joke back in the '60s about going back to Africa. You know the one where the boat hits the shore and all these greasy motherfuckers get off in robes and plastic beads and want to know, 'Hey, do the welfare checks come on the first and the 15th or the 10th and the 25th?' That won't do it."

As we came down in Lagos, where the greens were even more various than in Monrovia, the pilot announced that the use of camera equipment was forbidden. I was pushed back down into gloom, wondering what Nigeria's new regime preferred to keep off the photographic record. I bid farewell to the businessman and listened to a missionary explain how conversion worked and what he had learned through dealing with the spiritual concerns of Africans. "The Western version of the Joseph story is that wherever Joseph went, he never forgot God. The African version is that wherever Joseph went, he never forgot his *family.* So when asked what salvation means in African terms, you always got the answer that a man who goes home to his village and follows his father's orders will be a safe and happy man. The point for a missionary is that God the Father can be explained in those terms. That the Father of everyone is, finally, spiritual, and that doing his moral bidding will make one safe and happy." Much later, in Nairobi, I met a superbly dressed Irish lawyer, his hair silver, his gin tonic atilt, and the lines of intelligence and wit sectioning off his face, who soberly told me something I would never have imagined:

In the next century, this continent will be the center of Christianity. When the pope came here three years ago, we had the biggest crowd ever seen in Kenya. Kenyatta never drew crowds like that. In the West, we think Christianity is old hat. For the African, it is the good news. It is a release from the grip of superstition. Everything takes time to seep through, and our first legacy—our worst—was ravenous materialism. Now, very slowly, mind you, we are seeing the arrival of Western high-mindedness. It is very humbling and has that peculiar intensity you come to expect of Africans. At their best, they seem as though they could make stones come alive through the power and the sincerity of their emotion.

II. EAST AFRICAN ENTRY

We landed in Nairobi at half past midnight and the array of Africans was as provocative as that of any people I have ever seen: Africa, like a long and legged serpent, writhes over the chessboard of time, at once primeval and contemporary. There were Africans splendidly dressed in tweed jackets, silk shirts, and magnificently woven trousers who carried themselves as though they were to the rest of the world what the sun is to our solar system. Then there were others in brilliant robes and glistening Italian shoes; Africans in cowboy hats who had gold teeth, tribal scarification, and remarkably mismatched attire; Africans in deeply wrinkled $400 suits and terribly scuffed shoes, their hair as filthy as unshaken dust mops; Africans in berets and military dress, in smocks with official airport buttons. I appreciated most the arrogance and the enthusiasm, those eyes exuding temperaments as aloof as the ears of a giraffe but given the grace of bristling affection.

Everything fit together, I have long thought of this century as polyrhythmic, an era at one with the transmogrified African sensibilities of jazz, perhaps the most sophisticated performing art in Western history. But ours is also a century of speed. In that respect, the speed with which Africans moved from prehistory to software and the telex has provided a shattering but impressive compression of European history: the move from the world of magic to that of speculation, deduction, and scientific experiment. Sophisticated technology bespeaks an accurate understanding of natural law far beyond the explanation in metaphor of animist superstition. The agony of the long fight to separate church and state happened more quickly and with a brutality that did not allow African convention to suppress science or new political ideas. The moment Africans were colonized, their church was separated from the government, and the imposition of borders agreed upon by Europeans in Berlin in 1884 created pluralistic nations that tribalism in contemporary Africa has yet to truly accept. Though they were colonized, their conquest also meant access. Just as the white man changed Africa and Africa changed him, the adventure of the African in Europe's and America's libraries and laboratories means a safari into the intellect and technology that will, eventually, lead to a mutual transformation, a fresh combination, yet another bittersweet conjoining rife with uplift and destruction. It is one of the signal ironies of our time that the totally selfish or geopolitical concerns of empire also made for a redefinition in the wake of rebellion and decolonization which expanded our conception of human talent and dignity.

The drive from the airport was comfortable and the pleasantly heated Kenyan air came in the open windows after passing through fields of tall grass. It was early in the morning and I checked in at the New Stanley Hotel, located at the intersection of Kenyatta and Kimathi avenues, names that acknowledged the combination of eloquence and bushlord bloodshed that coaxed and hacked the way to independence: Jomo Kenyatta was the first president of Kenya and Dedan Kimathi had been the last butchering desperado of what the British call Mau Mau. In a few hours, I was looking out from my seventh-floor balcony as Nairobi came to, with night some dark capsule that dissolved into the morning light. Cars and old buses filled with workers began roaring and rattling down Kenyatta Avenue and the people of the city—walking swiftly, ever so swiftly—appeared from every direction and in every size, shape, skin tone, and imaginable sort of dress. There was a wood smell in the air and a chill that leaned subtly inside the wind and I could see the rectangles and cylinders of modern architecture surrounding the golden peaks of a mosque from which the muezzin chanted his guttural calls to prayer. Five times a day, above the percussion of jackhammers, car horns, and whistles, the caustic melancholy of Islam flared, taking control of an unplanned orchestration of human and mechanized sound.

It was time to hit the streets. I put on my black knit shirt, my olive British khakis, my slender leather Italian dress suspenders, my silk and wool Irish motoring cap, my beige Henri de Vignon high-topped shoes. That sartorial combination was in keeping with the cosmopolitan qualities of my bloodline—African and Asian from Madagascar, Irish from Atlanta, Choctaw from Mississippi, and some tribe I will probably recognize on another trip, perhaps to West Africa.

The pulsation out in the streets had its own uplift and I found myself wandering around, looking this way and that, not focusing on anything, only seeking the feeling of the city. It was a city all right and the populace ranged from the very rich to the terribly impoverished. The beggars came crawling forward, eyes crowded with the harsh lessons of penury. One man, his legs bone-thin and twisted around each other, pulled himself down the street with a long pole he used in rowing strokes; it struck me as I looked at all the people who had been reduced to cripples by polio that what we consider abstraction in African sculpture might just as often be realistic. Then there were others with slashes in their cheeks or their ear lobes stretched to brown loops that dangled against their collars. Those who shined shoes were setting up their businesses, as were people who sold elephant-hair bracelets, batiks, carved statues, and the machetes called pangas. As I walked it was obvious that they knew I wasn't an African. Some assumed more than that.

When I neared what I later heard was a dangerous part of town, I passed three young African men sitting on the ground, barefoot, ragged, and filthy. Soon one had passed me and was walking in front while the other two were behind, close enough to smell. I knew what that was. I suddenly put my back to a wall and they turned to face me. I let them know that I would defend myself. There was a brief exchange and they moved on. Had they been armed, things might have been different.

That was my first brush with street crime, and I was to have a second that was almost identical on a Sunday morning walk, though it didn't get as close to attack. In front of the New Stanley, I spoke with a man I'll call Boniface, who dealt marijuana, cocaine, and provided walking tours and sex with a chocolate topping for German women especially. A cosmopolitan man who had traveled as a sailor and was quite wily, Boniface told me about Nairobi crime.

> These people, they come in from the bush every day. Every day. They think there is work here and there is none and they do not want to become beggars. They are too proud. They would rather rob. But you were lucky. You were near River Road. There you can hire a man to kill someone you want dead for 50 shillings. They kill him. They come back and you don't have the money, they kill you. You see that white woman over there, the one crossing the street? That man right behind her, he can see she is too busy enjoying to know she is in danger. When she turns a corner, he will rob her. He will snatch her purse. If he cannot get her purse, he will take one of the bags she is carrying. He will get something and she will be disappointed in Africans. But Europeans they are scared in their heart of the black because if the child is bad, they say, "Go to sleep or I call the Negro." This happened to me in a small village in Germany. I was working the lift. This German girl see me when the door open: AHHHH! And she go down. We had to pick her up. All her life she was told as a threat: "If you are bad I will get the Negro." If that woman across the street whose money is doomed to be stolen is from Germany, she might feel she is punished for coming to Africa!

Since then, wandering robbers known as the "five-minute gangs" have been breaking into homes in the suburbs, taking what they can and getting away before the police arrive in the conventional six minutes. Even so, like any modern city, Nairobi doesn't feel dangerous and isn't, except for those who don't know where the limits are or who are "too busy enjoying" to feel the presence of a predator.

III. THE ONLY MODERN BLACK MAN

By the time I got back to the hotel on that first morning, breakfast was being served and the waiters in green coats, white shirts, black ties, and black pants moved quickly. The New Stanley's restaurant and the Thorn Bush, the hotel's enclosed sidewalk patio where drinks and food were served, became my meeting places. When I wasn't there, I was taking long rides in a cab I hired daily, listening to the driver disparage other tribes or explain how the tea and coffee plantations worked when we traveled far out of the city into the Aberdare. Or I was at the Jockey

Club, a remarkable race track, sitting up in the boxes with the Anglo-Africans who owned horses, betting the way they suggested and winning almost every time out. Or I was on foot, walking here and there, striking up conversations with every kind of African I could talk with, most friendly, some con men playing on what they expected would be a black American sentimentality about "the motherland." I could hang out with the rich black son of a coffee business owner, an athlete who had played rugby in Scotland and wondered why Africans who went to America came back so big. Or I might be dancing at the New Florida or the Skylight Room or partying with the teams of the NBA, the Nairobi Basketball Association. In all, it didn't take me long to know that I was an American, which was no news, or that the kind of American I was had a special significance to Africans, at least the Africans of Kenya. As one young man told me in the Nairobi market:

> We keep wanting you to come back, to help us build our country. The American black man is the only black man in the world who is his own man. You send an African to France, he comes back a *French* African; to England he comes back a *British* African. He will not come back the way you American black people are. You are the only ones who have learned all of the white man's knowledge and have put it out your *own* way. In his heart, the African knows this. In our country, this is what we need. We need to be Africans in a modern way. Now we are half old-fashioned and half European, or all of one. When we see you on the television and in the movies, on the cassettes of the basketball games and such things, we see a truly modern black man. That is our struggle and we hope you will come back to Africa and help us build this new thing completely.

I heard that many times and from many different levels of society, always said with an earnestness that made a bigger joke of the ersatz Africans of America who confused identity with pretentious name changing, costumes, and rituals that turned ethnicity into a hysterically nostalgic social club. But ethnic nationalist black Americans had no corner on imbecility. One conversation that was as illuminating as it was terrifying reminded me how unreasonable defense of African tradition could sustain barbarism. At breakfast one morning, I talked with a couple on vacation who lived in the Sudan, where Numeiri had recently sought support from the Muslim majority and allowed them to slaughter thousands of Christians in the south. Numeiri had refused to let the press into the areas where the murders were taking place, but those who lived in the country knew the facts and the rough figures. (Numeiri recently fell to a group of military men whose epaulets are large enough to suggest—if my epaulet theory is correct—that they will be as repressive and vicious as he was.) They also went on to talk about how tribal customs called for a clitoridectomy following the birth of each child. "They continue to cut away until nothing is left but an opening." I wondered how the ersatz Africans of Brooklyn would justify that. Who knows? After all, when the issue of female circumcision was raised at an international women's conference held in Europe a few years ago, the delegation from Upper Volta (now Burkina Faso) stormed out in protest, castigating the European feminists for imposing their standards on a Third World culture. Well, there's nothing like uncompromising ethnic self-regard at high tide.

IV. THE OLD MAN

It was the end of June and the drought was on. The Railway Club golf course, where Africans in floppy hats and plaid pants strolled in front of their caddies, was filled with green trees, but a long hay-colored stretch showed the effects of the devastating wait for rain. The Kenyatta Mausoleum, across from the Hotel International Nairobi, next to the Nairobi City Council, across from the Kenyatta International Conference Center, was parched. The grass was yellow or replaced in patches by brown or red earth, the bushes interrupted by the stone and steel gate were faded and sagging toward what looked like death from thirst, but through that gate, in a black cap with a shining badge on it, rifle at rest, in a red jacket that stopped halfway above the knees with five brass buttons lining down to a white belt, the legs covered by dark trousers either-sided with a red stripe and glistening boots, was a single African soldier as impressive as any soldier I've ever seen, standing guard out in front of the monument that contained the old man's remains. On each side of the guard were ten flagpoles from which the red, black, green, and white national colors flew, their emblem crossed spears behind a shield. Across the street, the green pavilion next to the conference center had long stretches of earth turned red by relentless sun, only three of the spotlights intended to light the path leading to the old man's statue over an empty fountain were left intact—the other forty-odd metal poles, victims of the intended coup in August of 1982, stood like dead and slightly bent gray stalks. The pavilion itself was falling apart and the octagonal and square motif of its pavement gave way to rebellious patches of uncovered stone, combining the structured and the anarchic as perfectly as anything in Kenya. The steps were loose and some of the stone was missing. But the bronze of the old man stared into the desiccation with a stoicism that bespoke his endurance and eloquence on the long trek to independence. That African voice is still legendary and the name "the old man" calls forth the culture.

> In Africa, it takes a long time to really become a man. A man is one who *knows*. When you have become a man, your respect is very big. The years give you the gift of *power*. Each hour, each day a man lives turns him stronger in knowledge. So the African has, as the European says, reverence. Our old people are respected because their spirits take on the strength that the body loses to time. When the old man spoke, he could make the air around your ears very hot. He could raise bubbles in your blood. Kenyatta was *force,* an African voice. That is why he put on the symbol of the country a shield, two

lions holding spears, and a cock with a hatchet in the center of the shield. This is not the British lion; this is the African lion. There are no lions in England; the lions are in the British mind. They took from us that symbol and Kenyatta took it back just as he took our land back. The cock is the power. It is all African and it is all very simple. It is also very strong and very patient. In Africa you must learn to wait and to remain powerful. That is the test of the world and all old men who are not mad or foolish know how it is done. Kenyatta knew. He was the old man. Yes.

Jomo Kenyatta was a Kikuyu born around 1892. His was a life that embodied the transition of the African from the world of magic and superstition to the complexity of modern life, which he could learn about only through contact with the Western world. Were it not for surgery, Kenyatta would have been dead early on, the victim of a spinal disease corrected at a mission when he was ten. It was there that Kenyatta became fascinated by papers that the missionaries referred to as objects that said things or gave orders. Once, when everyone had left after a proclamation had been read, Kenyatta returned and spoke to the paper. The paper did not answer. He raised his voice. The paper remained silent. Kenyatta decided that he had to get to the bottom of that magic, and once he did, he so intensified the power of his oral tradition that he developed into a spokesman for nascent tribal nationalism and anti-colonial feeling. The handsome and charismatic African traveled to Europe, flirted with communism, increased his skills as an orator, and returned in 1946 to Kenya, where he quickly came to symbolize the desire for independence and an end to the inferior status of the African in his own land. When the so-called Mau Mau Emergency took off in 1952, Kenyatta was arrested and accused of leading the guerrilla forces which were slaughtering Africans, whites, and livestock. The Kikuyu rebels were defeated in 1956. As David Lamb wrote in his excellent *The Africans,* the death toll following the rebellion "stood at 11,500 Mau Mau guerrillas and African civilians, 2000 African troops fighting for the British, 58 members of the British security forces and 37 British settlers." Nonviolent agitation continued, and, finally, Kenya became independent a few years after Kenyatta was released from prison in 1959, then exiled. In 1960, he was elected president of the new Kenya African National Union. He became prime minister of the independent nation on December 12, 1963. Those who wished him to follow the largely unsuccessful path of African socialism were disappointed. Kenyatta turned his back on the Marxist models and made sure that Kenya maintained its status as a capitalist, multiracial society, albeit one dominated by his own tribe. His decision to downplay race in favor of pluralism and incentive made him a hero to Africans and Europeans. Though the investigation was dropped when Kenyatta's daughter was discovered at the center of an ivory-smuggling ring, though Tom Mboya and a few other political enemies were assassinated, though there were some politically motivated arrests, the corruption and bloodletting were so comparatively modest that the old man is still revered. Since the nature of African independence has reduced almost everything to good or bad kings, Kenyans are largely philosophical about Kenyatta and see him as an essentially fair and intelligent ruler whose occasional ruthlessness never overshadowed what he gave to his country. Perhaps his greatest achievement was cooling the tribal animosities to such a degree that there was no national outbreak of violence when the old man died in August of 1978 and was succeeded by Daniel arap Moi, a member of the small Tugen tribe. Since the attempted coup of 1982, however, Moi has been replacing the Kikuyu in the armed services with the Tugen, which makes Kenyans nervous across ethnic lines.

V. THE UNIT

In the backwaters of our minds hovers the nightmare of the bestial African, human blood dripping from his panga. This is what many think of when they hear the term Mau Mau, a name accepted by the British but still denied by the fighters who had to reach for a primordial savagery to express their outrage in face of colonial repression. They committed the murders of rebellion in the most unspeakable ways, sometimes drinking human blood, eating human flesh, mutilating livestock, burning. It all ended with the demon run of Dedan Kimathi, the last desperado. A clerk who would be king, who seemed to have gone mad in the middle of his journey, whose fury against colonial domination created an appetite for blood among his followers, Kimathi had called himself Field Marshal, Commander-in-Chief, Knight Commander of the African Empire, Prime Minister of the Southern Hemisphere. None of those names protected him in court, and none of the magical powers he claimed for himself traveled beyond the Aberdare forest where he fell, wounded in a leopard-skin coat. His photograph after capture shows long woolly snakes of hair matted beneath his head as he lies supine, the British handcuffs looking like metal bones or talismans, the light cast from his eyes that of a man nearly overcome by contempt for his captors. Kimathi was hanged and the revolt crushed.

Pages upon pages have been written, reports made, accusations leveled and denied, the breakthrough coming when a British soldier, an Anglo-African who had been reared near the Kikuyu, began interrogating the captured rebel General China, making his way through the labyrinthine meanings of a protean tongue. By achieving linguistic entry into the Kikuyu world, the British were able to isolate the rebels, and an end came to four years of terror, manic whiskey-guzzling, and gauche flamboyance of the sort exhibited when white ladies wore pistols with their evening gowns. Most important was the fact that the British were able to enlist ex-rebels to help them track and fight the continued resistance, a device as important as General Crook's recruiting Indians to fight with the American cavalry in the wars of the Plains and the Southwest. As Fred Majdalany wrote in *State of Emergency:* "The whittling down of the increasingly disrupted gangs was from now on left more and more to Special Forces, whose use of ex-terrorists had reached the point where they were now regularly tracking down and killing their former leaders."

I had read about it, I had heard about it, I was told stories by the leftover British from the days when Africans felt smothered under the heavy red robe of empire. The central clash was with those who had fought for British control when far outnumbered—30,000 settlers to a million and a half Kikuyu—and had long been admonished by dignitaries back in England to give up the ship and let the Africans sail or flounder; and there were those baptized in the inevitably bloody dream of change, who took oaths in the bush and came away remade, the steel of pangas in their hearts, pangas that eventually made their way into human flesh. They would fight. Yes, they would fight. One of them told me about it. A cab driver.

My regular cabbie was Juma, a Kikuyu whose love for White Cap beer kept him from showing up on my final Sunday in Nairobi, when I went to the track for the last time. Irritated, I hired another driver and he took me out on the road to the Jockey Club, passing the African women who carried loads on their heads, the trees, the occasional spavined dog, the homes that were large and the buses that were raggedy, making a left turn into the track, where the backdrop became green and the Indians ran much of the gambling, where the owners had a clubhouse and talked excitedly about their horses, where tar-black Africans in British khaki sat under poles and a tarpaulin roof tooting marches, where the members of various tribes would entertain with exciting dances and drumming between the races. The African, European, Asian, and Arab crowd, filling the stands and the field, betting, cheering, and drinking with friends, family, and children, had an entrancing epic variety, ranging from those in robes and tribal beads to Saudi Arabian silk suits and diamonds, from the palest skin tones possible to the deepest ebony, from the squat and homely to the breathtakingly tall and handsome. Then there were the jockeys, jet-dark Africans and rosy-faced Irishmen armed with crops and educated knees. They came out of the stables seated on little saddles, the brims of their caps in the air, the straps beneath their chins, their silks brilliant in the afternoon sun, all moving on the backs of the bays, the chestnuts, and the grays, the creatures' musculature pulsive insignias of breeding.

They are coming out on the track now, some bucking and rearing, cantering to the gate. The sky is a particularly African blue, gray, and white; the vegetative geometry of the green shaping the horizon beyond the track has its own textures; and invisible patterns are cut across it all by big and little African birds that redefine the meaning of their hues in the light.

When it is all over and the sun is going down, my driver is waiting for me. He takes me to see a friend who lives near the Jockey Club, where I chat for an hour, and we head back for the New Stanley. When we are stopped by African policemen who have spread a long white piece of wood run through with spikes across the road, my driver is delighted instead of annoyed, and suddenly intuition pushes me to ask him if he knows anything about the Mau Mau. He is silent, leaning forward against the wheel, then back, slouching. He asks me why I want to know. I tell him I am a writer and I have heard what the white people have to say but I have found no one who was on the other side who could tell me what the Africans really thought and really did. He smiles and tells me he is very happy that I am a writer, that I can put my words on paper. There was no Mau Mau. He has never told anyone this before but he will tell me. He says he likes me. He has watched me every day when I rode with Juma. I remind him of a black American who came back to Africa and dedicated his life to educating Africans. Because of this and this only, he will tell me. His voice has a melancholy so thick the words seem to sink in the air after they are uttered.

I am a poor man but somehow I am happy for what I see. Africans can go to the New Stanley, Norfolk. It used to be European here, the Asian there, the African back down. You could own nothing. If you are there you must only service. You must only whisper. I saw this. My father was a cooker. If you want food—no. Water—no. Coffee— no. A European could write D.C.—district commissioner—that you are wrong. No word from you, no fair trial. But in 1945 the African learned from the war—if you cut a European, he bleed; if you shoot him, he die. This was new! The old people did not go to learn this. The European could not be killed. If you strike him, *you* die. Ah! Old was wrong. This was very important.

We needed *unit*, unit: *our* people, our land. We Kikuyu took the oath. I have been shot in the leg one time, two times. Two bullets in me right here and behind the ear. But all people are not equal. Some they do not have heart. Courage is to them the poison you spit out. They were royalist. We make it if you loyal to the British here, you die. You *die!* It was necessary because the British is very clever. He had command us, but he did not know us. How we live, how we move, Kikuyu knew. If he tell, he must *die!* In the bush in one month you become like animal. Smell, hear, quick, strong. You cannot eat for seven whole days. You can go for six months, for a full year without a wash, and now, even after 30 days, the animals let you pass. *Ha!* You see, you see?

The British thought the Kikuyu had lost to remember the forest, that we could not lie still as the trees and wait to kill them. We did not have the good guns of them. Ours had been made by ourselves and had only the *one* bullet. When you shoot, barrel is hot. You must wait to cool. Our orders were to use the rifles we had made ourselves only to defend. Only *defend*, you understand. To kill, we use only the long silent knife. If you use a bullet not to defend, you *die*. The knife because the European hates the sharp edge. He would rather be shot. He hates to burn covered with petrol. You kill him this way it is an African way. The knife, the flame make his heart stampede. It stampede.

I was scout. Young boy. Go here. Go there. No one knows what it is I am doing. We cut him here. We disappear. We smile to talk to him. We say we know nothing when he ask. Soon, when he looks at us and he does not know, he sees his own grave, his own family, his horses all floating in a grave of warm blood, all covered with petrol and he smells the flesh of British burning.

But the most we kill are not British—the loyal Royalist African. Why do we kill him most? I want you to understand this. He did not know that the African is a human being. He did not that the British is not God. He did not that he was more important than the British was to England. If he believe British is God, the European go home and rule with the royalist right here for him. Do you understand? The British will not have to be here. If an African must cut another African to death so that more will know the European is not God, it must be so. From that blood come the tree of respect. You must—only for emergency—fear the Kikuyu more than British.

We all must die, but what must we die for? If we must die to prove we are human beings, if we must kill to prove so, if we must love to know so, it is these things to do that are done. My heart has happiness somehow, even though I am a poor man. I hope you understand this because I did not get an indication—to read, to speak, to write. My eyes, my ears, my skin, what all I remember: This is my indication.

VI. A PANGA IS NOT A FEATHER

Given the history of postcolonial Africa, all Kenyans are concerned about the ever-present possibility of a coup, something they learned about when the air force attempted to take command of the country in the August dog days of 1982. The insurrection was put down quickly by the army, when the radio was recovered and broadcasts announcing a new regime were ended and the violent animosities of the African poor were beaten down. Those animosities sweep color, culture, and even class before them. As the wife of a coffee grower said to me, "They were going to get the Wahindi—the Indians; the Wabenzi—the rich Africans who drive Mercedes; and the Wazungu—us, the white people. They got a bit of the first two, but they never really got around to the Wazungu."

The hatred of the Indians is the enduring contempt for the go-between, the person who has risen with absolute determination and mercantile wiles but relates to those below in the condescending terms established by the rulers of the society. Three young men who worked in the market selling chess sets, carved statues, and printed cloth that women wrapped around them as dresses told me over beer in my hotel room that the Indians printed fake batiks which they sold for almost nothing or gave away as bonuses so as to corner the market. That was but one of the tricks Indians used to push Africans out of the business world, wanting everything for themselves. But they also admitted that the Indians were often more industrious than the Africans and that they were willing to sacrifice in order to build income.

> The Indian will be your friend only if he is fooling you! He is no good. One of the independence we do not have is economic. But we are different from the Wahindi. He will pile his money up and up and up. I cannot do this. I must go to the disco and drink beer and I must have a new pair of "levees." If I do not do this, I will have much sadness. I will feel like I am a dirt road and life is rolling over. But when I buy new clothes and dance and drink, then I am more.

A German businesswoman in her eighties told me that the Indians worshiped a god given over to currency, a ruthless mythological bitch whose vision of life was that anything done to gain money was all right. But she was equally aware of the notorious African inclination to corruption: "In the African mind, there is no stigma to corruption. It's just being smart." So a bribe in the hand is far more important than skill or talent in too many instances. Though Kenya claims a more honest governmental and social structure than almost any other African country, both black and white complain of the bribery in everything from licensing to acquiring land. Where things are not decided on the basis of tribal or familial allegiance, money commands favors. A Kikuyu businessman's son told me: "These men in government can be no good! When it was proposed that we might get a loan to build an underground so that people could travel better, when they could not discover the way to steal most of the money, they would not accept the loan and said that Nairobi was too small a city to have an underground!" This kind of hanky panky has led to a bitterness that found its limited release during the attempted coup and said a great deal about the changes in the country since independence. Twenty-five years ago, the whites might have been the most hated, then the Indians, then the Africans loyal to empire. But time and bribes and tribes had changed that pecking order, which was dwarfed by the fire and terror that resulted when the air force tried to throttle the Moi regime.

> Before the army, the people did not know what is coup. But the army teach them. At first, there is running and shouting. The people were happy in the streets, then they see. They see what is coup. Is when you can do nothing but watch and hope nothing happen to you or happen to your family. This is what took place on those few days. The people were happy to destroy business of Wahindi because they have been treated so bad by them. But the army took whatever they want. This was the pay they give themselves. Many Indian homes were broken into and they took sex with the Indian girls and the Indian wives. They feel this is their only chance because in certain places the Indian will threaten to kill an Indian woman if she is seen with an African. What the army did to them is not in the newspapers. So many disgraced their fathers had to marry them, or their brothers or their cousins. This is not talked about. But the Wahindi, they do not learn *ever*. Money is all they understand. Money will not stop the

soldier who kicks in the door. He will take the money and then still do what he came for—to kill you, to rape you, to wound you. Wahindi do not understand that the African is a human being. This the British knows, this the Wahindi will never understand. A panga is hanging over his head and he pretends it is a feather.

One Sunday morning I took a long walk, traveling up Harry Thuku Road, and passed a fenced-in area where soldiers were living. It was the Ministry of Information and Broadcasting, Voice of Kenya, the radio station that had been taken by the air force. At the gate in berets and fatigues were the two surliest black men I have ever seen. Viciousness seemed to seep from their pores and the only answer they had to any question was a sullen, "We are all right." They weren't impressed in the least by a writer from America and it was clear that their job was to kill anyone who tried to come into that station without the appropriate papers. Beyond the guardhouse at the gate, as I moved on, was a lot filled with broken-down cars and trucks. I looked for bullet holes in them and saw none. All I could think of was how terrible it must have been when men like those at the gate were allowed to do what they wished. The idea of a country taken over by cool black killers was as nightmarish as anything I could ever imagine. But then, anything could happen in Africa.

Harry Thuku Road became Hotel Boulevard and I heard "Polly Wolly Doodle" in what sounded like Swahili floating from a restaurant. Eventually, after walking up a hill and passing eucalyptus trees and a large hotel, I began descending and the Aga Khan Nursery School came into view, next to a playground filled with Asian children joyously playing soccer in white uniforms and expensive tennis shoes. Against the fence of the playground was a shack made of slats, flattened rectangular three-gallon cans, and cardboard. It was a store and inside it old African men sat at a table eating maize with powdered milk. Every so often a Mercedes filled with giggling Indians passed. Directly across from the playground there was a sunken field of pineapple trees, corrugated shacks, ragged, shoeless people, stacked burlap sacks, and a child collecting coal, but near the end of the street, seated at a table in a torn and filthy dress, her feet wide from never having worn shoes, sat a young girl of about ten. She was playing a card game by herself, alternately excited or laughing, her big eyes, long neck, and long arms predictions of a great beauty. In the way she turned her head, stuck her tongue out of the side of her mouth, and sighed the accompaniment to what was possibly a dream, this girl suddenly became an index of the indomitable. I knew that as long as Kenya could produce children like her, it would have a chance to handle whatever burdens history and circumstance placed upon its shoulders. Or, as it was once written, "Isn't it pretty to think so?"

THE RAGE OF RACE
January 12, 1988

By 1963, when he published *The Fire Next Time,* James Baldwin's writing had become almost exclusively polemical, foreshadowing the narrowing of black commentary into strident prosecution or spiteful apology. Considered the intellectual component of the Civil Rights Movement, Baldwin was a seminal influence on the subsequent era of regression in which Stokely Carmichael, Rap Brown, LeRoi Jones, and Eldridge Cleaver transformed white America into Big Daddy and the Negro movement into an obnoxious, pouting adolescent demanding the car keys.

The increasing bile and cynicism of Baldwin's generalized charges and his willingness to remove free will from the black lower class through what he called the "doom" of color helped foster a disposition that put the Negro movement into the hands of those who had failed at taking it over before: the trickle-down Marxist revolutionaries and cultural nationalists whose flops and follies of imagination Harold Cruse documented so well in *Crisis of the Negro Intellectual.* Those people led many up paths that resulted in imprisonment, spiritual collapse, and death for goals far less logical than acquiring political power through inclusion into the social contract. The alienation of abstract facelessness that Martin Luther King and the civil rights workers had won so many battles against was given greater strength when black political talk became progressively anti-white, anti-capitalist, and made threats of overthrowing the system itself.

Before he was swept into the position of a media spokesman, Baldwin had been much more ambitious and much more willing to address the subtleties of being a serious writer. His first book of essays, *Notes of a Native Son,* contains "Everybody's Protest Novel," which was written in 1949 and observes that ". . . the avowed aim of the American protest novel is to bring greater freedom to the oppressed. They are forgiven, on the strength of these good intentions, whatever violence they do to language, whatever excessive demands they make of credibility. It is, indeed, considered the sign of frivolity so intense as to approach decadence to suggest that these books are both badly written and wildly improbable. One is told to put first things first, the good of society coming before the niceties of style or characterization. Even if this were incontestable . . . it argues an insuperable confusion, since literature and sociology are not one and the same; it is impossible to discuss them as if they were."

The turmoil that would so twist Baldwin's intelligence and abuse the possibilities of his talent is also evident in that first book of essays, much of the trouble circulating around his sense of himself as "an interloper," "a bastard of the West." "Stranger in the Village" finds him reeling toward the emblematic as he writes of some Swiss hicks in an Alpine town, "These people cannot be, from the point of view of power, strangers anywhere in the world; they have made the modern world, in effect, even if they do not know it. The most illiterate among them is related, in a way that I am not, to Dante, Shakespeare, Michelangelo, Aeschylus, Da Vinci, Rembrandt, and Racine; the cathedral at Chartres says something to them which it cannot say to me, as indeed would New York's Empire State Building, should anyone here ever see it. Out of their hymns and dances come Beethoven and Bach. Go back a few centuries and they are in their full glory—but I am in Africa, watching the conquerors arrive."

Such thinking led to the problem we still face in which too many so-called nonwhite people look upon "the West" as some catchall in which every European or person of European descent is somehow part of a structure bent solely on excluding or intimidating the Baldwins of the world. Were Roland Hayes, Marian Anderson, Leontyne Price, Jessye Norman, or Kiri Te Kanawa to have taken such a position, they would have locked themselves out of a world of music that originated neither among Afro-Americans nor Maoris. Further, his ahistorical ignorance is remarkable, and perhaps willful.

But breaking through the mask of collective whiteness—and collective *guilt*—that Baldwin imposes would demand recognition of the fact that, as history and national chauvinism prove, Europe is not a one-celled organism. Such simplifications are akin to the kind of reasoning that manipulated illiterate rednecks into violent attempts at keeping "their" universities clean of Negro interlopers. Or convinced black nationalist automatons that they were the descendants of "kings and queens" brought to America in slave ships and should, therefore, uncritically identify with Africa. Rather than address the possibilities that come both of ethnic cultural identity and of accepting the international wonder of human heritage per se, people are expected to relate to the world only through race and the most stifling conceptions of group history. The root of that vision is perhaps what Shaw spoke of in *Major Barbara,* hatred as the coward's revenge for ever having been intimidated. Baldwin would call it rage, and write, "Rage can only with difficulty, and never entirely, be brought under the domination of the intelligence and is therefore not susceptible to any arguments whatever."

Though his second book of essays, *Nobody Knows My Name,* is the work of a gritty and subtle intelligence, there are more than a few indications of the talent that would soon be lost to polemics. Perhaps the most illuminating is "Princes and Powers," where he takes a remarkably sober look at the Conference of Negro-African Writers and Artists, held in Paris in 1956. Baldwin was faced with an international gathering of black people who were rejecting the justifications used to maintain the colonial structures they groaned under. Here Baldwin introduced themes he would later adapt to the American context: the denial by Europeans of non-Western cultural complexity—or parity; the social function of the inferiority complex colonialism threw over the native like a net; the alignment of Christianity and cruelty under colonialism, and the idea that world views were at odds, European versus the "spirit of Bandung," or the West in the ring with the Third World.

At the time, Baldwin understood quite well the difference between colonized and Afro-American people, whom he rightfully referred to as "the most real and certainly the most shocking contributions to Western cultural life." Though Afro-Americans also suffered under institutionalized prejudice, the nature of their experience was the manifestation of a very specific context. "This results in a psychology very different—at its best and at its worst—from the psychology that is produced by a sense of having been invaded and overrun, the sense of having no recourse whatever against oppression other than overthrowing the machinery of the oppressor. We had been dealing with, had been made and mangled by, another machinery altogether. It had never been in our interest to overthrow it. It had been necessary to make the machinery work for our benefit and the possibility of doing so had been, so to speak, built in."

In assessing the performance of Richard Wright, Baldwin understood the danger of apologizing for brutal, Third World politics that the older writer was condoning. Baldwin didn't miss the implications of Wright's address:

> . . . that the West, having created an African and Asian elite, should now "give them their heads" and "refuse to be shocked" at the "methods they will be compelled to use" in unifying their countries. . . . Presumably, this left us in no position to throw stones at Nehru, Nasser, Sukarno, etc., should they decide as they almost surely would, to use dictatorial methods in order to hasten the "social evolution." In any case, Wright said, these men, the leaders of their countries, once the new social order was established, would voluntarily surrender the "personal power." He did not say what would happen then, but I suppose it would be the second coming.

Listening then to Aimee Cesaire, Baldwin wrote, "I felt stirred in a very strange and disagreeable way. For Cesaire's case against Europe, which was watertight, was also a very easy case to make. . . . Cesaire's speech left out of account one of the great effects of the colonial experience: its creation, precisely, of men like himself." Baldwin could see that Cesaire was a modern man, a writer whose bearing and confidence were proof that "He had penetrated into the heart of the great wilderness which was Europe and stolen the sacred fire. And this, which was the promise of their freedom, was also the assurance of his power."

Such good sense wouldn't last long in Baldwin's writing. Once he settled into astonishingly lyrical rants such as *The Fire Next Time,* Negro

neighborhoods were described as relentlessly grim and so inevitably de-
forming that only the most naïve could accept Baldwin's having come
from such a "ghetto." Ignoring the epic intricacy of Afro-American life,
Baldwin began to espouse the kinds of simplistic conceptions Malcolm X
became famous for: "It is a fact that every American Negro bears a name
that originally belonged to the white man whose chattel he was. I am
called Baldwin because I was either sold by my African tribe or kidnapped out of it into the hands of a white Christian named Baldwin, who
forced me to kneel at the foot of the cross."

Actually, a good number of Negroes named *themselves* after freedom
came and the issue of converting slaves to Christianity was a subject of
major debate because it broached the idea of slaves having souls. But
such facts were of no interest to Baldwin. Rather, he chose to combine
the Nation of Islam's venom toward Christianity and toward whites with
an overview so committed to determinism that it paralleled the explana-
tory recipes of the left. When mature thinking was most desperately
needed, Baldwin was losing the ability to look at things the way they actually were.

In effect, Baldwin sold out to rage, despair, self-righteousness, and a
will to scandalize. The mood he submitted to was one he had pinned
down in "Princes and Powers." Alioune Diop, editor of *Présence Africaine*, had delivered a talk and Baldwin perceptively noticed this: "His
speech won a great deal of applause. Yet, I felt that among the dark people in the hall there was, perhaps, some disappointment that he had not
been more specific, more bitter, in a word, more demagogical." In America, there was a very similar attitude among those fat-mouthing Negroes
who chose to sneer at the heroic optimism of the Civil Rights Movement;
they developed their own radical chic and spoke of Malcolm X as being
beyond compromise, of his unwillingness to cooperate with the white
man, and of his ideas being too radical for assimilation. Baldwin was
sucked into this world of intellectual airlessness. By *The Fire Next Time*,
Baldwin is so happy to see white policemen made uncomfortable by
Muslim rallies, and so willing to embrace almost anything that disturbs
whites in general, that he starts competing with the apocalyptic tone of
the Nation of Islam.

Perhaps it is understandable that Baldwin could not resist the contemptuous pose of militance that gave focus to all of his anger for being the
homely duckling who never became a swan, the writer who would perhaps never have been read by so many black people otherwise, and the
homosexual who lived abroad most of his adult life in order to enjoy his
preferences. Baldwin's increasing virulence had perhaps more than a bit
to do with his homosexuality. As a small, even frail, man who wrote of
being physically abused by his father, the police, and racists in Greenwich Village, Baldwin was prone to admire and despise those who handled the world in a two-fisted manner (which comes out clearly in his
essay on Norman Mailer, "The Black Boy Looks at the White Boy"). He

was also given to the outsider's joy when intimidation was possible: "black has *become* a beautiful color—not because it is loved but because it is feared." This same attraction to fear permeated his ambivalent attitude toward Christianity. Condemned to hell as an erotic pariah by Christian doctrine, he was understandably relentless in his counterattacks; at the same time, his alienation did not prevent him from being awed by the particular power and majesty Negroes had brought to the religion. Boldly, though unconvincingly, in *Another Country* and *Tell Me How Long the Train's Been Gone*, he presented an alternative order in which homosexuals served as priests in a religion based on love.

Baldwin's prose was sometimes coated with the effete sheen of the homosexual straining to present himself as part of an elite, or it could be pickled with the self-defensive snits and bitchiness Lionel Mitchell called "our macho." Beware ye who would condescend: Baldwin's attitude wasn't substantially different from the aggressive defensiveness of any outsiders, be they black nationalists who celebrate Africa at Europe's expense, those feminists who elevate women over men, or any other group at odds with or at a loss for social and political power.

It is also true that Baldwin was the first of his kind, and perhaps the last we shall see for some time: The Negro writer made a celebrity and thrust into the national political dialogue. He had no models to learn from and settled for sassing the white folks when ideas of substance would have been much more valuable. His considerable gift for making something of his own from the language of Henry James and the rhetoric of the black church was largely squandered on surface charges and protest fiction. The talent for writing fiction that Baldwin showed in his first novel, *Go Tell It on the Mountain*, never achieved maturity. Though the rest of the novels are uniformly bad, almost every one contains brilliant passages in which Baldwin's long, long sentences were indicative of his intricate sense of consciousness, boasting finely orchestrated details, declarations, and nuances of feeling. But they are, with the exception of the all-white homosexual melodrama *Giovanni's Room*, ruined by the writer's contrived and sentimental conception of race. The purple trumpet in his soul played the same tune over and over, one which depicted Negro life as insufferable, saintly, and infinitely superior to that of whites.

Though homosexuality loomed ever larger in his fiction as the years passed, by the last long essay, *The Evidence of Things Unseen*, Baldwin streaks away from the issues surrounding the Atlanta child murders, ignoring particularly the exploitation of so many impoverished Negro boys by the homosexual subculture of that city. His eloquence gone, Baldwin reads as though his mind had so eroded that he no longer knew how to build an argument. Very little connects and any subject is an occasion for a forced harangue against the West, the profit motive, Christianity, and so on. It is a disturbingly dishonest book.

One cannot deny James Baldwin his powers, but it is tragic that he was never strong enough to defend and nurture his substantial talent and become the writer even such imposing gifts do not make inevitable. Finally, Baldwin's description of his success as a boy preacher in *The Fire Next Time* says much about the decay of a writer who once seemed poised on greatness: "That was the most frightening time of my life, and quite the most dishonest, and the resulting hysteria lent great passion to my sermons—for a while. I relished the attention and the relative immunity from punishment that my new status gave me. . . ."

MESSENGERS OF JOY
December 27, 1983

I asked to write about Lee Breuer's masterwork because I thought there were things that hadn't been discussed fully enough in Michael Feingold's scholarly and insightful review. I was particularly surprised by his final statement, "The occasion is daunting because it does something so basic to the theater, and so foreign to the culture and thought of our century, that putting it into words is a shock: *Gospel at Colonus* makes you feel good about being human." I found that odd because the international impact of African-American innovations in everything from speech to sports has communicated joy and awe, most consistently and most powerfully through *swing*, which means rhythmically remaking with a sensual enthusiasm both earthbound and transcendent. And what makes *Gospel at Colonus* such a successful extension of the domestic techniques of theatre is how well Breuer senses that black rhythm is a form of confrontation and transformation that is aimed primarily at humanizing, not trivializing.

Perhaps the most important aspects of African-American culture as expressed through the music is its double consciousness, its emotional counterpoint: melancholy lyrics will float or flit or swing over percussive rhythms that are the essence of celebration. The result is a combination of joy and sorrow, a fusing of tragedy and exaltation, proof of Senghor's dictum: rhythm is the architecture of being. For that reason, the music is the star of the show, finally. Not just the literal music, but the rhythms of different ways of preaching, teasing and punching words, shaving down the distance between speech and song, sometimes rendering lines as though the voice were a drum giving fresh swing to the iambic pentameter that dominates the text. Then there is the way Bob Telson's score pushes the work forward but also gives it many shadings because of the combinations of lead singers, small groups, full choir, and so on.

The visual ideas are one with the sound, since there are layers of associations. Dressing the choir in African robes but allowing them their inevitable fans, having the figures in the church painting on the wall black instead of the customary white, costuming the small vocal groups in suits and tuxedos, is a statement about the ways in which black Americans have synthesized many contributions. Just as important is the use of microphones and electric guitars, basses, and keyboards, since the humanizing of technology is what the use of any musical instrument has always meant. One of the Soul Stirrers uses a controlled—and comical—screech coated by the microphone that makes most electronic music (including Telson's synthesizer) sound like no more than cold contrivance. All these things show off the complexity that is beneath every truly black *American* sound or gesture, and how that complexity speaks profoundly to the story of Oedipus.

It is now no news that Breuer studied the structure of black church ceremony and brilliantly transferred Sophocles, but I found one of the cleverest ideas about the ritual expressed when the ushers, who usually subdue and remove people overcome by the spirit, turn into Creon's agents kidnapping Oedipus's daughters! But what is probably most important is that Breuer, though using an innovative idea, is in the line of those American artists who have recognized the moral, tragic, and jubilantly heroic symbolism of the Negro—Melville (*Moby-Dick's* Pip), Faulkner (who grafted Greek tragedy into a miscegenated Southern tale with *Absalom, Absalom!*), and Ellison (whose *Invisible Man* put Negro swing to Western classical literary tradition). In so doing, Breuer has discovered something about the possibilities of modern theatre that Peter Brook went all over the world looking for, that intersection where primitive intensity and sophistication combine for a timeless expression of vitality and grace.

DO THE RACE THING
June 20, 1989

The problems Spike Lee and his new film, *Do the Right Thing*, represent cannot be discussed outside the context of contemporary Afro-American media success and the reemergence of black power thinking. But a good place to begin is Brooklyn on June 5, the evening that Lee and Robert Townsend of *Hollywood Shuffle* were given tribute by the Black Filmmaker Foundation, a nonprofit organization that distributes independently made Afro-American films. Not only were Lee and Townsend praised but the ten-year existence of the foundation was cause for an awards presentation acknowledging the mostly white funders and the best films made since 1979.

The numerous film clips shown that glamorous evening at the Majestic Theatre of the Brooklyn Academy of Music demonstrated that Lee and Townsend are but examples of the many people making films, looking at historical figures, and attempting to address the joys, ambiguities, and dilemmas central to being an American of color in our time.

But at the press conference that preceded the ceremonies, it was obvious that such problems are of less interest to Lee than the chance to express a rather muddled vision of black cinema. When I asked him what exactly constitutes black film in terms of cinematic style, Lee could only answer that there isn't a large enough body of work to say, which suggests that he has yet to think out an aesthetic that would determine the visual style of his work. But there is no doubt that he has high regard for his new film: he claimed he had been robbed at Cannes because "they are always looking for a golden white boy." Depicting himself as a victim, Lee complained he'd had to fight for the $6 million that this film cost and "I'll probably have to fight for the $12 million for my next picture." In discussing whether *Do the Right Thing* is racist, Lee said, "White people can't call black people racist. They invented that shit."

Lee's glibness and his stage hostility weren't particularly fresh, but there was an especially disturbing quality to his bootlegged '60s pronouncement about racism. There is far too much proof that racism is no more the invention of white people than white people were, as Malcolm X taught so many while under the thrall of Elijah Muhammad, invented by a mad black scientist. The statement, however, seemed to be an attempt to parry what will become a central part of the discussion of the film, its very existence proof of what one can bring off with the necessary ambition to lead, the energy for self-promotion, and the ability to manipulate the simplistic ethnic ideas that pop leadership demands.

As *Do the Right Thing* proves, Lee is a miniaturist in more than size. His vision is small and lacks subtlety, but it continues to raise a luster of surface brilliance. The new film is such an advance in technical terms over the amateurish *School Daze* that one is surprised by it, even taken in— initially. Lee's control of the contemporary cinematic language—which is so influenced by television commercials, rock videos, and the techniques of the '60s European avant-garde—has been found impressive. All who would dismiss his gifts as a framer, lighter, and editor of images must now leave the room. He is clearly learning how to do it with exceptional speed.

But Lee, whose truest gift appears to be comedy, either lacks the intelligence, maturity, and the sensitivity necessary for drama, or hasn't the courage and the will to give racial confrontation true dramatic complexity. At heart, he is for now a propagandist, one who reduces the world to a shorthand projected with such force that the very power of the projection itself will make those with tall grass for brains bend to the will of the wind. Though there is much cleverness, the film has no feeling for the intricacies of the human spirit on any level other than that of fast-food irony, no sense of the trickiness of both good and evil, none of the emotional scope that brings artistic resonance. *Do the Right Thing*, for all its wit, is the sort of rancid fairy tale one expects of the racist, whether or not Lee actually is one.

One must always face the razor's edge of the fact that race as it applies to American identity has a complex relationship to the grace, grime, and gore of democracy, and that an essential aspect of democracy, of a free society's exchange of ideas, is that we will inevitably be inspired, dismayed, and disgusted by the good, mediocre, and insipid ideas that freedom allows. The burden of democracy is that you will not only get a Thurgood Marshall but an Alton Maddox, a Martin Luther King *and* an Al Sharpton—the brilliant, the hysteric, the hustling. And in terms of film opening up to more and more black people, there is no doubt that most will follow trends and appeal to the spiritual peanut galleries of society as long as there is money to be made, while a few will say something of importance, not only to American society but to the contemporary world. Few in this country have ever wanted to be artists, have wished to challenge or equal the best on a national and international basis. Most want no more than a good job and—in our time of the rock-and-roll elevation of the brutish, the superficial, and the adolescent—pop stardom. Those who believe that such American tendencies will fall before the revelations of the sword of the Negro soul are naïve.

That naïveté, like an intellectual jack-in-the-box bumpkin, periodically popped up through the Black Filmmaker Foundation's ceremonies. There was much talk of "controlling our images," a term suggestive of the worst political aspects of black nationalism, one far more dangerous if taken in certain directions than, say, *expanding* our images. Such "control" without attendant intelligence and moral courage of the sort we saw so little of during the Brawley farce or rarely hear when Louis Farrakhan is discussed, will make little difference, since the problems Afro-Americans presently face extend far beyond the unarguable persistence of a declining racism. Intellectual cowardice, opportunism, and the itch for riches by almost any means necessary define the demons within the black community. The demons are presently symbolized by those black college teachers so intimidated by career threats that they don't protest students bringing Louis Farrakhan on campus, by men like Vernon Mason who sold out a good reputation in a cynical bid for political power by pimping real victims of racism in order to smoke-screen Tawana Brawley's lies, by the crack dealers who have wrought unprecedented horrors, and by Afro-fascist race-baiters like Public Enemy who perform on the soundtrack to *Do the Right Thing*.

In more than a few ways, *Do the Right Thing* fits the description Susan Sontag gave fascism in her discussion of Leni Riefenstahl, "Fascinating Fascism." Sontag says fascist aesthetics "endorse two seemingly opposite states, egomania and servitude. The relations of domination and enslavement take the form of a characteristic pageantry: the massing of groups of people; the turning of people into things; the multiplication or replication of things; and the grouping of people/things around an all-powerful, hypnotic leader-figure or force."

In *Do the Right Thing*, the egomania and the servitude, the massing of people into things, and the irresistible force are all part of blackness. That blackness has the same purpose Sontag recognized in the work of Riefenstahl: it exists to overcome "the dissolution of alienation in ecstatic feelings of community." Lee's vision of blackness connects to what Sontag realized was "a romantic ideal . . . expressed in such diverse modes of cultural dissidence and propaganda for new forms of community as the youth/rock culture, primal therapy, anti-psychiatry, Third World camp following, and belief in the occult."

In order to bring off his romantic vision of race superseding all, Lee creates a fantasy Bed-Stuy neighborhood. No villains such as drug dealers ever appear to complicate things, nor any middle-class would-be street Negroes like the filmmaker himself. The variety of black people Lee chooses to sentimentalize, capture accurately, or to show admiration for are all lower-class. Some even feel animosity for each other. But when the racial call is given, all forms of alienation dissolve and the neighborhood merges into ANGRY BLACK PEOPLE led into a riot by a rail-tailed ne'er-do-well named Mookie, who throws a trash can through the window of a pizzeria owned by an Italian he works for. In the logic of the film, the Italian, Sal, is the real villain because, even though he has had his shop in the neighborhood for 25 years and has watched people grow up and die, he refuses to put the pictures of "some black people" on his wall, which is covered with the images of famous Italian-Americans.

Sal's refusal enrages a fatmouthing Negro named Buggin Out, who wants to boycott the pizzeria but can find only one supporter, Radio Raheem. To Lee's credit, Buggin Out is shown as a fool and Radio Raheem the kind of social bully who commandeers audio space with his noise-blasting boombox. Raheem brandishes gold-plated brass knuckles and explains why one pair is lettered "love" and the other "hate" in a soliloquy that connects him to Robert Mitchum's psychopath in *The Night of the Hunter*. Near the end of the film, the two enter Sal's place as it is about to close, the boombox obnoxiously loud, demanding the placement of black faces on the wall. Sal tells them to turn off the radio or get out. They refuse and tension builds until the Italian utters THAT WORD: *nigger*, then smashes the box with a bat. A fight ensues and Raheem is put in a choke hold and killed by the police during the struggle. When the police pull off with Buggin Out handcuffed as they drive billies into his stomach, Mookie throws the trash can and begins screaming at Sal that Raheem "died because he had a radio." The neighborhood Negroes then realize that Sal is the villain, that he is THE WHITE MAN, and that they, regardless of how much they have been irritated by Raheem and Buggin Out are, like them, BLACK. They exact their revenge—the young, the old, the crippled, the crazy. To maintain obligatory Third World solidarity, the mob decides not to destroy the Korean store across the street after the owner shouts, "I'm black, too."

When the firemen arrive after the pizzeria has been looted and torched, they hose the crowd blocking their work, and Lee commits the kind of vulgar distortion of history one is familiar with in the work of fascists. Are audiences to believe that Negroes bent on stopping firemen from putting out a conflagration are the same as those who met the force of water in Birmingham during a nonviolent demonstration? Apparently so, but that is only one example of Lee's moral confusion. His character, Mookie, rises from the bed of his Puerto Rican girlfriend the next morning, ignoring yet another of her foul-mouthed demands that he come visit her and their baby more often, and goes back to see Sal for his $250 salary. Sal throws five $100 bills in his face. Mookie throws two of them back at Sal, then finally picks them up and walks off, perhaps providing us with a metaphor for what Lee expects of his career—that he will be able to make irresponsible films white people will angrily pay him for.

It all seems, like much of LeRoi Jones's agitprop work, a little man's fantasy twisted up with a confused morality that justifies itself in the name of racial pride and outrage against historical and contemporary injustice. Throughout, pipe-stem Mookie talks bad to Sal and his two Italian sons, even tells Sal he had better not try anything with his sister. If you are Mookie's size and expect to talk that rough to a "let's step outside" Italian, you had better be sure that you wrote the script, directed the movie, and that he is working for you!

But *Do the Right Thing* is already being celebrated by white critics who would never have accepted such a polluted political vision from one of their own. It is, for one thing, a perverted version of *My Beautiful Laundrette*, where the white guy who works for the resented Asians helps defend his employers against a skinhead riot, not out of obeisance but in reaction to anarchy. Had that rightly praised film been made by a white director and had it shown the ex-skinhead *leading* his buddies in the destruction of the laundrette and the assault on the Asians, it would have been sanctimoniously shouted down, regardless of the personal shortcomings of some of the Asian characters.

In fact, had *Do the Right Thing* been the work of a white actor/writer/director, the picket lines would stretch to the Red Sea. But the gullibility of those white people who would pretend that this film is a comment on racism and not perhaps the real thing itself is proof of what Sontag calls "pop sophistication," the ability to perceive the actual political meaning as no more than "aesthetic excess."

Lee's success with the critics at this point goes beyond the fact that those whites who feel they are being treated to "the real thing" have rarely been disturbed by the exotic experience of having a turd pushed into their faces through an aft hole on the social deck beneath them. What makes Lee special is that fascists are never very good at comedy. Few, if any, are known for the quality of witty remarks made during their addresses or for bursts of humor in their work that provoke universal laughter. It is precisely because Lee can make audiences laugh that the fascist aesthetic he follows with such irresponsible deliberation slips the critical noose. Intellectually, he is like John Wayne Gacy in his clown suit, entertaining those who cannot believe the bodies buried under his house.

Postscript:

As it turned out, the game that Spike Lee was running went down very smoothly. Though as sticky and blurred as militant cotton candy, it melted in the mouths of the masses. But what was most bothersome, even occasionally depressing, was the way in which white film critics and supposed black intellectuals postured and breathed heavily over it, talking as though there was not only real content to the film but greatness as well. What Lee had done, as a playwright friend said, was "play white liberals perfectly." In the process, he proved that there is such enormous goodwill toward black people in the media, such a desire for actual seriousness and complex thought about racial issues, that if something appears to even look in the direction of that social swamp goo, many will impose their own seriousness onto it. But Lee, whose true achievement, according to one Hollywood producer, was making it possible for scripts with predominantly black casts to be discussed in production meetings free of the question, "Will it cross over to the white market?," will probably bring about his own undoing. Though he quickly changed keys and tunes when unvarnished questions were asked of him about the film and claimed that Do the Right Thing *was made to ask only the question of whether or not Americans can live in peace together, he also gave out interviews in New York's* Seven Days *and* Penthouse *that revealed much murk beneath his b-boy attire of baseball cap, huge glasses, and diamond earring. He also published* Do the Right Thing, *a journal of the making of the film and his original script. Each should have been rather revealing to those who thought him more than a pop, agitprop black nationalist with a gift for self-promotion.*

In Seven Days, *he told Jonathan Van Meter, "You see, we get the audience. First they see the King quote, and they breathe a sigh of relief. 'Whew! Thought we was gonna have black folks going crazy this summer.' Then we hit 'em with Malcolm X!" As for his own character, Lee opened the bag by observing, "I've heard a lot of people say to me, 'You're not like the rest.' Mookie is that character who's 'not like the rest.' He's that one black person that white people can identify with and who's not*

threatening . . . and then [Lee was described as laughing "devilishly"]
at the end of the movie he's the one that starts the riot. So people who
trusted him in the beginning, now their world's really fucked up."

Of the two quotes that end the film, one by Martin Luther King that
takes a position against violence and the other by Malcolm X that calls
violence in self-defense "intelligence," Lee told Penthouse, "Personally, I
side more with Malcolm X. Most young black people today would." Of
the riot at the end of the film, which he somehow confuses with self-
defense, Lee said, "What are black people supposed to do? They've lost
all faith in the judicial system. They've been seeing blacks get murdered
for too long—from Eleanor Bumpurs on down—and the cops get away
with it. I have perfect sympathy with the character in my film, Mookie,
who throws a garbage can through Sal's pizzeria window after the cops
kill a black kid." Later, he said, "Racism is about white people—they'll
have to change, not us."

In the journal of Do the Right Thing, Lee's desire to be seen as one of
the world's most important young filmmakers is stated clearly as are the
featherweight perceptions of social complexity, the deeper meanings of
political actions, and historical connections. He quite definitely meant to
bootleg the radiant morality of those who met the forces of Southern
racism with nonviolence to justify an irresponsible action in his film:
"About the riot. As the crowd torches the pizzeria, the Fire Department
arrives on the scene. Before firemen turned their hoses on the fire, they direct the water toward the people to disperse them. So we're back to
Montgomery and Birmingham, Alabama; the only thing missing is Bull
Connor and the German shepherds." Beneath it all, there appears to be
the ambition to take on the position of a race leader cloaked in slogans
and using the manner of a rap star, the nappy-headed Napoleon seeking
the seat at the big table reserved for the boy who's paid to be bad. If the
reader misses the quote from Malcolm X that follows the first page of the
script, said reader should see from the parenthetical directions throughout
what the filmmaker thinks. If those don't work, the final paragraph should.
"Am I advocating violence? No, but goddamn, the days of twenty-five
million Blacks being silent while our fellow brothers and sisters are exploited, oppressed, and murdered, have to come to an end. Racial perse-
cution, not only in the United States, but all over the world, is not gonna
go away; it seems it's getting worse (four years of Bush won't help). And
if Crazy Eddie Koch gets reelected for a fourth term as mayor of New
York, what you see in Do the Right Thing will be light stuff. Yep, we have
a choice, Malcolm or King. I know who I'm down with."

But, finally, what Spike Lee may have accomplished is the convention
of a new black exploitation film. As the script and interviews have revealed, the elements that give Danny Aiello's character Sal such humanity
and make the cardboard Negroes that much thinner, were improvised by
Aiello himself. That Lee was willing to allow his white actor to bring so
much humanity to his part while keeping his black actors locked up in

stereotypes suggests something quite unfortunate. Where the white actor sought and was allowed to move beyond the superficial, Negro actors like Paul Benjamin, who complained to Lee about the stereotypical depictions, were kept in their places. This implies that Lee is perhaps not the man he would have so many think he is. Knowing that he could not buck Aiello's demands, he bent for them, aware that Aiello, unlike his black counterparts, was not so desperate to be seen on screen "by any means necessary." If I am correct in this assessment, I am still not given to despair. The progress of the Afro-American through the thickets of this society has been constant and will continue to be. Only preparation, courage, and vigilance are necesssary. As one of Mr. Lee's characters might say, "It's not over, Rover."

BODY AND SOUL
December 27, 1983

I. THE LAST DAY

During the day, Rome has the feeling of rot and revelation one experiences when in the private domain of a handsome old woman, where sweat, sex, cologne, rouge, yellowed notes and papers, bottled remedies with indecipherable labels, crumbling flowers, photographs that seem to have been taken in a brownish gray mist, clothes stained with experience but never worn anymore, and the smells of countless meals have formed a heavy collective presence in the air. Its ruins are like the sagging and corded throatline of a beauty once too sensuous to be believed and now too soulful to be perfectly understood. Of course, nothing we worry about is old in the halls where the laws of nature were written, but in our human effort, with everything over so fast, a city like Rome seems very, very old.

On the last morning there, I decided to beat the summer sun to the punch. All of the notes, timbres, rhythms, and harmonies of the festival called Umbria Jazz, the feelings of awe and mystery, blood sacrifice and integrity that resonate from the cathedrals and museums of Perugia, Assisi, and Florence were moving from my memory to my spirit, and it was fully an hour and a half before dawn. The forthcoming heat of the day was presaged by the quality of subtly repressed steam given to the morning air by the slight humidity. Two stars shone in apparent sympathy

with the slow and gooey low notes of a brood of pigeons clustered somewhere up on the roof of our hotel, and outside in the street men were
loading a white newspaper truck. From the distance of perhaps 70 feet,
they seemed to be singing as they spoke in the sleep-laden, grumbling,
dictatorial—even celebratory—Italian that makes so much of vowels that
the most mundane order or response can sound like kindling for an aria.
I thought again of how the flares and loops of Italian speech remind me
of the sound and feeling of jazz, where the sensual weight, inflection, and
rhythm of notes count for so much.

Within an hour I was on the street, intent on an early morning walk.
After seven or eight blocks I turned, and nearly a mile away stood the
Coliseum. As I walked toward it, part of the pleasure was watching the
structure grow even larger and more distinctive as I grew closer. There
had been a light rain sometime in the night and the wetness gave the
Roman oval an evaporating sheen that seemed to fuse past and present,
since the droplets that fell from one place or another made it appear
freshly excavated and washed down. But mostly the Coliseum looked like
a huge crown of chipped and perforated stone. Its circumference and
height were less breathtaking than hypnotic, giving off an imagined hum
of history much like that of a movie projector as my mind computed the
emotion accumulated through a montage of associations, from Hollywood
to the history book: decadents and gladiators, religious fanatics and lions.
Of course, the greatest gladiator of our age came from Kentucky and attempted to immortalize his Olympic victory in 1960 with some poolhall
doggerel—"How Cassius Took Rome"—at a press conference held on the
newly painted red-white-and-blue steps of his home in Louisville, where
his father broke out with a patriotic song in his best Russ Columbo imitation.

II. ON THE WAY

In the winter of 1982, I had been invited to Umbria Jazz by Alberto Al-
berti, an alternately melancholy and exuberant ex-soccer player who books
the bands. He described Perugia as a charming medieval town in the hills,
and guaranteed me that I would love it and the music and the people. I
thought he might be right, but I also figured that there would be much
more to write about than fine jazz playing, since I could do that in New
York. That section of the world, stretching from the Greco-Roman era to
the Renaissance, had inspired in me a repository of images: Poseidon
hanging out down Africa way, enjoying fast women of river hips who
baptized him nightly; the tugs of literal war between the Greeks and the
Carthaginians for control of Sicily; Hannibal; the genetic footprints of
boots in the boudoir that left an olive complexion and a twisted wooliness
to the hair of certain Italians; and the Renaissance paintings in which the
solemn black king is right there in the manger at the beginning of Christianity. No doubt about it: I would go.

The flight itself was quite swinging, given its complement of Negro jazz musicians. For all their ego and sometimes crippling pursuit of hipness, they bring with them a downhome quality that personifies the best the race has yet produced. Among them I know again the barbershops and the pool halls, the big family dinners and the counterpoint of whist and domino games, the back porches and the locker rooms, the street corners and the church parking lots where I had learned so much while tested against the gruff friendship and gallows wit that have come, sometimes as slowly as the proverbial molasses in January, all the way from those slave cabins where the partying and the singing went on late into the night, puzzling old Thomas Jefferson, who knew his human property had to meet their mules and their labors in the dawn morning, to grunt and sweat until dusk. Standing at the back of the plane, swapping tales and jokes as the jet's windows opened to darkness on the left side and light on the right, I thought of how the old people had always said, "Justice may not have delivered our mail yet, but we still had a lot of goddam fun along the way—and raised as much sand as the alligator did when the pond went dry! You can believe *that*."

III. PERUGIA

We arrived in Rome and took a bus to Perugia, the headquarters of Umbria Jazz, traveling north on roads that passed between hills that supported both simple tiled houses and, now and again, castles embodying the will to security and civilization that resulted in armaments as well as the quarrying and dragging of the stone up that terrain. From those heights, the citizenry fought for sovereignty from invaders and rival provinces or, much later, against the control of the church. Perugia, whose history stretches back to the Etruscan age, is at the pinnacle of an especially steep group of hills, now partially surrounded by walls that provided the Romans with models of unscalable protection. Because of its very long past, Perugia, like all of Italy, is so steeped in a complex range of human time that it pulls together the superficial incongruity of the historical periods that create its atmosphere—the ancient walls, the misty and green and faded-orange landscapes already familiar from Renaissance paintings, the churches, the town squares, the sloping stone streets, the small cars designed to get through them, the motorcycles, the buses whose wide turns barely miss the walls and pedestrians, the opera house, the sidewalk cafes in which the culture of the city slowly sizzles, and the clothes that look a season or two ahead in elegance and verve of style.

IV. HANNIBAL AD PORTAS

Later, on the train to Florence: Out that window, where Italians are presently sunbathing, had come Hannibal, fighting at Lake Trasimene in 217 B.C., utilizing the beginnings of tank warfare, his Negro mahouts on elephants, the pachyderms girded for battle, their voluminous bellowing in the Alpine air behind them, their tusks and tonnage ready for the Roman legions that would be whipped to their knees and crushed. The survivors of slain Flaminius's decimated army fled throughout Etruria and Umbria, some hiding within the walls of Perugia, Perugia that was to send doomed volunteers to the terrifying Roman defeat at Cannae, where Empire seemed at end, and Perugia that was to furnish wood and grain for Scipio's fleet, helping to bang the gong on the big Punic dream of victory within the bastion of the boot, since Hannibal—great, wily, eloquent, and treacherous Hannibal—after 17 years of fighting, would return to an invaded Carthage, sue for peace, be refused by a bitter Scipio, and face his multitongued army's destruction at Zama, elephants and all.

V. UMBRIA JAZZ

Umbria Jazz wasn't like any other festival I had attended because it included jazz clinics, films, and concerts for audiences that sometimes had better ears than I expect even in New York. Those ears were also evident in the Italian tenor players I heard in the clinic, many of whom startled me with more soulful sounds than the canned Coltrane you hear so often in New York. Somewhere down the steep stone streets and around this corner and that, passing through the cool shadows of buildings that date back to the Middle Ages, the classes were held in an edifice that bore the inscription "Charlie Parker School of Jazz," an insignia that bespoke a conquest much different than the Roman seal of "Augusta Perugia." Dan Morgenstern of Rutgers University was brought over to lecture on jazz history, while tenor saxophonist Paul Jeffrey headed a faculty of musicians who ranged from their early twenties to their fifties—trumpeter Terence Blanchard, alto saxophonist Frank Strozier, pianist Harold Mabern, guitarist Kevin Eubanks, bassist David Eubanks, and drummer Jimmy Cobb. Jeffrey, a repository of jazz fact and lore and a model of patience and inspiration, said of the students, "They want to know about the soul part, about phrasing, time, and sound. Soul. They come looking for that." Mabern taught with the fervor of a deacon assigned a recalcitrant Sunday school class and had similar observations. "The reason cats come over here and have a good time is that they hear the truth. These people want the best they can get. They don't let this skin scare them into some other stuff. They want the real deal."

Carlo Pagnotta's plan for the festival included David Chertok's jazz films, music in the piazzas, in the tent—Teatro Tenda—20 minutes away, and a concluding performance in Narni, an hour from Perugia. Other than the excessive treble from the sound crew, who botched the first few concerts in the tent, there were no problems, unless one considered some well-deserved booing and cat-calling problems. But it had not always been that way. When Pagnotta began producing concerts with the cooperation and financing of local government in 1973, many of the young people who came treated the performances like rock and roll happenings polluted with radical stances. Music with melody, harmony, and instrumental control was considered the art of repression and the symbol of the enslavement of black people, while the opportunists of the "avant-garde" were celebrated as the voices of freedom. The concerts moved from town to town with the unruly young people following them, and things became so bad that the owners of local shops began to board up their windows and doors when the festival arrived. But in 1978, Pagnotta pared down the traveling aspects of the festival, adding a resident American group every night at Il Panino, a club at the end of a twisting street that descends and descends, testing the mettle of those who drink too much and try to walk home. Professor Germano Marri, an old friend of Pagnotta, was elected president of Umbria that same year. With his handsome seriousness and idiomatic wit, Marri appears to represent a communism as distinct from that of Russia and its totalitarian satellites as his superb suits are from their bad tailoring. Perhaps because aesthetic quality is so thick in the air and ambience of Perugia, Marri and his staff appreciate the human complexity that has eluded almost all socialist creation. The communist organization ARCI puts together the concerts in conjunction with Perugina Chocolate and Al Italia Airlines, and allows the music to exist free of avant-garde fashion. Perhaps they know it makes more sense for the new order to spread public joy than to risk the bitterness and stoic paranoia that pervade *The Book of Laughter and Forgetting* and *Man of Iron*. But this is in keeping with the history of Italian art, which provides strong proof that variety and divergence of taste are what have made the country and the culture what it is.

VI. DEAR OLD SOUTHLAND

In the warm afternoon light of the courtyard of the Hotel La Rosetta, over meals served under big umbrellas by waiters in white coats, Italy, as unfamiliar and foreign as it was, recalled the best in the American South. But in the streets, people seemed to float or sit in a meditative silence, or fashion their own angles on an effortless aristocracy shaped equally of confidence, curiosity, and sympathy, all of which could explode into lucid laughter or the metallic chatter of argument. The disdain for excessive activity during the hottest part of the day meant that Perugia's streets were nearly empty from one in the afternoon until four, when the shops opened up and the people filled the outdoor cafes, drinking mineral water or coffee or beer or wine, often mulling over ice cream, then strolling or stretching. I was convinced of the parallels when I found out that what we call hanging out is known there as *dolce fan niente*—sweet time for nothing. As Albert Murray was to say when I asked him about Italy later, "Long before there were Southerners in the U.S.A., there were Southerners in Italy, and it also meant a certain climate, a certain hospitality, a certain musicality in the language, and sometimes even a certain kind of violence and tendency to vendetta. In the more learned circles, the European vision of the Southerner is much like that of anyone who understands our South: the feeling created is that of an easeful relationship to culture and a spontaneity that says, deep down—the point of learning how to cook all this food and talk this way and wear these fine clothes is to have a good goddam time, man!"

In that atmosphere, usually in the courtyard or the hotel's bar, the moody and attractive George Coleman, who has the demeanor of a powerful Memphis deacon, would move from mournful aloofness to earthly humor, from impassive sullenness to buoyancy, carrying his ex-fullback bulk in a relaxed march, his arms swinging almost straight up and down, his long elegant fingers ever ready to throttle from the tenor saxophone virtuoso passages that manifested the loneliness of many years of discipline. In residence at Il Panino with the wonderful Ronnie Mathews Trio, Coleman was to play every night as he always does, giving everything he had, working mightily for his money and not backing up until he'd forced roars and loud applause from the audience. He is clearly one of the lords of his instrument, but, above all, he is a house-rocker.

VII. TUNES IN A TENT

Rocking a house is not the same as rocking a tent, and that is what was expected of the players the first few nights. The procession of events began at lunch, after which many of the musicians, observers, and listeners would go to see Chertok's films in Teatro Pavone, the opera house with painted ceilings, gold-leaf railings, five tiers of boxes, and an atmosphere reminiscent of the finest American movie palaces. The splendidly photogenic faces and forms of artists like Louis Armstrong and Duke Ellington, Lester Young and Charlie Parker, Jo Jones and Thelonious Monk, recalled Kenneth Clarke's description of the men in a Masaccio: "They have the air of contained vitality and confidence that one often sees in the founding fathers of a civilization." After Chertok's films, an American band would play in the opera house, followed later on by an Italian group heard in the open air of a piazza. Then there was dinner and the choice of a bus ride to the tent concert or an American group in a piazza. I always went to the tent.

The bus ride was brief and there was an excitement to riding downhill, passing the foreign signs and shops while lolling back in the pleasant air of Umbrian summer as it flowed in through the windows, and seeing the lights thicken on the right as we neared the blue striped tent patterned with Union Jacks. We leaned to the left as the bus wheeled around the tent in a big arc and let us all out at a gate near the artists' trailers. There was also a small tent where you could buy beer and snacks. Given the history of Umbria Jazz, if one bought a beer in a can or a bottle, it had to be transferred to a paper cup in case the buyer got riled during the performance and decided to throw the container at the stage. Everywhere were fans, including families with small children in tow, all surveyed by a number of good-looking young Italian men in splendid khaki uniforms, carabinieri serving the years of their mandatory military terms. There is something attractively civilized about young policemen who can represent authority with neatness, confidence, pleasant manners, and a physical strength reserved for lawbreakers, not the victims of their own boredom or problems with aggression. I thought that if the law ever became important again in America, the draft could supply an antidote to the fatigue and cynicism of the understaffed and overworked police, who would be provided with a constant influx of young fresh blood. There would be enough police to have them strolling beats again. If the uniforms were as fine as those in Italy, the cop might even become a heartthrob for the ladies, a role young men have always found attractive.

In the tent there was playing both excellent and deplorable, while in the late-night jam sessions in the sweatbox of Il Panino, the music was alternately blistering and romantic. This was made clear on the first evening, when the Italian audience showed its taste by booing the grotesque flute playing of Herbie Mann, though they applauded Freddie Hubbard, whose mixture of Clifford Brown and Clark Terry has resulted in a sound now as golden and streaked with red as a ripe peach. Hubbard was inventive with Mann's terrible rock band, but he got what he needed later that evening when he sat in with the group at Il Panino, building motives from the line of "Rhythm-a-Ning," shaping harmonic charges prickling with dissonance, and firing staccato punctuations that now and again gave way to smears which arced through the air like big, bright fish. George Coleman sustained the excitement with his style of perpetual substitutions—note-laden arpeggios as slippery as beaded curtains of polished stone dipped in boiling oil—while the rhythm section of pianist Ronnie Mathews, bassist Walter Booker, and drummer Hugh Walker coalesced into a mighty engine of harmony and percussion. It had been a long night, but I left Il Panino rekindled and ready for the next day, greatly satisfied by the dragon blasts of inspired artistry I had heard in that boiling club down that long and winding street.

VIII. WERE YOU THERE?

Italy is a land of many masters, and it would have been provincial not to take advantage of what was available on walks or at the National Gallery of Umbria right there in Perugia, or at the Cathedral of St. Francis in Assisi, less than an hour away by bus. On a morning when I had decided to explore the city or travel someplace near, I would be out on foot, feeling the uneven stone of many of the streets as the people seeped from their homes and the sounds of footfalls, rustling clothes, and voices replaced the silence. As I made my way to the Assisi bus past the farmers wheeling their produce into Perugia, I saw a Gypsy boy with a concertina and a frazzled cat on a chain. For some reason, he reminded me less of a kid imitating an Italian organ grinder than of the street preachers of my youth who used to stand at the bus stops, chanting the promises of damnation for most and salvation for the rest each time one of the big yellow and green vehicles would stop and release passengers.

After taking a bus down from Perugia into a valley, then through flat lands backdropped by low hills, where little farms were pressed together as closely as possible, going on through small towns with their second-story windows covered by wooden shutters that kept out the day's early heat, ascending again on roads that rolled and weaved until arriving in Assisi, only to see the Cathedral of St. Francis at the highest part of the city, I experienced the calm such places must have provided for their congregations as soon as I entered the huge church, felt its easy coolness, and began to concentrate on the craft and the emotional radiation of its painted walls. And though there are still those who think that the Negro, like Caliban or the gigantic Moor in Bernini's *Fountain of the Four Rivers* in Rome, should recoil in bitterness, disgust, and alienation at the abundance of those works that document a star-bumping plateau of Western Civilization, I felt that the painted walls were as familiar in feeling and function as the religious and secular music I had heard as a child in church and at home. People are exalted by a great religious painting hung in a gallery in much the same way they are by a superb recording of Mahalia Jackson.

Whether in biblical tales or annals of the suffering of the saints, perhaps the most important religious vision projected through the Italian plastic arts is its sense of moral responsibility. It can cost your life, or tear your heart, but it can also separate you from savages. They understood the costs in blood and also, as one sees in Donatello's *The Sacrifice of Isaac* in Florence, the costs in overwhelming anguish. Oh, yes, I had encountered that sense of life in those Negro churches, where the deacons stood before us, big men humming and singing in their soaked white shirts and dark suits, where the choir would enter from the rear in their swishing robes and so fill the room with mighty song that the roof seemed in danger of loosening and blowing away, where the tales and dreams of the Bible became almost three-dimensional as the worshipers rose to an impersonal oneness with what they expressed, preaching or crying or singing of the rumblings and the ruthlessness—and the *rightness!*—in the bosom of this old world.

Just as biblical lore had provided a comprehensive range of human situations for the painter, the sculptor, and the architect, Christianity had proven a perfect conduit for the movement from the vital though superstition-ridden world of Africa into the accumulated complexity of theme and ethics inherent in the biblical stories, an accumulated complexity that stood them well in the society of successive riddles that is America. Not only did the body of reinterpreted Old Testament beliefs born in rebellion against the Roman Empire speak to the slaves, but they sometimes fought to give voice themselves, reenacting the sedition of their forebears in Rome. I recalled how I had been told in Texas that, since old evil master didn't want his chattel property practicing religion, the slaves would wet down the walls of the cabins at night and gather many buckets and bowls and basins of water to also absorb the sound so that they could preach and pray in secret, separating themselves from the savages who owned the big house and the beasts of the fields.

In much the same way the Italian painters made their religious figures look Italian rather than Middle Eastern or even Negroid in features, facial expression, and dress as they personalized the lessons of Alexandria and Constantinople, the Negro slaves modified the stiff hymns to fit sensibilities that demanded richer conceptions of melody, percussion, and call-and-response. By adding an African-American dimension to religious material that remained Protestant, they made music that would provide an essential model for secular Negro musicians in the same way the mastery of perspective is essential to secular Renaissance painting. And eventually the sermons of the most imaginative ministers evolved into a poetry that functioned as an oral equivalent of Dante, who brought to the vernacular literature of Italian Christianity what Homer had to the mythology of Greece. A perfect example is this selection from a sermon Zora Neale Hurston took down in Florida in 1929:

> I heard the whistle of the damnation train
> Dat pulled out from the Garden of Eden loaded wid cargo goin to hell
> Ran at break-neck speed all de way thru de law
> All de way thru de prophetic age
> All de way thru de reign of kings and judges
> Plowed her way thru de Jordan
> And on her way to Calvary when she blew for de switch
> Jesus stood out on her track like a rough-backed mountain
> And she threw her cow-catcher in
> His side and His blood ditched de train.
> He died for our sins.
> Wounded in the house of his friends.

In short, a metaphoric and epic sense developed that proved perfectly compatible with how Vincent Sheean described the sweep of the spirituals Marion Anderson selected after sailing through Bach and Schubert in Salzburg in 1935; "At the end . . . there was no applause at all—a silence instinctive, natural, and intense, so that you were afraid to breathe. What Anderson had done was something outside the limits of classical or romantic music: she frightened us with the conception, in musical terms, of course, but outside the normal limits, of a mighty suffering." Had Sheean heard Anderson in the Cathedral of St. Francis, I believe he would have found himself surrounded by visual expression of the same sort.

IX. UPLIFT AND FRUSTRATION

The feelings left after the last notes on the second and third nights fused uplift and frustration. V.S.O.P. II, under the leadership of pianist Herbie Hancock, also featured bassist Ron Carter, drummer Tony Williams, trumpeter Wynton Marsalis, and saxophonist Branford Marsalis. Except for Williams, who proved a great drummer can sound as insensitive as a four-year-old, the group performed with invention, fire, and dazzling taste. Wynton Marsalis played shocking pedal notes at fast tempos; Branford Marsalis was never less than a split second behind Hancock's often complex chords, spelling them out as he twisted and bent them; Hancock pulled his unique timbre out of the instrument and spaced his ideas with dramatic effectiveness; while Carter inspired and supported as he crafted bass parts and rhythms of such drive that they almost made up for the drummer's incessant banging. On the third night, the Rutgers University Saxophone Ensemble under the direction of Paul Jeffrey was a casualty of the sound crew: guest soloist George Coleman was either distorted or inaudible, Jeffrey's orchestrations of Coltrane improvisations were so muddily amplified that they might as well have been written in unison, and only the extraordinary piano and drums of Harold Mabern and Jimmy Cobb could be heard throughout, with the good bass beat of David Eubanks appearing and disappearing. Protests resulted in vast improvements the next evening and, after Richie Cole's aggressively mediocre set, Sphere—tenor saxophonist Charlie Rouse, pianist Kenny Barron, bassist Buster Williams, and drummer Ben Riley—displayed distinct arrangements that primed the ear for their improvised command of the subleties of inflection, color, and rhythm. From the first note, the chill on the patina of the evening air lifted and the huge tent felt intimate. It was one of the best performances I have heard all year.

X. THE RELIGION OF GLORY: CAKEWALKING BABIES

The new religion, as I have called the love of glory
. . . a thing of this world, founded as it is on human
esteem.

> Bernard Berenson, *The Italian Painters*
> *of the Renaissance*

When I considered how the development of African-American music telescoped the evolution of Italian art, I had no difficulty seeing slavery and segregation as American versions of the Dark Ages, or recognizing how the soaring self-assertion and mocking false faces of the parades and social clubs of New Orleans provided the local musicians with a Renaissance sense of carnival. After all, Berenson says, "The moment people stopped looking fixedly toward heaven, their eyes fell upon earth, and they began to see much on its surface that was pleasant. Their own faces and figures must have struck them as surprisedly interesting. . . . The more people were imbued with the new spirit, the more they loved pageants. The pageant was an outlet for many of the dominant passions of the time . . . above all (the) love of feeling . . . alive." Given the attempts to depersonalize human beings on the plantation, or reduce them to the simplicity of animals, it is understandable that a belief in the dignity of the Negro and the joyous importance of the individual resulted in what is probably the century's most radical assault on Western musical convention. Jazzmen supplied a new perspective on time, a sense of how freedom and discipline could coexist within the demands of ensemble improvisation, where the moment was bulldogged, tied, and given shape. As with the Italian artists of the Renaissance, their art was collective and focused by a common body of themes, but for jazzmen, the human imagination in motion was the measure of all things.

As I thought of turn-of-the-century New Orleans, the Crescent City with its street songs and its opera houses, with the visual stretch of African-Americans from bone to beige to brown to black, with its Negroes dressed as Indians or parodying the Mardi Gras in their own Zulu Ball, with the bands riding on wagons and battling for the affection of the listeners, with the grief of the music on the way to the bone orchard and the zest of its celebration on the way back, the frescoes reminded me of the aural palimpsests of the old 78-rpm recordings with the red or blue-black labels that my mother had saved, those fragile discs that carried the hissing documentation of blues divas and jazzmen on their worn surfaces, from which the music struggled through the haze of primitive engineering. Just as Kenneth Clarke observed that the Italian Renaissance contributed its ideas in visual terms rather than reasoned argument or speculation, the same can be said about jazz, since its thoughts about American life arrived not in the philosophical text but in the well-picked note on moment's notice and the physical response of dance. You can tell that those people believed in an African-derived sense of infinite plasticity that lent to the bending and drastic rearranging of songs, just as they believed in the molten democracy of the *groove*, when a band catches its stride and every decision made by every individual not only carries his stamp but makes for a collective statement that transcends the particular. You can hear their frothing exuberance as they recognize that they can control the formless rush of the present and paint their faces on its canvas.

XI. DIZZY ATMOSPHERE

It was the next night and the last night of tunes in the tent, and Dizzy Gillespie looked less handsome than angry. He had been loudly booed after kicking off his performance with two dull would-be funk numbers. I was told later, "In Italy, we feel if a musician is great, he should be great. In America, it may be necessary for Miles Davis or Sonny Rollins to play rock and roll—or perhaps it is less painful to act young than wise. Here we feel sad or angry when a great man will abandon wisdom for ignorance. The more polite would say innocence. Why should they travel this far to put on a silly mask?"

The booing was to the good: Gillespie, who had been sulking on the piano bench, rose and roared forth with a succession of improvisations of such savage invention it must have been somewhat difficult to be Jon Faddis standing there next to him, knowing the only thing you could add that night was higher notes. The old master feinted, ducked, and worked out phenomenal accents that italicized the abstractions within his long phrases, proving that when angered, a sore-headed bear will rise to beat the band. Trombonist Curtis Fuller was exquisite and guitarist Ed Cherry worked some pulsive variations on the voicings of McCoy Tyner. Everyone left that evening aware that they had witnessed a master in matchless form.

XII. RENAISSANCE IN RED BEANS AND RICE

You cannot have a Renaissance without a Giotto. He stripped away what Clark calls the "decorative jumble" of images that made the medieval school both highly stylized and emblematic, offering in its place the weight and the sacrifice, the disappointment and the exaltation of human beings concurring and conflicting. In a sense, he discovered the individual in the pageant and, sometimes with the aid of bas-relief halos, pushed the force and substance of experience right at us, settling for neither mush nor surrender. Berenson points out that all of his lines are functional, that they are defined by movement, that he charged trivial objects with a power that not only transformed them but ignited the consciousness of the viewer.

In his own way, Louis Armstrong did the same. He discovered that his powers of imagination could stand alone, with the clarinet and the trombone of the conventional New Orleans band silenced, no longer needed to express the intricate and subtle musicality provided by the multilinear antiphonal style. His monumental ideas swelled a fresh world above his accompanying improvisers. In Armstrong's work there is a new kind of confidence that had never existed in Western music, an aural proof that man can master time through improvisation, that contemplation and action needn't be at odds. A quantum leap of control heralded a new relationship between the artistic consciousness and the body that has yet to inspire what could be a new school of brain research. Armstrong found that he could hear a chord, digest it, decide what to play, tell his lips, lungs, and fingers what to do, and express his individuality within the mobile ensemble as rhythms, harmonies, timbres, and phrases flew forward around him. He had mastered what A. E. Hotchner calls "the ability to assimilate simultaneous occurrences."

Unlike Giotto, Armstrong had immediate impact. He became a hero of epic proportions to fellow musicians. One remembers first hearing him sound like an archangel from a riverboat, another touching him just as he was going on stage and feeling an electric shock. Yet another recalls him taking the measure of a challenge at a cornet supper in Harlem and standing the listeners on their chairs, tables, and plates as he played notes that were like hot, silver solder splashing across the roof that supports the heavens. In his sexuality and the daredevil displacements of his abstractions, Armstrong is more in spirit with Picasso, but his position in an African-American Renaissance is unarguable. He delivered a virtuosity fresh from the frontier of his imagination, giving the trumpet an expressive power it never had. Armstrong brought a purer sound to the instrument's upper register, playing high notes that were functional rather than decorative, and his strings of eighth notes lifted the horn from a vocal, shouting riff style to a standard-bearer of melody interwoven with virtuoso rhythms. And it is clear that in the spirit of Giotto, Armstrong ignited the consciousness of his listeners by charging often uninteresting songs with artistic power, spontaneously transforming them through both an editing and embellishing process. When you hear Armstrong at his finest, he is like the Negro acrobat in the Roman sculpture, calmly balanced on the head of the crocodile of the moment. Berenson says that what a major artist does is show that human beings can cope with the complexities of life—and who could deny that in the face of Armstrong's greatest improvisations?

XIII. BLUES FOR JULIUS III

The final night of Umbria Jazz in Perugia, before the festival's actual conclusion in the mountain town of Narni, took place at Piazza IV. A bandstand had been set up next to the Great Fountain, which dates from 1275, and in front of the Cathedral of St. Lawrence, where a bronze statue of Julius III sat facing the back of the stage and the eyes of the assembled masses. In a way, the feeling of festival that had been building all week was now swelling in the streets with the people. There were African students in small clusters, Americans who were there studying Italian, Europeans on vacation, but, most of all, Italians, from the very young to the older women with calf muscles built from walking the inclines of the stone streets. There were no costumes and no streamers, yet the air felt full of colors and thick with the moisture of dance.

Before joining the dinner group, I listened to some of Ray Mantilla's Space Station, as it started the people near the bandstand dancing to the rushes and thumps of its Afro-Hispanic rhythms. Especially entrancing was the orchestral use of the traps by Joe Chambers, whose spare musicality gave the impression of a pianist playing timbres and multiple rhythms instead of lines and chords. Next, in the summer air, Jackie McLean played with a passion as scarlet as a fall maple and notes as bright and golden as an October birch. In the spirit of the Pagliacci lyricism of

Charlie Parker, McLean's sound was as brutish in timbre as it was plaintive and prideful. But his tone could also glow when he swung on the hard New York blues, or floated his ballad notes on the stream of flesh and memory. Yes, he was in fine form, skittering his lines across the chords set by vibist Bobby Hutcherson, whose music rushed forth or lulled in the air like hankty and piss-elegant chimes. Billy Higgins balanced both instruments on his ride cymbal and buffed them with his stripped-down snare accents, now and again using his toms and bass drum like nearly inaudible thunder. Bassist Herbie Lewis had the heavy and dark effect of a tonal percussionist. A very hot stage was set for the Umbria Jazz All-Stars.

It was late when the All-Stars took the stand, bringing with them the lore of many a dancehall, night club, jam session, and party rich with fine women, handsome men, whiskey, whist, coon can, dominoes, and the smells of downhome food steaming in the pots. On the front line were the Texas tenors: Arnett Cobb, who stands on his metal crutches and shapes each saxophone note like an individual bellows crafted to build heroic fire; Illinois Jacquet, a barrelhouse bull on wheels roaring into red capes; and Buddy Tate, who can rattle the pulpit of the bandstand with his sensuous renditions of blue-toned scripture. There was Al Grey, a master of the plunger who sometimes plays as though coaxing bulbous notes into his trombone rather than pushing them out. The rhythm section of pianist John Lewis, bassist Eddie Jones, and drummer Gus Johnson strung and loosened the bow of the bat with wit and encouragement. Then there was Scott Hamilton, less a seasoned star than a young man still in search of himself, wavering back and forth between recitations of Lester Young and Tate. But on song after song, with the rhythm section simmering and steaming under them, the veterans tore away everything that stood in the path of celebration, creating a pulsation that could be answered only with dance. And dance they did engender, especially with the inevitable encore—"Flying Home"—lifting the crowd with the bells of their horns into a massive articulation of unsentimental happiness. As green Julius III gave his blessing and the medieval Great Fountain bubbled over a democratic series of reliefs spanning local politicians, Christianity, astrology, history, education, Roman origins, and the most popular fables of Aesop, I heard the sound of American democracy become an international phenomenon and thought that if Hannibal had these kinds of troops, he would have easily taken the Roman Empire. With a song.

XIV. BIRD OF PARADISE

The next day I went to the National Gallery of Umbria, again watching the figures slowly change from dark-eyed and dark-skinned to Northern Italian. When I got to Piero della Francesca's polytych, it was like an explosion. Even though he was working with the new level of virtuosity that full-blown control of perspective allowed, della Francesca carried everything with him—the gold leaf and steepled frame and the sacrificial themes. There was an arrogance to his lyricism, especially in the perfectly measured distances and details of the section depicting the annuciation, but there was also the aloof idealism most confident virtuosi have in common. He used "no specialized expression of feeling," as Berenson observed, and the effect at first is one of coldness. Thomas Craven describes his figures as "masked in sullen gravity . . . their attitudes majestic and defiant." But what actually is taking place is a protest against the limitations of painting and an expression of unruffled confidence in the command of detail, a mastery that can concentrate on subtlety and overall effect rather than a conventional display of emotional states. That may account for the absolute stillness another writer sees in his figures.

In two cases, della Francesca's version of what Clarke calls "the new pessimism" rivals—or exceeds—Giorgione's *Col Tempo,* where a whithered beauty stares with the remorse of age at the viewer. In della Francesca's *The Flagellation of Christ,* we see a whipping in the background while a group of well-dressed men converse about other business in the foreground, presaging the modern theme of public indifference to personal pain and degradation. On the right side of *The Death of Adam,* he comments on the loss of Eden. An old man who had once been vibrant and handsome now sits feebly on the ground as his wife stands behind him, equally aged and with her flaccid dugs drooping and uncovered, a deadpan comment on the Renaissance ideal of physical beauty that no paintings of fine faces and figures—or prayer—will diminish.

As I examined della Francesca's work, his absolute stillness and his rejection of conventional expression reminded me of Charlie Parker. Parker brought a fierce and fresh virtuosity to the saxophone, protesting its limitations, and discarded the vibrato many considered necessary for the expression of deep feeling in the work of his predecessors. He depended on the voluminous details of his loquacious melody notes, his high-handed harmonic sophistication, and the seemingly impossible gradations of attack he brought to rhythms that themselves seemed beyond enunciation. Like that of the Italian painter, Parker's work brims with sullen gravity, majesty, and defiance; it is an art possessed by an idealism which says that only in the transcendence of the difficult can we know the intricate riches and terrors of the human soul. Both the painter and the saxophonist created continuity and contrast through echoing and near-echoing. The painter used figures and faces as motifs while varying features and skin tones, hair color and texture, dress and body position; the result is a series of geometrical calls and responses from one end of a painting to the other. In Parker's best work, he constantly reshapes phrases and rhythms, extending them, leaving something out here, adding something there, or compressing what he has previously played into a swinging board from which he bounces into more elaborate linear variations. Parker also left nothing behind, revolutionizing every detail of the jazz tradition. Parker became a colossus of human consciousness who could process and act upon material with a meticulous lyricism at any tempo. In his finest improvisations, you hear an imagination given the wide dimension of genius, running up a hill potted and mined with obstacles, but delivering its melodies with a sometimes strident confidence in their imperishability.

XV. NOT UNTIL NARNI

Traveling from Perugia, we crossed frightening gorges and saw the terrain become steeper until we arrived at a gas station and had to switch to buses small enough to get through a gate and up the narrow road to our destination. Narni is made almost completely of stone, with arches that cast shadows and lead into the descending side streets or into buildings that crest the city on the other side of the square where the concert was held. A big bandstand had been set up in front of a large fountain and, though the music was more than an hour away because of a power failure, Italians of all ages had begun to gather around the stage and were staring at us with overt curiosity and pleasure as we made for the bars or the little stand beyond an imposing Roman arch where sandwiches and beer were sold.

I found myself wandering through the city and its back streets, imagining the time when the clop of shod hooves and the rattling of wagons had filled the air, when word of Garibaldi's triumphs arrived, when the problems of putting in telephone service and electric lights and plumbing had been met with wires and fenced-in generators and the sewers full of turning pipes. Then I wondered if the first jazz notes had arrived by phonograph or radio. Narni had the look and feel of a place where modern life was but another loop on a very long tape of time. As I had been told by an Italian named Maurice Cohen: "In Italy, you can stand in the middle of your past and feel the present and dream about the future. You know that what is adaptive is what is lasting and that the key to Italian civilization, what some mistake for exceptional friendliness, is a confidence in the fact that though you might be influenced, you won't be consumed. You will merely take what is good and make it Italian. After all, the spaghetti first came from China with Marco Polo, but the Chinese did not make *pasta*. Italians did. Merchants came from all over the world to Florence, but Italians invented *banking*. And so it goes. That is our way and that is our safety." (I later found out that Cohen had been born in France.)

By the time I returned, the klieg lights were on, an Italian television crew was at work documenting the event, the square was filled with many people either standing or sitting on the ground, and in the houses that surrounded the square were families seated and crowded in their second-floor windows or old women leaning on sills with their elbows. A big band from Rome had finished their set and I was soon to wish they would kidnap American tenor saxophonist Bob Berg and teach him to cook. Even with the same rhythm section that had so perfectly supported George

Coleman and Freddie Hubbard, Berg managed to never swing a note, only bluster through the tunes with the aimless intensity of a fly caught between a closed window and a screen. The staff Paul Jeffrey put together played quite well until monitor problems led to tempo waverings even stable swingers like Harold Mabern and Jimmy Cobb couldn't set right. There were also early conflicts between Mabern's thick voicings and the obbligatos of Kevin Eubanks until the guitarist let Mabern have it and made his statements with good lines in his features. Frank Strozier invented bittersweet alto saxophone melodies, built tension with circular breathing, and delivered his ideas with rhythms both fluid and bumptious. Terence Blanchard, always a poignant player, surged through the trumpet with big intervallic leaps and an almost impersonal sense of heartbreak interwoven with desire that stung the audience, while Jeffrey, caught in the memory of the Umbria All-Stars, reached in the bucket and swung the bell off the tenor. I admire Woody Herman's refusal to sit down and moulder away, but his Young Herd concluded the concert with more precision than passion and swung about as hard as a buried log of teakwood, while the leader's singing was an unpleasant memento of minstrelsy.

It was after two in the morning and the streets were still filled with listeners who seemed reluctant to turn in, especially the old women in the second-floor windows, who were apparently determined to watch everything dismantled and packed before they called it a night. As for us, we were all taken to a banquet on the elevated patio of a hotel in Turni, where the staff showered Pagnatta with champagne and I stared at some of the most beautiful women I had ever seen in my life. By the time we returned to Perugia, it was almost dawn but I was still lit up and ready for the train ride to Florence, all the jazz notes behind me but the memory of an extraordinary people and their thirst for festival still in the front of my mind.

XVI. FIRENZE

One of the first things that impressed me in Florence was the army of well-dressed men and women on motor scooters shooting down the streets, their double-breasted summer suits, their striped dresses and sheer stockings, their briefcases and purses in place as they rounded corners or deftly moved between cars. There was also the sunlight that would smooth itself across the sky and loom in its seemingly imperishable weight just beyond the city's many shaded spaces, the cypress trees and the hills where Michelangelo designed the snaking fortifications, the huge cathedrals that maintain their grandeur in an almost ancient skyline dominated by tile the color of dried red mud, the infinity of shops with everything available from custom-made shoes to the most remarkable suits and dresses, wallets, purses, and scarves; the street market near the Duomo that the sellers would build each morning from poles and rectangles of plywood or formica, the horse-drawn carriages in which you could travel near the Ufizzi, the squadrons of pigeons that would light near the Fountain of Neptune, hustle a few bread scraps, and march in place behind the platoons of Japanese tourists, who faced the labor of lugging around their many cameras, packages, and guide books with determination and explosive smiles. The smallest sandwich stand might provide a simple but delicious snack, a glass of mineral water, and the parting choice of 42 imported beers. It was hard not to be impressed.

But I met a small, dark man from a town in Calabria who had been living in Florence for 20 years. He gave an impression of the city that was less hostile than sarcastic and indicative of the hometown pride you consistently encounter in Italy. He felt that the Florentines were very closed and unfriendly because they thought they were "too civilized." Yet they made more grammatical mistakes than anybody, he went on to say, and suggested that when Frederick II conquered Sicily and opened schools in which Italian was taught, he may have inspired Dante to write in the language. "The Florentines cannot say it is not so. Like all of us, they do not know. But I will bet you they have *never heard* of Frederick II."

I mentioned that I had been surprised by how softly people spoke during dinner the previous night—when I joined some Americans and we began laughing and joking, the people at the other tables kept staring at us.

"On the bus," he smirked, "where people should be talking and enjoying themselves, you would think they are whispering inside themselves in church. They do not like the loud."

It would be silly to come to Florence, where they do not like the loud, and not join those who line up in the morning outside the Gallery of the Tribune to see *Prisoners* and *David*, standing huge and lighted by the sun beneath the cupola at the end of the room, its musculature and the stare of the eyes familiar as the remembered images of the greatest boxers. Kenneth Clarke says that the look of the head "involves a contempt for convenience and a sacrifice of all those pleasures that contribute to what we call civilized life. It is the enemy of happiness." Looking at it, I could not help but think of Muhammad Ali, fresh from the attrition and the tuning of the training camp, coming up the aisle to face Sonny Liston, the Goliath of the boxing ring; or Ali standing in his sullen poignance as he recited with charming bravado one of his rhymed predictions of how he would fell the big ugly bear from Philadelphia or going to his locker room after his victory and suffering through the ice-covered and blackening cummerbund of bruises left by the bear's body punches.

There is also an air of gloom surrounding *David* because we know, as Michelangelo must have, how he was torn down by temptation and megalomania. There is perhaps no story of forbidden love quite so great and heartbreaking as the tragedy David enters when struck by the wonders of Bathsheba's lush body bathed in the morning light. Though he knows from firsthand experience the power and wrath of his God, David will still commit adultery, thus spitting upon the laws he is bound to uphold, then further corrupt his powers as king by eventually using them to design what was perhaps the first example of bureaucratic murder as he moved to rid himself of Bathsheba's husband, Uriah the Hittite. Next he must face the whirlwind of incest and fratricide among his children that culminates when Absalom, groomed in princely privilege as favorite son, rises to try and smite down his father. When I think of David moaning the name of his slain and seditious son, finally aware that even the chosen and the most gifted have no guarantees against the wages of obsession, I also think of Ali: his ego and addiction to celebration, his victory over the second Goliath of George Foreman in the humid bush of Zaire and the almost mythological grandeur of his third fight with Joe Frazier in Manila, then his desire for one last dance in the light of international praise and awe shaping in him a belief in magic that helped result in the once-quick tongue now battling ruefully—at the pace of a child reading his first schoolbook—to enunciate a simple sentence. Even so, just as we know that *David* is at the edge of a journey to a pinnacle from which he will fall, dragged in the dirt by his lust, we will always also know that there were moments when Ali, expanding our expectations of a heavyweight's grace, courage, and cunning, won and made it New Year's Eve all over the world.

The Duomo nearly overcomes the visitor through the grandeur of its collective art and design. I was most surprised by the black, gray, white, salmon, brown, and plum patterns of its marble floor. In an apparent attempt to simultaneously prove the glory of mathematic precision and illustrate the perfect construction of the universe, a series of rhyming geometrical images on either side of the huge church reveals the contemporary painting that begins with Mondrian's *Broadway Boogie Woogie* as little more than contrived decoration.

But the Florentine sensibility also encompasses the Medici chapels, where the gargoyle narcissism of the room honoring the Medici princes makes technical mastery revolting. Its overdone green, gray, plumb, red, and apricot marble has the garishness associated with drag balls and expresses not the resonance of a culture but its hollowness. By contrast, there is the consonant poetry of the white and green marble Michelangelo used to design the New Sacristy under the same roof, diminished only by the predictive science fiction of the female figures who are dangerously close to transsexuals, with their male thighs, muscular bodies, and tacked-on breasts.

I will never forget how many times I circled Michelangelo's unfinished *Pietà* in the museum behind the Duomo, fascinated by the possibilities for style it suggested. Its mix of the finished and the unfinished gives the impression of an intersection between realism and expressionism, between living flesh, dead flesh, and the spirit. For me, the big figure that hovers over the expired Christ seems to be death lifting his body beyond the equally spiritual figure of Mary, who is lost in lamentation for her son. I floated back much faster than I could have by plane and much further, all the way to a street not far from my old home in Los Angeles and into the living room where a wake was being held, with food and liquor everywhere, with men and women in dark clothes, and was memory-listening to a mother talking about how she had been with her dead son in the chapel for the last time as he lay in state, his body waiting for the ritual next morning that would take him to the burying ground. "I took Oran's hand and put it in mine, just like I did when he would get sick and ask me to rub his arms. The hand was cold but it wasn't stiff and it felt like it always did. The only difference was the fingertips had turned blue." She looked up, her face the color of mustard with a subtle undertone of beige, worn with grief and surely knowing what Mary had known.

XVII. ROMA

On that last morning in Rome, I stood before the Coliseum, relaxing into the thought of how much of my own experience had been clarified by exposure to foreign forms. It had been a steaming afternoon the day before when I arrived, bedding down in a hotel near the train station, in a section popular with the vacationing Arab middle class. A cab ride had taken me around the ancient city, which combined past and present even more startlingly than the others. Rome is both sad with the knowledge of the mystery of fate and vital with the awareness of how clearly human passions can speak through the ages, whether from the Egyptian obelisks that shoot up toward the sun or the ruins and fountains that detail the carcasses of empire and the glory of invention.

Because it was summer, many of the residents were vacationing and avoiding tourists, but there were still plenty of Italians at work who never gave the impression of oppressive boredom you become accustomed to in New York. One feels the presence of time with a special intensity here because the drive that brought those obelisks back from Egypt and pushed up the Pantheon or the Vatican or the Coliseum or the many fountains seems almost tangible. There is also a glow of confidence that comes from having survived monsters from antiquity to Mussolini, who used to speak from that balcony there. At the same time, there is the silt and the brown dust that has accumulated from the exhaust of automobiles and mutes the surfaces of streets and buildings with the gloom of the modern age. But perhaps that gloom has been overstated by pessimists who ignore the modes of redress and the reduction of degradation and squalor that have come in the wake of the Magna Carta and the Continental Congress. After all is said and done, the world has a richer human image of itself now despite its problems, but the way those Italians carry themselves is not so much an assertion of hope as of the ironic continuity that a long history provides.

On my only evening there, I saw a tall and darkly attractive group of African women walking in line as the Italians covered the streets on the way to shop or eat. One was especially striking, with brilliant black eyes, a long neck circled by the lines that are often seen by Africans as marks of beauty, and a long red dress that billowed and stopped just short of her ankles. She reminded me of the bas-reliefs at the Tazza D'Oro coffee shop where an African woman is depicted showering Rome with coffee beans, but not of a brace of Brooklyn ersatz Africans I had met in Florence, with their hair looking like sooted mops, their noses run through by rings, their bodies reeking the overwrought oils sold with incense in New York, and their attire the tacky and misbegotten emulation of an Africa that exists only in the minds of romantic primitivists rather than the continent which may someday rise to shake the world with its natural resources as Hannibal shook Rome with his elephants.

As I looked at those African women, I wondered if the descendants of slaves owned by fellow Africans would ever influence the world in the way those who were brought to America had. I knew then that slavery in America was as much ironic luck as it was enormous misfortune, since what U.S. slaves had endured made for a culture in which celebration was a form of protest that remade social, aesthetic, and athletic conventions. We are indeed fortunate to live in a period when we can see changes that began when the first slaves ran away from the plantation or learned to play the fiddle or sing hymns or read. Of course, that was only the beginning. E. Franklin Frazier once observed that certain field slaves, never having seen the master and the mistress work, thought freedom meant preening and kicking back behind mint juleps. It is pretty clear that too many African regimes haven't understood that a well-oiled and functioning infrastructure that marshals and markets all resources must precede the underhanded luxuries of success. The attempts to leap-frog directly to corruption have cost their economies dearly but, given the history of France since the Revolution, there is no need to count them out prematurely. Africans will probably learn their lessons the hard way, as others have, and then push more chairs to the big table of world power.

XVIII. PRECIOUS LORD

On the returning flight, I struck up conversation with a group of Negro pilgrims from Florida who had just been to the holy land, where they had walked in Jerusalem just like John. I had noticed them almost as soon as the plane took off, for they sat together and exuded a familiar combination of sobriety, wit, and warmth as they listened to one another, joked, or mused. The men all wore dark or gray suits with vests and the women either pantsuits or straight and simple dresses, their occasional diamond rings shining below knuckles and above their liver-colored nail polish. As I had first looked at them, recalling the heat of the churches and the steam of the sermons, I was reminded of the old saying, "Our race is like a flower garden, everything from lily-white to blue-black." When an African-American painter masters mixing all the colors necessary to capture such a range of skin tones, the painting of figures might be revitalized.

The pilgrims were still excited by what they had seen in Jerusalem and were comparing emotional reactions to the religious art of Rome. One woman said that there was a lot wrong with the way Catholics practiced the religion, but that their paintings and the sculpture told the truth. "They knew how a mother feels when her child is in pain and she can't do nothing about it," she observed. Their pastor said, "If I had somebody like that Michelangelo to paint my church, a man that inspired, we couldn't stay in there. We would need a bigger place. They would feel the truth vibrating through that paint. Yes, sir, when you stand in that Vatican, you can't help but feel the glory behind everything."

The preacher's words brought me back to the Coliseum, where I'd remembered how the Christians who had been meat for the lions began the protests that led to the fall of the Roman Empire after it converted to Christianity and could no longer justify chattel labor. I then recalled the Civil Rights Movement, when an empire of segregation and lynch-law had been torn asunder by those radicalized pastors and their nonviolent troops cracking the pillars of a temple to injustice with their bodies while singing reworked old spirituals that stung with political messages and threats to the redneck kingdom of violence. Then I saw again Mahalia Jackson painting an aural portrait of the suffering of the southern saints as she sang "Precious Lord, Take My Hand" at Martin Luther King's funeral, her image projected by a television set, a wet handkerchief in her hand, her hair thick and dark above her head, the dress frilled and white, and her body trembling with the passage of each note. For some strange reason as I walked near the ruins of the Senate, it came to me how radio waves and phonograph recordings had beamed the disembodied songbird of jazz into the ears of many virgins, giving birth to an international body of listeners who had been transformed in some vital way by that annunciation. At that moment, it was easy to see that the melancholy I have often felt when staring at the sealed-up palace of bebop innovation that was Minton's Playhouse in Harlem, or the stripped-away testaments to the night life of Kansas City, is a melancholy unfounded. The human point is not that something has decayed, but that when the times and the spirits were right, men and women met their challenges, and their efforts rose as brightly as the sun did on that last Roman morning.

NAME INDEX